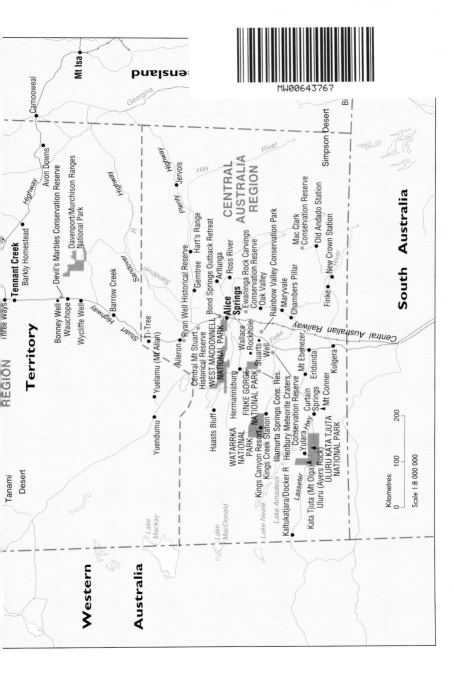

Outback Australia

A GUIDE TO THE
NORTHERN TERRITORY AND KIMBERLEY

Above Left: The enormous dome formations of Kata Tjuta
Below Left: Sunset over Uluru, the world's greatest monolith

Outback Australia

A GUIDE TO THE
NORTHERN TERRITORY AND KIMBERLEY

Malcolm Gordon

 Little Hills Press

Malcolm Gordon
Malcolm Gordon, 1989, Revised edition 1991, Revised Edition 1994,
Fourth Edition, 2000

Maps and Illustrations
Little Hills Press, created by MapGraphics
© 2000
Diagrams
Hospital Benefits Association Ltd. pp128-129.

Photographs – for credits see acknowledgements

Little Hills Press Pty Ltd
Unit 3, 18 Bearing Road
Seven Hills, NSW, 2147
Australia.

ISBN 1 86315 112 5

Printed in Singapore

DISCLAIMER
Whilst all care has been taken by the publisher and author to ensure that the
information is accurate and up to date, the publisher does not take responsibility
for the information published herein. The recommendations are those of the
author, and as things get better or worse, places close and others open, some
elements in the book may be inaccurate when you get there. Please write and tell
us about it so we can update in subsequent editions. In addition, the publisher and
author accept no responsibility for injury, loss or inconvenience sustained by any
person using this book. It should also be noted that any prices the author has listed
will be affected by both the introduction of the GST on 1 July, 2000, and general
economic trends that may cause them to rise. They should be regarded as a guide
only, and the reader is advised to confirm prices closer to the date of travel.

Little Hills™ and are registered trademarks of Little Hills Press Pty Ltd.

CONTENTS

Part One:

Northern Territory and Kimberley - A General Guide

ACKNOWLEDGMENTS

Without the generous help and encouragement of many organisations and individuals, this book would not have been possible, and I sincerely thank the following for their contribution, and for the kind use of material: The Australian Tourist Commission; Northern Territory Tourist Commission; Western Australia Tourist Commission; Regional Tourist Bureaux or Association or Visitor Information Centres in Alice Springs, Tennant Creek, Katherine, Pine Creek, Darwin, Kununurra, Fitzroy Crossing, Derby and Broome; Outback Queensland Tourist Authority; Parks and Wildlife Commission of the Northern Territory, in particular, to officers who checked drafts and gave advice on parks; Department of Conservation and Land Management (Kimberley); The Central and Northern Land Councils, Alice Springs and Darwin; Tiwi Land Council; Parks Australia; The National Trust; The Bureaux of Meteorology, Northern Territory and Western Australia for the use of their data; Fire Authorities, Northern Territory and Western Australia; The NT Department of Mines and Energy for use of their excellent detailed geological material on the National Parks; The NT Government Information Centre for the use of the NT Profile material; The Department of Transport and Works Roads Division, Alice Springs; The Royal Flying Doctor Service in Alice Springs; The WA and NT Police Departments; and Hospital Benefits Association, Victoria, for permission to use their first aid material and diagrams; Kaltukatjara Community Council; Territory Rent-A-Car (Alice Springs); and Ayers Rock Resort.

Assistance from the following people was much appreciated: Heather and Sam Goldsworthy, Maryvale Station; Leigh Goldsmith (The Outback Experience Tours), Alice Springs; Irma Versluijs (Outback Travel Shop), Alice Springs; Rod Mortison and Mike George (Coach Tours of Australia), Melbourne; Peter and Sue

Ackland, Mornington; Dr David Price, Mornington; Neil Taylor, Mornington; Jan Irons, Elliot; Stephen Moore (Uluru-Kata Tjuta National Park); Bev Kozolowski, Val Craiker and Joan Small (Tennant Creek Regional Tourist Association); Jan Christian (Fitzroy Crossing Tourist Bureau); Helena King (Derby Tourist Bureau); Jenny Tooke (Broome Tourist Bureau); Meg Nicholas (Central Australian Tourism Industry Association); Gail Eastaway (Kununurra Tourist Bureau); Chris Done (C.A.L.M.), Kununurra; Jenny Haines and Kathy Williams (Parks and Wildlife Commission, N.T.), Alice Springs and Palmerston respectively; Sharyn Innes (Katherine Regional Tourist Association); Manfred Haala (Kakadu National Park); Andrea Martin (N.T.T.C.), Alice Springs; Rose Holmes, Balfes Creek; Robert Ivers and Barry Neck, Richmond; Grant Achen, Dept. of Environment, Charters Towers; Noel Robertson, Cloncurry; Joe Freckleton, Camooweal; Anne Webber, Mt Isa; John Stewart, Hermannsburg; Felicity Mallon and Mick Lang (Mt Nancy Motel, Alice Springs); Ron Tremaine (Bojangles, Alice Springs); Wayne Kraft (Overlander Steakhouse, Alice Springs); Jan Heaslip (Bond Springs); Jan Hayes (Ooraminna Bush Camp); Noel and Michelle Fullerton (Camel Outback Safari, Stuarts Well); Sonne Faucett (Adelaide River); Sue Bayley (Humpty Doo); Tiwi Tours (Tiwi Islands); Lorraine Chidgey (East Arnhem Land Tourist Association); the Stockyard Gallery (Mataranka); John Lucas (Douglas Daly Park); and Peter Yates (Red Centre Resort), Alice Springs.

 And my thanks to the station and roadhouse owners, the tour operators and the many others in the tourist industry with whom I met, or had long telephone conversations.

Thanks also to my editors, Charles Burfitt and Mark Truman, and to Chris Hatcher at Artitude for his design work.

A special thanks to Douglas and Joyce Stephen for all their help, and above all, to my family, without whose support the project would have been impossible, in particular to my wife Gill for her valuable advice on the manuscript, and for her much needed support when the task at times seemed overwhelming; to Hannah for checking parts of the original script, and most recently for her editing and typing work in the preparation of this considerably revised fourth edition and for use of her historical outlines on the Northern Territory and Australia, which provided a basis for the Cultural History Section; and to Simon for his computer expertise.

Along the Gibb River and Kalumburu Road section is based on material kindly provided by the Derby Tourist Bureau, and with permission to use.

The section on Tourist Drives, Trails and 4WD Tracks is based on Central Australian Tourism Industry Association materials, with kind permission.

Maps

For their kind permission to reproduce maps: NT Parks Wildlife Commission - Maps of the NT Parks and Reserves. Parks Australia - Kakadu and Uluru. Central Australia Regional Tourist Industry Association - maps. Tennant Creek, Katherine, Darwin - NTTC and regional associations.
Kununurra, Fitzroy Crossing, Derby, Broome - WA Tourist Commission and regional/local associations. Department of Conservation and Land Management - Geike Gorge Geological Map. John Deckert, Westprint Heritage Maps

Photographs

For their kind permission to reproduce photographs:
Gonzalo de Alvear: cover, opp. half-title page (top), title page, 17, 144, 166, 423, opp.576
John Deckert: opp.16, 60, 63, 149
Hospital Benefits Association Limited: 128, 129
Katherine Region Tourist Association: 306
Little Hills Press: opp. half-title page (below), 66, 141, 245, 399, opp.592
Malcolm Gordon: opp.17, 43, 379, opp.577, 142, 294, 363
NT Tourist Commission: 20, 44, 283, 291, 386, 491

ABOUT THE AUTHOR

Malcolm Gordon was born in Hastings, New Zealand, attended Victoria University, Wellington, and graduated with a Bachelor of Arts degree in geography. He then taught in New Zealand (Wellington College, Hastings Boys High School and Kings College, Auckland) before moving to London for a four year teaching (John Lyon School, Harrow) and travelling stint. After a brief return to New Zealand, he moved to Melbourne with his family in 1976 where he headed the Geography Departments at Haileybury College and Camberwell Grammar School.

A six-month camping trip around Australia with his family - Gill, Hannah and Simon - in 1986 began a fascination with the outback, the culmination of which is this book now in its fourth edition. The first edition of "Outback Australia" won a Northern Territory Tourism award in 1990 in the Interpretive Category of the annual Brogla Awards. His latest travel guidebook, "Victoria's Mornington Peninsula", has been favourably reviewed.

Now an Australian citizen, Malcolm left his senior teaching position in 1997 to direct his own business, Edutour, in association with the Melbourne-based company, Coach Tours of Australia. He regularly visits the Northern Territory with inbound and domestic school and adult Edutour groups. He lives with his family at Mount Martha on the Mornington Peninsula, near Melbourne.

PREFACE

Since the original publication of "Outback Australia" in 1989 (the first comprehensive guidebook to the Northern Territory ever produced and recipient of a 1990 Northern Territory Tourism Award), the book has undergone several revisions. This fourth edition has been extensively rewritten with the addition of sections covering places and attractions along major routes leading to the Northern Territory, namely the South Australian part of the Stuart Highway from Port Augusta to the border, and the Flinders and Barkly Highways in Queensland from Charters Towers to the Territory border. A section on 4WD explorer routes, tourism drives and heritage loop roads are also included to provide adventurous travellers with further options for experiencing Northern Territory landscapes.

The format of this guide is to provide easy access to the large amount of information it contains. Part One is a general guide to the Northern Territory and Western Australia's Kimberley region including features along major routes leading to the Northern Territory. Part Two is a systematic coverage of the three geographic regions of the Northern Territory (Central Australia, Barkly and Top End) and The Kimberley region of Western Australia.

Within each region, places are listed alphabetically (except where an outstanding range of features give a particular identity to an area, in which case they are arranged in order of appearance), and contain a detailed coverage of their features, including history, attractions and services.

Regional boundaries at times are arbitrary and I hope that no offence is taken by those who consider they are more Central Australia or Top End, rather than the transitional zone dwellers in the region where they are included called The Barkly. I have also tried to redress an imbalance noted in much written material on the Northern Territory; namely the scant attention given to the

The Devil's Marbles; where granite boulders can be seen
balancing precariously on the rocks below

smaller, out of the way places. Highlighting these as well as the main tourist centres and attractions, is a way of acknowledging a much wider and colourful outback picture.

The outback is a beautiful mosaic of colour, mood, space, freedom, frontier, dreamtime and characters that along the way, and at the end, form amazing, often indescribable patterns that may evoke deeper awareness.

This is The Outback, take time to enjoy it.

Malcolm Gordon

Aboriginal Rock Art in Kakadu; indicative of a deep spiritual and cultural connection with the natural environment

AUSTRALIA

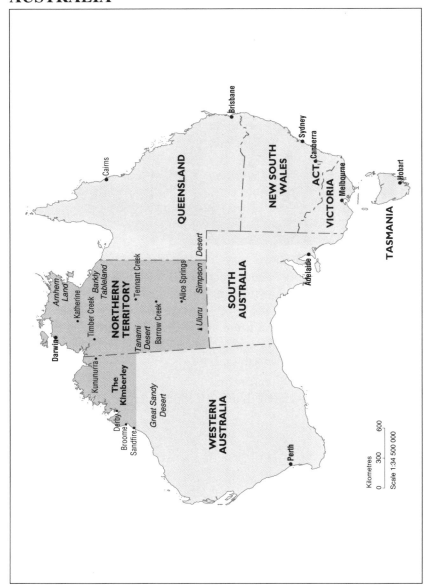

NORTHERN TERRITORY AND KIMBERLEY - A GENERAL GUIDE

Introducing the Outback

OUTBACK IMAGES

At its simplest, 'outback' is an Australian word that describes the remote, sparsely populated back country. But it is much more than that. While all mainland states have their outback, nowhere is it more closely associated than with the Northern Territory, and the Kimberley region of Western Australia. Even vehicle number plates in the Territory boldly proclaim "NT Outback Australia".

The varied, perhaps even comfortable, perceptions of where and what the Outback is, are likely to be shattered when confronted with the real thing. While it is difficult to define and map, road travellers in particular will definitely know when they have arrived there. A few random pictures and incidences suggest something of its unique character, colourful lifestyle, and a place that remains the defining characteristic of Australians.

It begins when fences and farmhouses slip off the landscape. A sand-blasted road sign points along a red track to a homestead, 100km (62 miles) into the lonely horizon. On the highway, on-coming drivers who are strangers, wave, reassured by fleeting communication. On a dirt road, a 50m-long road train bellows and bursts through a huge ball of red dust. At Timber Creek, two policemen patrol their beat - an area nearly the size of Tasmania. A millionaire businessman from New York is captivated by a 60,000-year-old Aboriginal culture in Arnhem Land, and finds revelation in their art and continuing way of life. On the McArthur River at Borroloola, children are prevented from getting to school because the boat which carries them across the river is threatened by huge crocodiles. An Aboriginal man saunters from the side of the Great Northern Highway in the vast wastes of the Great Sandy Desert and politely asks for the time. In the Kimberley, at a remote homestead on the Gibb River Road, a pastoralist and his family dine formally in the high-ceiling, corrugated iron, partially open-walled dining room with a party of overseas tourists, while at one of the property's outstations, stockmen cook over a fire and prepare for another night under the wide, starry skies. At Katherine, a teacher begins a lesson in the world's biggest 'classroom' - the School of the Air where children on the far-flung station homesteads receive their schooling by radio. The Outback

is where the mailman and the doctor do their rounds by air. In Alice Springs, an upside-down boat regatta is held - the river flows underneath its sandy bed and the boats have no bottoms. The images roll on...

The Outback is space, freedom and wilderness: a landscape of colours, botannical oddities, stunning wildlife, electrifying landforms, an ancient, mystical culture, and deep, piercing blue skies. The symbol of it all is the sometimes benign, sometimes brooding rich-red monolith, Uluru (Ayers Rock), which guards the ochre-dusted desert and anchors to its heart the soul of a continuing Aboriginal culture. After a visit to Australia, Mark Twain's general comments perhaps best sum up the Outback ... *it is full of surprises, and adventures and incongruities, and contradictions, and incredibilities, and they are all true.*

OUTBACK PEOPLE

The first Outback people, the Aborigines, form a significant group, and attitudes towards them since the time of the first white explorers and settlers have been ambivalent, to say the least.

Underlying racial tensions exist in places, as Aboriginal people get a new-found independence through the return of their traditional land, via Aboriginal Land Rights. Whatever the views and feelings engendered by this, the reality is that Aboriginal clans now own - under contemporary Australian law - a significant proportion of the land in the Territory. Since land rights implementation (it is still a contentious issue, with a number of unresolved elements in the legislation), options to live traditionally, semi-traditionally, operate economic enterprises, administer with white organisations some national parks, and to continue to play a significant role in the tourist industry through their art and heritage, have been exercised. In contrast, the town fringe-dwellers form a very small, but highly noticeable, impoverished minority.

Aboriginal people have been settled on these lands for at least 50,000 years, and most retain the long-established ancestral bonds with their traditional lands, even although modification to their lifestyle, through European contact, has occurred.

There are plenty of opportunities to meet Aboriginal people, particularly through organised cultural tours. Cross-cultural experiences can be all the more rewarding provided you have time and patience, and are prepared to accept differences, and have an open mind. Aboriginal people have value systems and codes of behaviour very different to other cultural groups in Australia. Often these are not understood or fully appreciated by non-Aboriginal Australians. One of the reasons for this, is that in the most populous regions in Australia (the southern and south-eastern seaboard), Aboriginal people constitute less than one percent of the population; in the Northern Territory, they make up around 27 percent of the population. Similarly, Aboriginal people form a significant proportion of the population in the Kimberley region of Western Australia. It is therefore not surprising that for many Australians, their first contact with Aboriginal people is in Outback regions. Visiting people from another culture highlights differences in manners, customs and ways of communicating with each other. In meeting Aboriginal people, particularly in more remote areas, it is helpful to bear in mind the following customs and etiquette. Aboriginal people do not like being photographed without the common courtesy of first being asked (in some places all photography is prohibited). More often than not, English is their second language, or even third, fourth or fifth! In some areas it may not be spoken very well or not at all. Speak clearly and reasonably slowly without being patronising in tone, and accord them the respect you would expect given to yourself. Generally they tend to be reticent with people from another culture, but if your attitude is genuinely friendly, you'll be well rewarded with warm responses.

Any assistance that you may require directly from Aboriginal people (eg. vehicle problems or seeking directions), is more likely to occur in areas off the major tourist routes (in remote areas, the dominant population group is Aboriginal). If you require obvious assistance, Aboriginal custom is generally not to offer to help until actually being asked. And if you have occasion to approach a group of Aboriginal people in the bush, be it a settlement or camp, wait for a few minutes at a clearly visible distance until someone approaches you. If this does not happen then generally treat the situation as you would at home when meeting new people - in particular, engage in sociable small talk to establish friendly rapport. The first person to address directly should be the same gender as yourself and the most senior.

Be mindful, too, that in Aboriginal culture, there were once strict rules about looking people in the eye. You may find that some Aboriginal people still observe this custom and avoid eye contact with you. Also, most Aboriginal clans have no formal greetings (close-knit family groups made them generally unnecessary), so don't be offended if your greeting is not returned. Another major difference between Aboriginal and Western culture in a meeting situation is the handshake, particularly between males. Aboriginal males generally do not have the Western custom of a vigorous handshake. Instead, hand contact may be a soft clasp of the hands, if at all. In most Aboriginal languages there are no words for please and thank- you; it is understood that at a later time you will reciprocate. There are many other differences. Provided you are respectful and aware of cultural differences, you will get all the help you need, and make new friends too.

At Aboriginal settlements, the best place for local area advice or information is the community store or council offices, where usually there are non-Aboriginal people up front. If you stop at these isolated places, it is courteous to contact the store or council office first. This is Aboriginal land where the residential areas of these communities are closed to visitors.

Alcoholism is a major social problem affecting a very small proportion of the total Aboriginal population. As those Aboriginal people who consume alcohol tend to do so in public places, this unfortunately attracts undue visitor attention. The fact that this practice is highly visible, has led to the rather absurd and hypocritical assumption by some non-Aboriginal Australians that most Aboriginal people drink to excess. In fact, a much smaller proportion of Aboriginal people drink alcohol in comparison to non-Aboriginal Australians.

To counter the problem, most Aboriginal Councils have prohibited the possession and consumption of alcohol in their communities, while some isolated roadhouses and hotels have agreed not to sell liquor to Aboriginal people. If Aboriginal people ask you to buy alcohol for them, please support the efforts of Clan Elders to combat alcohol problems by politely refusing.

To put this problem in proper perspective, you only have to reflect on the number of positive pursuits of Aboriginal people that you have seen. And consider how great natural features such as the MacDonnell Ranges, Uluru and Ubirr to name a few, are all the more evocative for the powerful spiritual imprints of their ancient but continuing belief system.

Another one of the delights of the Outback is meeting the roadhouse owners, stockmen, pastoralists and tour operators. And some are real characters. Often unsung, these people too are among the prized assets which give the Territory and Kimberley some of its unique flavour.

The 'tyranny of distance' which fostered a particular outlook on life in earlier times is often reflected in these men and women today, despite the advent of modern communications.

While much Australian history focuses on the eastern and southern States, it is clear that those much revered character traits of Australians regarded as typically 'Aussie' today, stem largely from outback roots. This is reflected in, and reinforced by the rich store of literature and song that the Outback has spawned. And although famous Australian poet, A.B. "Banjo" Patterson was alluding to drovers when he wrote in Clancy of the Overflow, Outback people have "... pleasures that townsfolk never know ...", the words help explain why people choose to live here.

There are a few common courtesies that you should be mindful of in the cattle station country (see also under *Cattle Station and Homesteads* in General Information Section). If you have need to visit a station homestead (for directions or permission to camp), the first rule is to always leave gates as you find them (if the gate is open, leave it open; if it is shut, then close it properly). By closing a gate which was open, you could deny livestock access to water; conversely, by leaving a gate open, you could be responsible for stock wandering to where station owners do not want them to be.

Always get permission to camp on station property and treat all water supplies with respect (see also under *Wildlife and Environmental Respect* in General Information Section). You won't endear yourself to pastoralists if you take cross-country short cuts by using private station roads. One 4WD driver certainly didn't when found on a station road - the driver abused the station owner for the poor quality of the road! It should be remembered by those who choose to be ignorant, that news of this type of trespass and behaviour, travels fast in the bush.

Friendliness, a dry sense of humour and plenty of good stories, best experienced in the quaint, often ramshackle bush pubs, characterise many of the outback people. When a 10-year drought broke in the Centre, there's the story of Ashley Severin at Curtin Springs, who as a youngster and having never seen rain, panicked and fainted - revival was quick after his father threw a bucket of bulldust over him!

Outback people have strong links with the past and you can learn much from them; in some places they will tell of fascinating things to see, where the best fishing is, and some good yarns (best advice is to be a good listener). It's worthwhile catching some of the races, rodeos and campdrafts for some unforgettable Outback entertainment and people, too.

Northern Territory Profile

SIZE

The Territory covers 1,346,200 sq km (519,633 sq miles), which represents about a sixth (17 percent) of the Australian continental land mass. Comparatively, the Northern Territory is 3.7 times the size of Germany, 5.5 times the size of the United Kingdom, and 5 times the size of New Zealand! It extends 1610km (1000 miles) from north to south, and 934km (580 miles) from east to west. Eighty percent of its area lies within the tropical zone, north of the Tropic of Capricorn.

POPULATION

It has 1% of Australia's population (approximately 180,000 people), of whom just over 60% live in the two major centres, Darwin (88,000) and Alice Springs (27,000). The remaining population is spread thinly (apart from Tennant Creek and Katherine), mainly in smaller townships, Aboriginal communities, tiny wayside settlements, station homesteads, and mining areas. The population density is only 0.1 persons per square kilometre - the lowest in relation to other states in Australia.

Over one quarter of the population is Aboriginal (27%); living mainly in nearly 100 small communities scattered throughout the Territory.

The blend of European, Asian and Aboriginal cultures and lifestyles gives the region a distinctive flavour and character, with Darwin being the most cosmopolitan. Another distinctive population characteristic is that it is weighted towards the young - nearly 80% are below 40 years, and around 50% below 25 years of age.

POLITICAL STATUS

The Commonwealth of Australia is a federation of six States (New South Wales, Victoria, Tasmania, Queensland, South Australia, Western Australia) and two territories. The Northern Territory, while established as a self-governing territory in 1978 with most Commonwealth powers transferred to it, has yet to reach full statehood. It has some differences in titles: instead of a Governor and Premier, there is an Administrator and Chief Minister respectively, and the 25 member Parliament sits at Darwin. Two major problems have yet to be resolved before statehood is declared. One is the emergence of a cultural dualism in the Territory as a result of self-determination in process of being restored to Aboriginal communities, and how to bridge cultural gaps for the social unity and cohesiveness that statehood demands. Another is financial. The small population is seen as being insufficient to generate the finance needed for statehood status.

FLAGS

The Territory flag incorporates 3 colours - black, white and red ochre. The five stars on the black panel represent the Southern Cross constellation, while the 7 petals of the Territory's floral emblem, Sturt's Desert Rose, are etched on the ochre. The 7 petals represent the 6 Australian States and Northern Territory. It is the only state or Territory flag without any element of the Union Jack.

The bird depicted on The Northern Territory Tourist Commission logo is the delightful brolga (Grus rubicunda). In the creation time, according to Aboriginal belief, there lived a beautiful girl named Bralgah, who loved to dance. She would dance all day long, whirling around with her arms outstretched as she fluttered about. Bralgah rejected the advances of one of the clan and was banished in the form of a whirly-wind. She returned as the dancing Brolga. Also known as the Native Companion, Brolga is one of the few Aboriginal names retained after European occupation.

ECONOMY

The Territory's vibrant economy is reflected in above the national growth rate figures in many sectors. Plentiful reserves of natural resources provide a strong base for the mining industry which contributes over 21 % of gross state product compared with around 5% in other states of Australia. The major minerals extracted are: bauxite(for aluminium) with Australia's third largest bauxite mine at Gove; gold, with major ventures in the Pine Creek district, Tanami Desert and Tennant Creek areas; manganese on Groote Island; Zinc, lead, silver with one of the world's major resources at McArthur River and Uranium with over 15% of the world's reserves occurring on leases surrounded by Kakadu National Park. Natural gas reserves are tapped from the Mereenie fields south west of Alice Springs and piped to major settlements including Darwin. A range of other minerals are also mined.

Tourism is another major industry which services over 1 million visitors annually. The pastoral industry based on approximately 239 leasehold properties, produce cattle for domestic and overseas markets including live cattle shipments to Asian destinations. These station properties range in size from 198 sq.km. (123 sq.miles) at Billytodd and Opium Creek to massive holdings such as Brunette Downs (12,254 sq.km/7600 sq.miles) and Victoria River Downs (11,885 sq.km./7370 sq.miles). Fishing is another important primary industry while defence establishments are significant employers.

THE ARTS, SPORT AND RECREATION

The variety and quality of the Arts in the Territory come as a surprise to many visitors. The region is rich in multi-cultural experiences, and various Arts and Performing Arts organisations are active in Alice Springs and Darwin, where they have fine facilities. Festivals add further colour.

The Territory climate and outdoor lifestyle are conducive to sport and along with the younger age characteristics, there's a high degree of participation in organised sports, and as a consequence there are magnificent facilities which visitors can share too.

Top End activities include fishing, canoeing, hunting, swimming, water-skiing, sailing, skin diving or pleasure cruising. Darwinites involve themselves in sporting activities from indoor bowling to football, athletics and cricket. Racquet sports and golf are popular, too. Alice Springs has over 40 sporting clubs, and even tiny Outback settlements might have a golf course (of sorts)! Horse racing, rodeos and campdrafts are popular and important social events in the Outback.

A profile of the Kimberley Region of Western Australia is included in the introduction to that region in Part Two.

USEFUL BOOKS

References found to be among the most useful are contained in the following list of books. It should be noted that a number of these publications (particularly *History*) are unfortunately out of print, but copies may be obtained in libraries or good second-hand book shops. The wealth of excellent specialist papers and tourist information type of publications produced by State and Territory Conservation and Wildlife Commissions, Parks Australia, other Government Departments and motoring organisations, and various Tourist Organisations, are acknowledged elsewhere in the text.

General

Australia's Flying Doctors; R. Woldendorp and R. McDonald
Alice on the Line; D. Blackwell and D. Lockwood
Big Run, The; J. Makim
Camels and the Outback; H. Barker
Drovers, The; K. Willey
My Country; a poem by D. Mackellar
Outback; T. Keneally
Outback Cooking in the Camp Oven; J. and R. Absalom
People of the Inland; J. Carter
To Ayers Rock and Beyond; Bill Harvey
Top End of Down Under, The; P. Jarver
Up The Track; D. Lockwood
West of the Centre; R. Ericksen
Yulara; P. Cox and A. Park

Geography

Australian Geographic
Australian Environments and People; M. Martin, G. Allenby
Geomorphology; C. Twidale
Heinmann Atlas

History

A Short History of Australia; M. Clark
A Land Half Won; G. Blainey
European Occupation; Ed. T. Gurry
Far Country, The: A Short History of the Northern Territory; A. Powell
Fatal Impact, The; A. Moorehead
Flynn of the Inland; I. Idriess
Front Door, The; D. Lockwood
Never-Never Line, The: The Story of the North Australia Railway; J. Harvey
New Frontier: Australia's Rising Northwest; J. Carter
Riches of Ancient Australia: A Journey Into Prehistory; J. Flood
Territory, The; E. Hill
Triumph of the Nomads; G. Blainey
Tyranny of Distance, The; G. Blainey
White Man in a Hole: Coober Pedy; R. Briande

Aboriginal

Aboriginal Australian Art; R. and C. Berndt, J. Stanton
Aboriginal Australians; R. Broome
Aboriginal People of the Northern Territory; A.T.S.I.C.
Aboriginal Words; Macquarie
Art of Utopia, The; M. Boulter
Dispossession: Black Heritage and White Invasion; H. Reynolds
Kakadu Man; Bill Neidjie
Killing Me Softly: The Destruction of a Heritage; P. and N. Wallace
Life Among the Aborigines; Bill Harvey
My Place; Sally Morgan
Other Side of the Frontier, The; Henry Reynolds
Papunya Tula: Art of the Western Desert; G. Bardon
Rock Art; A.T.S.I.C.
Rock Paintings of Aboriginal Australia; E. Godden and J. Malnic

Natural History
A Biological Survey of the Tanami Desert; D. Gibson
A Field Guide to Australian Birds, Vols. 1 & 2; P. Slater
A Field Guide to Central Australia; P. van Ooserzee
Discover Australia: National Parks; Ed. R. and V. Moon
Discover Wilderness Australia: Ecotours; N. Hermes
Kakadu; D. Ovington
Kakadu National Park: Plan of Management; Parks Australia
Key Guide to Australian Trees; L. Cronin
Living Centre of Australia, The; A Blomberry
Mingkiri: A Natural History of Uluru; compiled by L. Baker
Natural History Guide to Kakadu, Australia; I. Morris
Nature of Australia: Portrait of an Island Continent; J. Vandenbeld
Plant and Wildlife Identikits; Parks and Wildlife Commission of N.T.
Plants of the Tropical Woodland; M Clark and S. Traynor
Uluru - Kata-Tjuta and Watarrka: National Parks and Field Guide; A. Kerle

Travel and Fiction
A Town Like Alice; N. Shute
Australian Explorers Handbook, The; J. Carter
Australia's Coast of Coral and Pearl; P. Brown
Call of the Kimberleys, The; I. Shackcloth
Cattle King, The; I. Idriess
Crocodiles and Other People; D. Lockwood
Explore Queensland; B. Elder
In the Tracks of the Camelmen; P. Rajkowski
Kimberley, The: An Adventurer's Guide; R. and V. Moon
Kings in Grass Castles; M. Durack
Life on the Daly River; N. Polishak
One For the Road: A Hitchhiker's Outback; T. Horwitz
Ribbon and the Ragged Square, The; L. Christmas
Safe Outback Travel; J. Absalom
We of the Never Never; A. Gunn

Natural Features

Features broadly outlined in this section are in more detail in the regional introductions and at appropriate places in Part Two.

CLIMATE

The Northern Territory has two broad climate regions. The Top End experiences a tropical Wet (monsoon) and Dry Season regime, while the Central Australia Region is subject to a drier, arid zone climate pattern. The Kimberley has a pattern similar to the Territory's Top End Region. Climate tables in the regional introductions in Part Two detail patterns.

LANDFORMS AND GEOLOGICAL HISTORY

On a continental scale, the Northern Territory and Kimberley lie within the Great Western Plateau landform division - one of the world's most ancient and geologically stable regions (it has been relatively undisturbed by mountain building or tectonic forces for tens of millions of years). Within this region, some of the oldest rocks in existence are found, many dating back over 3000 million years to Precambrian Times (see Geological Time Scale Chart).

Subdivisions within the Great Western Plateau landform region - Arnhem Land Plateau, Barkly Tableland, Kimberley Highlands,

GEOLOGICAL TIME SCALE

Years Ago	Epoch	Period	Era
10 000	Recent	Quaternary	
1 000 000	Pleistocene		
12 000 000	Pliocene		
25 000 000	Miocene		Cenozoic
35 000 000	Oligocene	Tertiary	
	Eocene		
60 000 000	Paleocene		
70 000 000			
		Cretaceous	
130 000 000			
		Jurassic	Mesozoic
165 000 000			
		Triassic	
200 000 000			
		Permian	
235 000 000			
		Carboniferous	
285 000 000			
		Devonian	Palaeozoic
325 000 000			
		Silurian	
350 000 000			
		Ordovician	
410 000 000			
		Cambrian	
500 000 000			
			Pre-Cambrian
3 000 000 000			

MacDonnell Ranges and Amadeus Trough (where Uluru and Kata Tjuta are located) - indicate major breaks in the broad landform pattern, and areas where many of Australia's most dramatic wilderness landscapes are found.

Australia's landforms have evolved over hundreds of millions of years, the result of two major geological processes. Internal energy forces originating from the earth's core, caused tectonic activity (mountain building and major crustal rock movement such as folding, faulting and uplift), which gave initial shape to the continent and its landforms. External forces or agents of erosion (mainly running water, wind and temperature) have dramatically modified original landform features. Over the aeons, these erosional processes have worn the Great Western Plateau region to an almost flat surface, now only 400-600 metres (1312/1968 feet) above sea level.

Great fold mountain systems such as the MacDonnell Ranges, and botanical oddities in the arid, Central Australia region can be attributed directly and indirectly to internal geological forces known as plate tectonics or continental drift. Put simply, the earth's outermost layer or varying thickness is the crust of solid rock, which provides a bed for the oceans and base for landmasses. The total crust area is not an unbroken piece of rock. Instead it is divided into a number of separate pieces or plates, delineated by major fault or fracture lines. These plates ride on the mantle (an underlying layer of soft, red-hot rock or magma, extending from about 70kms/43miles to 2900kms/1798miles below the earth's surface. Convection currents within the mantle (these stem from radioactivity and consequent heat energy at the core), move these great crustal plates a few centimetres each year (Australia is currently drifting north-east at a rate of 3-4cm per annum).

When plates are pulled apart, molten rock pushes up to form new crustal surface as it solidifies. Where plates collide, one may be over-ridden or rock layers may be buckled by the compressional forces to form massive fold mountains. Forces within the plates can initiate major uplift. Such tectonic activity pushed up the

Petermann Ranges (Central Australia) over 500 million years ago - the outwash of eroded rock debris from these ranges laid the basis for Uluru and Kata Tjuta. The MacDonnell Ranges mark the welding together of ancient crustal rock in the formation process of the continent. But these ranges were worn down long before Australia became a continent.

Continental drift forced the plate on which the embryonic Australian continent was situated, to roam the globe. Six hundred million years ago, Australia formed part of a land mass which included Antarctica, South America and Africa called Gondwana, (the other continents as known today, formed another single landmass called Laurasia - it is thought that several times in the earth's history, the continents have joined into one single landmass called Pangea before breaking away again). At this time (600 m.y.a.), Australia was located in the tropical zone of the Northern Hemisphere.

The huge Gondwana landmass drifted south and around 144 m.y.a., began to break up. Australia, still attached to Antarctica, continued a southerly drift until about 60 m.y.a. when they separated. About this time Australia's northerly drift began. In the course of drifting, Central Australia in particular has been in tropical zones where high rainfall gave rivers the energy to carve great gorges through mountain ranges and to transport and deposit eroded rock debris. Under more arid conditions millions of years later, this eroded material provided a base for extensive stony plains and deserts.

Australia's latitudinal swings in location due to continental drift, created an environmental sieve for plants and animals. Relics of the rainforest are evident in Central Australia today. In the micro-climates of gorges in the MacDonnell Ranges, some of the world's oldest plants survive - ferns and cycads. The Cabbage Palm in Finke Gorge National Park is also another plant of a past, tropical period. Green tree frogs are an echo from rainforest days, while a number of fish species would normally be more at home in tropical waters.

DESERTS

Hot deserts now occupy approximately 70 percent of the Australian continent including high proportions of the Northern Territory and Kimberley land areas. Such areas are defined by an annual average rainfall of less than 250mms (9.75 inches) and evaporation rates which far exceed precipitation. Rainfall is erratic, occurring at unpredictable intervals when moisture-laden tropical air intrudes into the interior. Generally, the nature of desert landscapes is such that during the day the sun rapidly heats the land (temperatures up to 50 degrees Celsius in places), but under cloudless skies at night, rapid radiation of heat into the atmosphere causes extremes of daily temperatures - hot days and cold nights. What makes Australia's deserts distinctive in relation to popular Saharan images, is the variation of landform from place to place, and the great range of wildlife and vegetation that has adapted itself to arid conditions.

Landform provides the basis for classification of Australian deserts. North from Port Augusta, the Stuart Highway traverses or near fringes the five major desert types found in Australia; claypan or clay plain; stony or gibber desert; mountain desert and sand and shield desert.

Claypans and saltlakes characterise the landscape between Port Augusta and Glendambo. These features are formed by natural depressions into which intermittent streams have drained and deposited great amounts of fine sediment. Lakes which form are often short-lived; rapid evaporation turns them into claypans or playas, or where levels of salt are high, into saltpans or salinas.

Stony deserts or gibber plains were the bane of the first European explorers. Burke and Wills and Stuart, among others, experienced in the course of their expeditions, great stretches of ground strewn 'with sharp, dark-brown stones that were terrible to walk on' - the gibber plains. These stony deserts are the remains of rock debris dumped by rivers on the flanks of eroding central mountain ranges. Over time, winds have blown away the sand, leaving a mantle of stones. The passage of sand across the gibber plains causes the gravel and stones to be polished and worn by the wind to form ventifacts (a pebble faceted by the abrasive effects of wind-blown sand). Often shapes are triangular, and many gibbers have acquired a veneer of iron and silica rich material or "desert varnish" which colours them various shades of brown, ranging from yellow-brown to deep, blackish-brown. These landscapes extend discontinuously from Port Augusta to the Territory border and beyond.

The Musgrave, James and MacDonnell Ranges groups in the Northern Territory, and the ranges comprising the Kimberley Uplands, are classified as mountain desert regions. Within these groups of once great mountain chains, a variation of habitats, from ridges and broken, rocky range country to broad, sandy valley floors, give them a distinctive landscape identity. While mainly elevation has given a unity to the mountain desert type, geology has determined shield desert classification. Because deserts have developed on stable, Precambrian rock structures such as the Barkly Tablelands, they have been classified according to the underlying geological structures - a shield. These shield deserts in the Territory and Kimberley support a surprising variety of vegetation that from a moving vehicle, gives an illusion of complete plant cover.

Another common illusion experienced when travelling through the arid lands is heat haze. This phenomena is caused by the layer of air near the ground becoming less dense as it is heated. As a result, the light rays reaching your eyes are curved as they pass through the less dense air. Therefore, instead of the ground, a reflection of the sky is seen. These mirages, which often look like a lake or sea, no doubt caused as much anguish to the European explorers as did the gibber plains.

The most popularly known feature associated with deserts are sand dunes. In the Northern Territory, the Simpson Desert, parts of the Tanami Desert and areas around Uluru-Kata Tjuta National Park are characterised by sand dunes. Dunes are formed from granules (sourced from weathered rock) and shaped into distinctive mounds or drifts by the wind. In the Simpson Desert, the dunes are predominantly longitudinal in shape, asymmetrical in cross-section (the eastern face is the steeper), rise 6-30 metres (22.8/98.4 feet) above the interdune corridors and are about 360 metres (1180 feet) apart. They are also continuous over long distances - some extend for over 320 kms (198 miles). Sometimes rivers briefly flow in the interdune corridors. Studies suggest that these dunes are blown by winds from the south-west and south-east, with the steeper face of the slope changing according to wind direction. The surface sand is most mobile and the trend of the dune is governed by the stronger of the two prevailing winds.

About 75kms (47 miles) south of Alice Springs, sand dunes trend north-south and in this area, they mark the western extremity of the Simpson Desert. Further southwest, in areas around Uluru and between Uluru and Kings Canyon, the sand is essentially all that remains of the huge mountain ranges that once straddled Central Australia. For millions of years, great rivers carried the rock waste from the eroding ranges and deposited the material in low-lying areas. The reduced rock was blown back over the landscape to form the sand deserts seen today. Over the last few thousand years, the dunes have been stabilised by vegetation and are relatively immobile.

These dominant features of Central Australian landscapes are quite young geologically. The dunes of the Simpson Desert are estimated to be around 30,000 years old. This is perhaps not surprising when aridity developed in Australia only about one million years ago. As previously mentioned, throughout most of Australia's natural history, rainforest has been the dominant vegetation.

RIVERS

The Roper River flowing into the Gulf of Carpenteria, is the Territory's largest river. The other main river systems include the Daly and Victoria, which flow to the west, the Adelaide, Mary,

South and North Alligator (flowing to the North), and the Cox and McArthur (flowing into the Gulf of Carpenteria). The Katherine River forms part of the Daly River System, and all permanently flowing drainage systems in the Territory are located in the Top End Region.

There are no major rivers in Central Australia. Those which appear on maps rarely flow; after heavy rains, creeks and rivers can become raging torrents, but quickly contract to a series of billabongs before drying up. The Finke and Todd Rivers are well known examples. Vegetation fringing dry creek beds are sustained by moisture deep below the surface.

In the Kimberley, major rivers include the Ord, Durack and Drysdale, all flowing north into the Timor Sea. The mightiest river in the Kimberley is the Fitzroy, which flows into King Sound.

FLORA AND FAUNA

Within the Northern Territory, the range of natural habitats (mangrove coast and freshwater swamps and billabongs; rainforests; savannah woodlands; mulga and spinifex plains; gibber and sandy deserts; broken range country and sheltered, rocky gorges) provide a niche for nearly 3000 species of plants, over 350 types of birds, over 100 native mammals including 40 marsupials, more than 50 species of fish and other aquatic creatures in inland waters, a great range of reptiles and a large number of insects including 100 species of butterfly. The Kimberley Region is also characterised by prolific wildlife and a great range of plant species.

Flora and fauna are best seen in National Parks such as Kakadu and at specialist parks, in particular, the Territory Wildlife Park at Berry Springs and the Alice Springs Desert Park.

Cultural History

'DISCOVERY' OF AUSTRALIA

Since the time of the Greek philosophers, the supposed existence of a "Great Southern Land" (logically reasoned to exist in order to counterbalance the known Northern Hemisphere continents), or Terra Australis Incognita, intrigued European societies. From a European perspective, who 'discovered' Australia is subject to much conjecture. Although Englishman, Captain James Cook, is popularly credited with the first European discovery of the continent in 1770, there is some evidence to suggest that this is not true with visits by Chinese, Portuguese and Dutch maritime explorers occurred during the fifteenth, sixteenth and seventeenth centuries. Evidence of Chinese exploration is inconclusive, but a number of historical relics and maps (Mota Alves Map found in Timor, circa 1602 and the Dauphine Map, with markings pointing to Portuguese origin, circa 1536) give much credence to a Portuguese discovery. McIntyre, in his book "The Secret Discovery of Australia", propounds a compelling argument favouring the Portuguese.

The Dutch were active in Australian waters in the seventeenth century. Dirk Hartog landed at Sharks Bay, Western Australia in 1616, while Abel Tasman "discovered" Tasmania in 1642 and navigated around Australia's northern coastline in 1644. Although the Dutch embarked upon several voyages of exploration to the land they called New Holland, their interest waned when the continent was perceived to be of little economic benefit.

Frequent, early visitors to Australia's northern shores were Macassarese traders from the south-west tip of Sulawesi (Indonesia), who came mainly for catching trepang (a giant sea slug) and to trade with Aboriginal people. It is thought that visits to the Arnhem Land coast began around 1650.

The first Englishman to explore any part of the Australian coast was William Dampier, who landed on the northern coast in 1688 and navigated the Kimberley coastline. His scathing description of Aboriginal people etched negative imprints deeply into the European psyche - a mindset still evident in some Australians today.

To Europeans, Australia was the last great landmass awaiting discovery. Although not recognised or even considered at the time, what they really discovered was a land long inhabited by a people whose culture constitutes the longest continuing belief system of any society in the world's cultural history. What remains of academic interest is who from the Northern Hemisphere, discovered a continent settled in an orderly manner by Aboriginal people.

ABORIGINAL SETTLEMENT

ORIGINS

According to the beliefs of Australia's indigenous people, their ancestors have occupied the continent since the beginning of time or the creation period. However, from a Western scientific perspective, prehistorians agree that because Australia had no primate stock, people could not have evolved here. It is therefore assumed that Aboriginal people migrated to Australia, most probably from somewhere in south or south-east Asia. With improved dating technology, occupation dates of at least 50,000 BC in Kakadu National Park have been established. It is now generally accepted by prehistorians that the continent was initially occupied in the period 50-70,000 BC. However, ongoing research is pushing the dates further back into prehistory.

The timing and nature of Aboriginal migration and occupation are still subject to much opinion, but there is a preference by prehistorians for a pattern of migration termed the "porous northern perimeter" model. This model contends that occupation occurred as a result of steady migration rather than episodic waves. Contributing to the plausibility of this model is the different geographical conditions which existed between 70,000 and 10,000 years ago. During this time, the earth was experiencing the last great 'ice age'. As massive volumes of water were locked up in ice sheets, sea levels at times fell to between about 120 and 150 metres (394/492 feet) lower than today. As seas contracted, the configuration of the continents changed - under these conditions, New Guinea and Tasmania were joined to Australia to form the Greater Australian continent. Apart from a few shallow stretches of water, the ancestors of Australian Aborigines would have been able to move freely along the land bridge that existed between India and Australia during this glacial period. At this time too, environments that are extremely arid today, such as Central Australia, were far moister climatically, making them more habitable.

Of interest to prehistorians is the racial affiliation of Aboriginal people. Most now accept on cranial and skeleton evidence, that Australia was settled by two types of Aboriginal people identified as Robust (archaic skulls) and Gracile (modern skulls). It is contended that Robust people arrived between 50-70,000 BC, possibly related to Homo erectus in Indonesia. Gracile people are thought to have migrated about 35-40,000 BC and spread quickly through the continent, displacing and absorbing Robust people (both peoples were 'modern' in that they were Homo sapiens and so able to interbreed). Gracile people are generally accepted as being the ancestors of today's Aboriginal people.

CULTURAL DIVERSITY

The steady diffusion and orderly settlement of Aboriginal groups throughout Australia, along with different responses to the range of natural environments, contributed to clans developing a distinct cultural identity. There was no single homogenous Aboriginal society; clans differed in many aspects of their cultural and social organisation and in artistic expression. At the time of European contact, there were between 600 and 700 distinct clans in Australia, each with their own territory, political system, laws and language. Contemporary historians have likened the social structures and territory of Aboriginal clans to the nation states of Europe, but on a smaller scale, and without the visible manifestations (buildings and institutions) of such European countries.

Language gave particular identity and unity to each clan. And while the 600-700 'clan-nations' spoke between them 200-250 separate languages (as unlike one another as German and Russian), dialects also spoken by clans reinforced clan identity. There were an estimated 700 dialects (variants of a single language) in 1800. In some areas, of Central Australia, Pitjantjatjara language was spoken by hundreds of people over a huge area, whereas in parts of Arnhem Land, as many as ten distinct languages were spoken within a relatively small area.

Because of widespread social interaction between clan groups, people had to be multi-lingual to communicate. Prior to European occupation, over 100 languages were spoken in the Northern Territory alone. Many of these languages disappeared (as elsewhere in Australia) following massive societal disruption of the contact period (when Europeans arrived).

Despite many other differences (music and dance, kinship systems, art forms, rituals and ceremonies), underlying similarities brought clans together for trade, ceremonies,

intermarriage and maintenance of spiritual beliefs. Just as there are clear cultural differences between the German and French people, within the broader European grouping of people, a similar diversity exists within the wider Aboriginal race today.

The following outlines of Religion, Economy and Social Organisation are also designed to complement a representative description of one Aboriginal clan - Anangu - which appears under *Uluru-Kata Tjuta National Park* in Part Two.

RELIGION

Common to all Aboriginal clans is their belief system, the essence of which is best outlined from Kakadu National Park Plan of Management, 1986 (published by Parks Australia), and reproduced with permission:

"... According to Aboriginal tradition, the relationship to the land is an amalgam of spiritual, economic and physical bonds. These bonds are inextricably interwoven, and are set into a time frame which is often referred to by non-Aboriginal people as 'dreaming' or 'dreamtime'. These expressions are inadequate attempts in the English language to explain a system of belief which perceives the past, present and future as interacting with each other in an eternally dynamic relationship affecting the affairs of men, women and children in their everyday lives. A major aspect of the past which affects the present and future, is the creative behaviour of beings (creative spirits, beings or Gods), who moulded the landscape into its present forms and set in place people's languages, social organisations and values. Some features of the landscape, which mark the temporary or permanent abodes of these beings, are held to be significant by Aboriginal people. Many of these sites are seen as public and irrefutable evidence of the veracity of Aboriginal people's systems of belief. A few are regarded as secret or sacred and consequently have prohibited access ..."

In effect, spirit, country (or economy), kinship and "dreaming" or lore are inextricably linked. The stories of the so called dreamtime are not just stories for their own sake, but give moral guidance as to how to care for the country and for extended family. The laws set down in the creation stories may also be viewed as a system for sustainable living in a fragile, changeable environment. This concept was so complex as to be beyond the range of experience or understanding of most of the early European settlers.

ECONOMY

Since the Contact Period, European observers and social scientists have attempted to categorise Aboriginal lifestyle in terms of Western concepts of development. Invariably, literature describes their economy and lifestyle as hunter-gatherer, subsistence, primitive, or romantically, as 'noble savages'.

In effect, Aboriginal economy was the product of varied and deliberate responses to the range of environments in which they lived. And like any dynamic society, change and modification to meet differing needs was a continual process. Over time, technology became more complex, with change from a finer stone culture to more efficient bone and wood technology. Their economy was controlled, based on a stable considered management of the environment through the acquisition of intimate knowledge of ecosystems, and an effective division of labour. There is little doubt that the Aboriginal clans were settled on the land in an organised way; the constant movement over the land for economic or social purposes was no different in concept to movement of Europeans on the later pastoral holdings. The fact that Aboriginal movement was invariably seen as 'roaming' or 'walkabout' (implying an aimlessness), indicated that few, if any, Europeans really understood the system of Aboriginal landuse, or the subtleties of inter-clan relationships which necessitated obligatory journeys.

The apparent resistance of Aboriginal groups to develop intensive agriculture has been commented on by a number of historians.

Prehistorian D.J. Mulvaney, points out that the matter of Aboriginal agriculture is "... a non-problem of European making, for its presuppositions are Western concepts of progress and the moral virtues of industry ...". It has been assumed that because the Australian economy in post-contact times was based on intensive agriculture and pastoralism, the Aboriginal people should have done it too, and, that something must have prevented them. The possibility that Aboriginal clans saw no reason to change their obviously successful system of 'natural farming' practices, was for a long time, not even considered (refer to Anangu under *Uluru-Kata Tjuta National Park* for Aboriginal agricultural practices). Everything they needed was readily accessible from a great variety of foods and medicinal plants to raw materials for tools and weapons. And trade widened access to scarce commodities. Aboriginal people had better health when compared to the emerging industrial societies of Europe and were able to satisfy all their needs with just a few hours daily labour. It's ironic that the nineteenth century European mindset not only failed to recognise such efficiency, but also implied Aboriginal endeavour was lazy. But it's interesting to note the comments made in the 1960s of American anthropologist, Marshall Sahlins who described the pre-contact Aboriginal economy as the "original affluent society".

SOCIAL ORGANISATION

It is estimated that at the time of European contact, about 126 clan groups had all, or most of their territory or range in the Northern Territory, and collectively had a total population of around 35,000. Within these territories, bands or small family groups of 15-30 constituted the basic residential and economic unit. Groups of bands formed the larger social unit that anthropologists have classified as 'communities', 'tribes', 'culture blocs' or 'clans'. Of these terms, 'tribe' and descriptor 'tribal' are arguably misnomers. The main reason is that Aboriginal society is egalitarian - there is no single leader or chief, instead, authority is vested in a group of Clan Elders who give collective guidance and delegate responsibilities to suitably qualified clanspeople in accordance with Aboriginal law.

Bands are made up of extended families - grandparents, parents and children, and also affines; people related to clan members by marriage only. The bands have rights to resources in an area within the broader clan territory, but the land is collectively owned by the clan. There is no concept or practice of individual or family ownership of land. Members of clans trace their descent to the creation period and are spiritually bonded to their area of land (and features within it), inherited from generation to generation.

ABORIGINAL ART

The international art world has acclaimed contemporary Aboriginal artistic expression, while the numerous natural galleries of rock art are widely acknowledged as the world's oldest and finest collection of prehistoric paintings, engravings, drawings and stencils. Aboriginal art is unique in style, symbolism and form - there is nothing like it elsewhere in the world.

In one sense, Art is the "written language" of Aboriginal clans - a means by which spiritual beliefs are reinforced, children educated, history recorded, stories told, and communication of messages which could embrace a range of subjects from environment to politics. This subject and function aspect of art has changed little from prehistoric times.

It was only when (as in other aspects of Aboriginal culture), European cultures ceased to use Western technological and material values, as a basis for evaluating Aboriginal Art in very recent times, that the true value and significance of their symbolic, linear style came to be appreciated.

Ancient Aboriginal art is valued by anthropologists for its cultural insights while artists derive inspiration from its traditional and contemporary visual forms, spareness of technique, colour, motifs and symbols. Noted artists, Sidney Nolan and Clifton Pugh were among a number who viewed Aboriginal art as a rich source of new forms and ideas.

Rock art, found on exposed rock faces, in rock shelters or overhangs and in caves, is captivating to visitors, as much for its visual appeal as the sense of wonder it evokes in such ancient landscape settings. Some of the spiritual figures depicted on rock surfaces are, according to Aboriginal belief, the outlines or impressions of creative beings themselves as they returned to the land, rather than the work of any human artist. Aboriginal people inherited these sacred pictures, and it is their responsibility to maintain them with paint from time to time.

As in all Aboriginal art, style and form varies considerably from place to place. In places like Arnhem Land and Central Australia, symbols and motifs painted on rock also appear in other mediums of expression such as painting on bark or canvas, reflecting a continuing artistic tradition.

It is on the basis of technique, form, motif (recurring theme), size and character, that Australia's rock art is classified into one of three major styles or groups of styles, with paintings and engravings separated only at the level of technique (this classification is based on the work of L. Maynard "The Archaeology of Australian Aboriginal Art", in S.M. Mead's book, "Exploring the Visual Art of Oceania"). Panarmitee style (named after a site in South Australia) is an individual style containing pecked engravings examples of which may be seen at N'Dhala Gorge, Eastern MacDonnell Ranges.

The Simple Figurative styles are considered to form the next major rock art phase. Generally, animal or human figures are simplified in presentation. The third category is the complex figurative style. This includes Mimi and X-ray painting styles of Kakadu and Arnhem Land and are characterised by a higher degree of stylisation and decorative features (refer also to art sites outlined under *Kakadu National Park* in Part Two).

The efflorescence of Aboriginal Art during the last two decades, is as much a response to clans resuming control over their ancestral lands, as the adaptability of artists to experiment with design motifs and artistic techniques and to use new mediums.

Revival has been aided too, by increased interest in, and demand for, paintings and craft works. In many Aboriginal communities today, art and craft has become a major economic activity providing a significant source of income for the townships.

Examples of new elements incorporated into contemporary art include the acrylic 'dot' paintings on canvas from the Western Desert Clans, the batiks from Utopia and Bathurst Islands, silk-screen prints from Tiwi Island and woodcarvings from Central Australia. Despite the employment of new elements, modern Aboriginal art retains the essential traditions of subject, symbols and motifs. In this way, the unique form of Aboriginal art is maintained, while distinctive clan symbols continue to contribute to diversity of style from place to place. While art has become an economic activity, its traditional functions are faithfully maintained. Traditional materials are still used as may be seen in the wood sculptures of Tiwi Island, bark paintings of Arnhem Land, and in a range of practical, fibre crafted products. Also, the human body continues to be a major 'site' for painting - this and sand paintings were the original places where the dot-art style was used.

Many Aboriginal Communities have their own art and craft centres where you may purchase and appreciate the importance and vibrancy of art as an economic and cultural activity. Today, much of Aboriginal Art is marketed through Artists Associations, and to ensure integrity in the marketing of art works and equity for the artists, a label of authenticity including the creator's name, is attached to all items.

CONTACT PERIOD

As elsewhere in Australia, British colonisation of the Northern Territory and Kimberley brought about massive upheaval to Aboriginal economy and culture. Many contemporary historians are now interpreting British colonisation of the continent as an invasion and conquest of Aboriginal land - a cultural collision and human tragedy of epic proportions, the legacies of which are evident in Aboriginal society today.

To the colonisers, settlement of Australia was a great event of British imperialism. When they arrived they saw no visible signs of civilisation within their experience range. To the European mindset, land that was not used for buildings associated with urban development, nor for agriculture or grazing, was not regarded as being settled. This situation as perceived by the British, formed the basis of the principle of 'terra nullius' - that in 1788 when Australia was first colonised by the British, the continent was documented as an 'empty land' and, until claimed by the British, it belonged to no-one.

Because of this assumed 'right of occupation', along with its implications of Aboriginal inferiority as a race, and non-existence as a people, it became clear that the interests of two such totally different cultures could never be accommodated. And apart from those Aboriginal people who could be 'civilised' (this meant using them in a beneficial way to settlers, for example as cheap labour on pastoral runs, and women used for sexual purposes), there was no permanent place in white man's society for Aboriginal people. As there were few European women on the frontier at this time, a number of colonists had Aboriginal women as partners. Some had genuine affection for them and raised children; others treated their women like slaves.

It was not until 1992 that an Australian High Court ruling implicitly rejected the doctrine of 'terra nullius'. This ruling related to a successful native title court action in which a claim by five Torres Strait Islanders, led by Eddie Mabo, over the Queensland Murray Islands was upheld on the basis that 'terra nullius' had wrongfully usurped their title to these lands. They proved that their attachment to the land included a concept of ownership. This ruling is known as the Mabo Decision 1992. While the ruling was specific, its implications give rise to such interpretations as official recognition of Aboriginal settlement on the mainland. And to some contemporary historians, the ruling is a basis for interpretation of the Contact Period as an invasion and complete, often brutal subjugation of the conquered clans. The effects of

British occupation on Aboriginal society is subject to much research by historians. While there is much evidence to support the 'fatal impact' view (one which broadly supposes that Aborigines were passive victims of white contact), recent research is looking at the range of Aboriginal responses during the colonisation period for further insights into conflicts on the frontier.

  Questions such as the power Aborigines had at the time, what actions of reactions they made on the frontier, and to what degree they were complicit in the changes they experienced, are strands of enquiry which indicate the complexity of European-Aboriginal race relations in the Northern Territory and Kimberley as elsewhere in Australia.

IMPACTS

As the Northern Territory and Kimberley were, by virtue of the 'tyranny of distance', among the last areas of the continent to be systematically settled by the British, impacts of land dispossession were experienced by Aboriginal clans well into the Twentieth Century. Impacts varied from area to area. There were bloody conflicts between clans who resisted intrusion of their lands by white pastoralists. These conflicts often resulted from reprisal raids by Europeans after killing of cattle by Aborigines. An Aboriginal attack on the Barrow Creek Telegraph Station in which two whites were killed, resulted in a swift punitive raid of massacre proportions. Other massacres occurred at Tempe Downs, Loves Creek, and as recently as 1928 at Coniston Station. Indiscriminate killing of Aboriginal people was widespread; the fact that few Europeans were ever prosecuted, implied tacit approval by authorities.

  The nature of clan organisation and lack of equitable weaponry prevented an effective, coordinated response by Aborigines to Europeans colonisers. Consequently, clans were driven from their land, introduced animals (cattle, sheep, camels, horses, donkeys, water buffalo and rabbits) destroyed many traditional food resources, and Aboriginal populations were decimated by the effects of introduced virulent diseases such as smallpox, influenza and tuberculosis, against which they had no natural immunity. Many Aboriginal people, severely affected by disease, malnutrition and inhumane treatment, began to gather at frontier stations, missions and ration depots. Christian Missions and some European individuals, displayed humanitarian empathy. Generally, the missions provided refuge and although their organisations had a religious motive, they played a major role in ensuring the survival of Aboriginal culture (however in some places they were responsible for wiping it out). A number of Europeans associated with the missions showed great moral courage in the face of prevailing colonist attitudes. They generally viewed the work of Christian missions as misplaced sentimentality, and that Aboriginal people were expected to die out in the natural course of events.

Government established reserves provided a refuge of sorts. Other Aborigines camped on cattle stations where they were employed as highly skilful, but poorly paid stockmen or domestic servants. Some lived in squalor on the fringe of towns, while a relative few, mainly in the most remote outback areas, maintained (as far as was possible) traditional lifestyles. Those in closest contact with white settlements, invariably depended on European foods and often developed an alcohol and tobacco dependency.

Living conditions on both stations and settlements were generally poor, with no sanitation, water supply or medical services. The change to a mainly European diet of flour, sugar, tea and meat, led to a variety of nutritional disorders such as diabetes, obesity and impaired growth. It also contributed to a high infant mortality rate. The reserves, set up as part of a deliberate policy to remove Aboriginal people from the land, had major effects on family life. By 1911, fertility levels reached a point unable to sustain the Aboriginal population. The Aboriginals Ordnance Act 1918 accelerated family disintegration through the enforced removal of children from mixed parentage (White/Aboriginal) families. Children were placed in foster homes or in institutions where it was felt that chances of 're-education' to European ways were higher.

Further subjugation of Aboriginal society occurred with the official adoption of the policy of assimilation in the post-Second World War period. In practical terms, it supposed that all Aboriginal people would live like white Australians. Despite its attempts to socially engineer change, Aboriginal culture was remarkably resilient. Townships such as Papunya (1959) and Kaltukatjara (Docker River, 1968) were deliberately established in remote localities to facilitate the assimilation policy.

By the late 1960's, the policy of assimilation was increasingly being questioned. A referendum in 1967, which saw 90 percent of Australians vote in favour of citizen status for Aboriginal people, and the power of Federal Government to legislate for them in all states, reflected a change in attitude by non-Aboriginal Australians. Under a Labour Government in 1972, the assimilation policy was abandoned, and replaced by a policy of self-determination, through which Aboriginal communities could be actively involved in decision making about their own lives. Prompting this change of policy were strikes by Aboriginal stockmen at Newcastle Waters in 1966, and at Vestey's Wave Hill Station in 1967. These events drew national attention to the poor living conditions of Aboriginal people generally, and was a factor contributing to the referendum outcome previously referred to. A prerequisite for self-determination was land.

LAND RIGHTS

The Aboriginal Land Rights (Northern Territory) Act 1976, aimed to provide simple justice for people deprived of their land; the provision of a land base for a people who had no real opportunity to achieve economic equality with other Australians; and the maintenance of Aboriginal spirituality and cultural identity.

The Act gave Aboriginal people inalienable freehold title to all Aboriginal reserves and a means by which they could claim unalienated Crown Land. The Act also established three Land Councils which now administer land and generally act on behalf of the traditional owners, including negotiation of royalties for any minerals allowed to be extracted from Aboriginal land.

Land Rights is a contentious issue particularly for vested interests such as pastoral leaseholders and mining companies. The issue has become very complex. Following the implications of the Mabo Decision 1992, national governments have been attempting to legislate for an equitable Native Title Act to cover all of Australia. However, the Mabo Decision failed to define the extent to which native title existed in Australia. The Native Title Act 1993, was the first attempt to clarify native title but ambiguities in the Act has currently incurred often bitter debates as to equitable amendments.

The resolution of land rights is not only seen as critical to the well-being of Aboriginal people, but also a means by which conciliation between non-Aboriginal and Aboriginal Australians may occur. Whether politicians can achieve this, remains to be seen.

CONTEMPORARY SITUATION

With policy shifts from assimilation to self-determination, there is reason for some optimism about the future of Aboriginal communities. However, uncertainty about native title, attitudes of racial prejudice in some sections of the non-Aboriginal population, and Aboriginal poverty in many places, are among a number of impediments to social and economic equality.

While poverty is a fact, it should not mask the considerable achievements of Aboriginal communities. There are many cases of welfare dependency reduction by Aboriginal communities, through converting the strengths of cultural heritage to economic advantage. One example is the art and craft industry, which has become an economic mainstay in some communities. Aboriginal cultural tourism is another. In Alice Springs, the range of enterprises and services controlled by Aboriginal people includes Imparja Television Station (which covers almost one-third of Australia), primary school, adult education facility, CAAMA Radio, art and craft outlets, community store networks and three Aboriginal-owned airlines (Ngaanyatjarra Air, PY Air, Ngurratjuta Air). Similar examples are evident in other major Northern Territory centres.

In contrast, since the 1970's, small groups of Aboriginal people have chosen for cultural reasons, to live away from settlements by establishing outstation communities in the bush. This does not mean that they have resumed a fully traditional lifestyle; outstations use European technology, many have reticulated water and are linked to major centres by modern telecommunications.

Apart from those mentioned, there are some other contentious issues to be resolved before a more secure future can be achieved for Aboriginal people. One is to reconcile Aboriginal law with Australian law, while an official National Government apology to Aboriginal people for past acts of deprivation (including "the stolen generation" - when children were taken away from their natural families), is seen as an important gesture for conciliation by many Australians. So far, the Federal Government is reluctant to do so, and negotiations for a treaty between Aboriginal people and the Commonwealth of Australia have currently stalled.

EUROPEAN HISTORY

The following is an outline designed as a broad overview; historical details are included in the most appropriate places in Part Two.

EARLY BRITISH SETTLEMENTS

The British began the colonial garrison era at Port Essington on the Northern Territory's northern coast in 1824, when in the name of King George IV, Captain Gordon Bremer claimed the land as part of New South Wales. Three days later, he moved his party of 57 soldiers and 44 convicts to a new site at Fort Dundas (Melville Island). It was shortlived, as was a later attempt in 1827 to establish a garrison settlement at Fort Wellington, Raffles Bay. While fear of French settlement and the spread of the Dutch Trading interests in the region prompted the British settlement action, the harsh climate, isolation, and poor economic prospects brought about the end of Fort Wellington in 1829. All the old arguments for a permanent settlement on Australia's northern coast were revived when Bremer was ordered once more to establish a settlement in 1838. Port Essington was chosen, and the settlement named Victoria, was abandoned after 11 years. The northern coast was neglected until the landward approaches of the 1860's.

OVERLAND EXPLORATION

In 1845, Leichhardt was the first of the overland explorers to cross any part of the Northern Territory after a 5000 km (3100 miles), nearly 15 month journey from Brisbane to Port Essington. The expedition sought a route to Port Essington to facilitate demand by Queensland and New South Wales pastoralists for cheap Asian labour as well as a route for the export of livestock.

Perhaps the greatest explorer of the Northern Territory was John McDouall Stuart, whose epic attempts to cross the continent south to north resulted in success in 1862. His favourable reports paved the way for development by the colonists.

DEVELOPMENT

Pastoralists from South Australia began a steady push northward following Stuart's trail-blazing effort. At this time, the Northern Territory was under New South Wales jurisdiction. As a result of pressure from the South Australian colony, the Northern Territory was excised from the mother colony and became part of South Australia in 1863. It was called the Northern Territory of South Australia. Escape Cliffs, near the Adelaide River mouth was the site of the colony's first attempt at settlement. Established by the Territory's first Government resident, Colonel Boyle Finniss in 1864, the settlement failed and was abandoned two years later. Surveyor-General George Goyder finally established the first permanent settlement on the north coast at Palmerston (Darwin) in 1869.

Despite its limited resources, South Australia made bold attempts to develop its newly acquired territory. Its greatest achievement was the construction of an Overland Telegraph Line between Port Augusta and Darwin - a cable which connected with submarine cables to link Australia to England. The Telegraph Line, along with gold discoveries at Pine Creek, pastoral development, and a later railway to Pine Creek, assured Darwin's permanence. The importation of Chinese labour to help develop the goldfields at Pine Creek marked the beginnings of the Territory's cosmopolitan population.

Along the route of the Overland Telegraph Line, came the pastoralists, overlanders and drovers with their mobs, filling up the vast, rich pastoral lands of the Barkly Tablelands, Victoria and Roper River regions, thus laying the foundation for the cattle industry. In 1877, the first mission at Hermannsburg was established, and in 1888, the Northern Territory become a separate electorate. Mineral finds widened the developing Northern Territory economic base.

In 1911, The Northern Territory formally passed to the control of the Commonwealth Government. 1912 brought the appointment of Dr. J.A. Gilruth as the Territory's first Administrator, whose leadership saw industrial and social unrest emerge, culminating in the Darwin Rebellion of 1918-19. Between 1926 and 1931, the Territory was divided into two administrative regions; Northern Territory and Central Australia.

The World War II years saw military rule in the north, and after the bombing of Darwin in 1942, it became the first area to experience war on the mainland. Darwin was attacked 64 times by Japanese bombers and over 1000 people were killed. Katherine was also bombed as were a number of places in the Kimberley.

The devastation of Darwin by Cyclone Tracy on Christmas Day in 1974, saw a new city emerge from the rubble soon after, and the first big step towards a statehood was in 1978, when self-government was proclaimed.

Two books well worth reading for their historical insights and Outback character are: *Far Country - A Short History of the Northern Territory* by Alan Powell, and *Outback* by T. Keneally.

Main Routes to the Territory

NORTH TO THE TERRITORY BORDER - THE STUART HIGHWAY, SOUTH AUSTRALIA

"THE TRACK"

National Route 87 (Stuart Highway) is Australia's 3188 km (1977 mile) transcontinental highway that runs from Adelaide to Darwin, and basically follows the original trail of explorer Stuart in 1860, and the subsequent Overland Telegraph Line built in 1872. Although it's now sealed from Adelaide to Darwin, many Territorians still call it 'The Track', while some 'truckies' used to endearingly refer to it as 'Bitch-o-mine'.

David D. Smith was the engineer responsible for the highway's construction between Alice Springs and Darwin in the early 1930s. With little more than shovels, picks, crowbars and a 'motley crew', construction began. Road plant was non-existent, and camels were used for transport. Anticipating war, Smith exceeded his

budget by over $130,000 when he straightened and widened sections of the track, and his only comment when reprimanded was "Too bloody bad!". Smith was in charge of the upgrading and sealing of the road during the war (1943); a task undertaken by Australians, not the Americans, as widely believed. It must have been a good road, too. Les Taylor and Dick Rendle drove an XK120 Jaguar from Darwin to Alice Springs in 10 hours in 1951, averaging 155km/h (96mph)! For his effort, Taylor was given a speeding ticket by police in Alice Springs and fined 20 pounds.

Upgrading in recent years has resulted in a two-lane, all-weather highway, along which the various isolated settlements are like chapters in a book that unfold a fascinating history, captured best of all by Douglas Lockwood in his book *Up The Track*.

PLACES - PORT AUGUSTA TO THE TERRITORY BORDER

Many visitors coming from the southern states travel to the Northern Territory via the Stuart Highway, across the South Australian Outback. Places and attractions to the border are sequentially outlined.

PORT AUGUSTA
Population 16,000
This historic city, is located at the tip of Spencer Gulf, 306 km (190 miles) north of Adelaide. Established in 1853, it is characterised by some stately architecture and is today a busy tourist centre, port, transport cross-roads point (all traffic heading north, south, east or west must pass through here), and gateway to the Outback and "The Track". It is also a gateway to the beautiful *Wilpena Pound* in the heart of the *Flinders Ranges*.

Local attractions include Lookout Points (*The Water Tower, Mathew Flinders*); **Curdnatta Art and Pottery Gallery, Homestead Park Pioneer Museum, Royal Flying Doctor Service Base** and **School of the Air** (visitors welcome to both); **Australian Arid Lands Botanic Garden** and heritage walks.

The *Wadlata Outback Centre* is the region's Tourist Bureau which houses excellent interpretive displays as well as providing invaluable service up front for visitors. Allow 1-2 hours to experience the evolution of the Flinders Ranges and South Australian Outback through Wadlata's tunnel of time. For its own intrinsic charm, Port Augusta is worthy of at least an overnight stay.

Port Augusta offers many accommodation options and eating out places - for details contact Wadlata Centre (08) 8642 4511, *open weekdays 9am-5.30pm, weekends 10am-4pm*, at 41 Flinders Tce.

PIMBA
Population 50
Located 173 km (107 miles) north of Port Augusta, the well-worn collection of buildings features a licensed roadhouse, and has all fuels, restaurant, store and accommodation.

Campsites are available and cabins cost from $25. It's *open 24 hours*, credit cards accepted, EFTPOS, ph. (08) 8673 7473.

Pimba is also located at the road junction for motorists going to Woomera, Roxby Downs, Andamooka or the Oodnadatta Track. The Indian Pacific and Ghan trains roll past Pimba on the Trans-Australia railway line. Salt lakes are landscape features, one of which, Lake Hart, borders the highway north of Pimba.

WOOMERA
Population approx. 1800
Situated 8km (5 miles) north of Pimba, Woomera is best known
for its launching of experimental British rockets during the 1950s
and 60s. NASA operated a deep space tracking station nearby
during the 1960s and 70s. Today, the Defence Department operates
a Joint Facility Communications Establishment with the
Americans at Nurrungar near Woomera. And a new rocket
launching facility was begun in 1998. These are prohibited areas,
but you can visit the town. Attractions include a collection of old
missiles and aircraft at Missile Park and a museum at the
Woomera Heritage Centre.

   The town has a good range of services. **Accommodation** is
available at *Traveller's Village* ph. (08) 8673 7800 (backpackers
and camping, on-site vans); or *Eldo Hotel/Motel* ph. (08) 8673
7867. The hotel has a reasonable **restaurant**.

GLENDAMBO
Population 30
The small service township located 114 kms (71 miles) north of
Pimba consists of two enterprises; a Mobil Service Station and the
Glendambo Tourist Centre. Architecturally, the main building of
the tourist centre is a modern version of a traditional outback
homestead.

   The complex, provides a full range of services (fuel, repairs,
meals, take-away food, store, bar) and accommodation. It has
powered **camp sites** ($12), unpowered ($10); double
bunkhouse ($12 pp); **on-site vans** from $30 x 2; **rooms** from
$50 single and $55 double. Credit cards accepted, EFTPOS, *open
7am-10pm daily*. Telephone (08) 8672 1030.

   The *Mobil Service Station* has full vehicle services, fuels, shop and
takeaway food.

COOBER PEDY
Population 4000

Located 252 km (156 miles) north of Glendambo and 684 km (429 miles) south of Alice Springs, Coober Pedy is one of those places in the world that has to be seen to be believed. And at least an overnight stay is necessary to explore the features and outlying attractions of Australia's oldest and largest opal mining town.

The name is thought to be derived from two Aboriginal words - Kupa (white man) and Piti (hole). Put the two together and this is what Coober Pedy is all about - holes and gigantic mole-like mounds that spread dramatically over the surrounding landscape as man burrows for the prized opal.

Because of the torrid summer heat (up to 54C), many of the locals escape the high temperature by living comfortably underground. In fact, there's an underground hotel, bookshop, church and

bunkhouse accommodation. The town's population is one of the most ethnic in Australia with nearly 50 nationalities represented.

Attractions include around 30 opal shops (The Opal Cave demonstrates opal cutting and offers a wide selection of opal jewellery), visits to underground homes, churches, and art gallery; Umoona Opal Mine and Museum; lookouts (The Big Winch and above the Opal Cave) and noodling (this is sifting through the waste material from mines for opals) - check with the Opal Cave about their town tours which includes noodling and visits to underground homes and churches.

Outlying attractions include the spectacular "Breakaways" - an area of coloured low hills or outliers, detached, or literally 'broken away' from the Stuart Range, through processes of weathering and erosion. The moonscape-like features have spawned another industry in Coober Pedy - location for major films and more recently, a site for the shooting of TV adverts and the like. A good map of the area is available at The Underground Bookshop and The Breakaways are accessible by conventional vehicle to the main lookout point. A loop road, around 70km (44 miles) from Coober Pedy, exposes the wonders of the natural formations but 4WD is recommended.

To the east, the road meets the dog fence - a 2 metre high wire mesh barrier which stretches for 5300 km (3285 miles), across 3 states to protect the sheep country of the south from an invasion of native dingoes. And the homestead of the world's largest cattle station, Anna Creek, is located approximately 150 km (93 miles) to the east of Coober Pedy and covers a massive 30,114 sq.km. (18,670 sq.miles) area.

The town has a full range of **services and facilities** with a number of eating out options. **Accommodation** ranges from the 4 star *Desert Cave* to backpacker dugouts and caravan parks. Some samples are:

Desert Cave Hotel, single and double rooms from $145, ph. (08) 8672 5688.

The Underground Motel, single rooms from $65, double $80, ph. (08) 8672 5324.
Opal Inn Hotel/Motel, hotel rooms from $25 single, double $35, motel units from $75, ph. (08) 8672 5054.

Underground bunkhouse style from $12pp - *Bedrock Bunkhouse*, ph. (08) 8672 5028.

Camping - *Stuart Range Caravan Park* ph. (08) 8672 5179; *Oasis Caravan Park* ph. (08) 8672 5169.

CADNEY HOMESTEAD
Population 10
Located 151 km (94 miles) north of Coober Pedy, the modern roadhouse complex provides for most traveller's needs. Services and facilities include restaurant, bar, store, all fuels including aviation, repairs, airstrip, and accommodation.

The **caravan park** has powered sites from $16 x 2, unpowered from $6; **bunkhouses** from $25; **units** - single from $70, double - $77. Credit cards accepted, EFTPOS, *open daily 6am-11pm*, ph. (08) 8670 7994.

MARLA
Population 250
Located 82km (51 miles) north of Cadney Homestead, the small township was officially declared in 1982, and the name is derived from the Aboriginal word for kangaroo - *'Malu'*. The town site straddles the railway line but the town centres around the Marla *Travellers Rest Hotel/Motel* complex; other town facilities (school, police station, medical clinic and offices) are located on the other side of the railway.

The Travellers Rest has a bar, restaurant, takeaway food, supermarket, vehicle services (all fuels, repairs), camping area, swimming pool, BBQ and picnic facilities.

Accommodation; camping - powered sites from $10 pp, unpowered - $5 pp; **bunkhouse** from $19 pp; **motel units** - single from $59, double from $65. It's *open daily from 6.30am to around 11pm*. A night watch person is on duty for out of hours service (ring the night-bell), ph (08) 8670 7001.

The *Mintabi Opal Fields* are located 35km (22 miles) to the west of Marla, while to the east is the beginning of the 'Oodnadatta Track'. A permit is required from the Marla Police for entry to the Mintabi Opal Fields.

From Marla it is 160km (99 miles) to the Northern Territory Border. Just north of the border, the Victory Downs Road heads west and is an alternative 346 (215 miles), mainly unformed, sandy route to Uluru (Ayers Rock). A high clearance vehicle is advised and road conditions should be checked. There are no services along this route and the road swings north, passing Mt Connor before joining the Lasseter Highway near Curtin Springs. For details of places north of the border, refer to *The Central Australia Region* in The Northern Territory section.

QUEENSLAND TO THE TERRITORY BORDER - FLINDERS AND BARKLY HIGHWAYS

NATIONAL ROUTES 78 AND 66

In Queensland, the Flinders Highway (Route 78), stretches west from Townsville on the coast for a distance of 777 kms (482 miles) to Cloncurry. From Cloncurry the road becomes the Barkly Highway (Route 66) which crosses the Northern Territory border 323 kms (200 miles) north-west of Cloncurry. Colloquially, between Torrens Creek and Cloncurry, the Flinders Highway is known as 'The Dinosaur Highway'.

 The highway continues west across the Northern Territory to Threeways where it meets the Stuart Highway - a distance of 446 kms (277 miles) from the border. The total distance from Townsville to Threeways is 1545 kms (958 miles) - over one third of the width of the Australian Continent.

 The all bitumen road (both highways) traverses the wide expanses of the Queensland Outback and Gulf County margins, and the seemingly endless tableland terrain of the Northern Territory. Apart from a few topographical interruptions (Great Dividing Range crossing between Pentland and Torrens Creek, and the low range country between Cloncurry and Mt Isa), the landscape is dominated by undulating to flat, open and dry, grassy plains. Elevations rise imperceptivity from 336 metres a.s.l. (above sea level) at Charters Towers to around 400 metres a.s.l. on the Barkly Tablelands.

 For the appreciative traveller, the landscape is the antithesis of the developed coast - the subtle nuances and daunting scale of the plains and tablelands west of the Great Dividing Range, reinforce the imagery evoked in some of the lines of the second verse of Dorothea McKellar's classic Australian poem *My Country*:

"I love a sunburnt country
A land of sweeping plains ..."

"Her beauty and her terror -
The wide brown land for me!"

However, it's most unfortunate to note that the impression of monotony expressed by some writers in travel guide books tend to convey negative attitudes towards this vast landscape. In effect, you are crossing one of the world's greatest natural grassland and lightly-wooded plains - an attraction in itself.

The highways are narrow in places and some sections are subject to short period closures because of Wet Season flooding (between January and March). Beware of roadtrains, wandering livestock and the potentially mesmerising effect of the very long, straight stretches of road on drivers. Best advice is to change drivers frequently and stop for breaks - the tiny townships along the way often harbour surprising interest and a fleeting insight into life in the Queensland Outback.

Between Charters Towers and Cloncurry, the Inlander Railway almost runs parallel to the road. A good map is Westprint Heritage Map's 'Gulf Country' which covers the route west of Richmond, Gulf Country and Stuart Highway section.

SETTLEMENTS AND FEATURES - CHARTERS TOWERS TO THE TERRITORY BORDER

Routes 78 and 66 are the major road entry point to the Northern Territory for travellers coming from the eastern seaboard. The route is characterised by a relatively even spacing of tiny townships - the pattern a legacy of the Cobb and Co. Stage Coach days, when a day's run for the horses was around 43 kms (27 miles). Hence, equally spaced stopovers by natural water sources, spawned many of the settlements that feature on the route today.

PLACES AND FEATURES EN ROUTE TO THE NORTHERN TERRITORY/QUEENSLAND BORDER

Locations are sequentially listed east to west in this outline.

CHARTERS TOWERS
Population 10,000

Located 132 kms (82 miles) west of Townsville, the historic town owes its origins on Christmas Day in 1871 to a frightened horse and its sharp-eyed master, an Aboriginal boy named Jupiter Mossman. The story goes, that in searching for a strayed packhorse, Jupiter stopped for a drink at a local waterhole and spotted nuggets of gold in the creek bed. His boss, pastoralist and prospector, Hugh Mossman, registered his claim with the Ravenswood mining warden, William Charters, after whom Mossman named his field. Originally the name was Charters Tors (the Tors derived from the similarity of the surrounding hills to Charter's native English countryside). But over time, English usage changed Tors to Towers.

Following the alluvial gold find, the discovery of a rich auriferous reef turned a shanty-town into a more permanent mining settlement. In its heyday, nearly 100 mines were producing ore for the mills (stamp batteries), and nearly 100 hotels dotted the locality, 28 of which were located in the main street, along with a flourishing brewery (many of these hotels were in effect, no more than beer shantys).

The population peaked at around 30,000 in 1900. It became Queensland's second largest city and because of its attraction to wealth seekers, Charters Towers became locally known as "The World".

The *Day Dawn Mine* yielded more than 500,000 ounces of gold from nearly 600,000 tonnes of extracted ore. The legacies of the enormous wealth generated from the mines are reflected in the elaborate sometimes ostentatious architectural styles of the town's many historic public buildings. The Victorian Italianate style (Post Office), Classic Revival (features lots of columns as seen in the old Bank of NSW building) and combinations of both styles (the elegant Old Stock Exchange) are some features of Charters Towers' well preserved Gill Street building heritage.

When the gold declined in 1920, beef production kept the town's economy stable and helped to maintain the 19th Century townscape. Its Education function (there are four major boarding schools) also contributed to stability. The absence of later boom periods, spared the town from any re-development phases so that nearly all the buildings, including miners cottages and "Queenslanders" in the suburbs, are predominantly restored period structures. Collectively, the relatively intact nature of its period buildings gives Charters Towers a unique and very appealing historic ambience.

In more recent times, there has been a major revival of gold mining using modern methods in areas formerly deemed uneconomic, as well as the development of virgin mines. New agricultural enterprises in the district (grapes, citrus, olives and peanuts) along with the rapid growth of tourism have widened Charters Towers' economic base.

Other attractions include the restored **Venus Gold Battery**, organised tours to mines and some interesting events. The town hosts a popular annual country music festival, show, rodeo, goat races (sometimes) and the world's largest country cricket carnival where more that 100 teams compete for the "Goldfield Ashes".

The town has a full range of services and facilities, and plenty of accommodation and eating out options. For details of attractions and services, contact the Information Centre, Mossman Street, *open daily 9am-5pm*, ph. (07) 4752 0314. The National Trust Office in town has good heritage literature, ph. (07) 4787 2374.

CHARTERS TOWERS TO HUGHENDEN
(247 kms; 153 miles)

Balfes Creek (pop. 20) is located 43 kms (27 miles) west of Charters Towers, and was initially established in the 1870s as a staging post, then from 1884 as a railhead and service centre for the district's grazing properties. It consists of a hotel/motel and caravan park complex, which also offers snack foods, fuel (LP, ULP, diesel). The pub has an extensive beer can collection and a range of mineral and rock samples from the Thalanga Mines. It's *open daily*, credit cards accepted, EFTPOS facility, ph. (07) 4787 6688.

Another 31 kms (19 miles) west is **Homestead** (pop. 96), which had origins in 1870 with the discovery of gold in the area. Today it is a tiny service centre for pastoral and mining industries. The RGC Thalanga Mines, located about 8 kms (5 miles) from the township, extracts copper, lead, zinc and silver from a major ore body. The mine workers provide custom for Homestead and the pub at Balfes Creek. Homestead has a general store, post office and cafe, fuel (ULP, LP, diesel), tyre repairs and a school. The store complex *opens daily*, credit cards accepted, EFTPOS facility, ph. (07) 4787 6624.

Pentland (pop. 300)is a small pastoral service centre located 32 kms (20 miles) from Homestead. Originally it was a railhead settlement known as Betts Creek in the 1880s. The early township had a population of nearly 500 including 150 Chinese, many of whom worked in a number of small mines in the locality. Farming in the district subsequently gave greater stability to the township.
  Pentland has a hotel/motel (lunchtime snack food, evening meals, accommodation, credit cards accepted, EFTPOS facility), ph. (07) 4788 1106; caravan park, all sites, meals available from the kiosk, ph (07) 4788 1148; service station, fuel (ULP, LP, diesel), repairs; general store and post office; art gallery and craftshop; school; police station; railway station; golf course and race track.

Approximately 30 kms (19 miles) west of Pentland, the highway crosses the hills of the Great Dividing Range. At the *Burra Range Lookout*, there are magnificent views into the wilderness region of the relatively new White Mountain National Park. The 120,000ha park features beautiful wildflowers in late winter, deep sandstone chasms and a range of birdlife and reptiles. It's an ideal area for bushwalkers (no designated tracks) and wilderness camping (no facilities). The entrance is approximately 5 kms (3 miles) west of the lookout (near the shire boundary sign) and access is by a rough track (4WD recommended). **Campers** will need to be self-sufficient and must make prior arrangements with the ranger for *payment of $3.50 per person for camping fees*. It's advisable for all users to contact the ranger before entering the park, ph. (07) 4741 1113. Rangers regularly patrol the park.

Once across the Dividing Range, the relentless grassland plains dominate. The first township is **Torrens Creek** (pop. 18), which dates from the *Cobb and Co.* coach days, and is now a service centre. It has a hotel, built in 1917, which offers rooms, counter meals, fuel (ULP, LP), swimming pool and a challenging 9 hole bush golf course. The pub is also the local general store. It's *open daily*, credit cards accepted, EFTPOS facility, ph. (07) 4741 7342. There's also a garage (LP, ULP, diesel and repairs); railway station and an airstrip, once used by bomber squadrons during the Second World War.

No prizes for suggesting how the next settlement, **Prairie** (pop. 58), received its name. It's located 44 kms (27 miles) west of Torrens Creek, and consists of the ***Prairie Hotel***, which offers rooms, all meals, camping behind the hotel and is open daily, ph. (07) 4741 5121. Opposite the hotel is the ***Prairie Cafe*** - a small roadhouse with post office, store, fuel (LP, ULP, diesel) and EFTPOS facility. There's also a butchers shop, school and railway station in Prairie.

The biggest attraction in town is the old pub (circa 1868), with is amazing clutter of artefacts and memorabilia around the walls. It boasts holding the second oldest continuous liquor licence in Queensland, and for those with a penchant for ghost stories, the pub has a "ghost-in-residence".

HUGHENDEN
Population 1900

Located 43 kms (26 miles) west of Prairie, Hughenden is situated on the banks on the Flinders River (Queensland's longest river, over 840 kms or 521 miles in length). Explorers Frederick Walker and William Landsborough and their parties, passed by the town site in 1861 and 1862 respectively; both groups were searching for the lost expedition of Burke and Wills. A Coolabah tree blazed by the explorers can be seen near the showgrounds.

Hughenden is a busy service centre for a rich pastoral hinterland where cattle thrive on the red and black volcanic soil country north of the river, while sheep are better suited to the black soil downs country south of the town.

Local tourist literature boasts Hughenden as the home of "Beauty and the Beast". The "Beauty" can be found at **Porcupine Gorge National Park,** 63 kms (39 miles) north of the town. It features a spectacular gorge often referred to as Australia's "little grand canyon", with stunning views from two lookouts. Activities include bushwalking, swimming, wildlife observation and camping. If you have the time, it's highly recommended, but you are strongly advised to seek current information about the park (camping fees and unsealed road conditions) from the *Hughenden Visitor Information Centre*, or contact the ranger on (07) 4741 1113.

The "Beast" is a life-size replica (7 metres long by 3.5 metres high) of the bird-footed dinosaur, Muttaburrasauras langdoni, on display at **The Dinosaur Centre** and Hughenden Visitor Information Centre in Gray Street. The original skeleton was discovered on a grazing property near Muttaburra (205 kms; 127 miles) south of Hughenden in 1961 and constitutes one of the most complete dinosaur remains ever found. The area between Hughenden and Julia Creek were once part of an ancient inland sea, the receding fringes of which were frequented by the enormous plant eating dinosaurs (the replica would have weighed over 25 tonnes), over 100 million years ago. Because of the region's rich, ancient reptilian history, the Flinders Highway between Torrens Creek and Cloncurry is also billed as "The Dinosaur Highway".

The Hughenden Visitor Information Centre also houses a range of fossils and historical displays. A visit to the centre is rewarding, not only for its displays, but also for information regarding Porcupine Gorge National Park and details of the good range of accommodation places (caravan parks, hotels and motels), eateries, and general services and facilities that Hughenden offers. The Information Centre, including the Dinosaur Display, is *open Mon-Sat 9am-5pm; Sun (during season) 9am-5pm*, ph. (07) 4741 1021.

HUGHENDEN TO CLONCURRY
398 kms; 247 miles
Despite the sparsely populated plains and increasing distances between settlements, the route traverses some of the state's richest natural grasslands particularly south of Richmond, and one of the world's most significant marine fossil beds. At Marathon (65 kms; 40 miles) west of Hughenden, there's a roadside rest area with water, toilets and shaded picnic facilities.

The first major settlement is **Richmond** (pop. 800), located 113 kms (71 miles) from Hughenden. It's a colourful little town (magnificent bougainvilleas and gardens), which services pastoral and mining activities in the region. From the dry basalt country, 20 kms (12 miles) away, sweet-scented native sandalwood is harvested. The hardwood is milled in town and exported to Asia where it is used for incense and joss stick production (if you use joss sticks, chances are you are taking in the sweet aromas of Richmond Sandalwood). The mill is open to visitors and sandalwood souvenirs are available.

The town has a full range of services, including hotel, motel and caravan park accommodation and a few good eating out options. For details, contact the museum and Information Centre.

Richmond has achieved international recognition in the scientific fraternity for its unique marine fossil exhibits at the **Richmond Fossil Centre** - the steady stream of international invertebrate palaeontologists testimony to its world renowned status. So the major attraction is the Museum which houses an extraordinary range of species discovered within the Richmond Shire. These include the most intact (98%) vertebrate fossil ever found in Australia - a swimming reptile called the Richmond Pliosaur, recognised as the best fossil of its kind found in the world. It was discovered by grazier Robert Ivers on his property **Marathon Station**. Pride of place in the museum is an 100 million year old armoured dinosaur, an Ankylosaur (also found on Marathon Station) with even its fossilised skin still intact.

In ancient geological times, the region formed the floor of an inland sea which over the aeons, became the roof of The Great Artesian Basin. Millions of years of sedimentation has captured species in the layers, with subsequent erosion and weathering exposing the rare range of marine fossils seen in the museum today.

Also of interest in the museum and around Richmond are the moon rocks - their genesis well explained in the museum. The museum also houses an excellent information centre and cafeteria, and offers guided tours for schools and adult groups. It's *open daily 8.30am-4pm*, located in Goldring Street, ph. (07) 4741 3429.

Approximately 48 kms (30 miles) on is **Maxwelton**, once a staging post, now providing only a pleasant roadside rest area with shaded picnic facilities, water and toilets.

Julia Creek (pop. 600) lies 99 kms (61 miles) west of Maxwelton and is the administrative centre of the 40,818 sq.km. (25,307 sq.m.) McKinlay Shire. Julia Creek's first European settler arrived in 1862, when Donald MacIntyre established a grazing property in the district. Originally the creek was named Scorpion but the name was changed to Julia Creek in 1870 in honour of Macintyre's niece. Neville Shute in his famous novel "A Town Like Alice", used the Gannon Hotel in Julia Creek as one of the locations for fictional hero Joe Harman, and so gave much prominence to the town.

Today, Julia Creek services pastoral and mining interest (recent oil shale deposit discoveries have stimulated some initial development activity) and has most services required by travellers. There's a hotel/motel ph. (07) 4746 7103; motel ph. (07) 4746 7305; caravan park ph. (07) 4746 7108; supermarket; bank; hospital; roadhouse; vehicle services; a few eating out places; and EFTPOS facilities.

Attractions include the **McIntyre Museum** (Minmi Dinosaur fossils); events (campdraft and rodeo, races); water-based recreational activities at local waterholes (water-skiing) and the aptly named "Dirt and Dust Triathalon" - an annual event which attracts triathletes from interstate. For further information about the town, contact the *Shire Office*, ph. (07) 4746 7166, or accommodation places.

Four kilometres from town, the Burke and Wills Development Road heads north-west from the highway, providing a gateway to the savannah country of the Gulf Region and settlements of **Burke and Wills Roadhouse**, **Burketown** and **Normanton**. At 21 kms (13 miles) from Julia Creek, a turn-off to the south, leads to a couple of notable pubs. The first, *The Eddington Arms Hotel* (circa 1908) at Gilliat (5kms, 3 miles from the highway), is one of the few authentic corrugated-iron pubs still dispensing liquor in Western Queensland. The other pub is Crocodile Dundee's famous watering hotel, *The Walkabout Hotel*, located at McKinlay, a further 70 kms (44 miles) south of Gilliat.

CLONCURRY
Population 3180

Situated 133 kms (83 miles) west of Julia Creek, on the Cloncurry River, it was named by explorer Robert O'Hara Burke (of Burke and Wills fame) in honour of his cousin, Lady Elizabeth Cloncurry in 1861. Pastoralist and explorer Ernest Henry discovered copper in the locality in 1867, and founded The Australian Mine Company, which became the world's largest copper mine until eclipsed by Mt Isa. Mining operations by several large companies contribute to the town's vibrant economy today. The town also services the cattle and sheep properties in the region.

Cloncurry has an important place in Australia's aviation history. The Reverend John Flynn established The Royal Flying Doctor Service here in 1928 and the John Flynn Place Museum, captures the spirit of the service through an excellent interpretive display and period equipment collection. The museum complex also comprises an art gallery, Alfred Traegnar cultural centre, an outdoor theatre and Cloncurry Gardens.

The Mary Kathleen Memorial Park and Museum is also well worth visiting for some local history and an extraordinary collection of rocks and minerals (over 18,000 exhibits). It has picnic facilities, kiosk and tourist information. Cloncurry's period architecture of a number of public buildings and Chinese and Afghan cemeteries add further historic interest to the town.

The town has 3 hotels, several motels, caravan parks, eating out places, supermarket, banks, post office, medical services, variety of shops, vehicle services and a public swimming pool among its good range of services and facilities. For further details contact the *Tourist Information Centre* at Mary Kathleen Park, ph. (07) 4742 1361.

CLONCURRY TO MT ISA
117 kms; 73 miles

The plains give way to mainly broken low ranges and hill country with many rocky outcrops, and the road west becomes the Barkly Highway. Points of interest include a *memorial cairn to Burke and Wills* (by the Corella River, 43 kms or 27 miles from Cloncurry); the *Kalkadoon and Mitakoodi monument* 2 kms further west, has interesting inscriptions about the local Aboriginal clans. A further 19 kms (12 miles) is the turnoff to Mary Kathleen (site only), once the town site for a uranium mine which supplied the British Atomic Energy Commission with processed ore. There is little trace today of the once busy township of 1000 people which finally closed in 1982 after two relatively brief periods of operation. Some of the buildings were re-located to Mary Kathleen Memorial Park in Cloncurry. However, the terraces of the open-cut mine make interesting viewing as do the locality rock formations. There's a roadside rest area at the turnoff.

MT ISA
Population 24,000
It is Australia's largest, high-tech mining city based on very rich deposits of copper, lead, zinc and silver. Mining production first commenced in 1923 and Mount Isa Mines now ranks as one of the world's largest operations, with ores extracted from mine workings 5 kms in length, 1.2 kms in width and depths of 1.8 kms. Underground, the approximate length of openings are 950 kms (590 miles), whilst sentinel-like above ground, the towering exhaust stacks (the lead smelter stack is 270 metres high), dominate the city skyline and are impressive indicators of the mine's massive scale.

"The Isa" as the city is locally known, had a tough reputation in its early days. Today, over 50 nationalities give a distinctive cosmopolitan flavour to this isolated, but vibrant outback city, which nestles within the colourful and rocky terrain of the Selwyn Ranges (reputably among the oldest exposed rocks in the world). Mt Isa is also the second largest city in the world (the largest is Kalgoorlie-Boulder in Western Australia) by virtue of its administrative boundaries, which enclose an area of near-equivalent size to Switzerland - 40,977 sq.kms (25,406 sq.miles). But the world's longest city street is the 186 kms (115 miles) stretch of the Barkly Highway to "The Isa's" outlier western "suburb", Camooweal.

The awesome mining images tend to mask Mt Isa's diverse range of tourist attractions. Mine visits (surface and underground) combined with city sights; *Riversleigh Fossils Interpretive Centre* (a multi-tourism award centre with imaginative interpretive displays of the World-Heritage listed fossil sites at Riversleigh); Lookout sites for panoramic views of the city and Selwyn Ranges; *John Midlin Mining Display*; *The National Trust's "Tent House"*; the *Frank Ashton Underground Museum*; the *Royal Flying Doctor Service and School of the Air* bases; the *Kalkadoon Tribal Centre and Cultural Keeping Place* (Aboriginal history), are the main **city attractions**.

Outlying attractions include a fossicking trail; Lake Moondara (a popular spot for a range of water-based activities 16kms/10 miles, north of Mt Isa), and the beautiful *Lawn Hill National Park* which adjoins the World-heritage listed *Riversleigh Fossil Fields*. Lawn Hill National Park is to Queensland what Kakadu National Park is to the Northern Territory and is located approximately 333 kms (206 miles) by road, north-west of Mt Isa.

For details of all attractions, accommodation and tour offerings (particularly to Lawn Hill National Park), contact the *Riversleigh Interpretive Centre*, which is also Mt Isa's Tourist Information Centre, ph. (07) 4749 1555.

Mt Isa has an excellent range of accommodation places, eating out options and a variety of services and facilities in its modern commercial centre, and hosts Australia's richest rodeo - part of a very lively annual three day carnival held in August.

Approximately midway between Mt Isa and Camooweal, marks the beginnings of The Barkly Tableland.

CAMOOWEAL
Population 340

The town lies 186 kms (115 miles) west of Mt Isa and 13 kms (9 miles) east of the Queensland/Northern Territory border on the Barkly Tableland.

Historically the township has strongest links to Burketown - a major Gulf Port in the early European settlement days where goods for the newly established Barkly Tableland properties were wagoned to Camooweal, the most suitable site from which to distribute them.

Camooweal's name is thought to be derived from an Aboriginal word meaning "big winds" or possibly from the linking of Camoo (derived from Camel) to Weal, the name of an early European surveyor. The township was officially gazetted in 1884 but its settlement origins were much earlier.

The township continues to service surrounding pastoral enterprises and offers a basic range of services to travellers including good accommodation.

There's a hotel/motel ph (07)4748 2124; Shell Roadhouse (motel, camping) ph. (07) 4748 2155; BP Roadhouse (cabins), vehicle services ph. (07) 4748 2137; general stores and police station. Attractions include the heritage quality of some of the township's oldest buildings, in particular Freckleton's Store and the Shire Hall, both classified by the National Trust.

An outlying attraction is the Camooweal Caves National Park which protects some large caverns in a limestone landscape characterised by surface sinkholes. Visits are possible during the Dry Season, but best advice is to check first with local police or the ranger. The park is located approximately 15 kms (9 miles) south of Camooweal, access is 4WD recommended and facilities are limited. The ranger can be contacted on (07) 4743 2055. And if you wish to learn more about the township, Joe Freckleton at the old store is the local information guru ph. (07) 4748 2160.

For details of the Northern Territory section of the route (ie. west of Camooweal), refer to *The Barkly Region* in Part Two.

Territory Drives, Trails and 4WD Tracks

To enhance visitor experience of Territory landscapes and spirit of adventure, thematic tourism drives and heritage trails are currently being developed. Often these are loop roads from the Stuart Highway, thus encouraging motorists to venture beyond traditional routes to major destinations. Interpretive signage and information that is available at roadside stops and wayside inns, is indicated by logos. The Explorer Territory 4WD Routes cater for the adventurous 4x4 enthusiasts, while the heritage trails promote awareness of the region's rich natural and cultural history. All are initiatives of various Northern Territory Government Departments in association with regional tourism bodies. Details of places along these various routes are outlined in the appropriate regional sections.

For map recommendations, particularly for Central Australian 4WD Tracks, refer to *Information Sources* in Part One.

TOURISM DRIVES

Explorer Highway (All regions)
This follows John McDouall Stuart's route, the Stuart Highway, from Port Augusta in South Australia to Darwin, a distance of 2270 kms (1686 miles).

TOURISM DRIVES AND HERITAGE TRAILS

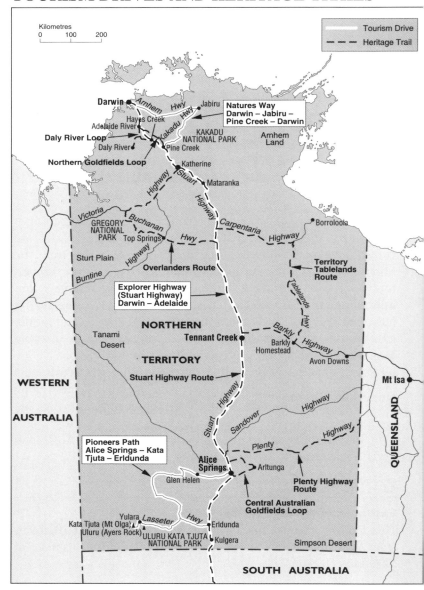

Kilometres
0   100   200

Tourism Drive
- - - Heritage Trail

Darwin
Arnhem Hwy
Jabiru
Hayes Creek
Adelaide River
Daly River Loop
Daly River
Northern Goldfields Loop
Pine Creek
Katherine
Mataranka

Natures Way
Darwin – Jabiru –
Pine Creek – Darwin

KAKADU
NATIONAL PARK

Arnhem
Land

Kakadu Hwy
Stuart

Victoria
GREGORY
NATIONAL
PARK
Top Springs
Sturt Plain
Buntine
Highway
Buchanan
Hwy
Highway

Overlanders Route

Carpentaria
Highway
Borroloola

Territory
Tablelands
Route

Tablelands Hwy

Explorer Highway
(Stuart Highway)
Darwin – Adelaide

NORTHERN

Tanami
Desert

TERRITORY

Tennant Creek

Barkly
Highway

Barkly
Homestead

Avon Downs

Stuart Highway Route

Stuart Highway

Sandover
Highway

Highway

Mt Isa

WESTERN

AUSTRALIA

QUEENSLAND

Pioneers Path
Alice Springs – Kata
Tjuta – Erldunda

Glen Helen

Alice
Springs

Arltunga

Plenty

Plenty Highway
Route

Central Australian
Goldfields Loop

Yulara
Kata Tjuta (Mt Olga)
Uluru (Ayers Rock)
ULURU KATA TJUTA
NATIONAL PARK

Lasseter   Hwy

Erldunda

Kulgera

Simpson Desert

SOUTH AUSTRALIA

Pioneer's Path (Central Australia Region)

This starts at the junction of the Stuart and Lasseter Highways (Erldunda), travelling to, and linking the landscapes of Uluru-Kata Tjuta National Park (Ayers Rock and The Olgas) and Watarrka National Park (Kings Canyon) guiding travellers along the Mereenie Loop Road through the Western MacDonnell Range National Park into Alice Springs, an approximate distance of 1150 kms (713 miles).

Nature's Way (Top End Region)

This begins at the junction of the Stuart and Arnhem Highways, 30 kms (19 miles) south of Darwin. It follows a sealed highway triangle through the Adelaide River and Mary River Wetlands and Kakadu National Park, and along the Kakadu Highway to Pine Creek - an approximate distance of 457 kms (283 miles).

HERITAGE TRAILS (SEE MAP)

Seven routes are devised to give insights into history.

1. Stuart Highway Route (All regions)

The signage at points of interest and wayside inns complement the Explorer Highway designation of the Stuart Highway from Port Augusta to Darwin.

2. Central Australian Goldfields Loop (Central Australia Region)

From Alice Springs this loop passes through the Eastern MacDonnell Ranges on to the historic gold mining settlement of Arltunga. A track north from Arltunga crosses pastoral properties to remnants of the Winnecke diggings and cemetery and back to the Stuart Highway north of Alice Springs. This route is recommended 4x4 or high clearance vehicles.

3. Plenty Highway Route (Central Australia Region)

This highway takes travellers coming from Queensland through the beauty of the Harts Range (the site of old mica mines) and on to the gem fields around Mud Tank.

4. Territory Tablelands Loop (Barkly Region)

This route exposes the wide horizons of the Barkly to the Gulf country and many legendary pastoral runs. The Barkly Tablelands and Carpentaria Highways Loop crosses the Mitchell grass plains to the spectacular "lost world" formations of the Abner Range south-east of Cape Crawford. North-east of Cape Crawford, the Gulf Country can be explored from Borroloola.

5. Overlanders Route (Barkly Region)

This loop traces the tracks of the old drovers - The Murranji Track was known as the ghost road of the drovers because of its torridness. It is parallel over much of its length by the Buchanan Highway where along the way interesting sites can be visited. The loop continues to Top Springs and the Victoria River District, passing the most legendary cattle station of all - Victoria River Downs. Jasper Gorge on the edge of Gregory National Park and magnificent mesa country are features of the Loop to Timber Creek on the Victoria Highway. West of Timber Creek is Keep River National Park, notable for its Aboriginal Art sites. The Victoria Highway joins the Stuart Highway at Katherine.

6. Northern Goldfields Loop (Top End Region)

Pine Creek and Adelaide River are gateways to a number of historic gold and tin mines and sites associated with the old railway and telegraph line. Reminders of past interactions between Aboriginal people, Chinese and European settlers from the frenetic gold rush days is depicted in interpretive signage at particular locations. In recent times, there has been a resurgence in mining activity.

7. Daly River Loop (Top End Region)

This route exposes the lovely Daly River country with its rich legacy of agricultural and mining activities and Aboriginal Mission station. The natural wonders of the Daly River itself, hot springs and tropical flora add to the region's scenic richness.

EXPLORER 4X4 TRACKS OF CENTRAL AUSTRALIA

Eight tracks are currently being designated (see map). Intending users are strongly advised to check with Central Australian Visitor Information Centre (Gregory Terrace, Alice Springs, telephone (08) 8952 5800), or contact police (08) 8951 8888 for information about current road conditions, permit requirements on some routes. There is an excellent detailed brochure of the tracks. Be aware that rental companies do not allow their conventional vehicles to travel on many of these routes; however they will allow 4WD but it's advisable to discuss this directly with companies.

Details of places including services are outlined in the Central Australia Region listing (where places are not included in this regional section, services are indicated in the following descriptions).

For a mantle of safety, you can register your radio call sign with the Royal Flying Doctor Service, and obtain operating procedures from the bases within whose area you may be operating.
Phone numbers for each of the bases are;
Alice Springs - VJD - (08) 8952 1033;
Port Augusta (South Australia) - VNZ - (08) 8642 5555;
Jandakot (Western Australia) - GPY - (08) 9414 1200.

I. Mereenie Loop Road
This unsealed road links the Western MacDonnell Ranges, Hermannsburg, Glen Helen and Palm Valley (Finke Gorge National Park) to Watarrka National Park (Kings Canyon). The condition of the road is variable; a 4WD vehicle is strongly advised - a 4WD is essential to visit Palm Valley and Tnorala National Park (Gosses Bluff) - and trailers and caravans are not recommended.

  As the road passes through Aboriginal land, a permit is required (immediately available from Central Australian Visitor

4WD Explorer Routes

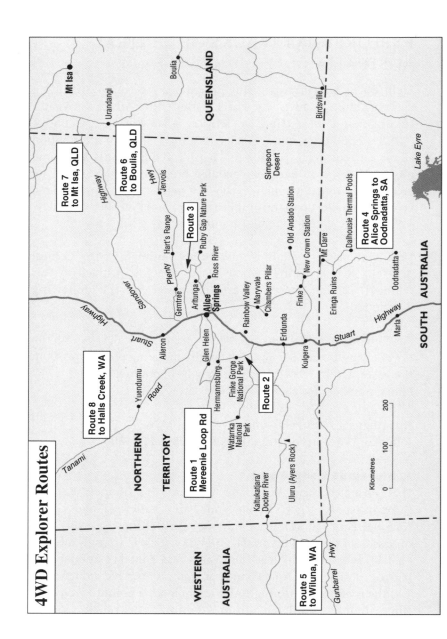

Information Centre in Alice Springs, Central Lands Council, Hermannsburg and Kings Canyon Resort, and Glen Helen Homestead for $2). This permit is also required for entry to Tnorala National Park (Gosses Bluff). The permit comes with a souvenir tour pass booklet.

Via Glen Helen (Namatjira Drive) from Alice Springs, distances are: 139 kms (86 miles) to Glen Helen on sealed road; 392 kms (243 miles) to Kings Canyon Resort. Via Hermannsburg (Larapinta Drive)distances from Alice Springs are: 109 kms (68 miles) to the Aboriginal Community of Wallace Rockhole, (services); 139 kms (86 miles) to Hermannsburg; 335 kms (208 miles) to Kings Canyon Resort.

Camping is prohibited along Mereenie Loop Road; stops allowed only at designated roadside areas.

2. Finke Gorge National Park to Kings Canyon (via Boggy Hole)

The route is mostly driving through a sandy river bed (4WD essential, no trailers) and travelling time to Watarrka National Park is about 7 hours. Bush camping is allowed along the Finke River with the best site at Boggy Hole where there's a large pool but no facilities. Traffic along this track is infrequent so it is advisable to travel with another vehicle, especially in summer. For latest advice on this route, contact the rangers at Finke Gorge N.P. ph. (08) 8956 7401. Travelling time from Palm Valley to Boggy Hole is about 2.5 hours.

3. Arltunga Historic Reserve to Ruby Gap Nature Park

The route explores the eastern extremities of the East MacDonnell Ranges, 150 kms (93 miles) east of Alice Springs. To Ross River, the road is sealed, after which a graded gravel road (suitable 2WD) leads to Arltunga. It's a 1.5 hour drive from Alrtunga to Ruby Gap (high clearance 4X4 vehicle is essential), and a 5kms drive along the sandy creek bed. Then a 2km walk to Glen Annie Gorge. Bush camping is permitted. See also *Heritage Routes* - Central Australian Goldfields Loop. A Parks and Wildlife Ranger is based at Arltunga Visitor Centre.

4. Alice Springs to Oodnadatta (via Chambers Pillar and Old Andado)

The road surface is characterised by large sections of sand, bulldust and corrugations. For current road conditions, contact Oodnadatta Police (08) 8670 7805. Conventional vehicles, trailers and caravans are not advised. No permits required, but a South Australian National Parks Pass is needed (available from State Automobile Associations) for areas south of the Northern Territory Border.

  Distances from Alice Springs: 36 kms (22 miles) to Ewaninga Rock Carvings(no services); 116 kms (72 miles) to Maryvale Station (services); 159 km (99 miles) to Chambers Pillar, no services or facilities; 343 kms (213 miles) to Finke (services); 373 kms (231 miles) to New Crown Station (limited services); 461 km (286 miles) to Old Andado Station (limited services); 564 kms (350 miles) to Mount Dare Station (South Australia), fuel (diesel, LP, ULP, Avgas by arrangement), store, repairs, credit cards, camping, accommodation, open daily ph. (08) 8670 7835; 681 kms (422 miles) to Dalhousie Springs (no services); 861 kms (534 miles) to Oodnadatta (Pink Roadhouse), fuel (diesel, ULP, LP, Avgas), store, repairs, credit cards, EFTPOS, camping, accommodation, open daily, ph. (08) 8670 7822.

  A good alternative route to visit Old Andado and Chambers Pillars is The Simpson Desert Loop - from Alice Springs via the Old Andado Stock Route Road to Old Andado, 327kms (203 miles) (see *Old Andado* listing for further details), then south to Mt Dare Homestead, northwest to New Crown Station and west to Finke. The loop heads north from Finke on the Old South Road (sometimes known as the Old Ghan Road) and back to Alice Springs via Chambers Pillar and places mentioned previously on this route. Or, from Finke you can travel west to the Stuart Highway on the Kulgera Road. For those with UHF, a growing network of repeater stations allows good communication with properties, and remote Simpson Desert areas.

  For further information on tracks in this region, contact Leigh Goldsmith (The Outback Experience) (08) 8953 2666.

5. Gunbarrel Highway

A high clearance 4x4 vehicle is needed particularly from Warburton to Wiluna. Conventional vehicles, caravans and trailers not advised.

From Yulara (Ayers Rock) distances are; 227 kms (141 miles) to Docker River (limited services); 329 kms (204 miles) to Giles (Western Australia), Warakurna Roadhouse, fuels (diesel, ULP, LP, Avgas), store, repairs, credit cards, camping, accommodation, open daily, ph. (08) 8956 7344; 559 kms (347 miles) to Warburton Roadhouse (Western Australia), fuel (diesel, ULP, LP, Avgas), store, credit cards, camping, accommodation, open daily, ph. (08) 8956 7656; 1025 kms (636 miles) to Carnegie Homestead (Western Australia), fuel (diesel, LP, ULP), store, repairs, credit cards, EFTPOS, accommodation, open daily, ph. (09) 9981 2991; 1375 kms (853 miles) to Wiluna, fuel (diesel, LP, ULP), mechanical repairs, store, credit cards, EFTPOS, accommodation, ph (08) 9981 7020.

An alternative route - The Great Central Road (Warburton to Laverton) - 577 kms (358 miles) is a formed, unsealed road on which conventional vehicles and trailers are not advised. As both roads can deteriorate quickly, seek information on conditions prior to travel. Permits are required on Northern Territory and Western Australia sections - available from relevant Land Councils - see addresses in *Practical Information* section in Part One.

6. Plenty Highway

From Alice Springs to Gemtree, the road is sealed. Gemtree to the Queensland Border is a graded, unsealed surface. Tobermorey to Urandangi and Boulia is dry weather access only and has sections of extreme bulldust and corrugation. 4WD is advised on these Queensland sections. Distances from Alice Springs are; 137 kms (85 miles) to Gemtree (services); 203 kms (126 miles) to Atitjere (Harts Range Store, services); 334 kms (207 miles) to Jervois Station; 553 kms (342 miles) to Tobermorey Station (on border), fuel (diesel, ULP, LP), repairs, store, credit cards, accommodation, open daily, ph. (07) 7748 4892; 648 kms (402 miles) to Urandangi

Hotel (Queensland), fuel (diesel, ULP, LP), store, credit cards, EFTPOS, camping, accommodation, open daily, ph. (07) 4748 4988; 831 kms (515 miles) to Mt Isa Shell Truckport (all services), open 24 hours, ph. (07) 4743 2488; or 805 kms (499 miles) to Boulia (Donohue Hwy), all services, open daily, ph. (07) 4746 3131.

7. Sandover Highway

4WD vehicles are recommended on the unsealed road from the Plenty Highway. Large sections of sand, bulldust and corrugation characterise this route.

Distances from Alice Springs are; 210 kms (130 miles) to Arlparra Store, fuel (diesel, ULP, LP), open daily, ph. (08) 8956 9910; 312 kms (193 miles) to Ammaroo Station, fuel (diesel, ULP, LP), store, open daily, ph. (08) 8956 9899; 717 kms (445 miles) to Camooweal (Queensland), all services, ph. (07) 4748 2155 (Roadhouse). There's a 4WD track leading north from Ammaroo Station, which connects to the Murray Downs Road (see under Davenport/Murchison Ranges National Park in Barkly Region).

8. Tanami Road

Better known as the Tanami Track, the surface is formed, unsealed with corrugated and sandy sections. 4WD recommended; caravans and trailers not advised. No permits required for the road; any deviation onto Aboriginal land requires permits. Refer also to Tanami listing in Barkly Region.

Distances form Alice Springs are: 188 kms (116 miles) to Tilmouth Well (services); 294 kms (182 miles) to Yuendumu (services); 598 kms (370 miles) to Rabbit Flat (services); 878 kms (544 miles) to Billiluna (Western Australia), fuel (diesel, ULP), store, repairs, open weekdays, ph. (08) 9168 8934; 1046 kms (649 miles) to Halls Creek (Western Australia - refer to Kimberley Region listing), all services.

Practical Information

INFORMATION SOURCES

OUTSIDE AUSTRALIA

The Australian Tourist Commission (ATC) is the first point of contact for intending visitors from overseas. It is a government body that functions externally in a promotional capacity, so get the materials they offer before you leave. Internet: The ATC's website - http://www.aussie.net.au has over 10,000 pages of searchable tourism information on Australia including state and regional information and images.

Singapore
17-03 United Square
101 Thomson Road
Singapore 307591
Republic of Singapore
ph 65 2555 4555

Japan
Australian Business Centre
New Otani Garden Court Bldg 28F
4-1 Kioi-cho
Chiyoda-ku Tokyo 102, Japan
ph. 81 3 5214 0720

Hong Kong
Suite 1501, Central Plaza
18 Harbour Road
Wanchai, Hong Kong
ph. 852 2802 7700

USA
2049 Century Park East
Suite 1920
Los Angeles CA 90067, USA
ph. 1 310 229 4870

Auckland
Level 13
44-48 Emily Place
Auckland 1, New Zealand
ph. 64 9 379 9594

London
Gemini House
10-18 Putney Hill
London SW 15 6AA, United Kingdom
ph. 44 181 780 2229

Frankfurt
Neue Mainzer Strasse 22
D 603111 Frankfurt/Main 1, Germany
ph. 4969 274 0060

Australia
Sydney (Head Office)
Level 3, 80 William Street
Wooloomooloo NSW 2011
ph (02) 9360 1111.

WITHIN AUSTRALIA

The Northern Territory Holiday Information Helpline, 1800 621 336 (free call within Australia only) provides instant information and a booking service. Alternatively, you can contact travel agents in your local area or check out the Northern Territory's internet website at http://www.world.net/Travel/Australia/NT_info/NTTC/.

The Western Australian Tourist Commission (WATC) can be contacted on 1300 361 351 (free call within Australia only) for information regarding the Kimberley region.

Whilst touring, visits to local information centres are good value for finer detail and maps. You can discover places of interest by talking to locals, particularly in the smaller centres.

National Park Organisations

Northern Territory parks are administered by the Parks and Wildlife Commission, the exceptions being Uluru (Ayers Rock and Olgas) and Kakadu, which are run by the Federal Organisation, Parks Australia. The West Australian Conservation and Land Management Department (CALM) controls Kimberley Parks. These organisations provide a great service up front, where at the actual parks information literature, displays, advice and provision of amenities are some of the things offered. Wildlife and Plant Identikit booklets are produced by the NT Parks and Wildlife Commission, and are highly recommended. Address and telephone numbers are listed in the appropriate sections.

National Trust

The Trust, with its affiliated state organisations, is a voluntary body that aims to preserve and maintain for future generations, Australia's heritage of buildings, landscapes and sites. It owns a number of properties which are open to the public while others privately owned are classified to ensure their preservation. Offices in Darwin and Alice Springs have excellent material, particularly historic walk guides. Membership is worth considering as it entitles free entry to all Trust properties in Australia and the UK.

  Direct enquiries to your state office, or write to: National Trust of Australia (NT), GPO Box 3520, Darwin NT 0801, ph (08) 8981 2848. For Western Australia: The Old Observatory, 4 Havelock Street, West Perth 6005, ph (08) 9321 6088.

Automobile Associations

Reciprocal arrangements operate between the state associations in Australia and their equivalents overseas. Up-to-date print-outs of road information, route maps, accommodation/camping guides and books are some examples of what is available. Membership has advantages of discounted prices and access to material, apart from the road services offered and their technical advisory section. Contact your respective state association office. AANT is at 81 Smith Street, Darwin, ph (08) 8981 3837.

Maps

Map producers do their best, but some things on the ground change quickly making accurate depictions very difficult. A useful map is the **NT Touring Map**. Strip maps and road maps of the Northern Territory, North-west and Kimberley are available from Automobile Associations.

  Highly recommended, particularly for 4WD Explorer Routes, are Westprint Heritage Maps. The series include a coverage of: Alice Springs-Uluru; Alice Springs-Oodnadatta; Plenty Highway; Tanami Track; Canning Stock Route; Gunbarrel Highway; Eastern MacDonnells and Gulf Country. The maps are well designed, easy to read, have a high degree of accuracy and contain informative text. Map publisher, John Deckert, focuses on Outback coverage and his expertise is the result of direct experience in these areas, including assignments for National Geographic and director of tours to the Simpson Desert. He also offers a personalised, advisory service, ph (03) 5391 1466.

Good map shops in Australia's major cities are: Perth, The Chart and Map Shop, 14 Collins Street, Fremantle, ph (08) 9335 8665; Adelaide, The Map Shop, 16a Peel Street, ph (08) 8231 2033 and Carto Graphics, 6 Young Street, Blackwood, ph (08) 8278 7748; Brisbane, World Wide Maps and Guides, 187 George Street, ph (07) 3221 4330; Sydney, Mapworld has several shops, ph (02) 9261 3601; Melbourne, Melbourne Map Centre, 240 Waverley Road, Chadstone, ph (03) 9569 5472 and High Street, Kew and Mapland, Little Bourke Street, Melbourne, ph (03) 9670 4383. Many of these shops also stock a good range of guide books and outback literature, as well as topographic maps.

Local tourist offices also have a range of maps including local interest ones and all types of maps are available at respective State Departments of Lands. Locations are:

NT - Dept. Of Land, Planning and Environment

Darwin Office; Cnr Bennett and Cavenagh Streets,
ph. (08) 8999 7032
Alice Springs Office; 21 Gregory Terrace, ph. (08) 8951 5316

HOW TO GET THERE

BY ROAD
Coach (bus)

Many see Australia by coach which is one of the best ways to experience the Outback's sheer size and variety of landscapes. There are two major national coach companies - Greyhound-Pioneer Australia (ph. 132030 toll free) and McCafferty's (ph 131 499 toll free). Both operate daily services in all states (McCafferty's does not operate in Western Australia). Both offer passes - Greyhound-Pioneer's Aussie and Kilometre Passes are popular with budget travellers; McCafferty's Territory Adventurer Pass is also popular. It is advisable to compare fare offerings of both companies as they can differ. Concessions are available for children and seniors.

Some sample fares for adult, one-way tickets are: from Perth to Darwin around $436; Kununurra to Darwin $102; Katherine to Kununurra $57; Melbourne to Alice Springs $135; and Sydney to Alice Springs $220.

Coaches enter the Northern Territory via the Stuart Hwy from Adelaide, The Barkly Hwy from Queensland and from Perth, via the Great Northern Hwy which links to the Victoria Hwy at the WA/NT border near Kununurra.

The Wayward Bus Touring Company offers a different style, popular with budget travellers with regular 8 day trips leaving Adelaide and an itinerary which includes Oodnadatta Track, Uluru and Watarrka before arriving in Alice Springs. Costs are $640 with additional $120 cost for return to Adelaide, ph (08) 8232 6646.

Organised Coach Tours

Tours organised for adult or school groups by coach companies is often the only way many people can afford to visit all those outback places dreamt about. A number of companies offer tours of varying duration and accommodation style (motels or safari camping style) to Central Australia, The Top End and Kimberley. Itineraries are tailored to meet group needs and costs reduce with increase in group numbers. The main advantages are cost savings, convenience and comfort, and organisational expertise of better companies (see under *Coach Touring* in Practical Advice Section).

Some companies are: Down Under Tours (Cairns and Alice Springs, ph. 08 8953 4455); Hopkinsons (Sydney, ph. 02 9632 3344); Coach Tours of Australia (Melbourne, ph. 03 9740 8411); Swan Gold Tours (Perth, ph. 08 9451 5333); Explorer Coachlines (Adelaide, ph. 08 8271 8866); and Sunstate (Brisbane, ph. 07 3868 2400).

For school or specialist groups, contact Edutour, (03) 5974 1288, an educational tours business which offers an innovative Edutourism package. It incorporates into a tour some structured learning relative to the school's syllabi (in areas of Social Science, Environmental Studies, Geology, Geography and History), and caters for overseas schools as well. Edukits, comprising a coil-bound booklet with maps, interpretive notes, study units and guide books are written and produced by Edutour's experienced teachers. Teacher Edukits (containing resource material), on-board library, pre and post tour classroom lessons, certificates and eduprizes along with luxury, modern, seatbelt equipped vehicles, and professional crews are the main elements of a unique, personalised package.

Safari style tours (tent and mattresses supplied; a safari trailer houses food, freezers and cooking equipment) to Central Australia cost from $650 p.p. for 10 days (based on 40 students with the provision for 1 teacher free of charge per 10 students). A 14 day tour to The Top End costs from $880 p.p. (Meals, entry fee to attractions, camping fees and Edutour component are included in costs). Contact Edutour (03) 5974 1288 for further details.

Motoring

For motorists, all main entry roads referred to under Coach are sealed and present no problem. The Tanami Road (often referred to as the Tanami Track) and Gunbarrel Highway from the West, and the Plenty Highway and Burketown Road from Queensland are four-wheel-drive entry points. Hired campervans are an interesting alternative to taking your own - check costs with major car rental companies.

BY RAIL

The famous Ghan runs between Adelaide and Alice Springs (1559km - 965 miles) and links the Outback town by rail to the rest of Australia. It takes 21 hours (adult fares; sleepers 1st class around $524, economy $325, seat $150 one way), and has a motor rail service too for vehicles ($290 per car, Adelaide to Alice

Springs). Connections are available with transcontinental trains from Sydney and Perth. The Ghan now runs from Melbourne to Adelaide, too.

Great Southern Railways have an Austrail Flexi Pass for overseas visitors obtainable in Australia on presentation of passport and return airfare ticket at capital city booking offices, or overseas from travel agents. An Austrail Flexi Pass (economy class only) costs from $400 for 8 days to $1045 for 29 days. For all rail information telephone 132 232.

BY AIR

Ansett Australia and Qantas Airlines are the two major carriers.

Ansett Australia is the only carrier in The Kimberley, and has an extensive network of services to and within The Territory. Airnorth is a secondary airline operating within the NT, based in Katherine. Telephone 1800627 474 for details of its services.

Both major carriers offer a range of holiday packages (conditions apply), child/student concessions, and airpasses.

Because of so many fare options, changes and discounted fares, it is better to contact carriers direct; Ansett 131 344 (national) and Qantas Airlines ph 131 415 (national).

COMBINATIONS

Combinations of transport modes can have cost and time advantages, as well as providing greater opportunities for seeing and experiencing the landscape. Air/coach or fly/drive combinations are worth considering. Apart from the 'Big Two' coach companies, there are many coach operators who run a variety of tours to the Territory and Kimberley from capital cities, (see *Organised Coach Tours*).

GENERAL INFORMATION

Best Time to Visit

The accepted tourist season is between April and October, when desert and tropical weather conditions are more tolerable. June and July are ideal months, as temperatures and humidity are lower (refer to outlines of climate for each of the regions in Part Two). Generally, at these times places are more accessible, and conditions for outdoor sightseeing are best. However, popular tourist spots do get crowded so it is advisable to book early.

Out of season visits are worth considering. Some advantages are often reduced rates, fewer tourists, the lush green of Top End tropical vegetation, and the spectacular water expanses and falls of the Wet or Green Season. Despite the Wet Season, Darwin has high sunshine hours (check tables), and air-conditioning and many all-weather roads reduce the impact of climate conditions. Off season in the Central Australia Region is hot, but visits are possible. Older visitors and young children may well find heat discomfort levels of the Outback in summer too stressful, and are best advised to plan their visits in the 'cooler' periods.

What to Wear

Light casual clothing, worn year-round, is a part of the Outback lifestyle. Cottons or similar are best as high synthetic content clothing can cause 'prickly heat' in the humid tropics. Drip dry, non-iron are most convenient. A useful hint for washing red dust out of clothes is to do so in cold water - hot water tends to 'fix' the ochre coloration.

Reasonable dress standards are maintained in restaurants and hotels in the larger centres, where in the evening for men, open-necked shirts and trousers are acceptable. Casino standards are stricter in the evening - no denim trousers and shirts must have a collar. The 'Darwin Rig' is common for men: shorts (or long trousers), long socks, shoes and open-necked shirt with collar. For women, light dresses, tops and skirts, tops and shorts are worn, and a dress to suit the occasion in the evening.

In the Central Australia Region, nights are cold to freezing in winter, so take warm clothing. For the bush, light trousers (jeans or similar), strong comfortable rubber-soled footwear and wide brimmed hats are advised for protection. Jeans are not advised for camel or horse riding - track suit trousers are better as they don't chafe.

What to Take

Health insurance documents are easily forgotten, as are vehicle insurance policy and spectacles prescription (in case of lost or broken glasses).

Protect Yourself

Sun strength and light intensity, particularly in Central Australia, are much warmer and stronger than people from other climates expect. Hats, sunglasses (for the children, too), sun lotions and block out creams are essential for comfort and skin protection. Bushflies and mosquitoes are plentiful in places, so take supplies of reliable repellents. Face nets are an effective bush fly deterrent. Take supplies of any medication you may require. Attune yourself as much as possible to the climate conditions - in and out of air-conditioned environments can increase discomfort levels.

Disabled Persons

Visitors confined to wheelchairs will welcome the attention given to their needs in recent years. Most new accommodation places have facilities, as do the major national parks. Local Tourist Information Centres have listings of facilities.

Pets

Domestic pets are prohibited from all Northern Territory Parks and Wildlife Commission parks and reserves (Guide dogs excepted only).

Parks Australia has banned all pets from Kakadu National Park. In the Kimberley, no pets are allowed in national parks. Many caravan parks don't allow pets. Given the restrictions, and climatic conditions, it's not much of a holiday for them! Dog owners are advised to have the animal checked for heartworm - the mosquito carriers are rife in the tropics. Those taking dogs should seek preventative advice regarding heartworm (tablets can be administered). Cattle tick is another problem for pets in the tropics. Kennels are few and far between, and most will not accept animals that have not been recently inoculated, ie. within 3 weeks. Kennel arrangements must be made several months in advance. Best advice is to leave pets at home.

ACCOMMODATION

A wide variety is available from luxury hotels to youth hostels, and well-appointed caravan parks to basic camping grounds. Many hotels, resorts and motels offer family group concessions, and have lower rates during the summer off-season period. While costs listed in Part Two were accurate at the time of writing, there may be some variation when you arrive there. Best advice is to check beforehand. A Tourism Marketing Duty of 5% of basic accommodation is levied on hotel and motel charges by the Northern Territory Government (caravan parks are exempt from this tax).

Hotels

Premier class are found in Darwin, Alice Springs, Yulara (Ayers Rock Resort), Jabiru and Broome. Old established and less expensive hotels are available for the budget-minded. The requirement of public bar among its facilities distinguishes a hotel from a motel.

Motels

They are well represented in cities, towns, resorts, and along the major highways. Developed to meet the needs of the travelling motorist, the motel industry now offers plenty of choice and fine facilities, particularly in Darwin, Alice Springs, Katherine, Tennant Creek, Broome and Kununurra. Like hotels, many have restaurants and swimming pools. In the Kimberley, many private hotels have standards similar to medium priced motels.

Roadhouses
On the highways, and in the rural areas of the Outback, roadhouses and wayside inns offer comfortable overnight accommodation, including airconditioned motel-style rooms, or cabins called dongas, or demountables and camping. They are relatively cheap, particularly camping.

Cattle Stations
Some enterprising station owners offer ranch style (bunkhouse) accommodation at their homesteads as an adjunct to normal station operation.

Hostels
Youth hostels offer an inexpensive alternative, but membership, irrespective of age, is sometimes needed. YHA Hostels handbook outlines membership conditions, lists locations, and is obtainable from National Head Office at 10 Mallet Street, Camperdown, NSW, 2050, ph (02) 9565 1699.

State office addresses applicable to this guide are 236 William Street, Northbridge, WA, 6003, ph (08) 9227 5122, and Darwin Transit Centre, 69 Mitchell Street, Darwin, NT, 0801, ph. (08) 8981 6344.

Hostels are located at Darwin, Border Store and Gagudju Lodge (Kakadu), Pine Creek, Katherine, Mataranka Homestead, Tennant Creek, Alice Springs and Yulara. In the Kimberley, there is one at Kununurra. YWCA has hostels in Darwin and Alice Springs.

Caravan Parks and Camping Grounds
Sometimes called tourist or holiday parks in the major centres, and despite frequent omissions from tourist literature, most do have areas set aside for tents. Cabins and on-site vans are available for renting at many. Powered sites are common in virtually all; shady grassed areas are not so common in arid

areas. Facilities include at least toilets and showers, and larger parks in towns and cities offer a range of recreation facilities and services. For an additional cost, air-conditioned cabins are available. Most roadhouses offer campsites - some free. Many national parks permit camping (fees now apply in all), with facilities varying from pit toilets only, to modern amenities. Alternatively, you can camp 'bush' - this is definitely the cheapest, provided you are geared for it. (See also *Practical Advice* section on Camping).

Bookings and Guides

Advance bookings are advised for places of your choice at popular spots, particularly during peak season months. Availability, types and costs are included for all places in regional sections.

  Local Visitor Centres are helpful. The Automobile Associations also handle bookings, and the RACV annually publishes a national accommodation guide (two books - one covering hotels, motels, B&B, resorts etc; the other covering Caravan Parks and camping), which is its recommended list of all types of accommodation - available from all AA offices.

FOR OVERSEAS VISITORS

Electricity

Power in Australia is 240 volts AC. Some of the large hotels provide a variety of power outlets at 240, 220 and 110 volts AC. However, it is advisable to include a small 110 volt transformer and plug conversion kit for the Territory.

Tipping

This is not obligatory in Australia, but visitors are quite at liberty to leave a tip if they so desire.

Currency

Australian currency is dollars and cents. Notes come in denominations of $100, $50, $20, $10 and $5, and coins in $2, $1, 50c, 20c, 10, and 5c. Overseas currency and travellers cheques may be exchanged at any bank and some larger hotels.

Driving

Vehicles in Australia are right hand drive, and travel on the left hand side of the road. A valid overseas driver's licence allows visitors to legally drive on Australian roads. Refer also to *Traffic Regulations* and *Road Surface Types* in the Practical Information Section.

SHOPS, SERVICES, COSTS

Larger centres offer a wide range of goods and services, and have excellent modern shopping facilities. Trading hours are generally between 9am and 5.30pm (in the Kimberley shops are open 8am to 5pm) during weekdays. Weekend trading is widespread, particularly in Alice Springs and other prime tourist centres. Great distances mean higher costs for a range of goods, particularly in the outlying areas.

Some foodstuffs in larger towns, such as fresh vegetables, are expensive, but it's not all bad news - a random survey showed some items only a few cents dearer in comparison with Melbourne supermarkets, a few items were cheaper, most about 10% to 20% dearer. Fuel costs are higher. For the budget-minded, it is possible to save on some durable food, photographic and vehicle items by purchasing in the supermarkets of Darwin or Alice Springs. Cold drinks can be a budget-biter for families, and takeaway beer can be expensive in some remote places.

Keep in mind that on 1 July, 2000, a Goods and Services Tax will be introduced in Australia. This will obviously have a marked effect on the prices of items and accomodation listed in this book. The overseas traveller should be aware of the change and prepare accordingly.

Shopping

If you are looking for something different and indigenous, you will not be disappointed. For interstate visitors, fly home with a special container of fresh barramundi or buffalo steak. And for wine buffs, a Chateau Hornsby red from the desert winery near Alice Springs. If beer is preferred, then try the world's largest bottle - the Darwin Stubby. Buffalo horns, replicas of outback road signs and crocodile warning signs, locally crafted leather, gemstones, and other items from natural sources, make interesting reminders. Genuine Aboriginal artifacts can be purchased throughout the Territory. Some fine bookshops in Alice Springs and Darwin have a fascinating range of Outback titles. Broome offers pearls and related items, while Kununurra has diamonds from the 'local' Argyle mine, and 'zebra rock'. Otherwise, for those gifts to take home there is the usual, often terrible, cheaper range of souvenirs and often of non-Australian manufacture.

MEDICAL SERVICES

Most visitors will never be too far away from medical help. Many small settlements have nursing clinics, providing initial care with a visiting doctor service on some days. The Flying Doctor Services are for everyone, including tourists, and are only a phone or radio call away for advice or action. They are called The Royal Flying Doctor Service in Central Australia, Aerial Medical Service in the Top End, and Royal Flying Doctor Service in the Kimberley. A full range of services are available in the larger centres, and in emergencies, medical services in the Aboriginal communities can be used. Full facility hospitals are in Darwin and Alice Springs; smaller regional or district hospitals at Tennant Creek, Katherine, Gove, Broome, Kununurra and Derby, Fitzroy Crossing, Halls Creek and Wyndham.

BANKS AND CREDIT CARDS

Banks, while well represented at branch level in the major centres, may have an agency only in smaller centres. Banking hours are Monday to Thursday 9.30am to 4pm, Friday 9.30am to 5pm.

 Locations of auto-tellers are listed in facilities for each settlement. Major national and international credit cards are widely accepted. It is advisable to carry sufficient cash for those long stretches between towns, as a few roadhouses do not accept credit cards for fuel or other services. Electronic Funds Transfer/Point of Sale (EFTPOS) facilities are becoming more widespread, even at remoter roadhouses.

FUEL AND VEHICLE SERVICES

Petrol (LP, ULP) and diesel are available on all major routes, and on some remote tracks. LPG for vehicles is now more widespread in its availability. Unless you go off the beaten track, there are few places where distances between services exceed 200km (124 miles). 24-hour fuel is available, and some places have varied opening hours (usually ranging between 6am and 11pm). Always check availability of fuel if travelling at night, as opening fees may be charged for after hours service. Supplies at some more remote places are unreliable, so check beforehand. The Automobile Associations provide detailed fuel availability information. Bottled gas is widely available. Aviation fuel is limited to a few locations.

It is best to get spares and have your vehicle serviced in larger centres, as smaller places are not geared for this - some will undertake emergency repair work, but you may have to wait for parts.

ROADS

First-time motorists may well be surprised by the extent and quality of bitumen, all weather-roads. In fact, most drivers see what they want to without leaving the bitumen. Road names can be misleading: don't always associate highways with sealed roads - the Gunbarrel Highway is a track; the Sandover Highway is a formed road; and part of the Buchanan Highway is a gravel road. Road surface types fall into three categories.

Sealed

Sometimes called bitumen or blacktop (Figs 1 and 2), these are mainly two-lane all weather highways, eg. The Arnhem. Most sections of the Stuart and many sections of The Great Northern Highway are to this standard. But, some may reduce to a width barely sufficient for two vehicles to pass. Other highways may have just one lane of sealed surface. Upgrading is a continuing process, and sealed roads generally present no problem for drivers.

Unsealed

Unsealed or gravel, dirt or sand surfaces may be formed, ie. engineered, to shed water quickly (Fig 5), while unformed are cut into the surface by a grader blade (Figs 3 and 4). The latter, in particular, can deteriorate rapidly after rains causing dangerous surfaces. After grading (usually once or twice a year after the rainy season), they can be good, passable even for some conventional vehicles. Many unsealed roads were built as 'beef highways', replacing the old stock-routes for the motorised roadtrain haulage of cattle.

Tracks

Generally have little traffic, and many are more akin to pathways worn by vehicles. Sometimes, sections of tracks are barely distinguishable from the surrounding terrain, while others are similar to unformed roads. Tracks are best suited to 4WD vehicles only.

  Users of all unsealed roads should always seek local, tourist authority, AA or police advice. Police stations have road condition postings, and regularly patrol major Outback highways in the Territory and Kimberley. Road conditions can alter rapidly, and many unsealed roads have 4WD only recommendations. Up-to-date road reports for the Territory can be obtained from AANT ph. (08) 8952 1087 or Tourist Centres or Police; for the Kimberley telephone 1800 013 314 for a recorded message.

Driving Hazards

Driving can be safe if the driver is aware of potential hazards, extends courtesy to others, and above all, adjusts speed to suit road conditions.

The main hazards are:

Tiredness

Distances and long straight stretches can have a mesmerising effect. Break your trip into realistic proportions, stop frequently, and change drivers to prevent 'dropping off'. Don't drink alcohol and drive.

Wandering Stock

Most station properties are unfenced, and dead, desiccated animals along the roadside are a grim reminder of stock and wildlife hazards. Camels, donkeys, horses, cattle, kangaroos and

ROAD SURFACE CROSS SECTIONS

Sealed, bitumen or blacktop:

Fig 1. Two Lane all weather highway (eg. Stuart Hwy)

Fig 2. One Lane sealed highway. Note frayed edges. (eg Victoria Hwy)

Unsealed

Fig 3. Unformed, flat bladed. Become more channel – like in sand country. Pot holes, bulldust and corrugations common.

Fig 4. Unformed rarely graded track. Deep wheel ruts and centre hump.

Fig 5. Formed earth or gravel road

emus are very unpredictable in their movements, particularly at night. Cattle sometimes seek the warmth of the bitumen to sleep on also. Best advice is to avoid night driving if you can.

Single-lane Bridges

There are a number of these on the Great Northern Highway between Derby and Wyndham. Others may be encountered too, on some unsealed roads. Slow down and be prepared to give way.

Cattle Grids

On some roads, cattle grids occur at intervals, and may be set above road surface levels. Iron-grid joins in the middle can be out of line, with one edge protruding. Slow down to prevent tyre damage.

Road Surfaces and Edges

If you are unfamiliar with driving on dirt roads, reduce speed until you get used to travelling on such roads. Speed generally on dirt roads should be about half that you would normally travel. Dust from passing or on-coming vehicles on unsealed surfaces obscures vision, so slow down or stop and close your windows. Pot holes, sand, corrugations, ruts left by heavy vehicles, jump-ups, rough creek crossings, flash flooding and 'bulldust' (fine deposits of soil and dust of varying depth) are all possible hazards on unsealed roads. Edges can become soft and cause bogging after rains. One-lane sealed road edges may drop sharply to the natural surface (see Fig 2).

Single Tracks

Many roads have been constructed for one vehicle at a time. On unsealed roads, shoulders are sloped more to effect run-off after rains, so slow down to have complete control when you are passing vehicles approaching from the opposite direction. Loose gravel from road verges may be flung at your windscreen when passing on narrow, sealed roads - again slow down to reduce the danger.

Road Trains

These mammoth haulers of freight are often 50m long, and consist of a prime mover towing up to three trailer sections.

Be careful when passing or overtaking, especially on sections of the Barkly and Victoria Highways where the seal width is only 4m, and the road trains need 2.5m of that! There's not going to be much room for you - slow down and pull over. This action will also reduce the chances of stone damage to your vehicle. If following one, be patient - they take a long time to overtake, and at least a clear kilometre ahead is needed before doing so. Often drivers will assist by signalling when the way is clear. And don't expect road trains to move over for you - they are more difficult to control if driving on two surfaces at once.

Traffic Regulations

They are much the same in the Kimberley and Northern Territory as in other parts of Australia. The main differences are:

Speed limits of 60km/h in built-up areas unless stated otherwise, with open limits on some roads. 'P' plate licence holders must have 0% blood alcohol level, and not exceed 80km/h. Blood alcohol limit is .05%, and random breath tests are conducted. Seat belts are compulsory. Interstate vehicles that stay for more than three months require NT registration. All accidents involving injury or property damage must be reported within 24 hours to police. Motorists turning right must give way to all vehicles from opposite direction, including those turning left.

Speed limit has a 110km/h maximum. 'P' plate holders must not exceed 90km/h and .02% blood alcohol levels - others .08% blood alcohol level. Accidents involving injury or damage over $1000 in value must be reported to police as soon as possible. The wearing of seat belts is compulsory.

Crossing State Borders

Two things happen here - you need to adjust your watches as Eastern and Western Territory Borders are also Time Zone boundaries, and certain fruit and plant quarantine regulations apply.

Time Differences

Australia is divided into three time zones. Central Zone (South Australia, Northern Territory) is half an hour behind Eastern Time Zone (Queensland, New South Wales, Victoria, Tasmania) and 1.5

hours ahead of Western Time (Western Australia). This means when travelling east across the WA/NT Border, advance watches by 1.5 hours; going the other way, turn back by 1.5 hours. Across Eastern and Central Time Zones, advance by half an hour if travelling East, turn back half an hour if going West. Make further allowances when Eastern States adopt Daylight Saving during summer.

Fruit and Plant Quarantine

Manned stations on some state borders and other points of entry may be annoying, but necessary, to prevent pests and diseases from entering these parts of Australia. Multi-million dollar agricultural enterprises could be jeopardised by travellers unwittingly bringing infected plants or fruits. The WA Agricultural Department is strict at their WA/NT border station, about 40km (25 miles) east of Kununurra. Vegetables, fruits, seeds, soil, plants and honey are some of the prohibited items, so don't stock up with fresh foods at Katherine if you are heading to the Kimberley. Acquaint yourself with the regulations by reading *Travellers' Guide to Plant Quarantine,* available from Agricultural Department Offices throughout Australia.

ABORIGINAL LAND

Land previously designated **Aboriginal Reserve** became Aboriginal Land with the declaration of Aboriginal Land Rights (NT) Act in 1976. Aborigines now have freehold title, accepted in traditional and contemporary Australian law. In short, it is now privately owned land, the title of which is no different in law to that of suburban blocks in the cities, and subject to the same laws of trespass. The fact that it is not fenced, as with cattle stations, does not alter its status. Visitors must obtain a permit and have it in their possession, whilst on Aboriginal land.

Permits

When making application for entry to any Aboriginal Land, applicants must state the reason for entry, dates and duration of intended stay, names of persons travelling, and itinerary and routes to be used while on these lands. Permits can only be issued after consultation and approval of the relevant Aboriginal communities. Processing permit applications can take 4-6 weeks.

It should be noted that, as a general rule, Land Councils have been asked by Traditional Owners not to issue entry permits for unaccompanied tourist travel. This does not affect visitors travelling on one of the organised tours onto Aboriginal Land, where tour bookings include the necessary permit.

It is the right of Traditional Owners of Aboriginal Land to refuse entry permits. Applications and any enquiries must be directed in writing to the relevant Land Council listed below.

Public roads that cross Aboriginal Land are exempt from the permit provisions. However, the exemption covers the immediate road corridor only. You may camp on the side of these roads, or at roadside stops or parking bays. A transit permit is required for the Yalara-Docker River Road, but not for the Tanami Road, Lajamanu Road and Sandover Highway. Some roads crossing Aboriginal Lands are not designated as public roads, so please seek advice from the Land Councils before travelling.

Direct enquiries to the appropriate Councils at the following addresses.

Central Australia (Alice Springs and Tennant Creek regions)
Permit Officer
Central Land Council
PO Box 3321
Alice Springs NT 0871
Ph (08) 8951 6320

Top End and Tablelands (Darwin, Nhulunbuy or Katherine regions)
Permit Officer, Northern Land Council
PO Box 42941
Casuarina, NT 0811
Ph (08) 8920 5100.

Melville or Bathurst Islands
Tiwi Land Council
Unit 5, 3 Bishop Street
Stuart Park
Darwin, NT, 0800
Ph (08) 8981 4898

The Kimberley, Western Australia
Aboriginal Affairs Department
PO Box 7770
Cloisters Square
Perth, WA, 6850
Ph (08) 9235 8000

For those proposing to travel into WA via the Gunbarrel Hwy, contact the Ngaanyatjarra Council, PO Box 644, Alice Springs, 0871. Ph (08) 8950 1711 for permit details.

Sacred Sites
A large number of places and features have special, often spiritual significance to Aborigines. These sacred sites are protected, and visitors should be aware that penalties exist for entering or interfering with them. Some areas that have historic significance to Aborigines are open to the public, and while visitors are welcome to visit some sites, respect should be shown for them.

Photography
Commercial photography is not allowed in Aboriginal Lands, unless prior permission has been granted by the appropriate Land Council. Photographs for personal collections are permissible. If these photographs involve the people who live in the areas, please observe the normal courtesy you would expect for yourself. In fact, because this has not always happened, some areas do not allow photography or videos.

Alcohol

Most Aboriginal Lands prohibit the importation and/or consumption of alcohol. If travelling to, or through, these Lands, check with the appropriate Land Council, regarding these designated 'Dry Areas' (alcohol free). Severe penalties exist for disregard of alcohol regulations.

CATTLE STATIONS AND HOMESTEADS

Cattle stations are business enterprises that are not geared to meeting requests for supplies from tourists. However, owners are reasonable and willing to help in cases of genuine trouble, but expect a cool reception if, through poor planning, you have run out of fuel. Station property is private land, and while it may be unfenced and wilderness-like, accord it the respect you would to your own. Some owners have closed access to attractions because of wilful damage to fences and bores, and there is some measure of exasperation behind the blunt *No Shooting, Camping or Trespassing* notices erected on some properties.

It should be noted a number of tracks, particularly in Central Australia, are in fact private station roads. When planning your route, please check thoroughly because sometimes maps don't differentiate between public roads/tracks and private station roads on private property. These station roads are rarely graded and are potentially very dangerous to those unfamiliar with them. (See also under *Chambers Pillar* in Part Two). A few stations in remote areas offer mainly basic services to tourists.

WATER AND FLUID INTAKE

In remote arid regions, water is a scarce commodity. Always carry adequate supplies of drinking water, and motorists, don't forget to allow for the car too. In Central Australia, campers should allow at least 4 litres (one gallon) per person per day. The amount you carry in the vehicle will depend on how far off the beaten track you go, the degree of physical activity, time of the year, and the number of people.

Take water on walks, no matter how long. You'll be surprised how thirsty you get, and how much moisture the body loses. Alcohol (beer, etc) is not recommended as a thirst quencher on walks - in fact it hastens dehydration, as most will know!

Facts clearly indicate the need to replace moisture lost mainly through the skin pores (moisture is also lost through the lungs by expelled air). The normal fluid requirement is around 4 litres per day in temperate climates (less for children, but remember their regulatory system is more sensitive than adults' and so need frequent smaller intakes). Under normal temperate climate conditions, eg. Melbourne, about 1.5 litres is lost per day. In the arid and Top End regions, higher temperatures and the nature of activities are going to increase the loss at a faster rate, eg. in the Top End at least twice the normal intake is needed, and up to 3 times more with strenuous exercise. On longer treks and under hot conditions, walkers are advised to drink 1 litre every 3 hours (a rough guide). Also, they need to counter salt and sugar loss - use salt tablets and barley sugar (or similar), as well as some solid food such as raisins or nuts (muesli bars are ideal).

Always boil water from natural pools and billabongs before drinking, after all you don't know who, or what, has had their feet in the trough! Water purifying tablets are a practical way to ensure adequate drinking water for bush campers.

NATIONAL PARKS

They aim to preserve and protect the natural environment, including features of scenic, historical, archaeological, geological and other scientific interest, in a system of parks and reserves open for public enjoyment, education and inspiration. Parks exist for heritage preservation and rangers work hard to keep them in pristine condition - help them by following park rules. Larger parks have well appointed visitor centres and ranger stations; others have visiting rangers.

Fees

All Northern Territory Parks and Wildlife Commission parks and reserves charge very reasonable camping fees. Parks Australia has entry and camping fees for Kakadu and Uluru/Kata Tjuta National Parks. Camping fees are also charged for some Kimberley National Parks.

Camping

While some parks are day use only, many others permit camping.

Pets

Pets are prohibited from all Kimberley National Parks. Northern Territory Parks do not permit cats or dogs (guide dogs excepted).

Facilities

Many have well appointed facilities; others, in keeping with the nature and usage of the park, are limited.

There are no bookings taken, and camping areas can get crowded. Always check water supplies. Restrictions on night use of generators apply in some. Wood for campfires is scarce in arid areas, and dead litter, if used, destroys a micro-habitat for many small creatures - gas for cooking is preferred. Refer to regional sections for detailed outlines on Parks.

WILDLIFE AND ENVIRONMENTAL RESPECT

All native animals (kangaroos, euros, wallabies and other marsupials, etc), reptiles (lizards, fresh water and saltwater crocodiles and snakes, etc) and birds (all parrots, cockatoos, finches, eagles, emus, bustards, etc) are fully protected in both the Northern Territory and Kimberley. Most trees, shrubs and wildflowers are similarly protected (refrain from picking wildflowers, photograph them instead).

The environment is a fragile resource, and while crocodiles, snakes and the like, may give you the 'horrors', each has a vital role in the ecological balance of things. The landscape beauty is often marred by unsightly litter cast off along the highways, in rest areas, and along bush walking trails, by thoughtless people. The ancient Kimberley boabs and rocky outcrops on the way west, have not escaped crude desecration either by 20th Century vandals. The only things you should take are photographs, while footprints should be the only traces of your visit.

At all natural waterways, falls, waterholes and dams, do not pollute these wildlife and cattle drinking spots by using soap and detergents when camping. This causes fouling, kills unseen aquatic life, and has a negative ripple effect on the food chain and ecosystem.

WILDLIFE AND MARINE DANGERS

With good sense and a preventative approach, such dangers need not mar your visit. Potentially dangerous snakes are around (as they are in all Australian states) but will rarely attack unless provoked. Wear appropriate protective clothing in the bush. Snakes capable of killing humans include taipan, king brown or mulga, western brown, eastern or common brown, Ingram's brown snake, speckled brown or Down's tiger snake, desert whip snake, yellow-faced whip snake, curl snake, desert death adder and common death adder. Despite the lengthy list, most are rarely seen.

Crocodiles, both freshwater and saltwater, inhabit coastal and inland waters of the Top End and Kimberley regions, and the latter type is lethal (refer to *Top End Region introduction* for crocodile outlines). Feral buffalo and boar (wild pig) inhabit large areas of the Top End, and can be dangerous. Bull camels can be temperamental too, in Central Australia. Get your close-ups with a telephoto or zoom lens to avoid trouble. Dingoes and goannas can be unpredictable.

Tropical coastal waters harbour an array of nasty species. Between October and May, box jellyfish (sea wasp) invade the coasts, and stings from their tentacles can be traumatic and lethal. The simple precaution is don't swim or paddle in the sea during these times. Darwin beaches have warning signs posted. Other marine nasties are sharks, sea snakes, blue-ringed octopus, cone shell and stone fish. On the brighter side, some areas are relatively free of these, but always seek local advice.

Other things to avoid are scorpions, an ugly-looking larger insect that gives a nasty sting, and is found in the arid regions. Leeches, on the other hand, are not so easy to avoid in the tropical, damp rainforests. They latch onto lower leg areas in particular, and if these flat slug-like things attach themselves, scrape them off, or discourage them with a bit of vinegar.

SAFE SWIMMING

Despite the marine and crocodile dangers, it is not all bad news for swimmers. A range of safe swimming can be found: Cable Beach (Broome), Berry and Howard Springs (outside Darwin), some natural rock holes in the gaps and gorges of the Central Australia region and Kimberley, Mary Ann Dam (Tennant Creek), Low Level Park (Katherine), and Mataranka Thermal Pool, to name some. Many hotels, motels and caravan parks have pools for guests, and larger towns have superb public swimming pools. If in any doubt about places to swim, seek local advice. And, if you feel uncomfortable about a place, be guided by your instinct - don't swim.

It may be of surprise to learn that one of the greatest natural dangers is Uluru. Unless you are physically fit, climbing the rock should be avoided. It is a demanding climb and should not be attempted by those with a heart condition, high blood pressure or asthmatic conditions.

FIRE DANGER PERIOD

Northern Territory

A sign near Kulgera, near the South Australian/Northern Territory border, reads... *We like our lizards frilled not grilled*, and warns of the bush fire dangers, even in the arid zone. Bushfires in Australia are usually associated more with the southern states. It may be of surprise to many visitors to learn the extent of this hazard in the northern regions during the Dry season, when large areas can be ravaged. Between July and December, a fire danger period is declared north of the 21st parallel (about 350km [27 miles] north of Alice Springs) at which times there are restrictions on fires in the open - camp fires can only be lit in constructed fireplaces, or on properly cleared areas (at least 4m distant from flammable matter), and must be extinguished after use. In extreme fire danger periods, a total fire ban may be declared, when no fires in the open may be lit. Fire danger months in the Centre occur between October and March. Please note the *Fire Danger* index signs, and act accordingly.

Controlled burning in the Top End takes place in late April/early May to reduce rank grass and encourage regrowth.

Kimberley

Here they say *Beef runs on grass*, so help the great Kimberley pastoral industry to prevent bushfires by strictly observing the following regulations. Camping and cooking fires must not be lit within 3m of a stump or log, and a 3m radius from the fire must be clear of all inflammable material. Someone must always be in attendance, and the fire must be properly extinguished before leaving. Total prohibition for all fires in the open operates in all shires of the Kimberley during the Dry Season. Check with local authorities for the exact dates, as they differ from shire to shire.

FOSSICKING

Fossicking in the Kimberley is allowed on Crown land, and a Miner's Right is required. For details, write to The Department of Minerals and Energy, Mineral House, 100 Plain Street, Perth, WA, 6004, ph (08) 9222 3333.

In the Northern Territory, there is plenty of scope for rock hounds, too, and a fossicking permit, which comes with a package of information including maps of sites, costs $5 for one month; $10 for 4 months; $20 pa.; and $50 for 5 years. In association with Tourist Authorities, NT fossicking sites are being developed Territory-wide by the Minerals and Energy Department. A visit to their offices at 58 Hartley Street, Alice Springs, ph (08) 8951 5658 or Smith Street Mall, Darwin, ph. (08) 8999 5286 is well worth while for interesting displays and a permit. Permits are also available from Regional Tourist Information Centres.

HUNTING AND SHOOTING

There's a misconception in many quarters that shooting is 'open go' in the Outback - this is simply not so! While the Top End is one of the few wilderness hunting areas in the world, stringent regulations apply. Strict rules on firearms also apply, and on the way they are carried and used. Every shooter must have a licence, and every firearm registered. Check with the Northern Territory Police. No hunting or shooting is permitted in the Kimberley, and all firearms carried in WA must be registered with the Police.

There are some safari operators who have concessions to allow organised hunting safaris for Banteng Cattle, Samba deer, buffalo or pigs in the Top End Region. Contact Top End regional Tourist centres or refer to details listed in Top End places listings.

FISHING

Northern Territory waters, in particular, offer some of the best year round fishing in Australia. Fishing with hand lines or rods is generally permitted in rivers and billabongs throughout the year, without a licence. Amateur fisherman are not permitted to sell their catch. The prized fish is the barramundi, currently under a stringent management programme. Bag limits for barramundi are: 5 fish per person per day. Special limits for barramundi apply to the Mary River System, including Shady Camp and Corroboree Creek - 2 fish per person per day, 4 fish for any trip of more than one day, and a minimum size of 50cm (20 inches). The Mary River System is closed to fishing between October 1 and January 31 of the following year. It is probable the 2 fish bag limit will apply to all waters in the near future. Refer to Top End regional introduction for further details.

The Northern Territory Fisheries Department has a detailed guide booklet to recreation fishing, and they will answer any angling questions. It pays to check too, for any changes in licence policy. Contact Fisheries Department ph. (08) 8999 5511 for further information.

Fishing is good in the Kimberley, too. Fisheries WA produces an excellent booklet detailing types of fish and regulations. Phone Fisheries WA in Perth (08) 9482 7333 or their Broome office ph. (08) 9192 1121 for details.

EMERGENCY AND ROAD INFORMATION TELEPHONE NUMBERS

For medical, fire, police and ambulance, dial 000 for both the Kimberley Region and the Northern Territory. For Marine Stinger Emergencies, ph 1800 079 909 (free call). Poisons Information Centre, ph. 131 126.

For Advance Road Information for Northern Territory, telephone Transport and Works Department (business hours Mon-Fri) (08) 8951 5211. For the Kimberley, telephone Main Roads Department 1800 013 314. Alternatively, contact the nearest Police Station or Tourist Information Centre in the proposed area of travel. For vehicle breakdown, contact the nearest service - these are listed in the Regional Sections under places.

Practical Advice

MOTORING

A reliable vehicle is essential for safe and enjoyable motoring in the Outback states. Conventional 2 wheel drive vehicles are quite suitable, and research shows that most 2WD travellers see what they want to by rarely leaving the bitumen. While a 4WD vehicle and Outback touring are often strongly associated, it is not necessary to outlay such an expense - for the few tracks and dirt roads you may want to venture on, it would be more economical to hire a 4WD.

PREPARATION

Have your vehicle systems thoroughly checked. For older vehicles, replace all hoses, fan belts, filters, plastic sections of fuel lines; check electrical system - coil, condenser, plugs, points, and replace if required; check and repack wheel bearings with grease; check brakes; and undertake a systematic check for loose wiring and nuts. After travelling on corrugated roads in the Outback you will be surprised how the jarring loosens things. Give attention to the cooling system, and flush out. Trailers and caravans should be checked thoroughly, too - often light, city trailers require strengthening before being suitable for outback conditions.

It is a good idea to acquire some mechanical skills, too. Local TAFE Colleges generally offer excellent courses for beginners that give confidence, and allow identification of many potential and real mechanical problems. In fact, with these skills you may be able to rectify simple problems without the expense of getting outside help, and to do your own basic servicing.

By all means listen to the loads of advice you are likely to receive. Cross-check with mechanics, Automobile Associations, etc, and a sensible, practical list of spares and tools to take will emerge. Otherwise, you will end up towing a complete repair workshop!

SPARES

For most travellers, tyre and spare tubes, tyre repair kit, coil, condenser, distributor points, fuses, fan belt and radiator hoses would be adequate. If you travel off the main roads, an extra tyre and tube is advised. Obviously, the extent of spares will depend on how long, and where you plan to go. Roof-racks should be of a heavy-duty type to withstand vibrations on corrugated dirt roads.

TOOLS

A good set of tools is strongly advised. Socket set, open-end and ring spanners, shifting spanner, screwdrivers, pliers, insulation tape, hammer, jumper leads, jack with wide base plate for sand surfaces, wheel spanner, pump, fire extinguisher, tow rope, axe, shovel, tarpaulin (for shade) and a good torch, are suggested.

FUEL, WATER, LUBRICANTS

Much depends on where, and for how long, you are going. Extra oil, fuel, water (out bush allow 4 litres [1 gallon] per person per day) and brake fluid are advised.

MAPS AND MANUALS

Always carry an up-to-date set of maps (see under *Maps* in Information Sources section). Carry vehicle insurance documents. A car manual is useful, as are several specialist books on the market about Outback motoring, including how to solve vehicle problems and survival skills. Jack Absalom's *Safe Outback Travel* is good value, as is Jeff Carter's *The Australian Explorer's Handbook*.

GENERAL ADVICE

In the arid areas in particular, never leave children or pets in a parked car, and always leave the windows down a bit if parked in the sun, to avoid windscreens being blown out by expanding air. A patent sun shade for windows (or towels and the like) keeps the car cooler when parked. (When travelling, sun blinds or similar make life more comfortable in the back seat, and prevent sunburn too.)

Be aware of driving hazards. In remote areas, check the fuel availability beforehand. Keep a weather eye out and, if off the main roads, check road conditions prior to leaving. Summer in the arid zones and in some Top End and Kimberley places, is not the time to travel off the bitumen. Keep your load to a minimum, as excessive loads are a frequent cause of breakdowns. Carry plenty of food and water in case of breakdown.

If planning to drive across remote country, let reliable people know your plans and estimated arrival time, and don't forget to report in (searches are costly and endanger other lives too).

On long driving stretches, it is a good idea to change drivers if possible every hour or 100km, to avoid tiredness, particularly in warm conditions and with no air-conditioning. Also 'water' the children every hour or so.

Outback motoring is not as hazardous as made out to be, provided you plan well. Automobile Associations are extremely helpful, and should be consulted. Check that your membership is current!

BREAKDOWN

No matter when you break down, always stay with your vehicle. Erect some shade, conserve energy, and wait until you are able to attract attention. If you have good supplies of food and water as suggested, there will be little danger.

FOUR WHEEL DRIVE (4WD)

There are many publications, including magazines, which give a good guide to this specialist form of motoring. Well off the beaten track requires thorough preparation and good equipment, including an RFDS High Frequency radio set. At least two vehicles should make up treks along remote tracks such as Gunbarrel Highway, Tanami Track and Canning Stock Route. Escorted 4WD treks are an alternative for treks in the remote areas. 4WD Clubs are a good source of information, and way to acquire skills, so contact those in your local area.

COACH TOURING

While for adult and school group organisers, costs are an important factor when choosing a carrier, equally important is the question of reliability of service and vehicles including safety aspects, and experience of the company. The following checks are strongly advised to ensure value for money and quality:

- Get at least three quotes as a basis for comparison.
- Establish company credentials. Ask for a company profile and references they have from recent clients.
- Check the age of the coaches. Often there is a correlation between cheaper tours and quality of vehicles (10-15 years old, re-tread tyres etc.)
- Quality vehicles should bear Q.A.M (Quality Assured Maintenance or similar issued by relevant State Road Authority).
- Better companies will have seatbelts on newly acquired coaches.
- Ask to visit the company depot to see their coaches and equipment.
- Carefully check what the tour itinerary and cost includes eg. meals, entry fees etc.

It is advantageous to deal directly with the coach company. A number of tour operators do not have their own coaches; instead they contract tours to coach companies, so often you do not know who the actual carrier will be. There is also a cost advantage in dealing direct.

EXTENDED TOURING WITH CHILDREN

EDUCATION

Many Australian families camp their way fully or partially around Australia for periods of 3 months or more. Get school work guidance from teachers. The trip will be ideal for much project work, and there is plenty of scope for parents being teachers - costs of things, distances, map reading, etc, can be a practical form of maths and geography. Keeping a diary helps with English. It is not necessary to enrol at correspondence school, and your local school will provide worksheets for subjects. It is surprising how enthusiastic children do get when travelling.

TRAVELLING

On the long journeys, have frequent breaks to allow children to run off a bit of energy. Avoid too many sweets as too much sugar can cause hyperactivity - better to chew on some dried meat strips (Jerky) or dried fruit and nuts. To counter the heat, have water in the car. A water filled container with a spray nozzle is a good way to keep refreshed. If you carry ice in a fridge or esky, cubes are good to have in a small cooler in the car for the children to suck. Rotate the children to reduce boredom - let them have turns sitting up front with one adult in the back. Above all, have plenty of games, tapes (Walkman ideal), etc, to keep them occupied, including 'school work'. Children's books (adults too) can be easily and cheaply purchased at book exchanges along the way, and many children (depending on age) enjoy making things from a kit containing glue, sticky tape, scissors, paper, cardboard and coloured pencils.

For toilet stops in the bush along the roads, a whistle is a good idea if people have to walk some distance away for privacy (both on the walker and in the vehicle so they can call each other) - it is easy to get lost and lose a sense of direction in flat scrublands. A trowel rather than a shovel, is better for children for bush toilet stops.

FIRST AID

A first aid kit is essential for motorists and campers, and a reputable first aid book is strongly suggested too, and don't forget health insurance. The St John Ambulance and Red Cross produce good first aid books. A first aid kit should include a broad crepe bandage, an antiseptic, vinegar or other acetic acid (apple cider vinegar is good for minor insect bites and stings, and urine is a good vinegar substitute for bull ant bites too), band-aids, scissors. Ideally, all general problems such as burns, cuts, gashes, blisters, sunburn and minor injuries, should be provided for.

First aid treatment for less common injuries from potentially lethal venomous creatures and dehydration are given below. In all cases, seek medical attention as soon as possible.

SNAKE BITE

While a few hundred people get bitten each year in Australia, fatalities are few and there are antivenoms available.

Steps taken should be:
- Lay the victim flat and immediately apply a broad pressure bandage over the bitten area. As much of the limb should be bound up as possible. Crepe bandages are ideal, but strips of clothing will do (see diagram). Tourniquets are no longer used.
- DO NOT wash, cut or suck the wound. Washing may delay venom identification and the administering of antivenom. Completely immobilise the limb by binding some type of splint to it - any rigid object will do. Leave bandages and splint intact until medical care is reached.
- Reassure and calm the victim and arrange transport as quickly as possible to the nearest hospital or medical centre.
- If the victim suffers from asthma, any allergy, or has received antivenom before, inform the doctor or hospital. (Doctors can monitor the victim closely for serum reaction.)
- If breathing fails, apply Expired Air Resuscitation (mouth-to-mouth resuscitation).

Techniques that save lives

There are two basic life saving techniques that may be used in the case of a venomous bite.

However, if they are applied incorrectly, they can be dangerous.

Any person who is out and about regularly should get a more thorough knowledge, perhaps making use of the many excellent first aid courses available.

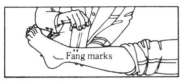

1. Apply a broad pressure bandage over the bite site as soon as possible. Keep the bitten area still.

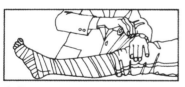

3. Extend the bandages as high as possible.

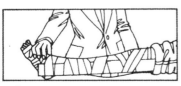

5. Bind it firmly to as much of the leg as possible.

Pressure Bandage and Limb Immobilisation.

1. Immediately apply a broad firm bandage around the limb to cover the bitten area as tightly as one would bind a sprained ankle. As much of the limb should be bound up as possible. Crepe bandages or any flexible material can be used.

2. Keeping the limb as still as possible, bind some type of splint to it – any rigid object will do.

3. Leave bandages and splint intact until medical care is reached.

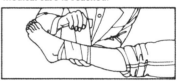

2. The bandage should be as tight as you would apply to a sprained ankle.

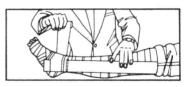

4. Apply a splint to the leg.

Bites on hand or forearm. **1.** Bind to elbow with bandages. **2.** Use splint to elbow. **3.** Use sling.

Mouth to Mouth Resuscitation

To be commenced immediately in all cases where breathing has stopped.

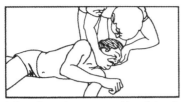

1. Lay the patient on one side. tilt head backwards and while supporting the jaw, use fingers to clear mouth of all foreign matter.

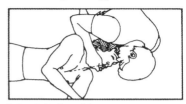

2. Look for breathing movements. Listen and feel for patient's breaths. If breathing leave on side.

3. If breathing stopped turn patient on back, tilt head backwards and, while supporting the jaw, seal nose with fingers.

4. Place your widely open mouth over patient's slightly open mouth and blow until the chest rises.

5. Watch the chest fall and listen for air escaping from the mouth. Then repeat steps 4 and 5 at a rate of 15 times a minute.

6. When breathing begins, turn the patient on to one side with head back, the jaw supported and the face pointing slightly towards the ground.

Continue resuscitation until the patient recovers and keep under observation until medical assistance arrives. For infants, cover the mouth and nose with your mouth and blow at the rate of 20 times a minute until the Chest rises.

As doctors can determine the type of snake from the venom by use of identification kits, there is no need to kill the snake and take it to the hospital (it can be helpful to identify and/or describe the snake).

STONEFISH

Stonefish can occur in shallow pools at low tide and, as the name suggests, it is very well camouflaged. A human hand or foot placed firmly on its back is likely to be pierced by one or more of the fish's 13 dorsal spines, and injected with deadly venom. Prevention is to wear strong shoes when exploring reefs and shores of known stone fish areas. A victim feels unbearable pain, and may collapse. Apply hot towels to the punctured area, or immerse in hot water to relieve the pain. Antivenom is available and medical help must be urgently sought.

BOX JELLYFISH OR SEA WASP

They inhabit northern coastal waters during the summer months from October to May, and they are deadly. Their venom has been known to kill within a few minutes. It is a jelly-like creature, box-shaped, and trails venomous tentacles several metres long. They are difficult to see. If stung, apply liberal doses of vinegar to the affected area (this action renders the tentacles harmless). Do not rub, as this triggers off more venom capsules. Do not suck the wound. Get the victim to medical help quickly. Apply mouth-to-mouth resuscitation if the victim collapses. Antivenoms are available. Marine Stinger Emergencies, Northern Territory, ph 1800 079 909 (free call).

DEHYDRATION

Lack of fluid intake has caused many deaths in the Outback. In serious cases, administer water or some other liquid (non-alcoholic) in very small sips. Add some salt and sugar to the liquid, too. Make sure the patient drinks slowly by only pouring small quantities into a utensil. Sponge the person down to lower body temperature. Medical attention depends on the recovery rate. Of interest may be the following death in the desert rate for various animals without water intake and in sun temperature of 40C: human beings 4-6 hours; pigs 1-2 days; cattle 4-5 days; sheep 6-8 days and camel more than 15 days.

CAMPING

COMMERCIAL CARAVAN PARKS

It is advisable to book ahead, during peak season periods, for sites at popular tourist spots such as Alice Springs, Mataranka, Katherine, Darwin, Kununurra and Broome. Tent sites are usually available at caravan parks.

NATIONAL PARKS

There are no bookings for sites, and many do get crowded. Check regional listings for Parks where camping is permitted.

BUSH CAMPING

In the Territory and Kimberley, camping in the bush, is allowed. Camping along main roads is not advised mainly for security and traffic noise reasons. Tourist authorities discourage camping in designated roadside rest areas. Instead, choose a spot well off the main road - adjacent to dry creek beds is ideal, but keep in mind the following:

- Do not camp in dry creek beds (flash flooding from storms miles away is a real danger).
- Don't pitch your tent directly under a tree (falling limbs, insect dwellers and moisture drip can pose problems).
- Keep sites well away from waterholes and bores (drinking habits of wildlife and cattle may be disturbed, and you may be in the midst of a cattle stampede if they are frightened).
- Be prepared for mosquitoes in many sites near water in the Top End (mosquito nets are advised).
- Seek permission from station owners to camp (it is private land).
- Do not pollute waterholes or dams by using soaps, etc; be careful with fire, and do not cut down any vegetation for wood

(all regions are fire prone and strict regulations on fires in the open apply - see *General Information* section).
- Store food away at night (dingoes and others enjoy a free meal!) and deeply bury toilet waste (dingoes easily scrape out shallow or covered sites).
- Do not bury rubbish (take it out with you).

Camping under the stars in the bush is one of the delights of the Outback, and provided bush campers do the right thing, this freedom to camp out will continue. When you leave the site, there should be no evidence of your stay.

CAMPING EQUIPMENT

The checklist included provides a starting point. Talk with your local camping dealer, most of whom offer better advice than the larger supermarket retailers, and have had experience in the bush. Tents should be dried before packing up - wet canvas will produce mildew and damage if not dried within a few hours. In the Centre, hard, sometimes stony ground can puncture the inner floor of tents - use a tarpaulin for underneath, but don't have it extending beyond the tent boundaries otherwise if it rains water will collect underneath! In hard ground, steel pegs are needed - use a mallet for driving them. Sand pegs are useful in sandy terrain. Blowing up airbeds each night can be a chore - alternatives are thick foam rubber rolls or self-inflating mattresses (the latter are ideal and less bulky).

Camping gas bottles are date stamped. Check that yours is valid, otherwise service stations will refuse to fill them. Older ones may need replacement fittings, and leaking gas is not desirable.

A camping fridge is highly convenient, but not absolutely essential; a 3 way type (gas, electricity, car battery) is ideal, and it can be run off a lead from the cigarette lighter fitting when travelling, then converted to gas or electricity at the campsite. If you do run it off the car battery, don't forget to turn it off when you stop the vehicle. It is not advisable to run it on gas while travelling - in fact, it is dangerous. If you do, it must be turned off at service stations. Also, gas should be kept out of inner tents where not only is there the risk of fire, but more significantly potentially lethal leaking gas. You should be thoroughly familiar with all gas accessories, and for first-time campers, a trial run is a good idea. A cooler or esky packed with ice is an alternative to a fridge for storing perishable foods. An extension lead is useful for caravan parks where there's a fee for such power uses.

Hire camping equipment is available from Darwin for visitors wishing to camp out, and many tours include bush camping in their itinerary. Hire campervans are another alternative.

Campers, in particular school groups, must observe rigid hygiene with respect to cleaning utensils after a meal. Bacteria love hastily-washed plates in the tropics, and sometimes outbreaks of stomach trouble can be traced to this source, or inadequate cold storage of perishable goods.

CAMPING CHECKLIST

Tents
  Family Tents
  Hike Tents
  Pegs

Sleeping
  Sleeping Bags
  Air Beds
  Camp Stretchers
  Space Blankets

Cooking
  Stove
  Barbecue
  Gas Bottle

Lighting
  Gas Lights (and spare mantles)
  Pressure Lantern
  Kero Lantern
  Gas Lantern
  Torch

Cooking Utensils
Camp Oven
Frypan
Jaffle Iron
BBQ Hot Plate
Kettle
Billy
Toasting Fork
Sausage Grill
Eating Utensils

Trouble Shooters
Wax Stick (for tent seams)
Spare Tent Pegs
Air Bed Patch and Plug
Puritabs
First Aid Kit
Insect Repellent
Waterproof Tape
Waterproof Matches

Other Equipment
Fridge or Cooler
Folding Table
Camp Chairs
Water Container
Bush Shower
Extension Pole for gas light
Stove Stand
Bucket
Porta Potti
Folding Toilet
Folding Spade
Air Bed Pump
Pocket Knife
Ground Sheet
Coil Rope
Fire Extinguisher

Clothing
Hat and Fly Veil
Poncho
Sturdy Clothing and Boots

PHOTOGRAPHY AND FILMS

In the Outback, particularly Central Australia, light intensities are much greater. Even with automatic exposure, it will in most cases be necessary to 'stop down' one or a half-stop to compensate for brilliance, unless you use a lens hood.

For those with a new camera, get familiar with it before leaving; shoot some film and check results. Discuss and seek advice from your local camera dealer, who will advise on film types, speeds and accessories you should take. Stock up with sufficient film as costs can be higher in remote, outback settlements. The major centres in the Territory have fast print-processing services.

CAMERA CARE

Avoid leaving cameras for lengthy periods in hot sunshine or in a confined space where it can get hot, as in a car glove box. A good inexpensive way to store camera and films is in a 6-pack polystyrene beer cooler. Protect your equipment from dust and sand by using lens covers, and use a sealed camera bag or similar for out and about. Use a blow brush, not a tissue, for cleaning lens. Do not break seals on films until ready to use. Get your films processed as soon as possible - if this is not practicable, then store exposed film in a cool spot, even in a refrigerator (camping fridge), provided the film is in a sealed container. Where camera and film have been in an air-conditioned (films in a fridge) environment for some time, avoid problems of moisture condensation by allowing them to 'warm up' at least one hour before use.

For photography in Aboriginal Lands and of Aborigines, see *Information* section.

CENTRAL AUSTRALIA REGION

Legend:
- Sealed road
- Unsealed road

Lake Mackay

Lake MacDonald

Lake Neale

Kaltukatjara/Docker River

Lasseter

Kata Tjuta (Mt Olga)

Uluru (Ayers Rock)

ULURU KATA TJUTA NATIONAL PARK

Yulara

Lake Amadeus

Kings Creek Station

Kings Canyon Resort

WATARRKA NATIONAL PARK

Mereenie Loop

Yuendumu

Mt Dennison

Yuelamu (Mt Allan)

Tilmouth Roadhouse

Lake Lewis

BARKLY REGION

Stuart Highway

Barrow Creek

Ti-Tree

Aileron

Ryan Well Historical Reserve

Central Mt Stuart Historical Reserve

WEST MACDONNELL NATIONAL PARK

Namatjira Dr

Glen Helen Gorge

Gosse Bluff

Hermannsburg

FINKE GORGE NATIONAL PARK

Illamurta Springs Cons. Res.

Henbury Meteorite Craters Conservation Reserve

Lunja Ernest Giles Rd

Mt Ebenezer

Rd

Curtin Springs

▲ Mt Conner

Finke

Wallace Rockhole

Stuarts Well

LaraPinta Dr

Alice Springs

Bond Springs

East Macdonnell Ranges

Outback Retreat

Arltunga

Gemtree

Hart's Range

Plenty Highway

Jervois

Hay River

Sandover R

Sandover

Highway

Ross River

Ewaninga Rock Carvings Conservation Reserve

Santa Teresa

Oak Valley

Rainbow Valley Conservation Park

Maryvale

Chambers Pillar

CENTRAL AUSTRALIA REGION

Mac Clark Conservation Reserve

Old Andado Station

New Crown Station

Finke River

Finke

Erldunda

Kulgera

Hwy

Central Australian Railway

South Australia

Simpson Desert

Kilometres

0   100   200

A GUIDE BY REGION

Central Australia Region

CLIMATE CHART

Alice Springs	J	F	M	A	M	J	J	A	S	O	N	D	Ann. av.
Temperature: C°													
Av. monthly max.	36	35	32	28	23	20	19	22	26	31	33	35	28
Av. monthly min.	21	21	17	13	8	5	4	6	10	15	18	20	13
Rainfall:													
Av. monthly mm.	38	45	34	14	17	15	17	12	10	22	25	36	285

CHARACTERISTICS

The Central Australia Region is most associated with the mighty monolith, Uluru (Ayers Rock), red sand-soils, and the best-known Outback town in Australia, **Alice Springs**. It is a vast sun-drenched desert region in which the features of the landscape evoke a powerful sense of pre-history, and leave lasting impressions for their vibrant colours; reds and golds at sunrise and sunset, blues and purples during the day.

About one quarter of the population is Aboriginal. Thriving threads of their ancient culture continue, mainly in the outstations or small communities in the arid interior, and many are also involved with cattle stations, arts and crafts industries and tourist ventures.

The heart of this uncompromising and sparsely populated region is Alice Springs. Today, it's a modern, small city that clings to legacies of its legendary pioneering days, despite rapid growth and sprawl brought about by the tourist boom. From its strategic, scenic setting, it has a buoyant economy based on regional administration, pastoral, oil and gas, railhead and tourist activities. Apart from Yulara (the gazetted town name for the settlement at Ayers Rock), other settlements are small and relatively few in number.

While Uluru is the best known and most popular scenic attraction, there are many other outstanding natural features: Kata Tjuta (the Olgas); Watarrka National Park (Kings Canyon); gaps and gorges of the MacDonnell Ranges; Mt Sonder; Palm Valley; Chambers Pillar; and Rainbow Valley.

The mysteries surrounding pre-historic Aboriginal rock engravings and Lasseter's lost gold reef, old mining settlements, outback pubs, cattle stations, prolific flora and fauna, an almost overwhelming sense of space and friendly locals, are other facets of this great arid region.

CLIMATE

Using Alice Springs as a guide, summers have long hot days, of which over 80 are above 35C (95F) and around 13 are over 40C (104F). Nights are mild to warm and humidity is low. Ground temperatures during the hottest parts of the day are higher in many places due to heat radiation from surface sand and rocks (temperatures can reach 50C [136F] at the Olgas), and strenuous activities are not advised during these times. Winter months have mild to warm days around the low 20C (54F), but a few can be cold at around 10C (27F). Skies are clear and there's plenty of sunshine. Nights and early mornings are cold, often freezing, particularly during June, July and August.

Rainfall is very erratic. The 285mm (around 11 ins) average, while tending to fall mainly in summer, can come at any time; occasionally it is in cloud bursts which cause dry creeks to rapidly become raging torrents.

The climate table for Alice Springs details patterns.

LANDSCAPE

Sand dunes, salt lakes, clay pans, rocky outcrops, small plateaux, low mountain ranges, and dry sandy creek beds provide relief, colour and fascination to a landscape dominated by relentless red sand and gibber (stony) plains.

The distinctive reddish-brown colour results from rainwater mixing with iron-oxides contained in the rocks to form a common rust. Along with the weathering of rock over millions of years, the huge amounts produced have effectively stained most surface soil, sand and rock in rich ochre tones. Walkers and campers will soon find that clothing is quickly pigmented, and bare limbs rapidly acquire a golden tan!

Unlike most desert regions in the world, Central Australia is clothed with a moderate but nevertheless distinctive cover of vegetation. In fact, after major rains, the proliferation of wildflowers gives it a glorious hue.

In one respect, the early explorers were right about the great inland sea - they were just a few million years too late! Immense geological forces associated with various orogenies (major mountain building periods between 350 and 450 million years ago) distorted the ancient sea bed, wrenched and uplifted, inclined and split great sandstone slabs, while buckling the more flexible bands of limestone and siltstone. Molten rock (magma) welled to the surface, fused and changed rock compositions creating complex structures for geologists to ponder over, and a wealth of minerals to tantalise prospectors.

Millions of years of heat, wind and water have worn down, sculptured or exposed rock into some of Australia's best known landmarks - Uluru (Ayers Rock), Kata Tjuta (The Olgas), The

MacDonnell Ranges, Watarrka (Kings Canyon) and Chambers Pillar. Sand resulting from the breakdown of rock provided substance for the great deserts. If you wonder how those infrequently flowing creeks carved great gaps through the MacDonnell Ranges, much of the wearing away and grinding down action occurred during times when the climate here was sub-tropical, and rainfall was much higher.

It is a land of infinite mood, enormous in scope and scale, yet also sharp and fine in detail and best understood by Aboriginal people, whose spiritual attachment to it adds another dimension to its character.

FLORA

The region is a botanical wonderland, not only for its variety of vegetation, but also in the adaptation of plants to withstand the arid conditions and drought cycles. Against a background of dominant red soil, the variety, shape and form of tree, shrub and ground plant soften and enhance the aesthetic quality of the desert landscape. More than 1000 species have been recorded, and the ability of the plants to avoid, counter and endure droughts is quite remarkable.

Tough, leathery and wax-coated; thick, fleshy and succulent; needles, spikes and thorns and fine hair-covered, are some of the leaf forms designed to counter and endure dry periods by reducing moisture loss or conserving water. Root systems of ghost gum and cyprus pine probe deeply into the most unlikely precipitous rock faces to tap moisture sources from seepage, or condensation from and air and soil trapped in the crevices. Shaded valleys and water in the MacDonnell Ranges allow the continued survival of relic cycad and cabbage palm. Large river red gums and coolabah, amongst others, line the sandy creek beds, indicating moisture presence deep below.

Masses of daisies, pea flowers, pussy tails, parakeelya are some annual and ephemeral wildflowers and grasses that grow rapidly after rains, and climax in a sweep of colour. They avoid the

droughts; their seeds germinate only when adequate moisture is available, and can change the red desert to green in a matter of days. Whilst plants in Central Australia can flower at any time, noticeable peaks coincide fortunately with the popular tourist months of April and September. Depending on winter rains, wildflowers are at their best around August and September.

Drought, rain and fire are the major elements that regulate vegetation cover. In fact, Aborigines developed a system of patch burning to promote new growth to attract animals and so ensure an adequate food supply - a practice which the Parks and Wildlife Commission is now using for conservation purposes. Grasses, roots, seeds, berries and fruits are a rich food and medicine source, and Aborigines have exploited this vast natural 'supermarket' for thousands of years. However, unless you have a good knowledge of edible 'bush tucker', it's best not to experiment as some plants are poisonous.

Melons often seen growing along the verges of roads are called Paddy Melons - a fruit introduced by the Afghani cameleers as food for their camels. They are not particularly edible.

Some distinctive trees on the sand plains are: desert oak (Casuarina decaisneana) a 'droopy' willow-like tree that grows particularly in the Ayers Rock, Kings Canyon area; corkwood (Hakea suberea), noted for its cork-like bark and delicate yellow flowers; desert poplar (Codonocarpus continifolius), a tall thin tree similar in shape to the English variety; ironwood (Acacia estrophiolata) with tough wood and drooping foliage; and beefwood (Grevillea striata). On both plains and rocky slopes are: bloodwood (Eucalyptus terminalis), noted for its red sap; mulga (Acacia aneura) matures from shrub to tree and has yellow flowers; and white-wood (Atalaya hemiglanca) characterised by small white cup-shaped flowers and waxy leaves.

Some common shrubs on the plains are: colony wattle (Acacia murrayana) with small, fluffy, yellow ball-like flowers; desert grevillea (Grevillea juncifolia) distinctive for its long yellow flowers loaded with nectar and a source of honey for Aborigines and honey-eating birds; and saltbush (Atriplex nummularia). Common to plains and rocky slopes are: witchetty bush (Acacia kempeana) and several species of cassia with their 5-petalled yellow flowers. Native fig (Ficus platypoda) thrives on the rocky slopes; tea-tree (Melaleucas) are associated with watercourses and soaks, and spinifex is widespread on plain, rocky slope and sand dune. Refer also to flora cross-section under *MacDonnell Ranges Region* for further plant characteristics.

A visit to The Alice Springs Desert Park and the Olive Pink Botanic Garden in Alice Springs are worthwhile introduction places to plants of Central Australia. *The Plant Identikit booklet, a Parks and Wildlife Commission publication is highly recommended.*

FAUNA

Wildlife is prolific, and like the vegetation, has adapted ingeniously to cope with the cycles of heat, drought and rain.

Larger animals include those of the kangaroo family which are marsupials (young raised in a body pouch): red kangaroo (Macropus rufus), the world's largest marsupial, two metres in height, very mobile and ranges the grassy shrub plains; euro or wallaroo (Macropus robustus), smaller, adapted to rocky outcrops and less mobile than the red kangaroo, survives for lengthy periods without water, and, like all kangaroos, the female raises three different aged young ('joeys') at a time.

At about 6-months-old, the joey leaves its mother's pouch and is replaced within a month by a newborn, hairless one about 2-3cm in length, whereupon the female gets pregnant again (joey number one suckles for another three months from outside the

pouch which is occupied by joey number two). This 'production line' can be slowed down during drought periods.

The black flanked rock-wallabies (Petrogale lateralis) are highly agile in their rocky habitats, and best seen at Simpsons Gap (McDonnell Ranges National Park).

Other larger animals are: dingo (Canis familiaris dingo), a dog thought to have been brought to Australia by Aborigines, howls rather than barks, hunts mainly smaller animals, usually belongs in packs although mainly seen alone, coloured sandy-yellow with an occasional black and tan, and extremely cunning; feral cats (Felis catus) are larger than domestic varieties and have adapted well to arid conditions; fox (Vulpes vulpes) is an introduced species as are the more observable donkey (Equus asinus), horse (Equus caballus), camel (Camelus dromedarius) and rabbit (Oryctolgus cuniculus).

There are many smaller animals which avoid heat stress by sheltering in burrows and the like during the day, and so are rarely seen. Some of these nocturnal species are: brushtail possum (Trichosurus vulpecula) a tree living marsupial; bandicoot (Macrotis lagotis), bilby or rabbit-eared are the only species now left; marsupial mole (Notoryctes typhlops), sandy-coloured, lives in desert sands; spiny anteater or echidna (Tachyglossus aculeatus), a porcupine-like, spine-covered creature; and several special of bats that live in caves, crevices and in tree trunks. Once rid of prejudices, native rats and mice are attractive little animals, and unlike their distant city relatives are disease and dirt free. The spinifex hopping mouse (Notomys alexis), among others, is fun to watch at night when spotted by torchlight. Small carnivorous mouse-like marsupials include the stripe-faced dunnart (Sminthopsis macroura), like many species can go into a type of suspended animation when food is scarce; fat-tailed marsupial mouse and hairy-footed pouched mouse.

Reptiles are plentiful and the spinifex habitats support the world's greatest variety of lizards, which include goannas, skinks, geckoes and dragons. Being cold-blooded, they rely on heat absorption to regular their body temperature and seek shelter when it's really hot or cold. Perentie (Varanus giganteus) grows to 2.5m and is the world's largest lizard - they are harmless, but like all reptiles, give them space!; Goulds goanna (Varanus gouldii), grows to 1.3m and is the most common variety in the arid region.

Skinks are a varied group, and best known as they are common throughout Australia. They generally have smooth skins and large headscales - the Central Australian blue-tongued lizard (Tiliqua multifasciata) with its striking blue tongue, is one example.

Geckoes are small velvet-skinned nocturnal lizards with large eyes and the ability to detach their tails as a protective mechanism.

Dragons are distinguished from skinks and geckoes by their dull, thick, rough scales, spiny projections and lidded eyes. Some species include: central bearded dragon (Pogona vitticeps); long-nosed dragon (Lophognathus longirostris), long bodied and a fast mover when disturbed; central netted dragon (Ctenophorus nuchalis) has distinctive mesh patterning; the thorny devil (Moloch horridus), the most fearsome in appearance with its yellow-brown colouring and projecting spines, while the frilled-neck dragon (Chlamydosaurus kingii) has a folded frill that can be raised into a wide collar around its neck as a protective device designed to scare.

  While rarely seen, be mindful that snakes do exist and you are best advised to give them a wide berth. Main snakes are: king brown or mulga snake (Pseudechis australis) which is widespread, grows up to 2.5m and is the largest and most dangerous; the western brown (Pseudonaja nuchalis) is about 1m, timid, moves quickly, and is dangerous if provoked; the children's python (Liasis childreni) and carpet python (Morelia bredii) grow to 0.75 and 2m respectively, are night hunters, timid and non-venomous.

Reptiles of Central Australia are well represented at the *Alice Springs Desert Park, Alice Springs Reptile Centre* and the *Frontier Camel Farm in Alice Springs*. These reptile houses are a useful introduction to the range of species.

Bird life is plentiful with over 200 types being recorded. Ground birds include: Australian bustard (Ardeotis australis); emu (Dromaius novaehollandiae); crested pigeon (Ocyphaps lophotes); spinifex pigeon (Petrophassa plumifera); brolga (Grus rubicundus); willie wagtail (Rhipidura leucophrys); zebra finch (Poephila guttata); and painted firetail (Emblema picta). Some shrub and tree dwellers are: black-faced cuckoo-shrike (Coracina novaehollandiae); grey shrike-thrush (Colluricincla harmonica); red-backed and sacred kingfisher (Halcyon pyrrhopygia and sancta); spiny-cheeked honeyeater, yellow-throated miner, white-plumed honeyeater and mistletoe bird (Dicaeum hirundinaceum).

Aerial birds include: rainbow bee-eater (Merops ornatus); varieties of woodswallows and martins.

The most colourful are the parrots: red-tailed black-cockatoo, little corella, pink cockatoo, galah, cockatiel, Port Lincoln ringneck, mulga parrot and budgerigar. Raven, crow, magpie, magpie-lark and butcherbirds are distinctive black and white birds.

Main waterbirds are: pelican, cormorant, duck, egret, heron, plover and grebe. Barn owl and southern boobook are night birds. Birds of prey include: wedge-tailed eagle, brown falcon, black and whistling kite, black-shouldered and letter-winged kite and Australian kestrel.

Aquatic life includes fish, frog and crustacea, which generally bury themselves and suspend body functions when the waterholes dry up. Desert squalls called 'willy-willies' have been known to suck fish, tadpoles, frogs, shrimps and crabs into the air where they eventually fall some distance away as 'fish rain'.

Best times to see wildlife are early morning, evening, or just after storms, when animals are more active, and waterhole localities are ideal spots.

Take your time on walks; frequent stops and patience may well be rewarded by wildlife activity happening around you, and there's much truth in the saying, *happiness isn't found at the end of the track, but along the way*.

The Parks and Wildlife Commission also has an excellent Wildlife Identikit booklet available which covers birds, reptiles, mammals, aquatic life, spiders and insects. A detailed bird checklist brochure for Central Australia is useful too. *A Field Guide to Central Australia - A Natural History Companion for the Traveller* by Penny Van Oosterzee and *The Living Centre of Australia* by Alec Blombery are excellent illustrated field guides to the region and recommended for those seeking greater detail on landscape, flora and fauna.

ATTRACTIONS AND CONSERVATION

Most of the scenic attractions of Central Australia are protected by Parks and Wildlife Commission Park or Reserve status. The accessibility and popularity of many features in the parks, particularly those in the MacDonnell Ranges, places pressure on facilities and the environment. These can be minimised if visitors are mindful of regulations with respect to litter, fire, firewood, flora and fauna, and use of vehicles.

The Parks and Wildlife Commission provides a wide range of interpretive displays, information boards, literature and facilities at the parks, and fees are levied.

DRIVING

Always check the condition of unsealed roads. 'Off the beaten track' travellers are advised to check fuel availability, road conditions and Aboriginal land permit requirements prior to leaving. The granting of land rights to Aboriginal people means that they now legally own large areas of land, so make sure you don't trespass. Keep to designated tracks, and users of all roads should be alert to livestock and roadtrains. Refer to *Information and Advice* Section for detailed outback travel comments.

TOURING SUGGESTIONS

Most of Central Australia's attractions are natural features and, although widely separated (Uluru is 450km [279 miles] from Alice Springs!), are located in distinct areas that with careful route planning can be seen without too much back-tracking, (see *Tourist Drives, Heritage Trails and 4x4 Tracks* in Part One).

PLACES AND ATTRACTIONS

A I L E R O N

Population 10

LOCATION

Half a kilometre off the Stuart Highway, 133km (82 miles) north of Alice Springs.

CHARACTERISTICS

The modern roadhouse offers a well-stocked general store, licensed restaurant (main course $7-15), accommodation, and a couple of entertaining kangaroos. There used to be a hotel here, but that was burnt down in 1980, and the homestead of the 4,000 sq km (1520 sq miles), Aileron Station, is next door. Of interest in the area are Ryans Well and Annas Reservoir (see separate listings), Native Gap, 20km (12 miles) south and Gem Shop at Aileron Station.

ACCOMMODATION

Motel style - single $55, double $65.

Old stock route well, Stuart Highway

Camping/Caravans - powered sites $15, unpowered $5; backpackers $10 p.p. Sites grassed and shaded; pets allowed, dogs must be leashed.

SERVICES AND FACILITIES

It has picnic/BBQ shaded area, an airstrip, ice, takeaway food, artifacts, souvenirs, showers for travellers ($2) and camping gas. For vehicles, there's LP, ULP, diesel, LPG, oil, basic spares, tyres and tubes, tyre repairs, minor mechanical repairs and towing service (within 30km-19 miles). Credit cards accepted, EFTPOS, open 7am-10pm, daily, ph (08) 8956 9703.

ALICE SPRINGS

Population 27,500

LOCATION

In the heart of the MacDonnell Ranges, 1482km (918 miles) south of Darwin and 1543km (958 miles) north of Adelaide, on the Stuart Highway. It also lies 31km (19 miles) south of the Tropic of Capricorn.

CHARACTERISTICS

It is Australia's premier Outback town destination, but don't expect to find hitching rails, 'ringers', or ramshackle pubs. Alice Springs, The Alice or simply Alice, has long since shed her frontier appearance, and with her sparkling shopping plazas, pedestrian mall, palm-fringed resorts and suburban sprawl, has become quite a modern, sophisticated Miss.

Dramatic growth brought about by the tourist boom has led to the destruction of all but a few remnants of the Old Alice; the only Outback reminders in the main street are the Inland Mission (Adelaide House) and the waft of leather from the saddlery.

In itself, the town is not Outback any more, and the place projected in Neville Shute's novel *A Town Like Alice* no longer exists - in fact, some long-time residents suggest that it was far from being the bonza (good) town which Joe Harman reminisced

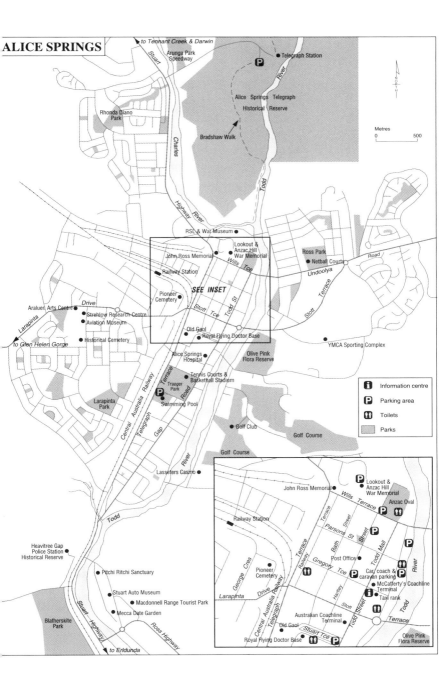

about. But the real Outback is not too far away, and this stark discovery fosters an acute awareness of the past, as well as lessening any conflicts between town image and city reality. Despite the outward changes in character, the continuation of The Flying Doctor Service, Aboriginal culture, and a host of new explorers and pioneers, such as the tour operators, still lend an air of excitement to Alice Springs.

CITY CENTRE

It's attractive, treed and compact, with modern shopping plazas, art galleries, museums, information centres, restaurants, essential services and historic buildings all within easy walking distance. Focal point is the Todd Mall with Yulara type 'sails' as its centrepiece. Some hotels and motels fringe the centre, while most other accommodation places, Casino and Cultural Centre are within 3km (2 miles). Apart from tourism, the commercial centre serves a thriving cattle and mining industry, as well as personnel from the highly secretive US communications establishment at Pine Gap. Government administration and railhead are other functions.

HISTORY

The area in and around Alice Springs is the traditional homeland of the Arrernte people whose ancestors have lived here for thousands of years. To the Arrernte people, Alice Springs is known as Mparnte - a region steeped in Aboriginal spirituality.

European history in the area began when the original Alice Springs was founded in 1871 as a Telegraph Station, situated alongside a Todd River waterhole discovered by surveyor W.W. Mills. He named it after the wife of the Superintendent of Telegraphs, Charles Todd. The completion of the Adelaide to Darwin Telegraph Line established a well defined and watered route through Central Australia. Along its umbilical-like line came explorers, prospectors and pastoralists, and the beginnings of 'The Track'.

The tiny settlement was not designed to cater for outsiders (it received once yearly supplies by Afghan camel strings) and the influx associated with mineral discoveries in the Eastern MacDonnell Ranges, among other factors, led to the establishment of Stuart Town. It was sited midway between the telegraph station and Heavitree Gap in 1888. Despite the promise of a railway, the first 96 blocks of land offered for sale saw only five buyers. William Benstead had confidence though, and built Central Australia's first pub, The Stuart Arms in 1889.

Francis Gillen described The Alice of 1901 as having nine buildings; three breweries, a pub, three stores and two houses. The breweries were closed, not through lack of demand for beer, but because the brewers drank the amber liquid before it had time to cool - or so it was claimed!

The railway came in 1929. Population rose from 40 Europeans in 1926 to 250 by 1932. Consolidation of the cattle and mining activities gave it a sound economic base. But it was also a tough, frontier cattle-town with a dusty street and the rowdy weatherboard Stuart Arms Pub, which offered the only accommodation in town, including beds on the veranda for latecomers!

Between 1926 and 1931, Stuart Town was a seat of government for the separate Territory of Central Australia, and the name was changed officially to Alice Springs in 1933. The population at this time was only 467.

During World War II, Alice Springs was a major military base and, with the bombing of Darwin in 1942, became the administrative headquarters for the Northern Territory. Supreme Allied Commander, South West Pacific Area, US General Douglas MacArthur spent some time here. Australia, north of Alice Springs, was under military control and many civilians were moved out of the town. In 1943, the Stuart Highway was sealed between Alice Springs and Darwin to facilitate rapid troop movements. On the lighter side, one Brigadier claimed that liquor constituted one-third of civilian supplies coming up from Adelaide - the Tennant Creek pub was selling beer at $28 a case, and the leasee at Dunmarra was buying grog in 30 to 50 case lots. In the interests of efficiency, the Brigadier restricted soldiers' drinking in Alice Springs hotels to just one hour a day, and placed a ban on all licensed places along the Stuart Highway. It's doubtful, though, if this order affected the rate of beer consumption by Aussie troops!

Partly due to glowing reports by ex-servicemen, the tourist industry started to develop after the war. There were tough times between 1957 and 1962, when virtually no rain fell and cattle numbers dropped dramatically from over 350,000 to below 175,000. Population in 1961 was 4648, rising to over 18,000 twenty years later.

The bituminisation of the Stuart Highway from Port Augusta to Alice Springs in 1987 provided a major boost to tourism - an industry which now caters for over half a million visitors each year.

TOURIST INFORMATION

The Telephone Area Code is 08.

Central Australian Tourism Industry Association. It offers detailed local information and an excellent monthly information booklet Welcome to Central Australia. They are also very much up front at their airport booth, which is open daily. The main office is open week days 9am-6pm, weekends 9am -4pm, Gregory Terrace, ph 8952 5199.

Outback Travel Shop, Irma Versluijs is a knowledgable, multi-lingual (English, Dutch, German, French, Spanish) and friendly proprietor, who offers a tour booking and a general information service at 2A Gregory Terrace. It's a good, relaxed place to check out the regional tour options, open daily, ph 8955 5288.

Automobile Association (NT), 58 Sargent Street, ph 8952 1087, and Shop 4, 105 Gregory Terrace, ph 8953 1322.

National Trust - heritage information and books. Open Mon-Fri 10.30am-2.30pm. Old Hartley Street School, Hartley Street, ph 8952 4516.

Parks and Wildlife Commission of Northern Territory - National Parks information and brochures. Stuart Highway, 7km south of town, ph 8951 8211, open Mon-Fri 8am-4.20pm. They also have a desk in the Tourist Association office.

The Department of Land, Planning and Environment - is a good map source, located in Gregory Terrace, ph 8953 1322.

The Department of Mines and Energy - have excellent displays and a range of literature for those interested in rocks or fossicking pursuits. Located Minerals House, Hartley Street, ph 8951 5658.

Institute for Aboriginal Development - located 3 South Terrace, has a good selection of Aboriginal literature and maps, including distribution of Central Australian languages. Ph 8951 1311.

Central Lands Council - located 31 North Stuart Highway, issue permits to visit Aboriginal lands, ph 8951 6211.

Disability Services - The Disabled Persons Bureau, Flynn Drive, ph 8951 5880 has a useful booklet "Access to Alice" available from its office.

ATTRACTIONS - IN AND AROUND ALICE

Anzac Hill, either walk up via the 'Lions' walk (starts opposite Catholic Church), or drive up for the best viewing and orientation point. Located just north of the city centre. Nearby in Schwartz Crescent, is the RSL Club Military Museum, which has an excellent collection of war memorabilia including photographs of Northern Territory troop movements during WW II. *It's open daily from 10am*.

Museum of Central Australia, after Anzac Hill, this is a good starting point to learn something of the natural history, pioneering days and Aboriginal culture of Central Australia. First Floor, Alice Plaza, Todd Mall. *Open 9am-5pm week days, weekend and public holidays 10am-5pm $2 admission. Children free.*

Historic buildings

Adelaide House, was built as the first Alice Springs Hospital by the Australian Inland Mission between 1920 and 1926, under the direction of the late Reverend John Flynn. It incorporates an ingenious cooling system. With the establishment of a government hospital in 1939, it became a convalescent home for outback women and children, and was declared a museum in 1980. The stone radio hut behind the building was where Traeger and Flynn conducted their first radio transmission in 1926. Traeger invented the first pedal radio transmitter used by Flynn for his Flying Doctor Service in 1929. This development gave the Outback stations a 'mantle of safety' for the first time. Todd Mall, *open 10am-4pm weekdays, 10am-noon Sat, closed Dec - Feb. Adults $3, children $2.*

Flynn Memorial Church, built in memory of the Reverend John Flynn in 1956. Todd Mall.

Old Court House/National Pioneers Women's Hall of Fame, was originally built as the Administrator's Council Rooms when Central Australia had its own government, between 1926 and 1931. Located in Hartley Street, it now houses a permanent display of artifacts and memorabilia honouring women who are pioneers within their chosen field, ph 8952 9006.

The Residency, was built in 1926 for John Cawood, the first Government Resident of Central Australia. It now functions as a museum of Northern Territory history. Parsons Street, *open weekdays 9am-4pm, weekends 10am-4pm.*

Stuart Town Gaol, completed in 1908, it's the oldest building in the town area. The gaol's first white prisoners were put away for such offences as horse stealing, and the last two for riding on the Ghan without tickets! The gaol closed in 1938, and it is now a National Trust property. Parsons Street, *open weekdays 10am-12.30pm, Sat 9.30am-noon, $2 adults, children free.*

Hartley Street School, this first government school opened in 1929 with Miss Pearl Burton as teacher. The building reflects contrasting styles of architecture, with the addition of the octagonal room in 1946. It now houses the National Trust, shop and local arts and crafts, *open weekdays 10.30am-2.30pm.*

Tunck's Store, a good example of an old-type store built in 1940 and run by Ralph Tuncks until 1979. Corner Hartley Street and Stott Terrace.

The Old Government Homes, built for government officers in the early 1930s, they give an idea of period styles. Hartley Street.

Other Attractions

Panorama Guth, Dutch artist Henk Guth started an art studio here, and conceived and executed an impressive 360 degree landscape painting of the Centre. You view it from a central elevated observation point. Also, there's an art gallery featuring many of the Hermannsburg School of water colourists. *Open 9am-5pm Mon-Sat, 2pm-5pm Sun, Hartley Street - Adults $3, children $1.50*, closed Sun (December-February).

Royal Flying Doctor Service, offers a window on Outback isolation and a unique Outback Medical Service. A visit is highly recommended. *Open 9am-4pm Mon-Sat, 1-4pm Sun. Tours half-hourly - Adults $3, children $1.* Stuart Terrace, ph 8952 1129.

Alice Springs Reptile Centre. The centre features imaginative indoor/outdoor displays of reptiles representative of Central Australia and the Northern Territory. It includes an entertaining and highly informative interactive reptile show, orchestrated in inimitable fashion by Rex Neindorf. In all probability, after experiencing this hands-on interaction with such reptiles as python snakes, bearded dragons, thorny devils and frill-necked lizards, you will never look at them in the same way again. The centre is *open daily; adults $6, children $3.* It is located at 9 Stuart Terrace (opposite Royal Flying Doctor Service), ph (08) 8952 8900.

Olive Pink Botanic Garden is a unique assemblage of Central Australian native plants in a reserve south-east across the river from the town centre. It was established by a rather remarkable woman, Olive Pink, who lived with the Arrernte and Walpiri people in the Tanami, worked hard for their advancement, and was a great stirrer of Government Departments. There are fine displays at the visitor centre. *Open daily 10am-4pm.* Access via Tuncks Road.

Aboriginal Art, Aboriginal paintings and artifacts by artists from the desert regions have captured the interest of art galleries from London to New York. This fascination with its subject matter and style has spawned a large number of galleries in Alice Springs. 1997 Australian Tourism Award Winner, Aboriginal Art and Culture Centre, is one place that should not be missed. Apart from its range of paintings and artefacts, it offers escorted tours of the Centre, didgeridoo lessons and a number of cultural tours including tailoring of special interest tours for groups. They also have an excellent cultural centre based at the Red Centre Resort (North Stuart Highway). It's owned and operated by the Pwerte Marnte Marnte Aboriginal Corporation, located 86 Todd St, open daily, ph 8952 3408.

Technology, Transport & Communication Museum includes and houses reminders of the early days of aviation in Central Australia in the former Connellan Hangar. It's also the site of Alice Springs' first airport. *Open daily 10am-4pm*, Memorial Drive. *Donation.*

Alice Springs Cemetery. Contains the graves of Lasseter (of Lasseter's lost gold reef fame, see *Kaltukatjara* listing), Albert Namatjira, a famous Aboriginal artist, and E.J. Connellan, founder of Connellan Airways, the Territory's first. Memorial Avenue, just beyond the Aviation Museum.

Araluen Arts Centre. It's a centre for visual and performing arts and cinema. Art and exhibition galleries include the Albert Namatjira Gallery which features original works of this famous artist. *It's open 9am-5pm daily.* See also under *Nightlife* listing. Larapinta Drive, ph 8952 5022.

School of The Air, is where teachers communicate with pupils who live on the remote Outback stations. It's a fascinating place that first started radio education in 1951. *Open Mon-Sat 8.30-4pm, Sun 1.30pm-4pm, costs $3 adult, children $1, family $8.* Head Street, ph 8952 2122.

The Old Telegraph Station Historical Reserve, covers 570ha (1407 acres) and is administered by the Parks and Wildlife Commission. It's the original settlement site, and there are ideal places for picnic lunches along the banks of the Todd River. It features the waterhole from which Alice Springs takes its name, a visitors centre, and many restored buildings that comprised the original Telegraph Station Settlement. There's an interesting walk to Trig Hill Lookout, which is a good spot for photographs and views. The Larapinta Trail links the reserve to West MacDonnell National Park. Facilities include shaded grassy picnic areas with tables, barbecues, toilets (including for disabled), and water. A wildlife enclosure adds interest, and rangers are most helpful. There's plenty of literature about the reserve available, too, and the area gives an insight into the pioneering lifestyle of a century ago.

 It functioned as the main station of a telegraph line laid across 3000km (1860 miles) of rugged, inhospitable and unknown desert terrain between Adelaide and Darwin. It was erected in 2 years, used 30,000 telegraph poles, involved hundreds of construction men, and was masterminded by Charles Todd. Opened in 1872, the line connected Australia to the rest of the world, which suddenly reduced the isolation of the country. Messages which took weeks could now be relayed in hours, and legendary cattleman, Sir Sidney Kidman, used it effectively for relaying instructions to his drovers moving herds down the stock routes (see *Bond Springs* listing for Kidman story). Stations were needed at intervals to boost the flagging signals, and as you travel up 'The Track', you'll see a few more smaller ones.

   Guided tours are available, and it's located North Stuart Hwy 3km north of town. *Open 8am-9pm Nov-March, 8am-7pm April - Oct. Entry is adults $4, children $1.*

Strehlow Research Centre. The centre's own description "Reflections of a rich Aboriginal culture and the evocative story of a man who pursued it" should be taken literally. While it gives an interesting insight into a dark period of European-Aboriginal relations at a time when Aboriginal culture was close to collapse, the Centre appears to be more about the singer (Ted Strehlow) than the song (an encompassing depiction of Aboriginal culture). Strehlow's work is outlined in the *Hermannsburg* listing. The display, incorporating creative uses of light, sound and photographs is impressive, but a lasting image for me was a large photograph of named Europeans alongside unnamed Aboriginal people.

   Facilities include a gallery shop (books, souvenirs) and light refreshments. It's located in Larapinta Drive, open generally 10am-5pm daily, adults $4, family $10, ph 8951 8000.

Mecca Date Garden. Date palms, the oldest known cultivated tree crop, established as early as 3000BC, were introduced to Central Australia by Afghan camel drivers. This 2ha (5 acre) date plantation is the only one of its kind in Australia. There's no entry fee. You can purchase dates and enjoy afternoon tea under the palms. Palm Circuit. *Open weekdays 9am-5pm, Sat 9am-1pm*, ph 8952 2425.

Frontier Camel Farm. It features a centre which houses a camel museum with pictorial display, incorporating Arid Australia Reptile Display. The camel farm offers a guided daily tour with short camel rides (*adults $10, children $5, family $25* - includes Reptile House) at 10.30am. Longer tours are available including 'Take a Camel out to Dinner or Breakfast' and a 3 hour Todd River ecotour. The Reptile House has a fascinating collection of arid zone species, grouped on the basis of shared habitat. The guided tour referred to includes a talk about snakes and other reptiles. A kangaroo enclosure adds further interest. Facilities include toilets, kiosk and picnic area, *open daily 9am-5pm*, located Ross Hwy, ph 8953 0444.

Wallaby Rock at Heavitree Gap Motel. You can watch the wallabies in the wild when they make their evening descent from the rocky slopes for feeding.

Old Timers' Folk Museum, is a museum with exhibits of the pioneering days, including Rev. Dr. J. Flynn display. South Stuart Highway, *open daily (April-Oct), 2-4pm. Admission $2*, ph 8952 2844.

Alice Springs Golf Course, is the first dunes course in Australia in a true desert climate and rates among the top 10 desert courses in the world. The first official Tournament was won by Greg Norman in 1985 on a 6196 metre, par 72, challenging, championship course. The course record of 66 set by Norman has only been equalled twice. It features fully grassed undulating fairways, well bunkered greens and a beautiful MacDonnell Ranges backdrop to most holes. There's a practice range, pro shop, hire clubs, motorised buggies and refreshments at the clubhouse. Visitors are welcome, *green fees around $30*, located Cromwell Drive, east of town centre, ph 8952 1921.

Outlying Attractions
Alice Springs Desert Park, refer to *MacDonnell Ranges* listing following Alice Springs.

Transport Heritage Centre. The centre incorporates the *Old Ghan Train and Road Transport Hall of Fame*. The *Old Ghan Preservation Society* have built a station to original design specification and restored a section of the old, narrow garage railway track at MacDonnell Siding. Also the railway enthusiasts have restored a number of locomotives including steam, and assorted railway carriages. There's an information centre and museum in the station.

The Old Ghan Railway and the Overland Telegraph Line once formed the Territory's two life lines, and the name Ghan honours the Afghan Camelmen who plugged the gap between Oodnadatta railhead and Alice Springs. A statue in the city railway station foyer bears the inscription: *In 1878 work started on the planned 1800 mile railway. It got to Oodnadatta where it stopped for nearly 40 years during which time camel trains run by hardy Afghans worked the country to Alice Springs ferrying passengers and freight up from Oodnadatta. The railway reached Alice Springs in 1929 and the train was affectionately known as the Ghan. It was variously known as Afghan Express, Afghan Special, The Royal Ghan and The Flash Ghan*. For more on Afghans and camels, see *Stuarts Well* listing.

Train rides are available at times (check with Centre) and Tuits Old Ghan Bush Kitchen Dinner includes a train ride (see under Eating Out)

Next door is the Road Transport Hall of Fame, which houses an amazing collection of old vehicles, reminders of man's ingenuity in countering the hardships in developing Australia's Outback. It includes the original AEC Roadtrain, built in the UK as part of a joint military/civil engineering project - it was found a few years ago in Darwin, rusting away along with three 'dogs' (trailer sections) and has been restored.

Facilities include toilets, souvenir shop, refreshments and BBQ/picnic area. It's located about 10kms (6 miles) south of Alice Springs, *open daily 9am-5pm*, ph 8955 5047.

Chateau Hornsby Winery. The only winery in the Territory has five grape varieties: Shiraz, Cabernet Sauvignon, Riesling, Semillon and Chardonnay. It's *open daily (Monday excepted) 9am-5pm* for lunches and wine tastings, and there's some lively Jazz music generally on Sundays. Located in Petrick Road, off South Stuart Highway, ph 8955 5133.

Cattle Station Visits, Bond Springs Outback Retreat (see separate listing) and Ooraminna Bush Camp offer opportunities to stay on working cattle stations. Ooraminna lies within half an hours drive of Alice Springs located on the 1640 sq km (1016 sq mile) Deep Well property, approximately 30kms (19 miles) south of Alice Springs on the Old South Road.

Jan and Bill Hayes, descendants of the original leaseholder, run over 5000 polled Herefords on a landscape of infinite variety between the rocky MacDonnell range country and margins of the red sandhills of the Simpson Desert. A range of options are available from half day visits to extended tours. Cattle station tours, bush dinners including the tastes of chemical free, locally produced beef, memorable chats about station life and history around a campfire, sleeping in the 'pioneer suite' (a swag on the ground), or guided bush walks and horseriding are among the range of simple, but captivating experiences offered. The Ooraminna Hut provides comfortable, settler-type accommodation and facilities include a well-stocked homestead store. Ooraminna caters for large groups and functions, bookings are essential, packages can be designed for particular needs, and transfers are available from Alice Springs, ph 8953 0170 for details.

ORGANISED TOURS

There is a great variety of tours of varying duration that cover scenic attractions, geography, historic places, Aboriginal Culture, cattle stations, and special interests, many of which are 'off the beaten track'. Alice Springs is the main departure point and base for Central Australian exploration, and large tour operators such as AAT Kings, are complemented by a host of smaller local companies, each with their own specialist niche and mode of transport. You can see and experience things by bus or coach, 4WD safari, camel, horse, chauffeured limousine, aircraft, helicopter and balloon. There are even operators who tailor tours to meet your specific needs. Most day and extended tours include a meal in the cost. Some tours offer last minute stand-by rates, and 'off season' touring can be a bit cheaper. The Outback Travel Shop (see under *Information*) and the Tourist Information Centre are places to point you in the right direction.

A sample of the types of tours available are;

Town Centre. For orientation and viewing of 13 town centre attractions, The Alice Wanderer is great value. It costs $20 for an all day ticket (9am-5pm); the 45km circuit takes just over one hour and you can get on and off as desired, ph 8952 2111.

Day Tours, AAT Kings, ph 8952 1700 offer half day tours covering local attractions, $45 adults, $23 child; Day Tours, Eastern and Western MacDonnell Ranges and Hermannsburg options, $89. Their extended tours include a 2 day Uluru tour. Centre Sightseeing Tours, ph 8952 2111 have half day Stanley Chasm and Simpsons Gap Tours among their range, $35 adult, $25 child. Centremen, ph 8953 2623 offer half-day Western MacDonnell tour $30 adult, $20 child; full day $75 adult, $50 child.

Extended and 4WD Tours, Sahara Outback Tours, ph 8953 0881, have an Uluru-Kata Tjuta/Kings Canyon 3 day camping safari tour, $320; 2 day Uluru National Park, $222 and a 5 day Red Centre 4WD camping trip, $520. Children under 11 at discounted rate. The Outback Experience, ph 8953 2666, have a focus on Rainbow Valley, Chambers Pillar and the Simpson Desert in their 4WD, full day tour of this remote desert region. Costs $95 p.p. Spencer Tours, ph 8952 2639, have a 4 day Uluru-Kata Tjuta/Kings Canyon tour from around $800 among their range of options.

Aboriginal Culture Tours. Aboriginal Art and Culture Centre, ph 8952 3408 (see also under *Attractions*) offers reasonably-priced and highly recommended "share, learn, participate and experience", cultural tours, at their Red Centre Resort base.

Other Tours (specialist interest/activity based). Cattle Stations Bond Springs (see separate listing) and Ooraminna Bush Camp (see under *Attractions*). Ossie's Outback Horse Treks, ph 8952 2308 offer half and full day rides in the spirit of stockmen and explorers; 3 day treks $660 p.p., sunset and bush dinner ride $119 p.p, Heritage rides $75 p.p., and tailor-made rides from $45 are some of the options. For Dining Tours see under *Eating Out.* Camel Tours see under *Attractions* and *Stuarts Well* listing. Outback Ballooning ph 8952 8723 and Ballooning Downunder ph 8952 8816 both offer a number of tours ranging from about $120 for 30 minute flights. Air North, ph 8952 6666 offer one day safaris to Uluru, $479 p.p.

EVENTS

April-May, there's The Alice Springs Cup Racing Carnival; Country Music Festival and Bangtail Muster - a lively parade of floats.

June-July, The Finke Desert Race, a motorbike race which runs between Alice Springs on rough tracks to Finke; Alice Springs Show, an agricultural and historical show and traditional country fair; Lions Camel Cup, Australia's premier camel racing carnival.

August, Alice Springs Rodeo where professional cowboys and cowgirls from all over Australia compete; Alice Springs Marathon, a 42.2 km (26 miles) race over a scenic MacDonnell Range area course.

September-October, Henley-on-Todd, a boat regatta with a difference - no water and bottomless boats; Honda Masters Games has become Australia's premier mature-age athlete's carnival; International Multicultural Festival celebrates the cultural diversity of Australia's society through song, dance, arts and food.

November, The Corkwood Festival features Central Australian arts, crafts, music, entertainment and food, culminating in a rollicking bush dance at night.

HOW TO GET THERE

(see also *How to Get There* in Part One)

By air: Ansett Australia and Qantas operate daily services from all states.

By Coach: Greyhound Pioneer runs daily services. The Wayward Bus is another option.

By Rail: The Ghan, between Adelaide and Alice Springs, takes around 21 hours, and offers a motor-rail service.

By Road: While it's a long way from anywhere, major roads from other States are bitumen.

Local Transport

Taxis and a bus service are the only forms of public transport. Many hotels offer courtesy coach transfer to and from the city centre.

Taxis: *Alice Springs Taxis*, ph 8952 1877 and *Alice Radio Cars*, ph 8952 3700. Both companies offer tours.

Airport Shuttle Service.

Bus transfers from the airport to your accommodation destination *cost around $9*, ph 8953 0310.

Vehicle Rentals: Renting can be an economical way to see attractions, especially for groups. Rates are competitive, and there are variable concessions. **Mokes** or similar are popular. Most have 4WD vehicles and all generally have a good range of vehicles. *Territory Rent-A-Car* offer good rates, ph 8952 9999. Others include; *Thrifty*, ph 1800 634 499; *Budget* ph 8952 8899; Avis ph 8953 5533; *Centre* ph 8952 1405; *Koala Campervans* ph 1800 998 029; *Hertz* ph 8952 2644; *Outback Auto* ph 89535333; *Brits* ph 1800 331 454.

Bicycles: There are a number of bicycle tracks, and many attractions are within easy cycling range. Bicycles *cost from about $12 per day*. Check with hostels which often hire or *Centre Cycles*, ph 8953 2966.

SHOPPING

There are many outlets for traditional and contemporary Aboriginal artifacts and paintings produced by Central Australian artists. Prices are reasonably uniform, but while you can expect to pay more than at the smaller settlements along 'The Track' and Outback places, there's a greater range. It pays to shop around, and genuine items should have the artist's name, place of origin, and descriptive notes, as a measure of authenticity.

Opals, gemstone, jewellery, crafts from local natural materials, pottery, fine arts, books on Central Australia, and Outback clothing, are further options.

ACCOMMODATION

Alice Springs has an excellent range of accommodation options. Most of the hotels, motels and resorts have swimming pools, a number have restaurants, courtesy transport and some cater well for disabled guests. The following is a representative sample with prices quoted for double rooms per night.

Hotels

The most highly rated includes **Rydges Plaza**, ph 8952 8000, Barrett Drive,with its luxurious appointments and facilities. Rooms from $190; suites from $360-$460. Nearby is **Lasseters Hotel Casino**, ph 8950 7777 with rooms from $180; suites $230. **The Diplomat Hotel**, ph 8952 8977, town centre, offers rooms from $150; suites $228.

Other options are the **Alice Springs Vista Hotel**, ph 8952 6100, Stephens Road, rooms from $140 and **Alice Springs Pacific Resort**, ph 8952 6699, Stott Street, with rooms ranging from $170 to $238.

Motels, Resorts and Apartments

There are many options in this accommodation style and $55-$120 range.

Mt Nancy Motel, ph 8952 9488, North Stuart Hwy, offers comfortable, good value accommodation, rooms from $58.
The Midland Motel ph 8952 1588, Traegar Ave has well appointed units from $65-$90.
The Red Centre Resort, ph 8952 8955, North Stuart Hwy has units from $65 and excellent tourist facilities in spacious surrounds.
The Swagmans Rest Motel, ph 8953 1333, 67 Gap Road has units from $63, while the *Territory Inn*, ph 8952 2066, Leichhardt Terrace, offers a more luxurious style with rooms from $120.
Alice Tourist Apartments, ph 8952 2788, Gap Road have one bedroom apartments from $72 to two bedroom apartments (up to 6 persons) from $104.

Hostels and Budget
There's plenty of choice with places offering good share facilities and services, particularly for backpackers.

The *YHH Pioneer Lodge*, ph 8952 8855, cnr Parsons St and Leichhardt Tce has 4 share rooms $14 (members) $17 (non-member); double rooms $18 (member) $21 (non-member), bicycle hire and pool.
Stuart Lodge YWCA ph 8952 1894, Stuart Tce, single rooms $30; double $40, pool.
Ossie's Homestead, ph 8952 2308, cnr Lindsay Ave and Warburton St, offers excellent value which includes breakfast. Dormitory style $12, 4 share room $14 and double room $32, pool.
Melanka's Backpackers Resort and Lodge, ph 8952 4744, 94 Todd St, offers a number of options ranging from dormitory $13, 4 share room $14 and double room $16, to shared facility motel rooms from $50.
Alice Lodge, ph 8953 1975, 4 Mueller St, a tidy little establishment with a pool, has dormitories $13 (8-10 share), $15 (4 share), double room $32.

Other options are *Elke's*, ph 8952 8134 and *Toddys*, ph 8952 1322.

Camping and Caravan Parks

Locations are a least 3km from the town centre. All have shaded, grassed sites, pools (except *Heritage*), BBQ's and shops. Only two have disabled facilities (*MacDonnell Range Holiday Park* and *G'Day Mate*) and all except Heritage do not allow pets.

For Coach/Camping groups, **The Red Centre Resort**, ph 8952 8955, North Stuart Hwy, has impressive amenities and recreational facilities.

MacDonnell Range Holiday Park, ph 8952 6111, Palm Place (south of town), has superb amenities and facilities; powered sites $18x2, unpowered $15x2, cabins from $36-$70.

G'Day Mate Tourist Park ph 8952 9589, Palm Circuit (south of town) is also highly rated for its facilities; powered sites $16x2, unpowered $14x2; cabins from $50.

Heavitree Gap Park, ph 8952 4866, Palm Circuit has powered sites $16x2, unpowered $14x2.

Stuart Caravan Park, ph 8952 2547, Larapinta Drive has powered sites $16x2, unpowered $13x2 and cabins from $42.

Wintersun Caravan Park, ph 8952 4080, North Stuart Highway, powered sites $16x2, unpowered $14x2, on-site-vans from $36 and cabins from $41.

Heritage Caravan Park ph 8953 1418, is the only park that allows pets and has basic facilities.

Other Types of Accommodation

Bed and Breakfast style is offered by **Orangewood,** ph 89524114, 9 McMinn St, from $140. Cattle Station stays are outlying options at Deep Well, Ooraminna Bush Camp *(see under Attractions)* and Bond Springs Outback Retreat *(see separate listing)*.

EATING OUT

The span and quality of dishes and the range of styles and settings at the various establishments are quite remarkable. And there is sufficient selection to satisfy both the discerning diner and carefree traveller from a palate and pocket perspective. For fine dining, the major hotels have casually elegant restaurants at competitive prices as do some smaller, more intimate restaurants. Contrasting styles include the modernisation of bush foods and gourmet dining out in the bush. As menus generally change frequently, prices are not given. All are licensed and open daily; few are BYO.

The ubiquitous fast food outlets are garishly visible - KFC, Hungry Jacks, Pizza Hut, Red Rooster and McDonalds.

In and around Todd Mall are numerous small eateries and cafes; a good one for light meals is *The Jolly Swagman* in John Cummings Arcade. Across the river in the small Eastside Shopping Centre are two pleasant surprises - an excellent fish and chip shop and *Le Coq En Pate*, a delightful French delicatessen run by a French couple from Brittany.

Restaurants

Kellers ph 8952 3188, Gregory Terrace is another Territorian oddity that would have been loved by Mark Twain - a Swiss and Indian Restaurant. It's highly recommended for its quality dishes at moderate prices.

For an intimate setting, a Mediterranean edge to its food and comprehensive wine selection, **The Midland Restaurant and Wine Bar** is also recommended. It's medium priced, located in Traegar Avenue, ph 8952 1588.

Centrally located in Todd Mall, **The Red Ochre** is a popular day and night-time spot for Australian bush cuisine.

Uncles Tavern at the Diplomat Hotel offers all meals at reasonable prices, while at their **Miss Daisy's Restaurant**, stylish surrounds, al fresco options and modern dishes, including Territorian meals, are features, ph 8952 8977.

Comfortable surrounds and good value Italian fare is a feature of *La Casalinga*, ph 8952 4508, located in Gregory Terrace.

Camel's Crossing, ph 8952 5522, Todd Mall, specialises in moderately priced Mexican and Vegetarian foods.

For Chinese foods, *Chopsticks Restaurant*, ph 89523873, Yeperenye Shopping Centre, Hartley Street, and *Golden Inn*, ph 8952 6910, located across the river in Undoolya Road, serve a good range of reasonably priced Chinese styles.

A good family restaurant is at *Mt Nancy Motel*, which among its traditional fare, has a good fisherman's basket. It's located North Stuart Highway, ph 8952 9488.

The Red Centre Resort has two poolside options; a stylish, medium priced restaurant and a more casual bistro style where you can also purchase and cook your own BBQ meat packs. It's located North Stuart Hwy, ph 8952 8955.

Avid carnivores should try 'The Drover's Blowout' at the *Overlander Steakhouse*. It's a dish of Territorian meats which includes some, or all if you wish, buffalo, emu, camel, kangaroo and crocodile, and while popular, it is expensive (other dishes are medium priced). It has a great bush atmosphere, bar and live entertainment at its 72 Hartley St location, ph 8952 2159.

Also in a similar outback pub decor mode is *Bojangles*, ph 8952 2873, located in Todd St. The medium priced 'bush bistro' has a focus on Territory meats and exudes a lively atmosphere when the live country entertainment begins.

Bush Dining Out

The Camp Oven Kitchen have resurrected some of the old bush cooking skills and implements in their preparation of outback gourmet cuisine. All foods are beautifully cooked in cast iron pots (camp ovens) heated by a covering of embers from a campfire. For details of this bush dinner tour, ph 8953 1411.

Tuits Bush Kitchen have a base by the Old Ghan Train, where a four course meal has local meats (camel, beef and kangaroo) in the mains, accompanied by chats about local history. Another memorable dining tour is their 60 minute Old Ghan Train Ride in the evening to a bush dinner site, ph 8952 2873 for further details. For another interesting experience, you can take a camel out to breakfast or dinner in a tour offered by *Frontier Camel Farm*, ph 8953 0444.

NIGHTLIFE
Venues for night-time entertainment featuring live action, include some hotels, *Lasseters Casino*, some restaurants, in particular *Settlers* where Bard of the Outback, Ted Egan often performs, and Araluen Centre for Arts and Entertainment *(live theatre and cinema)*. There's also a *cinema centre* in Todd Mall.

SERVICES AND FACILITIES
As one would expect in a small, dynamic city, Alice Springs has a full range of shopping, banking (all major banks) and medical services and facilities. Virtually all shops and supermarkets open daily. Churches include Anglican, Baptist, Catholic, Church of Christ, Jehovah Witness, Uniting, Lutheran, Salvation Army, Seventh Day Adventist, Latter Day Saints and Pentecostal.

Radio Stations and frequencies are: 8AL 783 (ABC); 8HA 900; 8CCC FM 102.0; and Tourist Radio Information 89.1 FM.

RECREATION FACILITIES
Racecourse (frequent turf activity); Bowls, Gap Road, visitors welcome; Tennis Courts, Traegar Park, available for hire; Golf Course (see under Attractions); swimming centre (Oct-Apr), Speed Street; Ten Pin Bowling, Gap Road; Squash Courts, Gap Road; and indoor Abseiling and Rock-climbing facilities are at the YMCA, Sadadeen Street.

THE MACDONNELL RANGES

Characteristics

Rising impressively from the vast Central Australian sand plains, the MacDonnells consist of a series of rugged ranges that extend nearly 300kms (186 miles) between their eastern and western extremities. The main range is characterised by a number of startling gorges - great slashes cut by the erosive power of ancient rivers, the largest of which provides southern access to Alice Springs.

To the west of Alice Springs, the West MacDonnell National Park encompasses spectacular arid range landscapes and steep-sided, colourful gorges and waterholes, formerly designated as a number of smaller parks and reserves. One of the world's greatest long distance walking tracks provides bushwalkers with unique insights into the Park's natural and cultural attributes, while those seeking wilderness serenity, wonderful scenery and encounters with wildlife in the MacDonnell Ranges generally, will not be disappointed. In the MacDonnells to the east of Alice Springs, outstanding natural and cultural features remain protected by a number of smaller parks and reserves.

The ranges are formed mainly from quartzite (sandstone) with some limestone layers exposed as serrated ridges in places. Erosion since their formation in Devonian Times (between 450 and 350 m.y.a. when the Alice Springs Orogeny, buckled and folded the massive sheets of sandstone to form the mountain range), has left long, parallel belts of steep-sided, folded ridges (anticlines), and deep and broad valleys that from the air, resemble crests and troughs of waves.

In effect, the MacDonnells today are the tilted, contorted stumps of mountains that once towered to over 3000 metres (9840 feet) above sea level. Erosion over the eons has reduced the tops of the folds, leaving the roots of the rock strata jutting out in the often

WEST MACDONNELL NATIONAL PARK

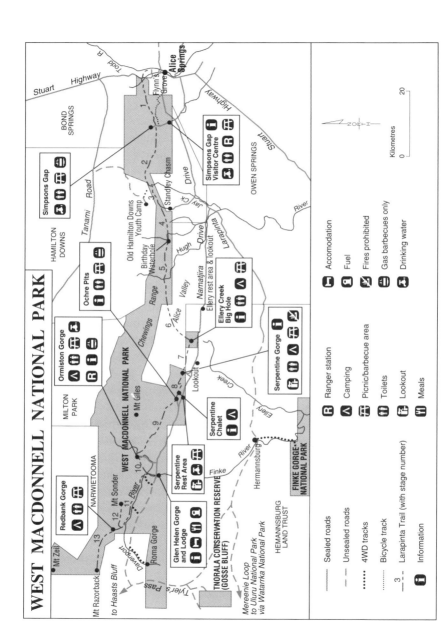

Simpsons Gap

Ochre Pits

Ormiston Gorge

Redbank Gorge

Glen Helen Gorge and Lodge

Serpentine Rest Area

Serpentine Chalet

Serpentine Gorge

Ellery Creek Big Hole

Simpsons Gap Visitor Centre

WEST MACDONNELL NATIONAL PARK

TNORALA CONSERVATION RESERVE (GOSSE BLUFF)

FINKE GORGE NATIONAL PARK

HEMANNSBURG LAND TRUST

Mereenie Loop to Uluru National Park via Watarka National Park

Alice Springs

Flynn's Grove

Stuart Highway

BOND SPRINGS

HAMILTON DOWNS

MILTON PARK

NARWIETOOMA

Mt Zeil

Mt Razorback

to Haasts Bluff

Tylers Pass

Davenport

Roma Gorge

Mt Sonder

Mt Giles

Tanami Road

Old Hamilton Downs Youth Camp

Birthday Waterhole

Standley Chasm

Ellery rest area & lookout

Lookout

OWEN SPRINGS

Stuart Highway

Todd R

Hugh

Chewings Range

Alice Valley

Namatjira Drive

Larapinta Drive

Jay Ck

Finke River

Ellery Creek

Ormiston Creek

Hermannsburg

1 2 3 4 5 6 7 8 9 10 11 12 13

	Sealed roads
	Unsealed roads
	4WD tracks
	Bicycle track
	Larapinta Trail (with stage number)

Legend icons:

- Ranger station
- Camping
- Picnic/barbecue area
- Toilets
- Lookout
- Meals
- Accomodation
- Fuel
- Fires prohibited
- Gas barbecues only
- Drinking water
- Information

Kilometres
0   20

vertical form seen today. The average height is now less than 500 metres (1640 feet) above the surrounding land level which is itself about 600 metres (1968 feet) above sea level. Towards the western extremity of the ranges are Central Australia's highest peaks: Mt Zeil, 1531 metres (5022 feet), also the highest point in the Northern Territory; Mt Leibig, 1527 metres (5008 feet) the second highest, with the most picturesque of all, Mt Sonder, rising to 1380 metres (4526 feet).

Arid zone habitats of Central Australian landscapes are well represented - sheltered moist gorges; exposed ridges; broken valley floors; riverine and woodlands. These environments provide niches for, and richness in botanical life-forms and wildlife, from relic palms and sublime ghost gums, to prolific birdlife, reptiles and black-footed rock-wallabies. Because the ranges are generally lightly vegetated (see vegetation cross-section), the delineations and colour hues of the inclined rock structures tend to dominate, and along with gaps, gorges and chasms, make the MacDonnells a place of unlimited, often stunning scenic beauty.

Complementing this extraordinary beauty is a cultural overlay given by over 40,000 years of settlement by Western Arrernte people, and the enduring and adaptable nature of their culture may be appreciated at various places in both the Western and Eastern sectors of the MacDonnells.

For fascinating insights into landform evolutions, ecology and Aboriginal interaction with the landscape, all of which will enhance your appreciation of this great arid region, a visit to the **Alice Springs Desert Park** before exploring the MacDonnell Ranges is strongly advised (see outline under *West MacDonnell National Park*).

Most of the features in the West MacDonnell National Park and parks and reserves in the East MacDonnell Ranges are accessible by conventional vehicles. And main sealed roads to both western and eastern areas of the ranges form part of designated loop roads and 4WD tracks (refer to *Tourist Drives, Heritage Trails and 4WD Explorer Tracks* in Part One).

In the following sections, places and features in the Western and Eastern MacDonnell Ranges are sequentially listed from Alice Springs. As most features of the Western MacDonnell Ranges (which include the Heavitree and Chewings Ranges) are now contained within the National Park, for convenience, all places in the Western MacDonnells are listed under the *National Park*.

WEST MACDONNELL NATIONAL PARK

Proclaimed in 1991, the Park encompasses an area of nearly 1500 sq.kms (930 sq. miles) and extends west from Alice Springs in unbroken lines along the main spines of ranges to Mt Zeil in the north-west, and beyond Tylers Pass to the south-west, a distance of over 160kms (100 miles).

Altjira, meaning the eternal land, is the name given to the MacDonnell Ranges by the Western Arrernte people. John McDouall Stuart was the first European to explore the area and named the ranges after the Governor of South Australia, Sir Richard MacDonnell in 1860. By following the course of the Hugh River, Stuart's party broke through the Chewings Range just west of Standley Chasm (between Paisley and Brinkley Bluffs) at what is now called Stuart Pass. And the number of features having Teutonic place names in the Park is attributed to explorer Ernest Giles on the instruction of his 1872 expedition patron, Baron Von Mueller, a notable botanist who founded Melbourne's Royal Botanic Gardens.

PRACTICAL INFORMATION

Access to the features in the park are by feeder roads (generally sealed) from the sealed main road from Alice Springs, Larapinta Drive. Namatjira Drive, which branches off Larapinta Drive approximately 46 kms (28 miles) from Alice Springs, becomes the main sealed road to the park's other major attractions. This road is sealed to Glen Helen Gorge.

There are no park entry fees, but camp fees apply where camping is permitted (around *$1 p.p and $3 family*). At many areas, you leave fees in honesty boxes. There are entry fees to Alice Springs Desert Park and Standley Chasm, both of which are outside the National Park. Pets are not permitted in the National Park.

While fires are permitted in designated fireplaces in some areas of the National Park, no firewood is supplied. It is illegal to cut or collect firewood from within the park (as in all Parks and Reserves), so you must bring in your own supplies.

A rather unusual hazard is the often ice-cold water in waterholes at gorge areas in the park. This can cause shock to the body and induce cramp. Wetsuits are a good idea.

Ranger Stations and Visitor Centres at *Simpsons Gap*, ph (08) 8955 0310, and *Ormiston Gorge*, ph (08)8956 7799, have excellent interpretive displays and a range of park literature and maps for sale. Rangers also offer free guided walks, slide shows and 'campfire' talks between May and October.

Good maps are produced by the *Parks and Wildlife Commission* and *Westprint Heritage Maps* are good value (see also under *Maps* in Part One).

Facilities at places and features are outlined at respective locations, including areas with wheelchair access. As there are generally short walks to actual features, sensible footwear, protective clothing and sunscreen lotion and your own supplies of water in this desert environment are a must. As there are limited treated drinking water supplies in the park, it is better to be on the safe side by taking your own.

A number of Alice Springs-based tour operators offer a variety of organised tour options from half and full day to extended excursions - refer to *Alice Springs* listing (Tours and Information sections) for details and advice.

MAJOR ACTIVITIES
Stretching 220kms (136 miles) from Alice Springs to beyond Mt Razorback is **The Larapinta Trail** - an exhilarating long distance,

wilderness bush walking track that traverses an arid landscape of infinite character and deep cultural spirituality. Many stages have been completed and virtually all of the planned 13 sections are within the National Park. It can be enjoyed as a series of overnight or day walks, or a very challenging, end-to-end walking safari.

Each section is classified according to degree of difficulty and detailed trail notes and maps are available from Visitor Centres in the *Park, Parks and Wildlife Commission Offices* or *Information Centres* in Alice Springs. Intending walkers should consult with Rangers prior to undertaking any sections and must be properly equipped. All overnight walkers must register with Rangers. There are many other fine shorter walking tracks in the Park and these are outlined at their respective locations.

The Simpsons Gap Bicycle Path connects Alice Springs with Simpsons Gap, a dramatic gorge gouged through the Chewings Range. The sealed path is an easy, family-friendly track that meanders through broken woodland country where in many places there are magnificent views. And shady picnic sites along the route provide quiet spots for rest and enjoyment of wilderness scenery and serenity. The 17 km (10.5 miles) path begins at Flynn's Grave on Larapinta Drive, 7 kms (4.3 miles) from Alice Springs. You can hire bicycles in Alice Springs and best advice is cycle in the early morning, returning later in the day. Take plenty of drinking water as there are no supplies along the path. The path is also suitable for wheelchairs.

Other activities (Ranger programs, swimming, wildlife appreciation) are outlined at appropriate places.

PLACES AND FEATURES

ALICE SPRINGS DESERT PARK
Characteristics
One of the most outstanding complementary features at major Northern Territory tourist attractions is the imaginative design and innovative display technology of their purpose-built,

environmental and cultural interpretive facilities. This new Desert Park is no exception. In effect, the integrated manner in which the varied habitats, plants and animals of Australia's deserts, and their traditional use and management by Aboriginal people are arranged, justify its billing as the world's first bio-park, and places the facility at the international fore-front of environmental presentations.

Located just west of Alice Springs along Larapinta Drive, and set in the foothills of the MacDonnell Ranges on a 1300 hectare (3211 acres) reserve, the Desert Park is a product of a Northern Territory Government initiative, managed by the Parks and Wildlife Commission. It is designed as a microcosm of the larger desert environment for purposes of environmental education, research and conservation, particularly of endangered desert species of flora and fauna.

The park's function and design at more subtle, practical and aesthetic levels is a reflection too, of the integration of a wealth of creative talent, much of it home-grown in Central Australia. Artists have worked closely with regional naturalists and Aboriginal custodians to collect the knowledge and inspiration needed to re-create the desert's inner most secrets. The linking of Aboriginal and non-Aboriginal expertise is a major element contributing to the park's trendsetting status.

The Alice Springs Desert Park offers enriching cultural and ecological perspectives that are not only refreshingly different, but ones that should not be missed. And the Park's claims that after visiting this facility "you will never look at deserts in the same way again", is no idle boast.

Information and Advice

The park *opens daily except Christmas Day, 7.30am - 6.00pm. Admission fees are adult $12; child (5-16 yrs) $6; under 5 free; family (2 adults, 4 children) $30; pensioner/student $6*; for group concessions, check with administration, ph (08) 8951 8788.

Allow at least 3 hours for your visit. Begin at the Exhibition Centre by first viewing the introductory film, then onto the interpretive displays and through the desert habitats including the Nocturnal House.

Core Facilities

Within the park's 50 hectare (124 acres) core area, there are representative samples of plants and animals that occur across Australia's arid zone, a region taking up 70% of the continent. The core area buildings house one of the world's largest *Nocturnal Houses*, which provides a rare window into the lifestyles of shy, night-time creatures; an *Education Centre* for schools and specialist groups, and a *Nature Theatre* for presenting raptor (birds-of-prey) behaviour. The *Exhibition Centre* features inspirational, inter-active displays interpreting desert ecosystems and a venue for a visually dramatic, 20 minute movie 'exposure' of the 4.5 billion year evolution of Central Australia. Projected in high resolution, 70mm format onto a 17x6 metre screen, 'This Changing Heart', is a cinematic masterpiece, with a climax linking virtual-reality to reality, a breathtaking experience.

Habitats

The reserve's natural landscape has been sensitively modified to create three of Australia's desert habitats - desert rivers (riverine); sand country, including dunes and salt lakes, and woodlands. In the near future, the addition of gorge, range country and mulga plains environments, will effectively complete a representation of all major Australian desert habitats.

Walking trails, suitable for wheelchairs, trace a fascinating 1.6km pathway through the completed living habitats, now colourfully embellished, in particular, by indigenous birdlife. Already these habitats feature over 320 native plant species and over 120 animal species, several of which are extremely rare or on the brink of extinction. Some animals are contained in unobtrusive enclosures.

Wildlife in these habitats are closely monitored as part of the on-going scientific research and conservation function of the park. Insights into the work of scientists, including captive breeding programs, is possible by prior arrangement. And talks by Park guides illustrate how indigenous people use and manage their desert 'supermarket', as well as other aspects of their culture, through some captivating story-telling.

Services and Facilities
Apart from those outlined, the park has toilets including facilities for disabled visitors; wheelchair and stroller hire; gift shop with an excellent range or quality goods; tourist information and literature; and a cafe catering for all meals. In the habitat area, there are shade and interpretation shelters, and drinking water sites. Guided tours by friendly, knowledgeable staff can be arranged, and school and specialist groups are well catered for, but bookings for classroom facilities are essential. Talks tailored to meet group needs can be arranged. For further information, telephone (08) 8951 8788.

JOHN FLYNN HISTORICAL RESERVE
The small reserve located on Larapinta Drive, 7km (4 miles) west of Alice Springs marks the resting place of Reverend John Flynn. The ashes of the man who founded the Australian Inland Mission, The Royal Flying Doctor Service, the first inland medical centre, and an outback padre patrol system, are encased here in a stone cairn. A large boulder crowns the cairn, and Mt Gillen stands sentinel-like in the background.

The memorial plaque inscription sums up the achievements of this Outback humanitarian: *The Very Reverend John Flynn, OBE, DD, of the Presbyterian Church of Australia 1880-1951. His vision encompassed the continent. He established the Australian Inland Mission and founded the Flying Doctor Service. He brought to lonely places a spiritual ministry and spread a mantle of safety over them by medicine and radio.*

SIMPSONS GAP

Conveniently located close to Alice Springs on Larapinta Drive, 18km (11 miles) away, Simpsons Gap was described by Overland Telegraph Line surveyor Gilbert McMinn in 1871 as *"one of the finest pieces of scenery I have met for a long time"*. Wide white sands, majestic river red gums and striking ghost gums lead to a quiet pool sheltering beneath the mighty gorge walls. The remnants of huge quartzite slabs, sheared from the walls, lie jumbled at the entrance base, and provide a precipitous playground for a colony of black-footed rock-wallabies (early morning and late afternoon are best times to see them). Picnicking here in the late afternoon is a delight when the mellow sun enhances the contrast between big and bold, soft and gentle.

  Interesting wildlife in the surrounding spinifex, mulga and witchetty bush plains include dingoes, euros, long-nosed dragons and the harmless little children's python, while for keen bird watchers there are eagles, kites and Port Lincoln ringneck parrots, among many others. Bond Gap, a narrow cleft with an icy-cold waterhole is a lesser known gorge in the range, accessible by the Larapinta Trail and Woodland Walk.

History

To the Western Arrernte people, the Gap is Rungutjirpa, the spiritual home of the Giant Goanna Ancestors or Big Lizard People. The ridge through which the gorge is cut retains this Aboriginal name today. The area is an important site to Aboriginal people, where a number of spiritual trails cross.

Prior to 1957, the whole area around the gap formed part of a large cattle station. In 1957, an area of one square mile was reserved around the gorge until 1970, when the 30,950 hectare (76,447 acre) Simpsons Gap National Park was declared. Prior to this, years of overgrazing severely damaged the landscape, and Alice Springs took the brunt of dust storms that originated from here when tonnes of top soil was blasted away by the westerly winds. Careful land management practices and removal of cattle by the

Parks and Wildlife Commission have largely restored the delicate natural balance between soil, plant and wildlife.

Geology

Here the quartzite (metamorphosed beach sand) of the Heavitree Range is down-faulted into 2000 million-year-old rocks of the Arunta block below. Massive earth movements during a major mountain building period about 350 million years ago resulted in faults or fracture lines running north-south at various intervals through the east-west trending quartzite ranges. Simpsons Gap is thought to be the last of an extensive continuous arched sheet of quartzite that unified the Heavitree Range before major faulting and erosion occurred. The gap was cut along a fault-line by the erosive power of Roe Creek, which maintained its relative level as the surrounding land was lowered by erosion. Even although Roe Creek flows intermittently, the fact that the creek maintained its level accounts for the gorge formation and the often deep scour pools that characterise Simpsons Gap and other gorges of the MacDonnells. Sometimes, a series of gentle creek flows will cause the pool to silt up until it's scoured out again by the next raging flood.

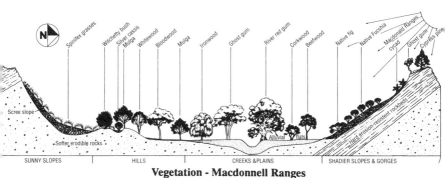

Vegetation - Macdonnell Ranges

Information, Walks, Facilities

A 6km (4 miles) sealed road from Larapinta Drive leads to the gap. One kilometre from the turnoff is the Visitor Centre and Ranger Station. It has an excellent interpretive display and a range of park literature. Rangers give a free half-hour guided tour at the Gap - check with centre for times as these vary, phone (08) 8955 0310. *Opening times are 5.30am - 8.00pm.* Swimming and camping are not permitted. The Gap has wheelchair access.

Walks include: *The Larapinta Trail* section (see previously under *Major Activities*); a short *Ghost Gum Walk* begins at the Visitor Centre and gives a good introduction to native plants of the area; *Cassia Hill Walk*, begins from a carpark near the Gap itself, and is a 500metre track giving fine elevated views of the region, and *The Woodland Trail* is a 17 kms (10.5 miles) return track to Bond Gap. Always check with Rangers first before undertaking any longer walks.

An area near the Gap has well appointed, shaded picnic facilities (free gas BBQs, tables), water and toilets including facilities for disabled visitors.

TWIN GUMS

Approximately 18km (11 miles) west of Alice Springs (just past the Simpsons Gap turn-off), are two ghost gums (Eucalyptus papuana), highlighted by the changing colours of Burt Bluff in the background and made famous and captured best of all on canvas by Aboriginal artist, Albert Namatjira. Unfortunately, one of the trees is dying, and as they are located on Aboriginal land, they can only viewed from a rough, roadside parking area. There are no facilities.

STANDLEY CHASM

At 24kms (15 miles) from the turnoff to Simpsons Gap is the 9km (5.5 mile) sealed access road to the chasm. Standley Chasm is a five to nine metre wide rock cleft in the jagged Chewings Range, and features sheer, rust-stained walls of quartzite that blaze vivid red when fired by the sun's 10-minute mid-day passage. It's a dramatic climax to a comfortable 20 minute walk along the winding creek bed where you can see some magnificent relic cycad plants. The chasm's a popular spot around mid-day, but despite the crowds, the 'magic moment' is well worth seeing and photographing.

Geology

Nearly 900 million years ago, enormous pressures within the earth squeezed magma (molten rock) into vertical fractures that extended north-south in much of the rock of the MacDonnells. The intruding magma forced the fractures apart, and when it 'cooked', a dark green rock called dolerite was formed between the quartzite. Such intrusions are called dykes, and as dolerite is much less resistant to weathering and erosion than quartzite, it was eroded away completely by a south-flowing creek, leaving the near vertical, 80m high walls seen today.

History

The chasm was named after Alice Spring's first school teacher, Ida Standley, who moved to Jay Creek in 1925 to teach Aboriginal children, and became the first white women to walk through the spectacular gap. Originally, it was known as Gall Springs, after Charles Gall, manager of one of the earliest pastoral leases taken up in the Centre, the 3625 sq km (1377 sq miles) Owen Springs Cattle Station.

  Today, the chasm is on land owned by the Iwupataka Aboriginal Community, and has the distinction of being the first all-Aboriginal tourist enterprise in Central Australia managed by an Aboriginal Corporation. It is not part of the National Park.

Service and Facilities

It has a kiosk where you can buy refreshments, excellent meals and snacks, souvenirs, and local crafts and artifacts; toilet and shaded picnic area with water and BBQ facilities, characterised by a few free-range dingoes and wallabies; ramps for wheelchair (no wheelchair access to chasm); a 40 minute loop walking track by the kiosk, gives elevated views. *Opening hours 8.00am - 6.00pm, a* modest entry fee *is charged, ph (08) 8956 7400.*

5km (3 miles) west from the turn-off to Standley Chasm is the *Namatjira Drive* road junction; south-west on Larapinta Drive leads to Hermannsburg, while Namatjira Drive takes you to Glen Helen. At 32 kms (20 miles) west of the junction on Namatjira Drive is *8 Mile Gap*, a roadside stop area with lookout and picnic facilities (tables and water).

ELLERY CREEK BIG HOLE

Located 10kms (6.2 miles) from 8 Mile Gap, on Namatjira Drive is another spectacular gorge characterised by high, red rock faces, a large deep waterhole, and a sandy creek fringed by river red gums. Explorer Ernest Giles came this way in 1872 and named it after Government Astronomer and Director of the Melbourne Observatory, R.L.J. Ellery. To distinguish the rock pool from others along the creek, locals added Big Hole to the name, while to the Arrernte, it's Udepata.

It's an appealing spot that's popular with picnickers and campers alike, and if you are energetically inclined, a climb to the top of the flanking ridges is well rewarded with magnificent views. The shapes and colours of the steep and narrow gorge walls are reflected in the still waters, creating fine subject matter for artists and photographers. The walking track to the waterhole is 20 minutes return. The Dolomite Walk takes 40 minutes return and will be loved by naturalists and geologists.

Geology

The gorge was formed by the south-flowing Ellery Creek, which cut across rock strata and carved a gap through a Heavitree Range quartzite ridge. Faulting has offset the alignment of the ridge across the waterhole, breaking the rock formation and causing a line of weakness which has been exploited by the creek. A few fine examples of folded rock strata here can be seen, giving some idea of the enormous energy associated with its formation. At the main road, directly across from Ellery Creek turn-off, an interesting lizard-like formation called 'Julie' highlights the ridge. This feature consists of a single two metre wide band of limestone in siltstone, and since the latter is more easily erodible, the limestone has been left projecting like a wall. Weathering of the limestone wall has produced the lizard-like silhouette.

Facilities
Wood barbecues, pit-toilets and picnic facilities (tables and shade shelters) are provided. While it may be very hot here, the water can be ice-cold. Camping is allowed (fees apply), and the 1.2 km graded, gravel access track is suitable for conventional vehicles.

SERPENTINE GORGE
Located 11kms (7 miles) west of Ellery Big Hole, the locality features two winding gorges where a south-flowing creek has cut through two quartzite ridges that have a fold between them. At the upstream site, the very narrow gap suggests that the creek has eroded along a nearly straight vertical joint, or fracture.

The gorge has an impressive, wide entrance, 60m high walls, and a deep and cold, permanent waterhole at the far end. At the entrance, another waterhole can prevent access after rains, but in summer, it dries up quickly. Many cycads make low green fountains of palm-like growth at the base of the cliffs. The walk to the waterhole take approximately one hour return, while from the waterhole, a further 15 minute climb to the lookout offers great views. The cool, gorge environment is an important refuge for many rare plants and animals.

Facilities
Picnic, wood barbecues, and pit toilet facilities are provided. Camping is allowed, firewood is strictly BYO. Access is via a 3km,

rough graded gravel track, with extreme care, negotiable by 2WD vehicles.

SERPENTINE CHALET BUSH CAMPING AREA

This relatively new site, located 6km (4 miles) west of Serpentine Gorge, features quiet, simple wilderness camping on secluded, designated sites, each with wood BBQ fireplaces. As with all camping areas in the Park, you must supply your own firewood. This style of camping is the main attraction; the other feature is of historical interest - the Chalet ruins which are the result of a short-lived tourist venture in the 1960s. A walk to the *Chalet Dam* takes about one hour return. As yet, facilities are minimal, although pit toilets are planned. A rough, 2km graded track from Namatjira Drive provides 2WD access (with care) to the first 5 independent campsites and ruins, after which is a 4WD track only to the remaining campsites. Back on Namatjira Drive, there's a roadside stop with tables, water and lookout, 3kms from the Chalet turnoff.

OCHRE PITS

This feature is located 12km (7 miles) west of Serpentine Gorge, on Namatjira Drive. There's a short, sealed road to a park area from where a sealed path leads to an exposed cliff face consisting of various coloured ochre clays. The swirls of red and yellow clays are used by Arrernte Aboriginal people as colour pigments for a range of decorative purposes such as rock painting and body decorations. It also has medicinal uses. The colours were derived from the changes to the folded siltstones and shales by weathering, which caused iron oxides (common rust), aided by water, to be moved. The various colours from yellow to deep ochre, emerged when different iron oxides mixed with water and stained the mineral particles in the soft rock. The Ochre Pits sealed path is suitable for wheelchairs, and takes 15 minutes return. The Arrernte Bush Walk takes 3 hours return and leads through Inarlanga Pass, a scenic gorge characterised by cycad plants. Along the way there are some interpretive signs giving insights into Arrernte use and care of the land.

Facilities include picnic (gas BBQs, tables and shade shelters), pit toilets and interpretive signage.

ORMISTON GORGE AND POUND

From the Ochre Pits, it is 17kms (10.5 miles) to the Ormiston Gorge turnoff, then a sealed 7km (4.3 miles) road to the feature. The turnoff is 136 kms (84 miles) from Alice Springs.

Ormiston Gorge's awesome 2km long red wall, permanent pool, and adjacent Pound wilderness, make it one of the most memorable spots in the National Park. The dominant feature is the gorge, a deep cut carved through a quartzite range by floodwaters of *Ormiston Creek*, leaving sheer 250m high walls towering above the boulder-strewn creek. High above, ghost gums and cypress pine cling tenaciously, while the rock face gives a remarkable parade of colour when struck by the sun.

The *Pound* is a rugged natural enclosure that measures about 10km across, and is almost completely surrounded by high ridges. The 2 to 3 hour, 7km (4 miles) walk through this area unfolds a stark beauty that can touch the spirit. It must be one of the most inspiring shorter wilderness walks in Australia. Dominating the eastern end of the Pound is the hump-shaped 1389m (4555 ft) Mt Giles.

Ormiston Creek is the most northerly catchment which, together with the Davenport River, form the Finke River a few kilometres north of Glen Helen. Ormiston Creek is thought to have been named by R.E. Warburton, son of explorer Colonel P.E. Warburton.

Geology

The area is a geologist's delight. Needless to say, it's very complex with much folding and bending back or overthrusting of rock strata. There's an anticline outlined by the Heavitree quartzite immediately past the entrance gates, while at the main waterhole, this quartzite in the base of the cliff has been overlaid by more of the Heavitree quartzite which was pushed southwards from a few kilometres away. The change of slope, about half-way up the main rockface, indicates the thrust surface on which this movement occurred. The quartzite or sandstone is the main rock type in the gorge area, while outcrops of schist, gneiss and igneous rocks can be seen in the Pound. The Pound rocks are over 1700 million-years-old and belong to the Arunta Complex - one of the Territory's oldest grouping of rocks.

Flora and Fauna

Many types of acacias can be identified around the public facilities area; river red gums line the creekbeds; bean trees and bloodwoods give scant shade in the Pound; and spinifex is widespread. In the spring and after rains, wildflowers add a delicate touch to the ground cover, particularly Sturt's desert rose.

The wildlife is varied. Rarely will you see dingoes, but you may hear them at night. Euros, rock-wallabies and smaller marsupials are shy. Reptiles include skinks, geckoes and the occasional perentie. In the pools, heron, grebe, teal, darter and cormorants may be seen. Plumed pigeon, spotted bower bird, mistletoe bird, Port Lincoln parrot and honeyeaters are other birds seen in the area. When the creek dries up, the spangled perch, one of Central Australia's 30 species of fish, bury themselves deep in the mud where they survive until the next rains come.

Bushwalks

The Ghost Gum Lookout Walk takes 30 minutes return and climbs to a good vantage point with great views of the gorge. It then descends from the lookout into the gorge and along its base. It takes about 1.5 hours return. The Pound Walk (previously mentioned) is one of a number of longer walk options including sections of the Larapinta Trail. Mt Giles walk is another option for experienced walkers. Check first with Rangers for advice on longer walks and routes for the Mt Giles walk in particular.

Services and Facilities

Superb facilities are provided here. There's a Ranger Station and Visitor Centre, well appointed camping ground (showers, toilets including for the disabled), camping fees apply, picnic tables and gas barbecues. Rangers have made noteworthy efforts to tune visitors to the bush by providing a sensory trail and a litter awareness track (try them out!). Ranger programs include a guided walk/talk at the waterhole, slide shows and Ranger chats around a campfire (without the fire). All are free and check with the Visitor Centre for times. Rangers can be contacted on (08) 8956 7799. The permanent rock-pool is ideal for swimming and is accessible by wheelchair.

GLEN HELEN GORGE

It's located 4kms (2.5 miles) west of the turnoff to Ormiston Gorge. Here, erosion by the *Finke River* (thought to be the world's oldest, having flowed along the same course for 350 million years), has produced an impressive gorge and large, 30m deep waterhole. A short distance through the gorge you can see two interesting rock formations: 'window in the rock' on the eastern side, and the 'organ pipes' on the western. The latter are the result of weathering along the bedding planes of vertical sandstone strata. A climb over the range, or a swim through the icy waters, allows access for views of these two features. It was here that Ernest Giles found his way north blocked by the waterhole in 1872, and attempts to build a causeway on the western side for a shortcut for vehicles to Hermannsburg, have met with failure. After the floods of 1975, the waterhole silted up and for a while it was possible to walk through on dry sand.

To the Arrernte people it was known as Yapalpe, the home of the Giant Watersnake, and according to Aboriginal belief, it's from these icy depths that the first creative beings emerged.

Geology

The sedimentary rock beds cut by the Finke were more resistant, thus causing a deeply scoured pool that's kept full by water permeating through the sand in the bed of the river. The rock faces reveal Pacoota sandstone or quartzite that is distinctive by its coarser grain, and formed during major earth movements about 350 million years ago, when white sandstone was broken and mixed with brown sand and rock fragments. It's also called breccia, and the weathering process, with the help of water, has caused the rocks to be coloured by the iron oxides.

Facilities
There's a walking track with information signage. From the car park, it's a pleasant walk alongside the ancient riverbed, and the date palms along the base of the red cliffs should not be mistaken for cycad or red cabbage palms found in the Finke Gorge National Park (they are a legacy of the Afghan cameleer days). Limited services and facilities are available at Glen Helen Lodge next door to the park.

GLEN HELEN LODGE
The homestead is set on a small freehold site surrounded by the National Park and shares the same entrance to Glen Helen Gorge, 139 kms (86 miles) west of Alice Springs. It features a long, low, white-washed lodge that nestles comfortably by the Finke River on what must be one of the most envied locations going. Massive, red quartzite cliffs provide a startling backdrop, while to the north-west, a softer landscape spread directs the eye to the beautiful Mt Sonder. The homestead has been restored and rebuilt with a 1930s atmosphere inside, and the Lodge is run by the Ngurratjuta Corporation who provide basic services, at this stage, to visitors.

History
It is possible that the station was named after Helen Bakewell, a relation of Grant, one of the partners who established the property in the late 1870s. The original homestead was built alongside Ormiston Creek and was called Munga Munga. It now lies in

ruins. Cattleman Fred Raggart built the first homestead on the Lodge site in the early 1930s, and a later owner of the property, Bryan Bowman, recalls the days of sheep, cattle and thoroughbred horses in his fascinating book, *The Glen Helen Story.* The 2165 sq km (823 sq miles) Glen Helen Station surrounds the lodge, and the homestead is 55km (34 miles) to the north-west. You may wonder about those donkeys on the road; no-one left the gate open, they are feral.

Services and Facilities

It has a shop selling basic foodstuffs, takeaway food, ice, softdrinks, souvenirs, tourist literature and Mereenie Loop Road passes. A lovely outdoor patio area overlooking the Finke River is a great spot for refreshments. Accommodation at this stage is camping, - powered sites $15, unpowered $5. Amenities include showers and toilets. Vehicle services are fuel only (LP, ULP, diesel and oil). It's cash only, open daily (shop hours 8am-5pm), ph (08) 8956 7489.

REDBANK GORGE PARK

It's located 20kms (12 miles) from Glen Helen and 4kms (2.5 miles) from the turnoff to the gorge. From Glen Helen, the graded formed road surface is suitable, with care, for 2WD vehicles as is the rougher, graded gravel track into the gorge. The area features a delightful gorge that is permanently blocked by several very deep and cold pools along its 800m length. It's a most appealing spot in an area of superb scenery that includes Mt Sonder.

The sheer walls of the gorge rise to 40m, and its 5m maximum width narrows at one point to just one metre. From the car park, it's a 30 minute walk, and if you intend exploring the chasm be warned; the water is ice-cold, there are few natural footholds underwater, and the walls are slippery. Unless you are a very strong swimmer, cold-blooded or both, an inflatable mattress to provide support in case of chill-induced cramp, is strongly advised.

The walk from the day-use area to the waterhole takes around 40 minutes return. The Mt Sonder Walk, Section 12 of the Larapinta

Trail, takes at least 8 hours return. It's a hard walk, and the effort is well rewarded for the unsurpassed views from the summit. Check with Rangers first.

Facilities
At the day use carpark area near the gorge, there are picnic facilities (wood BBQ, tables), pit toilets, shade and interpretive shelters. There are 2 camping areas - *Ridgetop*, closest to the gorge and *Woodland Camping Area* located about 1km along the access road from the turnoff. Both have wood and gas BBQs and pit toilets. There are camping fees.

West from Redbank Gorge the road leads to Tnorala with options of loops to Hermannsburg and Palm Valley or the Mereenie Loop Road to Watarrka and Uluru (see *Territory Drives, Trails and 4WD Tracks* in Part One).

MT SONDER
The eye-catching peak is located approximately 15km (9 miles) north-west of Glen Helen where it rises majestically and dominates the skyline. While it's not the highest peak at 1380m (4526 ft), it's certainly the most picturesque, and landscape painters and photographers will be hard-pressed to find a more aesthetically pleasing subject. Mt Sonder's steep faced peaks provide a challenge to the few who climb it, but they are rewarded with an astounding view of the ancient Finke and its tributaries, as well as the serene sweep of Centralian landscape. Redbank Gorge is an ideal base from which to climb Mt Sonder (see under *Redbank Gorge*).

Ernest Giles named the mountain after Dr William Sonder of Adelaide, and Arrernte people call it Rutjipma. It's also known as 'sleeping women mountain' - from certain angles it resembles a woman lying on her back. The geology of Mt Sonder is very complex with much folding and bending back of rock strata, particularly where Heavitree quartzite has overthrust onto itself.

THE EASTERN MACDONNELL RANGES

East of Alice Springs, the MacDonnells begin as a narrow range, gradually broadening into a complex, well eroded patchwork of parallel ridges that taper into the forbidding margins of the Simpson Desert. In contrast to the Western MacDonnells, the gaps and gorges are not as big or bold, but they do have a quieter, wilderness charm. Adding to their very different character, is a greater visible presence of a continuing Eastern Arrernte culture, seen in a number of small art sites, while N'Dhala Gorge is an extraordinary art gallery with thousands of rock engravings. And Arltunga provides insights in Central Australia's first town and the men who mined for gold there. The two sectors of the MacDonnells are complementary in terms of their natural and cultural assets.

Getting There

The Ross River Highway is the main route to a number of features protected by park or reserve status. The highway is sealed from Alice Springs to Ross River Homestead (82 kms/51 miles). N'Dhala Gorge and Ruby Gap Nature Parks are only accessible by 4WD vehicle. There are some loop track options for 4WD drivers - south from Ross River Homestead (see also under N'Dhala Gorge in this section) to Alice Springs is 95 kms and takes about 2 hours, while north from Arltunga via Cattlewater Pass Track to the Plenty Highway is 76 kms (47 miles) and takes about 3 hours. Always check road conditions first.

For a unique, adventurous 4WD journey into the timeless, rugged and remote lands at the extremity of the MacDonnells, Ooraminna Bush Camp (see also under Attractions in Alice Springs listing) offer 2-3 day tours. These explore gaps and gorges and old gold workings on private station properties (otherwise not accessible to the public), along tracks that also expose the quiet, stark and

EASTERN MACDONNELL RANGES

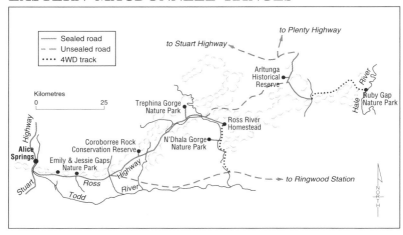

Sealed road
Unsealed road
4WD track

to Plenty Highway
to Stuart Highway
Arltunga Historical Reserve
Ruby Gap Nature Park
Hale River
Kilometres
0   25
Trephina Gorge Nature Park
Ross River Homestead
Highway
Coroborree Rock Conservation Reserve
N'Dhala Gorge Nature Park
Alice Springs
Emily & Jessie Gaps Nature Park
Highway
to Ringwood Station
Stuart
Ross
River
Todd
NORTH

stunning beauty of the broken range country. Tours can be tailored to meet group needs, "Tag-along" 4WD options are available, and for further details ph (08) 8953 0170. For other tour offerings to the Eastern MacDonnells, refer to *Tours* in the Alice Springs listing.

Camping

There are a number of excellent bush camping areas in some of the parks. Fees are around $1 p.p. ($3 family) payable in most areas in honesty boxes.

PLACES AND FEATURES

These are listed sequentially from Alice Springs.

EMILY AND JESSIE GAPS NATURE PARK

The park protects two small gaps in the range and surrounding ridgetops, with the short access track to Emily Gap located 10kms (6 miles) from Heavitree Gap, while the Jessie Gap entrance is 7kms (4 miles) further east of Emily Gap entrance.

The main features are two small gaps in the range which contain Aboriginal rock paintings depicting spiritual stories, one of which at Emily Gap, telling where the caterpillar ancestors of Mparnte

(Alice Springs) originated. These are significant, registered sacred sites for Eastern Arrernte people. At Emily Gap, the gorge is narrow, and it's from these cold, deep waters that the caterpillar ancestral beings emerged to create many topographic features in the region.

The sand-fringed waterholes and river red gums make both gaps a popular scenic spot for picnicking. You may also climb and walk along the top of the range between the gaps for some wonderful views and wildlife encounters.

Both features are easily accessed, and facilities include wood BBQ, tables and pit toilets. Camping and pets are not permitted.

CORROBOREE ROCK CONSERVATION RESERVE
Approximately 34 kms (21 miles) further east from Emily and Jessie Gaps Park are outcroppings of rocks, the most prominent of which is Corroboree Rock. It consists of a vertical remnant of dolomite strata (a pillar of limestone) which has been more resistant to the ravages of erosion that the surrounding shales. The rock is a registered sacred site and a place where Eastern Arrernte elders stored ritual objects in a small cave. To the Arrernte, the feature is known as Antanangantana, and the name Corroboree is a gross misnomer. Corroboree is not an Arrernte word, nor a Central Australian word. It was probably derived from an Aboriginal language from Eastern Australia and adopted by European settlers.

Interpretive signage and a short walking track around the rock helps appreciation of the area. Picnic tables and toilets are provided. Camping and pets are not allowed.

TREPHINA GORGE NATURE PARK
The turnoff to the park is 23kms (14 miles) east of Corroboree Rock, and the 9km (5.5 mile) access road is sealed for the first 4km, after which it is a gravel surface. If you are looking for some wilderness, solitude and attractive scenery, this park will not disappoint. It features two quite different gorges. Trephina Gorge

is notable for its sheer wall of quartzite formation which is visually impressive. A wide sandy creek bed, towering river red gums and tranquil pool make it a delightful spot for campers.

By contrast, John Hayes Rock Hole is protected by low cliffs, and its shaded seclusion provides an ideal refuge from the high temperatures summer can bring. Nearby, in the area below Mt Hayes, wedge-tailed eagles were once so common that it was called the Valley of the Eagles.

History

The precise origin of the name Trephina is not recorded, however one theory is that it was named after the wife of former prospector and cattleman, William Benstead, who also built Alice Spring's first pub. In 1907, the Hayes family established Undoolya Station that used to surround the park, and the rock pool was named after their son. William and Mary Hayes arrived in the Alice Springs district in 1884 with horses and bullock teams loaded with steel telegraph poles to replace the original wooden poles on the Overland Telegraph Line. Today, descendants Jan and Bill Hayes run Ooraminna Bush Camp and continue family association with the area through their 4WD Tours venture. The Undoolya Station was later reduced in size by the creation of the Garden Station Lease which now surrounds the park.

Flora and Fauna

Flora around the gorges and valleys includes river red gums, ghost gums, whitewoods and ironwoods, while precariously clinging to the cliff tops and faces are white cyprus pine, ghost gums and native fig. Spinifex is widespread, and delicate rock ferns thrive around John Hayes Rock Pool, home to tadpoles and other small aquatic creatures.

Common larger animals are dingoes (you will hear their nightly howls), euros on the spinifex slopes, and the large reptilian perentie. Smaller species include lizards and some bat colonies in the deep rock recesses (one roost entrance can be seen half-way up the left hand wall as you walk into the John Hayes Rock Hole). There's a colony of black-footed rock-wallabies at Trephina Gorge.

Birdlife is rich and varied. In the bush are Port Lincoln parrots, mistletoe birds, western thrush, pied butcher birds and grass wrens, to name a few, while dainty fairy martins build mud nests in the rock crevices. Birds of prey include little falcons, goshawks, kestrels and wedge-tailed eagles, while white-faced herons frequent the pools. You don't have to walk great distances to see the wildlife. Find a shady spot away from other people, sit quietly, and let the wildlife resume normal activities. This approach is quite rewarding.

Walks
Walks from Trephina Gorge all offer opportunities for landscape appreciation. The *Panorama Walk* and *Trephina Gorge Walk* are both loop tracks that take about one hour return. The *Trephina Ridge Top Trail* is an exhilarating walking track (6 hours one way) that leads to *John Hayes Rockhole* and is for experienced bushwalkers (check with the Ranger Station first). After the walk you can swim in the waterholes.

Facilities
The park has a Ranger Station (ph 08 8956 9765), information shelters which combined with free Ranger campfire talks, enhance a visit to the park. There are 3 superb camping areas varying in facilities from just pit toilets and wood BBQs to tapwater and free gas BBQs. Two areas are at Trephina Gorge. John Hayes Waterhole is a basic campground with pit toilets, fireplaces and tables, access to which is recommended by 4WD vehicles only. Camp fees apply (honesty boxes) and pets are not permitted.

ROSS RIVER HOMESTEAD
The property is located 82 kms (51 miles) from Alice Springs via the sealed Ross River Highway. The old, white-washed homestead has a backdrop of time-worn hills from its creek side site and

offers a taste of Central Australia's pioneering history. Formerly the headquarters of Loves Creek Station established in 1898, the homestead now offers visitors an economical base from which to explore the ancient Eastern MacDonnells landscape.

History

The river and homestead were named after explorer, surveyor and pastoralist, John Ross, a six foot, black-bearded, Scottish Highlander who in 1871 along with Harvey, Alfred Giles, Hearn and Tom Crisp, were the first men to follow John McDouall Stuart's trail-blazing route. Their brief was to survey a route for the Overland Telegraph Line, and some time was spent in the MacDonnell Ranges surveying.

Ross traced a northern trail from Adelaide for over 1500km (930 miles) using a prismatic compass, a tracing of Stuart's map, a lead pencil, and a two-foot ruler. Food consisted of flour, tea and 400 pounds of jerked meat ('boot-lace' or dried strips), and the medical supplies were Holloway's pills ('cure-all' patent tablets), boracic based eye lotion and castor oil. Water was collected and stored in canvas bags which were soon torn by scrub riding, so they shot wallabies, ate the meat, and used the ill-cured skins for water carriers.

At Chambers Pillar, they carved their names in the soft sandstone base before spending some time in the Eastern MacDonnells. Another survey party found Heavitree Gap and the Alice Springs. Further north, Ross unearthed Stuart's papers at Central Mt Stuart, and to Harvey, this was the appropriate time and place to open a bottle of rum that he had carried from Adelaide. They drank here in silent memory of a fellow Scot. They completed their survey work, and met up with engineers who were already pushing the line of telegraph poles south from Darwin. Plans for the route, and Telegraph Stations across the Central Australia, were based on Ross's survey work. The Highway, River and Homestead named after him, are fitting tributes to this hardy explorer.

The homestead with its characterful interior was probably built in 1909 by Alfred Tabe for Tom Wallis, who by the turn of the century, had acquired most of the land which now constitutes the adjacent 3670 sq.km (2275 sq. miles) Loves Creek Station. At this time the present 6202 hectare (15,319 acre) Ross River property was part of the Loves Creek Run. Wallis mainly bred horses, a practice continued by new owners, Barker and Bloomfield when they took over the lease in 1911. Horses were also bred to supply the British Army in India (Indian Remount Trade), but after the First World War demand for military horses declined. The number of brumbies (feral horses) running wild in the region today are legacies of the Remount Breeding venture. By 1933, the property was reported as running 1500 cattle, 700 horses, 6 camels and 400 goats.

In 1937 it was found that the homestead was actually located on the other adjoining run today, The Gardens Station. A new lease designed to protect the homestead was finally drawn up in the 1940s. The first tourist enterprise was established here in 1959 from which time its name became Ross River Homestead. It continues as a vibrant tourist venture today.

Services and Facilities
The homestead has a bar, restaurant (all meals, medium priced, with a good selection of Territorian meats for dinner), and sells ice-creams, softdrinks and souvenirs. Vehicle services are fuel only (LP, ULP, diesel).

Accommodation includes cabins $107 x 2; bunkhouse from $13 p.p. (without bedding); camping, powered sites $8 adult, unpowered $6 adult, (children half price). Sites are grassed and shaded with fireplaces (wood supplied), pets allowed, dogs leashed. There's a swimming pool for cabin guests.

The homestead opens daily, EFTPOS facility, credit cards accepted, ph. (08) 8956 9711.

N'DHALA GORGE NATURE PARK

It's located 11kms (7 miles) south of Ross River Homestead, accessed by a 2.5 km (1.5 mile) track leading from the primary track. The road from the homestead follows the Ross River Valley and has some wide sandy river crossings. A 4WD vehicle is necessary. From the turnoff to the reserve, the main track continues south to Numery Road where you can head east for 43 kms (27 miles) to join the Ross River Highway, 30 kms (18 miles) from Alice Springs.

At the gorge, a Ross River tributary has sliced a passage through the quartzite, and while the gap has a rugged beauty, it is the prehistoric petroglyphs (rock carvings), sheltered by the gorge walls, that are the main interest of the park. Several thousand engravings, some thought to be around 10,000-years-old, have been noted throughout the gorge, and local Eastern Arrernte people continue to have knowledge of the meaning of the designs (which are explained by interpretive signage). The carvings have been affected by weathering, and the best time to see and photograph them is early morning or late afternoon, when the low angle sun highlights the shallow engravings.

The petroglyphs are of two styles ; the finely pecked carvings through use of hammer and chisel type tools (constitute 97% of petroglyphs) and pounded impressions by using a stone directly on the rock surface. Over 5,900 individual engravings have been identified and are the equivalent of modern day libraries for the store of continuing spiritual and cultural messages they represent. A 1.5 km (about 1 hour return) marked walking track leads into the gorge containing these carvings as well as other art sites, shelters and spiritually significant places, of the Eastern Arrernte who call it Irlwentye (pronounced Eel-oon-ja).

The gorge is also an important site for several rare plants including the Peach-leafed Poison bush (Trema aspera) and Hayes Wattle (Accacia undoolyana).

The local geology is complex and has been described as an open book on earth's history. The curious rock formations and ancient rock petroglyphs combine to give an awesome sense of prehistory to the Ross River region.

Facilities
Facilities are basic and include wood BBQs, picnic tables and pit toilets. Camping is allowed (fees apply) but pets are not and you need to take in your own water.

ARLTUNGA HISTORICAL RESERVE
Arltunga is located 110kms (68 miles) east of Alice Springs and the Ross River Highway is sealed to the turnoff to the reserve. The Arltunga Road has a formed gravel surface that can get dusty and corrugated in places along its 36km (22.3 mile) length. With care, 2WD vehicles are okay.

  This reserve protects the scattered and rather eerie remains of an old gold-mining town that was one of Australia's most isolated and desolate. Within the reserve are the old Government Stamp Battery and Cyanide Works, Government offices and residences, police station and gaol. Old mines and miner's dwellings are scattered throughout the reserve, while two cemeteries and isolated graves are grim reminders of the hardships at the diggings. There have also been some major restoration projects including re-timbering of wells and reconstruction of the old police station.

History
In April 1887, Joseph Hele and Isaac Smith found alluvial gold in a dry watercourse downstream from the region's best natural waterhole, Paddys Rockhole, called Arltunga by the local Aboriginal people. But the 'ruby rush' at the nearby Hale River (Ruby Gap Nature Park area) was at its peak, and news of gold at Arltunga did not attract any immediate rush there. This was not surprising as the red stones were bringing $2.50 a carat (5 carats=1 gram) on the London market, until chemical tests on the 'rubies' proved them to be near worthless garnets. The ruby rush

collapsed. A few miners tried their luck at Arltunga, but hardships brought about by unreliable water supplies and periods of fierce droughts, deterred all but the hardiest and most desperate.

Although the field was not a particularly rich one, its spasmodic development, sometimes fired by the floating of short-lived mining companies, sustained a population of between 50-80 people for about 20 years. According to H. Brown, a South Australian Government geologist who visited the diggings in 1890, there were 12 men including a shopkeeper and a butcher, in residence at the shanty town beside the rockhole, and 15 diggers working only 5 of the 16 registered claims on the alluvial fields. Even though reef gold had been discovered at Mt Chapman, he found an equally bleak picture in these fields, too. After noting inadequate crushing and treatment equipment, and the band of dispirited diggers battling heat and flies for pitiful returns, Brown concluded that unless water supplies and equipment were improved, the field was doomed despite the good potential of the reefs. Consequently a 10 stamp battery and cyanidation plant for treating tailings was hauled 600km (372 miles) from Oodnadatta railhead and was in operation by 1898. It encouraged an influx of diggers at about the same time that Henry Luce discovered reef gold in the nearby White Range.

Between 1898 and 1916, the battery crushed 11,672 tons of ore-bearing rock, which produced 14,912 ounces of gold which today would be worth more than $6 million. Luce's mine was the richest in realising 2,556 ounces.

Conservation
Most of the old buildings are still largely intact. Deliberate acts of vandalism, such as removing door and window frames for firewood, and destroying stone walls to obtain gold that was falsely rumoured to be hidden there have however, considerably lessened the heritage value of some of the buildings. Graffiti inside buildings is a continuing problem. Visitors are asked to help

preservation by not pushing or climbing on stone walls, and by leaving historical artifacts where they lie.

Care needs to be taken when wandering through the reserve as there are many old mine shafts and wells. Young children should be well supervised.

Fossicking
Fossicking, metal detectors, or mining of any description is not permitted in the reserve. A Mines and Energy Department gold fossicking locality is located nearby.

Services and Facilities
Within the reserve, wood BBQs (please bring your own firewood as no fuel is available), picnic, toilet and water facilities are available (it's wise to bring additional supplies of water). Walking tracks and information sign-posts have also been provided. The Visitor Centre is open daily from 8am-5pm and houses a display of Arltunga's mining history incorporating artefacts and historical photographs. A 20 minute slide show outlining history and points of interest throughout the reserve can be viewed upon request when there is a Ranger at the centre. An outdoor display features domestic and mining equipment including a five head gold battery. Guided tours are available at certain times from May to October. There is wheelchair access, pets not allowed. For further details, ph (08) 8956 9770.

Just outside the park entrance is the Arltunga Bush Hotel. The pub is a corrugated iron and stone structure with a store selling basic supplies. Good value, nutritious farmhouse style meals are available (range from $5-$20) and includes roast dinners and BBQs.

Accommodation options include cabins from $35 to $55, camping $5 per person and swag hire. It's open daily, cash only, pets allowed, dogs leashed, ph (08) 8956 9797.

RUBY GAP NATURE PARK

Access to Ruby Gorge is via the Arltunga Historical Reserve, from where it is approximately 40kms (25 miles) to the park boundary. A 4WD high clearance vehicle is essential on this rough track. You must notify the Ranger at Arltunga of your intent to visit the reserve. From the park boundary, there is a 5km (3 mile) drive along the river bed and then a 2km walk to Glen Annie Gorge.

The park is characterised by a timeless, rugged beauty that surrounds a system of gorges and startling geological formations along the winding course of the Hale River. Ruby Gap is at the south-western entrance to the park, but the main Gorge, Glen Annie, is located about 7km (4 miles) further upstream.

History

It was here that explorer David Lindsay found some bright red gemstones in 1886. He named Glen Annie for his wife, rode off to break the news of his find, and started the 'ruby rush'. They came by camels, horses, or simply pushing hand-carts, and the area saw hundreds of diggers sifting through the river sands for rubies. Twenty-three companies were floated and the first gems to arrive in London were greeted with enthusiasm. However, when they arrived in increasing quantities, jewellers got jittery, and more detailed analysis revealed they were garnets. But some made money out of them and it certainly put Alice Springs on the map. Little remains at this desolate site today except for a lone grave, and garnets can still be found in the river sands north of the gap.

Geology

Of particular interest is the geological structure at Ruby Gap. About 350 million years ago, a huge slab of Heavitree quartzite was forced southwards, sheared and rose over existing layers of quartzite. A second slab or slice was then thrust over the first and these piggyback structures are called nappes. Each quartzite slice was topped with thin, tan-brown layers of limestone and siltstone, and being relatively flexible under pressure compared to other rocks, they have been contorted into many tight folds. Erosion has now cut through the nappes which can be seen as cliffs to the west and south of Hale River. This folded rock strata can be seen between Ruby Gap and Glen Annie Gorge. North of Glen Annie, the river bed widens where many fascinating river-worn stones can be found.

Facilities
There are some fine spots for camping along the river, but no facilities or water. The Hale River is susceptible to flash flooding after heavy rain - if it begins to rain heavily, get out fast. Do not enter the Hale River if the sand is soft and wet after recent rains. Always check conditions with Rangers at Arltunga before heading to this very isolated area. No animals are allowed.

ANNAS RESERVOIR CONSERVATION RESERVE

85ha (210 acres)

LOCATION
About 150km (93 miles) north-west of Alice Springs, 30km (19 miles) west of the Stuart Highway from the turn-off near Aileron.

CHARACTERISTICS
It features a natural rockhole, 10m wide and 2m deep, surrounded on three sides by rocky walls, reserved for its aesthetic and historic interest.

HISTORY
It was discovered in 1860 by explorer Stuart, who named it after the youngest daughter of his patron, James Chambers. On his return from his final and successful expedition to the northern

coast in 1862, Stuart rested here, seeking relief from the agony of scurvy. Alfred Giles saw the reservoir as an ideal watering place for sheep on their way to Springvale Homestead near Katherine. He even estimated that it contained enough water for two drinks each for 12,000 sheep. Giles achieved the remarkable feat of droving 12,000 sheep, broken into several mobs, across a 174km (108 miles) dry stretch between Alice Springs and here in 1878. It took 2 days to water the thirst-crazed creatures, and only 150 sheep were lost either by drowning in the reservoir or wandering off into the mulga scrub.

The waterhole also supplied construction gangs working on the Overland Telegraph Line, while in 1884 it was a homestead site for A.M. Woolridge's property. However, the rockhole was of importance to the Anmatjera people, and one night in 1886 they attacked the homestead with fire and sticks. The two occupants escaped, and Woolridge consequently moved his homestead to Barrow Creek. Today, little remains of the homestead except for the rock ruins of one building and walls of another.

The reserve is fenced, but damage by cattle has made it less than the idyllic spot that Stuart found, and the Conservation Commission is working on its restoration. There are no facilities, and visitors are asked to take out their litter. Camping is allowed. Animals are not allowed.

HOW TO GET THERE

Getting there is complicated and requires a good mud-map. It's on private property; you can easily get confused by the number of station tracks, and the last 200m is by walking. For advice, check with the Parks and Wildlife Commission.

ATITJERE (HARTS RANGE)

Population 120

LOCATION

On the Plenty Highway, 203km (126 miles) north-east of Alice Springs.

CHARACTERISTICS

This small, mainly Aboriginal township is situated on the northern flanks of Harts Range near the centre of one of the Territory's best mineral fossicking areas. In this model Aboriginal settlement there is a police station, school, the Atitjere Community shop (a small supermarket and general store), Council offices, registered airfield, and race course. While it is on Aboriginal land, no permits are required, but alcohol is not allowed.

The surrounding landscape is full of interest. The ranges are composed of rugged outcrops of strongly metamorphosed sediments and volcanic rocks with various intruded material. Many strangely shaped rock formations, and the interplay of light, provide plenty of subject variety for photographers. Vegetation includes mulga and witchetty bush on slopes and ridges; ironwood, whitewood and kerosene grasses on the flatter areas; tea-tree along the upper creek beds, and river red gums lower down. Keen fossickers will be pleased to know that spinifex is not widespread in the area and Zircon, magnetite, moonstone, garnet, muscovite, mica, blue quartz, beryl and apatite are just a random sample of what is here.

HISTORY

The area was the scene of much mining activity in the past, the remnants of which are mullock heaps (waste rock), scattered diggings, and the foundations of many stone-walled houses that used to shelter over 100 men and equipment. These structures are part of the Territory's mining heritage and should be left intact.

EVENTS

Picnic races are held during the first weekend in August, and everyone is welcome.

HOW TO GET THERE

By road, the first 102km (63 miles) of the Plenty Highway is sealed after which it is a reasonable gravel surface to Atitjere. It's suitable for conventional vehicles but check conditions first.

ACCOMMODATION

Spotted Tiger Camping ground has excellent facilities with wood BBQs at each site. Costs are $5 p.p. per day. It's located 3km past the racecourse.

SERVICES AND FACILITIES

Apart from those previously referred to, the store has a wide range of food and general store items, ice, limited take-away food, and sells gemstones. Fuel services include LP, ULP, diesel, oil and camping gas. *Opening hours are 9am-12noon, 3pm-5.30pm weekdays and Saturdays 9am-12noon.* It's cash only, ph (08)8956 9773. The community has an art and craft workshop, and artefacts and paintings are available from the store or workshop. For further information contact Atitjere Council (08) 8956 9787.

BOND SPRINGS OUTBACK RETREAT

Population 20

LOCATION

Approximately 16km (10 miles) north of Alice Springs.

CHARACTERISTICS

This privately-owned homestead is not only headquarters of the 1515 sq.km. (576 sq. miles) **Bond Springs Cattle Station**, but also the site of a characterful outback retreat in the surrounds of the scenic MacDonnell Ranges. Under the directions of Jan Heaslip, the retreat offers elegant accommodation for up to 12 discerning guests and a range of activity options from swimming and tennis to guided excursions including overnight and nocturnal safaris. Wildlife spotting, and the heritage attributes of the station's original buildings are further captivating features. Conveniently located close to Alice Springs, it not only provides accessible insights into Cattle Station life, but also gives you a 'break' from gaps, gorges and chasms.

HISTORY

The station was established in 1872 by Mr Bond, who, with his family, had a pretty torrid 12 month bullock cart trek from Adelaide. Their mulga slab house with wattle-and-daub is basically as it was when first built and is a rare example of an authentic settler's dwelling. Straight sticks cut from mulga, ironwood or witchetty bush were used for the walls and called 'wattles' - in fact, Australia's wattles got their name when these early settlers built wattle-and-daub huts using acacia saplings woven or 'wattled' together and daubed with wet clay.

  Other historic buildings include a saddlery and leather room, a 1930s two-roomed galvanised iron homestead and original school room and meat house. The present rambling homestead was built in 1940 by the Chisholm family from whom the Heaslips acquired the property in 1964. For a time, in the 1920s, Bond Springs was part of the Kidman Cattle Empire.

HOW TO GET THERE

For directions, please telephone Bond Springs (08) 8952 9888.

ACCOMMODATION

Corkwood Cottage is an immaculately appointed private cottage which features early Australiana decor. Rates are $240 per couple Bed and Breakfast, with a maximum of four persons.

The Homestead offers further finesse, *The Acacia* and *Witchetty Bush Suites* cost $200 per couple per night, including breakfast.

THE CATTLE KING

The late Sir Sidney Kidman was a pioneer and visionary cattleman who, during the early 1900s, acquired a vast network of sheep and cattle stations spanning Outback New South Wales, Queensland, South Australia, Northern Territory and Kimberley. He eventually controlled, or had interests in, more than 100 stations covering well over 161,000 sq km (100,000 sq miles) - an area larger than the UK. He made the Birdsville Track famous, and the sheer scope of his organisation earned him the title, 'The Cattle King'. Ion Idriess wrote a vivid, although romantic account of Kidman's life in his book of the same title. Kidman's entrepreneurial approach to cattle raising was matched only by James ('Hungry') Tyson, who preceded him, and his methods were a forerunner to such big meat company operations as Vesteys from the 1920s. At 13, Kidman ran away from home in Adelaide with only a tiny swag (bundle of belongings), a one-eyed horse called Cyclops, and 50c in his pocket. He headed north. This was during the 1870s; the last phase of exploration and when settlement began to push towards the vast unoccupied tracts of Central Australia, Top End and Kimberley. Through all manner of outback jobs and experiences, he became an expert bushman and a fine judge of horses and livestock. With his acute memory he retained the most intimate mental maps of the interior, and his later fortune was based upon this vast store of knowledge and astute droving.

It was his bold plan to get cattle in prime condition to the coastal New South Wales, Victorian and South Australian markets, and to the scattered mining settlements, that makes this man an extraordinary cattleman. His plan was remarkably simple: develop a system of stations through Central Australia that would enable the owner to buy stock cheaply from anywhere in the north, bring them down through the 'chain' (strategically located and owned stations) where they could rest, feed and water until they reached the railhead from where they were taken to Adelaide. In this way, droughts could be beaten, the stock would be in prime condition and premium prices obtained at market. 'Chains' were eventually established down along the three great rivers of Western Queensland, the Georgina, Diamantina and Cooper; across the north-west to the Kimberley; and down through the Centre, of which Bond Springs was a later link in the 1920s.

There were inevitable disasters, but Kidman's conception of the Outback as being divided into a number of 'paddocks' in which livestock were moved from one to another, was innovative and successful. R.M. Williams, who founded the well-known empire based on boots and bush clothing, said of Kidman *"... you have to remember he created his world, his empire in the horse and buggy days when there were no aeroplanes and no motor cars or trucks. He must have either ridden a horse or driven a buggy throughout the whole of Outback Australia"*. Kidman, along with Thomas Elder and others, also helped initiate the commercial use of camels, and his contribution to the pastoral development of Outback Australia is legendary.

Apart from the settlement aspects, there's some interesting natural history at Bond Springs, too. The property was under the flight path of a meteorite shower some thousands of years ago, and attained astro-geological prominence when a six gram stone meteorite was found. And the source of the Todd River that finally empties the water it infrequently carries into the Simpson Desert, is located on the station property.

Other meals can be provided.

The retreat offers a range of safari tour options and packages which include accommodation. For further details, telephone (08) 8952 9888.

CENTRAL MT STUART HISTORICAL RESERVE

0.3ha (0.74 acres)

LOCATION
On the Stuart Highway, 216km (134 miles) north of Alice Springs.

CHARACTERISTICS
Explorer John McDouall Stuart, along with companions William Kekwick and Benjamin Head, discovered the feature thought to be closest to the continent's geographical centre on April 22, 1860. His diary entry states: *"I find from my observations of the sun that I am now camped in the centre of Australia. I have marked a tree and planted the British flag. There is a high hill about two and a half miles to the north-west. I wish it had been in the centre, but on it tomorrow I shall raise a cone of stones and plant the flag, naming it Mount Sturt"*. Captain Charles Sturt was his old leader, explorer and friend. Stuart also buried some papers in a bottle, no more than names and dates, under the stones.

Subsequently an 'a' was added to the name, probably due to cartographic error, a fitting tribute anyway to the man whose expeditions established a route from south to north across the continent. The reserve and stone cairn alongside the highway commemorates their discovery, and the actual 'mountain' is about 12km (7 miles) to the north-west from here.

EXPLORER STUART

John McDouall Stuart, who was born in Scotland in 1815, was a member of Charles Sturt's expedition of 1844 which attempted to find the continent's heart, and had led minor expeditions west of Lake Eyre in search of grazing lands in 1858 and 1859. Surveyor and explorer, Stuart was fascinated by the mysterious interior, and it took three determined efforts to finally reach the Gulf. Turned back by hostile Aborigines and sickness at Attack Creek in 1860, and by harsh terrain and low supplies at Newcastle Waters the following year, Stuart's resolve to reach the north was successful in his final expedition, when the party struck the coast at Mary River mouth on July 24, 1862. But it was not without great personal cost. The epic pioneering success almost killed him; his eyesight impaired from taking solar observations rendered him blind in one eye, and such was his scurvy affliction and exhaustion, he had to be carried for much of the return journey. He never fully recovered, and died in London in 1866. Following his 1858 expedition, the Royal Geographical Society recognised this achievement by the presentation of a gold watch. For his subsequent efforts, the Society awarded him the Patrons' Medal, and only African explorer, Dr Livingstone before him had been twice honoured by this august body. Stuart had ridden over 16,000km (9,920 miles) in his relentless search for an overland route, and the 3025km (1875 miles) Stuart Transcontinental Highway between Adelaide and Darwin is a fine memorial to his indomitable spirit.

THE REAL CENTRE OF AUSTRALIA

Australia's precise mathematical centre of gravity has been calculated, and the point is on Lilla Creek Cattle Station, 335km (208 miles) east of Uluru, and 300km (186 miles) south of Central Mt Stuart and approximately 30kms (18 miles) west of Finke (refer to Finke for details of how to get there). The nearest settlement in its Simpson Desert location is Finke. The spot, located at a latitude 25 deg 36 min 36.4 sec south; longitude 134 deg 21 min 17.3 sec east, was determined by a team of three computer programmers, two Government surveyors and personnel from Queensland University Geographical Studies Department in 1988. They used the South Pole as a reference point, and marked off more than 22,000 points around the continent and criss-crossed the country with lines, taking into account such variables as the rugged coastline. This was a Bicentennial project of The Queensland Royal Geographical Society. The spot has been called the Lambert Centre, after Mr Bruce Lambert a noted surveyor and the first chairman of the National Mapping Council, and it's the precise point at which Australia can be divided into quarters.

CHAMBERS PILLAR HISTORICAL RESERVE

340ha (840 acres)

LOCATION
159km (99 miles) south of Alice Springs, via the Old Ghan or Old South Road.

CHARACTERISTICS
This reserve features a prominent column of red and yellow sandstone, which, including its 25m (82 ft) high pedestal, towers 58m (190 ft) above the surrounding plain. An eerie quality

pervades, and the names carved into the pillar's soft sandstone base by the explorers and early settlers, are a record of hardship and tenacity that gives it a genuine sense of history. The pillar was formed from sandstone sediments laid down under a shallow sea about 400 million years ago. Since then, wind, heat and rain have eroded away the weaker material, leaving this solitary column of pebbly sandstone.

Stuart discovered it in April, 1860, and simply described this giant pillar rising majestically from the scorched desert sands as a 'remarkable hill'. He named it after James Chambers, one of the expedition's sponsors. Stuart used the Pillar as a landmark on subsequent journeys, as did others such as Ernest Giles and John Ross, and it retained this function until the coming of the railway in the 1920s.

To the Aborigines, it has long featured in their belief as Itirkawara, the Gecko ancestor whose modern day descendants are the commonly seen knob-tailed geckoes.

The colour of the pillar is a pale cream-yellow except for the tip where oxidation of iron in the sandstone column has stained it a deep-red. Early mornings and late afternoons are best times for photography, when the pillar glows like a burning ember. It's a magic geological and historical place, and the only sad note is that a few visitors have added their names or graffiti to the sandstone. This action is not only illegal, it also lessens the historical significance of the reserve. Prosecutions have resulted in fines of over $5000!

HOW TO GET THERE

It takes about 4 hours on a flat bladed surface that is not recommended for trailers or caravans, even when towed by 4WD vehicles. It's 4WD from Maryvale Station. A number of tourists are causing inconvenience and annoyance to pastoralists on Maryvale, Idracowra and Horseshoe Bend Stations by using private roads to cut across to the Stuart Highway, rather than using the authorised access road through the station. Understandably, prosecutions may result if travellers ignore advice and show disrespect when crossing private property. Also these private station roads are infrequently maintained and are potentially dangerous.

The road to Maryvale Station is reasonable with sandy patches and plenty of dust. From the station, the first 12km (7 miles) is very dusty with bulldust patches; the next 23km (14 miles) slightly better, but care is needed at the washouts. At the 12km (7 miles) post, the road turns sharp left near a boundary fence and becomes rocky as it climbs to the top of a rise. Here the road divides - the right hand track is not all that distinguishable, so follow the other along the top of the rise (this section is very rough and requires extreme care during descent). The final 10km (6 miles) to the Pillar is over red sandhill terrain. If this is off-putting, there are plenty of tours to the Pillar from Alice Springs (a recommended one is *The Outback Experience*). For Stuart Highway entry, refer to the Maryvale Station listing. Please remember that the authorised track to the Pillar from Maryvale is also the only exit route.

SERVICES AND FACILITIES

Tables, pit toilets, information shelter, walking tracks, but no water. Camping allowed (honesty box for small fees), bring in own firewood and plenty of water (summer temperature often 50 degrees Celcius), and take out all rubbish. For further advice about route, contact Leigh Goldsmith (*The Outback Experience*), (08) 8953 2666.

CURTIN SPRINGS

Population 15

LOCATION

On the Lasseter Highway, 80km (50 miles) east of Yulara.

CHARACTERISTICS

There's plenty of character and hospitality at this working cattle property and roadside inn that offers travellers refuge from heat and highway in a comfortable cattle station setting. A pleasant brush-shaded area between the roadhouse and homestead has an interesting aviary, and even lush green grass; quite a contrast to the surrounding red sandhill, spinifex and desert oak country.

Peter and Ashley Severin not only opened the roadhouse in the late 1950s, but also the station homestead, where you can breakfast, lunch or dine with them. Ashley tells me they began tourist services here to help them through the drought years and only had six customers in their first year! Included within the boundaries of this 4162 sq km (1639 sq miles) station, is the Mt Conner monolith, as well as around 5000 Aberdeen Angus and Shorthorn cattle. Apart from sharing their table, you can also join tours of the station and Mt Conner (see also separate listing). After the hype of 'The Rock', this establishment offers a more down to earth outback experience that's a lot cheaper too!

HISTORY

Curtin Springs was founded in 1943 by Mr Andrews, when the vacant Mt Conner Crown lease (abandoned by Paddy De Connlley, whose homestead ruins can be seen near Mt Conner), was incorporated into the new title. The station takes its name from the nearby brackish springs and the Prime Minister of the day, John Curtin.

The Severins took over in 1956, managed to survive the drought years, built up the herds, and today are continuing their innovative approach to beef production by a breeding program of crossing Belgium Blue and Murray Grey with existing herd types. You can ask Ashley Severin what he calls his new bovine breed.

TOURS

Tours that include Mt Conner and Curtin Springs, with dinner and champagne at the homestead are operated daily by *Day Tours*, ph 08 8953 4664 for details (see also under *Mt Conner*).

ACCOMMODATION

Deluxe from $65 (single or double); Budget from $32 single, $42 double; Camping/Caravans - $10 per powered site; tent sites free; showers $1 p.p. Sites ungrassed, pets allowed, and dogs must be on a leash.

SERVICES AND FACILITIES

The roadside inn has a bar, general store, meals in the homestead (breakfast $10, lunch $14, dinner $22 for a 3 course meal), swimming pool (guests only), 1.2km airstrip, and showers for travellers ($2). Take-away food, ice, artifacts and souvenirs are available. Fuel includes LP, ULP, diesel, autogas, camping gas and oil. Basic spares, mechanical and tyre repairs, tyres and tubes, and towing services are offered.

Credit cards accepted; EFTPOS facility, opening hours 7am-10pm daily all year, ph (08) 8956 2906.

ERLDUNDA DESERT OAKS MOTEL

Population 30

LOCATION

On the corner of the Stuart and Lasseter Highways, 198km (123 miles) south of Alice Springs.

CHARACTERISTICS

Erldunda means lime or salty water, and the resort established here in 1980 is a combination of motel, hotel, roadhouse, tavern and caravan park. Its strategic location 95km (59 miles) from the South Australian border, and 258km (160 miles) from Ayers Rock Resort, makes it a convenient rest, refuelling or stop-over point. Surrounding the resort is the large 6705 sq km (2548 sq miles) *Erldunda Cattle Station* covering vast expanses of red sand and desert oak country. For those travelling to Uluru on the Lasseter Highway, a rest area 0.5km from the junction has an information bay that is worthwhile checking.

ACCOMMODATION

Motel - from $66 single, $75 double, $88 triple per night.
Budget - from $26 single, $36 double, $47 triple.

Camping/Caravans - powered sites $18 x 2, unpowered $14 x 2. Sites grassed and shaded. Pets allowed, dogs leashed.

SERVICES AND FACILITIES

The resort has tavern/bistro bar, dining room (fully licensed, approximately $20 for 3 course meal, bistro meals also); a shop selling groceries, takeaway food, ice, artifacts, souvenirs; picnic/BBQ/shaded area; swimming pool (non-guests $2.50); tennis court; telephone; and showers for travellers ($2.50). Fuel includes LP, ULP, diesel, LPG, oil and camping gas. Vehicle services available are: basic spares, tyres and tubes, tyre repairs only. Tourist information is available.

Open all year, opening hours 6.30am-10pm. Credit cards accepted, EFTPOS facility, ph (08) 8956 0984.

EWANINGA ROCK CARVINGS CONSERVATION RESERVE

6ha (15 acres)

LOCATION

36km (22 miles) south of Alice Springs on the Old South or Old Ghan Road.

CHARACTERISTICS

Set in red sand plain country beside a small claypan just west of the Ooraminna Ranges, this small reserve protects ancient intriguing rock carvings. Here, on outcrops of smoothed soft sandstone, are the art galleries, featuring a great variety of symbols and designs, including snakes, spirals and animal tracks.

Natural weathering has caused some damage and a cast of some of the carvings will at least be a record of the designs (the replica is on display in the Alice Springs Museum), and you can help preservation by not climbing on the galleries and remaining on the platform overlooking the main site.

There's plenty of wild life and plant life here, despite its arid surrounds. Two hundred species of plants, 100 bird types and thirty reptiles have been recorded. The claypan, when full of water, is irresistible to birds and larger animals such as red kangaroos, euros and dingoes.

The carvings are best photographed in the early morning or late afternoon when shadow effects highlight the shallow engravings more. Also, these times are more comfortable for viewing, particularly in summer.

HOW TO GET THERE

The Old South Road is flat bladed and has sandy patches and plenty of dust. With care, conventional vehicles are okay. South of Ewaninga, the road leads to Maryvale Station and Chambers Pillar, from where it is 4WD only.

SERVICES AND FACILITIES

Tables and a pit toilet have been installed at Ewaninga. Visitors are asked by the Parks and Wildlife Commission not to collect wood for fires from this area as this will upset plant and animal life. Information signs along the walking trail provide a guide to the carvings and Aboriginal use of the area. Camping is not permitted, and there is no water. Rangers patrol and maintain the reserve, and are most helpful with information and road advice.

FINKE

Population 300

LOCATION

On the fringe of the Simpson Desert, 150km (93 miles) east of Kulgera from the Stuart Highway on the Old Goyder Stock Route Road.

FINKE GORGE NATIONAL PARK

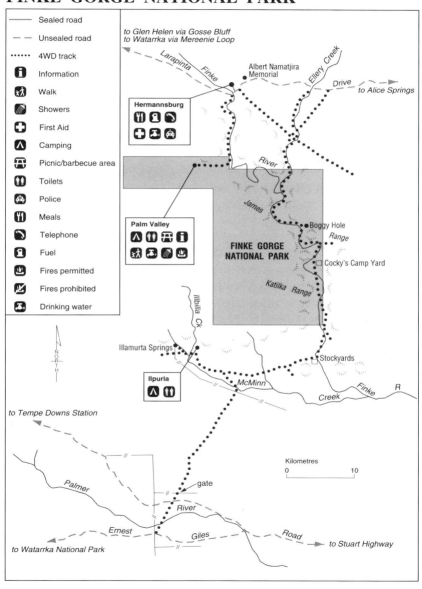

Legend:
- ——— Sealed road
- – – – Unsealed road
- ••••• 4WD track
- Information
- Walk
- Showers
- First Aid
- Camping
- Picnic/barbecue area
- Toilets
- Police
- Meals
- Telephone
- Fuel
- Fires permitted
- Fires prohibited
- Drinking water

NORTH

to Glen Helen via Gosse Bluff
to Watarrka via Mereenie Loop

Larapinta

Finke

Albert Namatjira Memorial

Ellery Creek

Drive

to Alice Springs

Hermannsburg

River

James

Boggy Hole

Range

FINKE GORGE NATIONAL PARK

Cocky's Camp Yard

Palm Valley

Katilka Range

Ilbilla Ck

Illamurta Springs

Ilpuria

McMinn

Creek

Stockyards

Finke R

to Tempe Downs Station

Kilometres
0   10

Palmer

gate

River

Ernest

Giles

Road

to Stuart Highway

to Watarrka National Park

CHARACTERISTICS

People of the Yankunytjatjara language group live in the town, governed by the Aputula Aboriginal Council. It is basically an Aboriginal settlement where tourists are welcome, and while no alcohol is allowed (it's a designated dry area by order of The Aboriginal Councils and Northern Territory Licensing Commission), permits to visit are not required. There's a general store, fuel services, garage, an art and craft centre, health clinic, police station, Council offices, school, and some old buildings associated with the town's earlier railway function.

While most Aboriginal settlements, for various reasons, remain closed to tourists, the Aputula Council has a positive attitude towards visitors and they are in the process of developing tourist facilities. Even for many white Australians, there is a similarity between being in an Aboriginal community and visiting a foreign country. Respect and sensitivity toward differences can be the basis for rewarding and genuine cross-cultural experience, and the area provides an ideal opportunity for this. Visitors are asked not to take photographs or use video cameras here without first asking permission. (Signs to this effect have been posted. Aborigines feel this is an invasion of their privacy, just as you would if some strangers poked a camera over your suburban fence and filmed your backyard BBQ party!)

HISTORY

The town was named after South Australian pastoralist William Finke, and developed as a railway settlement with the building of the line between Adelaide and Alice Springs. It was quite a flourishing township, and on a few occasions the pub's resources were exhausted when floodwaters stranded the Old Ghan train here. It hosted many a race meeting, and during one, the race was held up while Australian Inland Mission patrol padre, Arthur Cottrell, conducted a baptism. The proud parents persuaded him that it was the ideal spot as *"we're all here, you, us, the baby, and our friends!"*

The railway station, cranes and water tower are still there, while the pub has been renovated for the community's Art and Craft Centre.

An outlying feature is the Lambert Centre, the point at which the geographical centre of Australia is marked by a 5 metre flag pole which replicates the one on Parliament House in Canberra (see outline under *Central Mt Stuart*). You can leave your mark too by signing the visitors book. From a turnoff north from the Kulgera Road, approximately 15kms (9 miles) west of Finke, a sandy winding (4WD) track leads for approximately 12kms (7 miles) to the site. Directions are well sign-posted.

HOW TO GET THERE
From Kulgera, it is a formed gravel surface that's suitable for conventional vehicles, provided care is taken. Check road conditions at Kulgera.

SERVICES AND FACILITIES
The community store sells a wide range of food stuffs and has artifacts (from local artists). Vehicle services include fuel (LP, ULP, diesel) and full mechanical repairs. Opening times for the store are variable. For further information, telephone the Aputula Council (08) 8956 0966.

FINKE GORGE NATIONAL PARK
45,856ha (113,264 acres)

LOCATION
142km (88 miles) south-west of Alice Springs, via Larapinta Drive and Hermannsburg.

CHARACTERISTICS
Ancient palms, tranquil rock pools, and startling rock formations are the highlights of a visit to this national park that straddles the Fink River between the Krichauff and James Ranges. The park principally protects an amazing botanical oddity; the unique cabbage palms growing along Palm Creek, a tributary of the Finke.

Within this magnificent wilderness region, the variety of wind and water sculptured rock structures and prolific flora and fauna offer plenty of scope for naturalists, photographers and bushwalkers.

HISTORY

Explorer Ernest Giles came this way in 1872 on the first of his five expeditions into the Red Centre. He basically followed the Finke north-east from Chambers Pillar, and about 3km (2 miles) south of where Ellery Creek joins the Finke River, Giles found some cabbage palms, along with tall river gums, thin melaleucas, and a great variety of bird life. He named the grove, Glen of Palms. Here Giles collected many plant samples and from sketches, his patron for the expedition, Baron Von Meuller, a scientist and first Director of Melbourne's Botanic Gardens, identified the palms as Livistona mariae. It's clear that Giles did not explore Palm Creek or find Palm Valley. Stuart named the Finke River in 1861, after one of his benefactors, when he crossed it close to the present town of Finke.

The discovery of the greatest concentration of palms is attributed to three Lutheran Missionaries from the Hermannsburg Mission, Kempe, Schulze and Schwarz, in 1877. They explored the upper reaches of this Finke tributary and named it Palm Valley. The Horn Scientific Expedition to Central Australia, in 1894, spent some time here collecting samples and studying the environment, and few visited the region until Len Tuit and Jack Cotterill pioneered tourism in the area during the late 1950s. In fact, Tuit established a chalet near Palm Creek for the slowly developing touring industry at this time.

Apart from tourism, the discovery of sizeable reserves of natural gas and oil in the 1970s led to the establishment of the Palm Valley Gas Field. Its 9.2 billion cubic metres of recoverable gas is now being piped to Alice Springs and Darwin, via Tennant Creek and Katherine for domestic and power generation purposes.

Further west is the Mereenie Oil and Gas Deposits which have proven reserves of 38 million barrels of oil and 11 billion cubic metres of gas. Oil production began in 1984 and both fields are closed to visitors.

FLORA AND FAUNA

The park contains one of the most comprehensive collections of living central Australian plants, of which over 580 species have been identified with more than 30 classified as rare. After rains, wildflowers carpet the ground in a spectacular blaze of colour. Ghost gums, river red gums, melaleucas, cyprus pine and the palms provide a habitat for prolific birdlife, including pied butcher birds, black-faced cuckoo-shrike, western bower birds, Port Lincoln parrots and white-plumed honeyeaters. The central netted dragon, among other reptiles, is an interesting creature.

Cabbage palms have been growing here for millions of years and evolved at a time when the climate was more suited to these tropical plants. Their nearest relatives survive at Millstream on the Fortesque River in Western Australia and near Mataranka. These relics of the sub-tropical flora which flourished over Central Australia a million years ago require for their shallow root system, a stable soil structure free from scouring floods, and a permanent shallow water table. That they have survived climatic changes is due to the local geology where tiny fractures within the sandstone allow rainwater to seep gradually through to the solid base rock which prevents it from escaping. This seepage, despite lengthy drought periods, maintains a sufficient supply of moisture to the palms.

About 1200 individual palms in the Palm Valley area are of reproductive age, and the oldest trees have an age of between 100 and 300 years, based on their growth rate of 1m every 10 years. The tallest are about 26m. In Palm Valley, about 800 mature specimens grow in this narrow rocky valley along with cycads, river red gums and melaleucas.

Cycads (Macrozamia macdonnellii), like the cabbage palms, are relict plants, remnants of earlier geological time scale periods when higher rainfall occurred. But cycad are more akin to living fossils. They evolved 200 million years before the palms, at a time when dinosaurs roamed across a prehistoric Australian landscape. While palm-like, it does not belong to the palm family. It never flowers; instead it produces male and female cones. It is a slow growing plant with a thick, usually underground trunk, while its large greyish-green leaves, and sharply pointed leaflets crowd the stem top. The cycad usually grows at the base of cliffs where there is adequate shade and moisture. They are concentrated in Cycad Gorge and are in other parts of the MacDonnell Ranges.

Particularly after rain, crystal-clear rock pools remain in the valley and provide beautiful reflections of the long, narrow, red-cliffed walls. And the towering walls of Cycad Gorge are an impressive, colourful entrance to the oasis-like Palm Valley.

Kalarranga Walk is of great significance to the local Western Arrernte people and while Kalarranga is a highly important place to the Arrernte people, visitors are allowed to use the prominent rock within the valley as a vantage point, but are asked to respect and leave this sacred area unmarked. From this sacred rock site, there are excellent views of a natural amphitheatre. These unusual sandstone structures resulted from erosion of 400 million-year-old Hermannsburg formations, originally deposits of sand under a shallow sea that were welded together by great heat and pressure and subsequently uplifted. The surrounding rocks of this amphitheatre take on remarkable shapes, particularly at sunrise and sunset.

HOW TO GET THERE

From Hermannsburg, it's 4WD only along the Finke River bed. Tour operators in Alice Springs include the park in their tours.

SERVICES AND FACILITIES

Information is available at the entrance to Palm Creek. Shelters, tables, gas BBQs and toilets are available in the picnic area - please use them to assist in reducing the impact of visitors in the Palm Valley car park area. Camping fees - $5 p.p.p.n or $12 per family. Pets are not allowed in the Park. A large camping area features shower and toilet block (please use solar showers sparingly). It's an attractive area with plenty of shade.

GEMTREE CARAVAN PARK

Population 12

LOCATION

On the Plenty Highway, 70km (43 miles) from Stuart Highway turn-off, on a sealed road.

CHARACTERISTICS

A relatively new establishment in the Harts Range features natural bush camping sites amidst a rocky outcropped, mulga, ironwood and bloodwood covered landscape, where the main interest is gemstone fossicking (zircon, garnet, smoky quartz, moonstone are some). *Daily Fossicking Tours* (*cost $40 per set of equipment*) include experienced guides to accompany you to nearby gemfields where you will be shown how to find your own garnets and zircons. They also cut stones, have a fine gemstone display, and sell gemstones. Nearby attractions include exploration of the *Painted Canyon* rock pools (sometimes having water in them) and fossicking around old mica mines. Or, you can indulge in a round of golf on *Gemtree's 9 hole bush course* and on Saturday nights, play Paddy Melon bowls.

ACCOMMODATION

Camping: powered sites $16, 2 persons; unpowered $12, 2 persons; bush sites $6 per person; on-site vans $37, 2 persons; cabins $46, 2 persons. Pets allowed, dogs leashed.

SERVICES AND FACILITIES

Basic shop, food (pies, pasties, drinks), ice, souvenirs, local Aboriginal artifacts, fuel (LP, ULP, diesel), oil, camping gas and golf clubs for hire. *Opens daily 8am-6pm*, Credit cards accepted, EFTPOS facility, ph (08) 8956 9855.

HENBURY METEORITE CRATERS CONSERVATION RESERVE

16ha (40 acres)

LOCATION

On the northern slope of the Bacon Range, 145km (90 miles) south-west of Alice Springs.

CHARACTERISTICS

This reserve protects a series of at least 12 craters formed about 5000 years ago when a falling meteor shattered in the atmosphere, and its pieces struck the earth's surface. The craters range in diameter from 2 to 180m (588 ft), and up to 15m (49 ft) in depth; their distribution suggests that the meteorite shower came from the south-west. The meteorite's fiery path through the sky appears to have been witnessed by Aborigines, the clue being in the translation of one Aboriginal name for the area - *sun walk fire devil rock*.

Consisting of iron (90%) and nickel (8%), these high density meteorites weighed several tonnes and hit the surface at 40,000km/hr (25,000mph). The impact velocity caused 'explosive' craters; the immense energy released folded back strata of near-surface rock to form the crater rims, while fragments of nickel-iron alloy were dispersed shrapnel-like over a wide area. Over 500kg of metal has been recovered from the site, one fragment of which weighs in at 44kg, and can be seen in the Alice Springs Museum. It's suspected that a number too are used as door-stops in various places around Central Australia, but don't let that give you ideas; today, it's illegal to remove any specimens, if indeed they can be found.

The dry, rocky, crater-pitted plain resembles a small-scale moonscape that is of great scientific value. The United States National Aeronautic and Space Administration thought so, when personnel including astronauts used it for familiarisation purposes prior to and during manned moon missions.

Vegetation is sparse, except in the soaks created by the craters, there is little shade, and it gets very hot. Wildlife is migratory and includes red kangaroo, dingo, various reptiles such as bearded dragons, wedge-tailed eagles, spotted harriers and zebra finches.

HOW TO GET THERE

By road, access is from the Stuart Highway via the Ernest Giles Road (turnoff about 40kms; 25 miles, south of Stuarts Well), which is a formed gravel road that can get corrugated. The turnoff to the Craters is 11 kms from the Stuart Hwy - the 5km track to the reserve can be very corrugated. Exercise care with conventional vehicles.

SERVICES AND FACILITIES

Wood BBQs, picnic tables with shade shelters, and pit toilets, are provided at the entrance to the park. There is no water. It is a comfortable walk along a track (suitable for wheelchairs) that has detailed guide information about the craters. Please keep to the track, avoid unnecessary disturbance of the surface, and remember that these astro-geological features are unique. Camping is allowed and facilities are basic.

HERMANNSBURG

Population 600

LOCATION

On Larapinta Drive, 121km (75 miles) south-west of Alice Springs.

CHARACTERISTICS

An historic precinct of sun-scorched stone buildings set among palms and eucalypts on the Finke River plain bear testimony to the dedication of Lutheran pastors, who brought the gospel message, medical aid and European education to the Arrernte people over

114 years ago. Today, the Arrernte own the old Mission and, with the help of the National Trust, older buildings have been restored while others are retained for use by a thriving community. Hermannsburg maintains its strong links with the Lutheran Church through its Aboriginal and European pastors, whose role today is a spiritual one.

Buildings include the second church built in 1880, the Bethlehem Church, a smithy (built in 1882), a school-house, and old residences, two of which house a museum and tea rooms. A unique art gallery and works by local artists in a range of mediums adds further interest to Hermannsburg.

Although an Aboriginal settlement, visitors are welcome but a permit is required for an overnight stay. Most visitors use the settlement as a transit stop whilst on their way to Palm Valley. It has had a unique role in Territory history. Check with the Council Office or tea rooms as to what buildings you may visit, and be diplomatic with photography. There's an entry fee of $4 for admission to the precinct payable at the Kata-Anga Tea Room where a free cup of tea or coffee is included.

HISTORY

Original missionary Kemp said of the torrid 20 month journey from Bethany in South Australia in 1877 *"...that like the journey of St Paul to Rome, it was beset with all the privations imaginable"*. With missionary Schwarz, they led a party consisting of five lay workers, two Aboriginal stockmen, over 30 horses for the two large covered wagons, 2000 sheep (half of which died in the heat, and the long waterless stretches encountered), 20 cattle, 5 dogs and chickens.

The settlement, named after the Lutheran Training College at Hanover, was the first mission station in the Territory. It battled not only the harsh physical conditions, but also isolation, financial problems, sickness, apathetic governments, and constant opposition of vested interests among some pastoralists. The 1880s saw the beginnings of racial problems, with the arrival of the white pastoralists. Many settlers had little regard for Aboriginal needs or rights - in fact, in many instances Aborigines were regarded as a nuisance and primitive. Tensions and clashes between the races occurred. The drought of 1883 brought hostilities when Aborigines speared cattle for food. White reaction was swift; police stations were established, such as at Illamurta Springs (see separate listing), and Arrernte people were shot. Schwarz spoke publicly of Aboriginal treatment in 1886: *"In 10 years' time there will not be many Blacks left in this area, and this is just what the white man wants. With all the shooting that is taking place, it is hard to conceive that the native people have any kind of future, and our only hope is that they are rescued from this intolerable position"*. In later years, reserves were to be established, the first of which was at Haast Bluff in 1937, as a result of lobbying by Lutheran missionaries.

In the 1880s, about 100 Western Arrernte (at one stage the population was over 500) lived at the mission, and buildings consisted of a church, residences, shearing shed, wooden blacksmith's shop, and the second oldest remaining structure, 'the colonist's residence'. A vegetable garden and orchard, including date palms, were established. Under Pastor Carl Strehlow's leadership in the 1890s, the buildings that today constitute the historic core were constructed. A grammar and dictionary of Arrernte language was compiled in 1891 and such was the trust of the Arrernte people for Ted Strehlow (son of Carl who was born here and dedicated his life to study of these people) that they entrusted him with many items of spiritual significance at a time when their lifestyle and beliefs were threatened. These items are now held in the Strehlow Research Centre in Alice Springs, but cannot be viewed by the public.

Albert Namatjira

Albert Namatjira was born here in 1902, and with artist Rex Battarbee's encouragement, started to paint Central Australian landscapes, using European techniques combined with an Aboriginal eye for perspective and colour. His works achieved international recognition in a style of watercolour paintings that became known as The Hermannsburg School. Caught in a cultural cross-fire, Albert Namatjira died an unhappy man in 1952. A monument recognising his work is located on Larapinta Drive, about 2km east of Hermannsburg, and his grave may be seen in Alice Springs. The school blackboard was used in the 1940s to demonstrate drawing techniques to children. Pastor Albrecht was a powerful force behind the direction of the mission between 1926 and 1952.

Freehold title of the Hermannsburg lease was granted to the Arrernte in 1982.

ATTRACTIONS

The historic precinct with its tones of traditional Germanic farmhouse architecture in a timeless setting gives Hermannsburg unparalleled heritage status. The *Art Gallery* houses a unique permanent collection of original works by painters of the Hermannsburg Style including Albert Namatjira and his descendants. There's an *entry fee of $3* which includes a guided tour and outline of the life of Namatjira. It's highly recommended.

At the *Kata-Anga Tea Room*, the works of local artists may be purchased at very competitive prices. These include works of the Hermannsburg Lady Potters who have achieved international recognition for their style of pottery, paintings and hand-painted silk scarves.

The Kata-Anga Tea Room located in the former Mission Superintendent's residence is the best place for information and where the wonderful atmosphere is more than complemented by the quality and variety of the reasonably priced home made food. It's *open daily 9am-4pm March to Nov.; 10am-4pm other months*, telephone (08) 8956 7402.

HOW TO GET THERE

The road (Larapinta Drive) is sealed to Hermannsburg. There are plenty of tours from Alice Springs (see *Alice Springs* listing).

SERVICES AND FACILITIES

There are two supermarkets, tea room and fuel (LP, diesel, ULP and camping gas) and full mechanical repairs at the garage. The settlement has a police station, Council Offices, health clinic, school and church (Lutheran). The Kata-Anga Tea Room has facilities for disabled visitors and the historic precinct has wheelchair access.

As yet, EFTPOS is not available and only some credit cards are accepted. You are not allowed near the Aboriginal residential area, and photographing Aborigines strictly requires permission.

ILLAMURTA SPRINGS CONSERVATION RESERVE

130ha (320 acres)

LOCATION

Approximately 192km (119 miles) south-west of Alice Springs, via Stuart Highway and Ernest Giles Road.

CHARACTERISTICS

The reserve protects the permanent waters of *Illamurta Springs*, which was an important water source for cattle in this dry, sandy area. To prevent further environmental damage to this verdant oasis, cattle have been fenced out. The Spring is situated in the bed of a small Illbilla Creek tributary, at the foot of the James Range, and the ruins of a lonely police outpost, established here in 1891 in an attempt to reduce cattle killing by local Aborigines, is the only sign of man's intrusion. Thick scrub surrounds the old station and stockyards, which are rapidly decaying. It is a picturesque, quiet spot, where a range of wildlife can be observed at the now clear waters. The site is important to the Western Arrernte people. Access is via the Stuart Highway and Ernest Giles Road, or from

Palm Valley via the Finke River 4WD route (see outline under *Territory Drives, Trails and 4WD Tracks* in Part One). There are no facilities. No animals or fires are allowed, and camping is not permitted. However, you may swim in the pool. Camping facilities are available at the nearby **Ilpurla Aboriginal Community**.

JERVOIS STATION

Population under 10

LOCATION
On the Plenty Highway, approximately 335km (208 miles) north-east of Alice Springs.

CHARACTERISTICS
In addition to looking after about 8000 Polled Hereford cattle on their 5000 sq km (2000 sq miles) station property, Michael and Denise Broad offer some basic transit services to travellers going to, or coming from, Queensland.

Of interest on the property is an air raid shelter, built during the 1960s for protection against rockets being test-fired from the Woomera Range in South Australia. Jervois and other stations were under the test flight path, and before they pressed the button at Woomera, controllers would telephone the stations to let owners know that another rocket was on its way. In case the rockets fell short of their targets, the shelters were provided. Some fragments did fall on local stations!

HOW TO GET THERE
From Harts Range, it is a formed road surface, and beyond here 4WD is recommended. There are two river crossings just before the turn-off to the station.

ACCOMMODATION

You can camp at the ***Rest Area***, nearly opposite the Jervois turn-off, on the Plenty Highway. Facilities here include fireplace, table, shelter and water.

SERVICES AND FACILITIES

The station has a small shop selling basic items, ice, artifacts and souvenirs. LP, ULP and diesel, oil, and minor repairs are vehicle services available. There's no accommodation or camping, but you can have showers ($2). Credit cards accepted, EFTPOS facility, open during daylight hours, ph (08) 8956 6307.

KALTUKATJARA (DOCKER RIVER)

Population approximately 320

LOCATION

In the Petermann Ranges on the Northern Territory/Western Australian border, 227km (141 miles) west of Yulara.

CHARACTERISTICS

The *Kaltukatjara Community Council* administers this small Pitjantjatjara settlement which consists of a general store, council offices, health clinic and school among its main buildings. Visitors are welcome to use services provided by the store and are requested to observe and adhere to signs posted in the tiny township. While no permit is required for travellers, it's advisable to check with the Central Lands Council or Tourist authorities in Alice Springs. Alcohol is prohibited.

The road through Pitjantjatjara lands leads to an abandoned section of the Gunbarrel Highway and the Warburton turn-off, about 80km (50 miles) west of the border at Giles (see map advice, *Information Sources*, in Part One for map recommendations). Travellers crossing the border into Western Australia must have necessary permits.

HISTORY

Of interest, 41km (25 miles) east of Kaltukatjara is *Lasseter's Cave* and memorial plaque. Lewis Hubert Lasseter, better known as Harold Bell Lasseter was the central figure in one of the Territory's most intriguing mysteries - the legend of Lasseter's lost gold reef. His claim to have found a rich gold-bearing reef in central Australia was so convincing that the Central Australian Gold Exploration Company (CAGE) was formed in 1930 to find it. The expedition headed westwards from Alice Springs in July, 1930, and Lasseter was included in the party led by Fred Blakeley. Distrust of Lasseter's story by Blakeley, confusion and arguments over locations (Lasseter claimed their position in the Ehrenberg Range, about 150km [93 miles] due west of Haasts Bluff was nearly 200km [124 miles] too far north), and aerial reconnaissance halted by a plane crash, was enough for CAGE to order their return to Alice Springs. The fortuitous arrival of Paul Johns, a dingo trapper with a camel team, prompted Lasseter to engage him and together they struck out for the Petermann Range. But luck ran out soon after for Lasseter. Johns left him after a fight, his camels bolted away, and his supplies were almost depleted. Despite some help from Aborigines, he eventually made his way to Winters Glen where, in an emaciated and pitiful state, he lived for some weeks before his lonely death. His body was later found by Bob Buck who buried him at nearby Irving Creek. In 1957, the grave was reopened and the remains taken to Alice Springs and buried at the cemetery.

  In his last letter found in his diary, Lasseter claimed to his wife that he had found the reef again. Since his death, many have tried in vain to find it, and the legend is either supported or refuted in some books that make interesting reading: *Hell's Airport* by Cootes, *Lasseter's Last Ride* by Idriess, and more recently, Stapleton's *Lasseter Did Not Lie*. In 1981, *The Melbourne Sun* (February 11, 1981) reported that two men had sighted a lengthy metre-high gold quartz blowout reef to the north of the Petermann Range. Yet another expedition in July, 1988, reported finding 'oceans' of quartz and four buried items specifically referred to in Lasseter's diaries. Over 30 people have died in previous expeditions, something that Lasseter's fabled reef refuses to do!

HOW TO GET THERE

It's a flat bladed road, suitable for conventional vehicles driven with care. Check road conditions before leaving. The road by-passes Kaltukatjara. Take the turn-off to the settlement for the store and fuel.

Lasseter's cave and plaque are near the settlement.

SERVICES AND FACILITIES

There's a well stocked general store which also offers meals and snack food and fuel (ULP, diesel and Avgas). Opening times are variable and it's cash only, ph. (08) 8956 7373.

Camping is only permitted at *Lasseter's Cave* where there are no facilities except drinking water. It is advisable to notify the Council Office if you intend to camp, ph. (08) 8956 7337. Only emergency mechanical repairs can be effected in the township.

KINGS CREEK STATION

Population 9

LOCATION

On Luritja Road 30km (19 miles) east of Wataarka National Park.

CHARACTERISTICS

Apart from managing the camel and cattle side of things on this 2000 sq km (1240 sq miles) property, Ian Conway has developed a tourist enterprise that is conveniently located close to the magnificent Wataarka National Park. It features a camping ground with grassed, small, individual sites, separated by natural vegetation that is the next best thing to bush-camping.

Kings Creek Station was the first camel property of its type in Australia and now runs over 200 of these ruminants. Here they are bred for the live, world-wide export market and for their meat, which is on the menu is some Alice Springs restaurants. The property's innovative camel farming program has attracted much interest including the capture and "domestication" of wild desert camels.

ATTRACTIONS
Working camel and cattle station. Camel rides, helicopter flights and station tours (by prior arrangement) are the main attractions offered, and is a good base to explore the nearby *Wataarka National Park* (see separate listing).

HOW TO GET THERE
For access and road conditions, see *Wataarka* listing.

ACCOMMODATION
Serviced safari cabins including bed and breakfast, $32 per person. Camping costs are $8 adult; children $4.50, and sites are powered, grassed and shaded. Pets allowed, dogs must be leashed.

SERVICES AND FACILITIES
The station is expanding its facilities. It has a well stocked shop including Aboriginal artefacts, Camel leather products, souvenirs and ice, a bar, bough shed where BBQ meals and damper are available, take-away food, picnic/BBQ/shaded areas, disabled facilities, showers for travellers ($3.50) and swimming pool. Fuel includes LP, ULP, diesel, oil and camping gas. Vehicle services available are basic spares, minor mechanical repairs and tyre repairs. There's a 2.2km airstrip.

Opening hours as required daily, credit cards accepted, EFTPOS facility, ph (08) 8956 7474.

KULGERA

Population 21

LOCATION

On the Stuart Highway, 20km (12 miles) north of the Northern Territory/South Australian Border.

CHARACTERISTICS

Surrounded by the 1370 sq km (521 sq miles) Kulgera Cattle Station and an arid landscape of mulga plains with rocky outcrops, this small settlement consists of a hotel/motel caravan park complex, and a police station.

The hotel is either the first or the last in the Territory (depending on which way you are travelling), and its comfortable, friendly atmosphere gives a great introduction to the Territory, or vivid memories of it as you leave. For those entering the Territory, it is a worthwhile orientation and information spot, as well as being the gateway to the Dalhousie Springs area in South Australia. Explorer Highway information boards and Dalhousie Springs and Simpson Desert information boards have been established here. Since the recent discovery of the real geographic centre of Australia near Finke, the pub can now claim to be the most central in the continent.

EVENTS

The showground is the venue for the annual *gymkhana* held during the last weekend in September. Everyone is welcome, and evening barbecues and bush dances provide plenty of lively entertainment.

ACCOMMODATION

Hotel/Motel with self-contained units - $56 a double. Backpackers $10 p.p.

Camping/Caravans - powered sites $15 x 2; unpowered sites - $5 p.p. Sites are grassed, with some shade. Pets allowed, but must be under control.

SERVICES AND FACILITIES

The hotel has a shop, a bar, restaurant, picnic/BBQ/shaded areas, showers for travellers, and sells take-away food, ice, souvenirs and artifacts (locally produced and excellent value for money). A 1.3km airstrip is nearby, and the police station provides road condition information. An Information Bay near the hotel gives further detailed tourist advice.

Fuel includes LP, ULP, diesel, autogas, camping gas and aviation (by prior arrangement). Oil, basic spares, minor mechanical repairs, tyres and tubes, and towing service are vehicle services available.

Open daily 6am-11.30pm, credit cards accepted, EFTPOS facility, telephone (08)8956 0973.

MAC CLARK CONSERVATION RESERVE

LOCATION

In the Simpson Desert, 298km (185 miles) south-east of Alice Springs, via the Old Andado Track.

CHARACTERISTICS

It is an area set aside to preserve a rare occurrence of Acacia peuce, of which there are only two other known locations in the world - both in Queensland, near Birdsville and Boulia. At this Andado bore location, they are known as casuarina, while in Birdsville they are called waddywood. It resembles a she-oak in shape and foliage, but whereas the she-oak bears cones or 'apples' the peuce has seed pods, hence its acacia classification.

Acacias, more commonly known as wattles, generally live for about 20 years. Exceptions are mulga, blackwood and cedar wattle, which live to about 100 years, while peuce is thought to be over 500-years-old! They grow to heights of 17 metres. About 1000 mature trees are protected within the reserve with the major stands fenced to prevent interference by animals. An on-going research program includes assessing regeneration and growth rates, so it is important not to interfere with stakes and tree bands.

The reserve honours the late Mac Clark, who owned the surrounding Andado Station for many years. There are no facilities at the reserve, but you may walk through the fenced areas to appreciate these rare desert giants.

ACCESS
From Alice Springs, the reserve can be reached via the Old Andado Track or from Kulgera. 4WD recommended (see also *Old Andado Station* for road conditions).

MARYVALE STATION (TITJIKALA)

Population 120

LOCATION
On the Old Ghan or South Road, 115km (71 miles) south of Alice Springs and 44km (27 miles) from Chambers Pillar.

CHARACTERISTICS
A 3180 sq km (1208 sq miles) cattle station that now provides basic services to travellers, because of its location on the increasingly popular route to Chambers Pillar. It's run by Heather and Sam Goldsworthy, who don't mind caravans or trailers being temporarily left here, but they don't take any responsibility for their safety. About 115 Aboriginal people live on the property, and some of their artifacts can be purchased at the store. Camping is allowed for a small fee but there are no shower facilities.

HOW TO GET THERE

From Alice Springs, refer to *Chambers Pillar* listing for road description, and please keep to authorised private station roads only, which are signposted.

From the Stuart Highway, 9km south of Stuarts Well, a flat bladed (Old Hugh River Stock Route), public road runs east to Maryvale. It's sometimes graded with rough patches (Hugh River crossing). The distance is 94km (58 miles), 4WD recommended. Check conditions with Police or Roads Department.

SERVICES AND FACILITIES

There's a shop selling basic items, including snack type foods, pies, cold drinks and morning and afternoon teas and coffee. LP, ULP and diesel fuel are available, but there are no repairs or other vehicle services. Toilets and water are available.

Credit cards accepted, EFTPOS facility, *open daily 8.30am - 5.00pm*, ph (08) 8956 0989.

MT CONNER

LOCATION

Approximately 20km (12 miles) south-east of the Lasseter Highway at Curtin Springs.

CHARACTERISTICS

This flat-topped monolith rises 330m (1100 ft) from the plain, and was named after M.L. Conner, a South Australian Parliamentarian, by explorer William Gosse who discovered it in 1873. It is the eastern-most of the 'Three Great Tors' (residual prominent rock mass - mesa is a more accurate term to describe Mt Conner, as it is an isolated tableland area with steep sides). Unlike Uluru, Mt Conner has horizontal rather than near vertical strata, and the summit is flatter. Structurally, it is a mass of quartzite nearly 3.5km (2 miles) long and up to 1km wide, with much of its

surrounds boulder strewn at the base from which vertical rock faces rise sharply. Some softer layers have worn away, creating deeply honeycombed faces and cave-like rock shelters. The precipices glow red when lit by the mellow sun, providing another unforgettable desert image.

As to its geological formation, there are several theories. One suggests that the monolith is the remnant of a former land surface in which marine fossils are evidence that it was once the floor of an inland sea. A contrasting view is that Mt Conner comprises nearly horizontal beds of sandstone which was originally deposited by the meltwater of a glacier. Even more interesting is a recent notion that it has meteorite impact origins. It is thought that Mt Conner is around 700 million years old. To Aboriginal people, Mt Conner is known as Attilla.

There is plenty of interesting flora and fauna. Native pine and fig, corkwood, mulga, saltbush and spinifex soften the harsh red colours. On the summit, spinifex mainly grows. Wildlife in the surrounding area includes large goannas, euros, dingoes, camels, emus, grass-wrens, and rare peregrine falcons.

Mt Conner is situated on *Curtin Springs Cattle Station*, owned by the Severin family, who regretfully found it necessary to close public access because of constant damage to fences and bores. However, in conjunction with *Day Tours*, the station offers a range of activities such as sightseeing (ruins of Paddy De Connelley's homestead), and summit climb for Uluru-Kata Tjuta views, as well as a more distant vista of the Petermann and Musgrave Ranges. Contact Day Tours for details and bookings, ph (08) 8953 4664.

> On the Lasseter Highway, the Mt Conner Lookout and rest area is a pleasant 'cuppa' stop. Facilities include fireplace, tables, shade and water.

MT EBENEZER

Population 20

LOCATION
Approximately half-way between Alice Springs and Yulara; 188km (116 miles) east of Yulara on the Lasseter Highway.

CHARACTERISTICS
The original part of this roadhouse is built out of hand-cut desert oak, which contributes to its unpretentious exterior and inviting, comfortable atmosphere inside. It is managed by Barry and Cheryl Ganley for the owners, the Imanpa Aboriginal Community who have their settlement nearby. Apart from providing services to travellers, a positive feature is Aboriginal participation in the enterprise, which has a training emphasis for Imanpa people as well as a focus on their artifacts and paintings. Visitors are asked not to photograph Imanpa people.

The roadhouse also specialises in home-style cooking; the pies (kangaroo, beef and chicken) and pastries that they make are superb. In the distance opposite, the Basedow Range and Mt Ebenezer can be seen across the shimmering red sand landscape. And the meaning of Imanpa has a ring of optimism - 'land of hope'.

ACCOMMODATION

Motel style - rooms for approximately $50.
Camping/Caravans - $5 per person. Pets allowed, dogs leashed. Extra charge for powered sites.

SERVICES AND FACILITIES

The roadhouse has a bar; licensed restaurant (all meals are available and notable for their homestyle quality and reasonable price); gift shop and an impressive range of locally produced artifacts and paintings - excellent value. They are displayed in a rustic, rambling art gallery. Showers for travellers ($2) and ice. Vehicle services (LP, ULP, diesel and oil) are available. It's *open daily 7.00am-8.00pm*, credit cards accepted, ph (08) 8956 2904.

NEW CROWN STATION

LOCATION

On the fringe of the Simpson Desert, approximately 185km (115 miles) east of Stuart Highway at Kulgera and approximately 30 km (19 miles) east of Finke.

CHARACTERISTICS

Francis Smith runs this large 7720 sq km (2980 sq miles) cattle property, and frequent requests for fuel resulted in the station providing this basic service for travellers. Diesel and limited ULP supplies are the only services available during reasonable daytime hours. It is cash only, ph (08) 8956 0969.

HOW TO GET THERE

For road conditions, refer to the *Andado* listing.

OAK VALLEY

Population 28

LOCATION

On the Old Hugh River Stock Route, 60kms (37 miles) east of Stuart Well (on the Stuart Hwy) and approximately 40 kms (25 miles) north of Maryvale Station.

CHARACTERISTICS

Oak Valley is situated in the isolated and rugged beauty of the James Ranges, about 100 kms (62 miles) south of Alice Springs by road. In its north-western tip of the Simpson Desert location, it has sand dune, mulga plains and desert oak landscape surrounds, and is a beautiful spot to experience the ever-changing faces of the desert.

The enterprise is Aboriginal owned and operated by the Southern Arunta people and directed by Robert and Mary Lerossigna (the first French/Aboriginal tourist operator in Central Australia). It offers a range of excellent tours which include Aboriginal art, culture and lifestyle; natural and European history, and excursions to marine fossil fields. A *two hour Aboriginal tour costs $15 p.p.* Other special interest tours include wildlife and photographic.

HOW TO GET THERE

By organised tour from Alice Springs - Oak Valley Tours. By road, it's a flat-bladed, sandy track which can be negotiated with care by conventional vehicles but 4WD is recommended. Check road conditions first (see also under *Maryvale Station*).

SERVICES AND FACILITIES

It has a good camping ground (no powered sites), $6 p.p. Sites have shade shelters, wood BBQs (wood supplied), pets allowed, dogs leashed. On-site swags are also offered at $10 each.

It has a small shop selling basics. It's *open daily*, credit cards accepted, telephone (08) 8956 0959.

OLD ANDADO STATION

Population 1

LOCATION

In the Simpson Desert, 330km (205 miles) south-east of Alice Springs, via the Old Andado Stock Route Road.

CHARACTERISTICS

Historic Andado Station features the original homestead buildings of the huge 10,857 sq km (4126 sq miles) cattle property set amongst giant sand dunes of the Simpson Desert. Built out of timber and corrugated iron by the first lessee, Mr Robert MacDill in 1922, visitors can now enjoy its atmosphere in the red desert environment. 18km (11 miles) away is the current Andado Homestead, where by arrangement you can see the working side of things on a cattle station, but only if there are activities like a muster, branding or camp draft - check with Molly Clark who runs the Old Andado Homestead. Molly and her husband, Mac, used to own the whole station, and if you want to learn something about remote station life, Molly's a mine of information and is one of those often unsung characters who epitomises the indomitable spirit of Outback women in such remote, arid regions of the Territory. Her husband was tragically killed in an air crash in 1978, and the *Mac Clark Conservation Reserve* nearby is named in his honour. (See separate listing for this reserve.)

The drive to the station, via the Old Andado Stock Route, offers a stunning experience of endless stretches of the Simpson Desert, named after the President of the South Australian Royal Geographical Society by Dr Madigan, whose flights over the area in 1929 were financed by the Society. The Simpson Desert extends much of its 48,282 sq km (18,347 sq miles) into this corner of the Territory, and has Sahara-like ridges of rich red sand that are virtually straight, parallel and continuous for nearly 150km (93 miles). Wave-like, they roll north-west/south-east trending from horizon to horizon, often exceeding 30m in height and forming the world's longest parallel dune systems.

From Old Andado, worthwhile travel options include the Simpson Desert Loop Track, a magnificent scenic route that heads south to Mt Dare Homestead in South Australia (excellent facilities) and sweeps north west to New Crown Station and north from Finke on the Old South Road to Alice Springs (see details in the section on *Territory 4WD Tracks* in Part One, including map recommendations).

HISTORY

There was much truth in the old saying *"no wise man fools with the Simpson"*. Many people have died of dehydration, and it's thought that explorer Ludwig Leichhardt perished in its formidable sands, too. To cattleman Edmund Colson, it was a challenge. Convinced that after good rains, fresh water would lie in the claypans and grass would sprout between the ridges, he set out in May 1936, after some heavy rains had fallen, with an Aboriginal companion and five camels; two for riding and three for food and water. With temperatures over 45C by day, and below freezing point at night, the 55-year-old arrived in fine fettle at Birdsville after just 16 days and 321km (199 miles). He had conquered the unconquerable, and to dispel any doubts about his feat and satisfied that he had proved his theory, he returned by the same route. However, his crossing was the first southern crossing in the vicinity of the 26th Parallel (Northern Territory's southern border follows this line of latitude). David Lindsay attempted one of the earliest crossings in the same year he found 'rubies' at Ruby Gap, in 1885. It was Madigan's 1939 expedition that made the first crossing north of the 26th Parallel, and the story is well told in his book *Crossing the Dead Heart*. However, there were many undocumented crossings of the Simpson Desert.

HOW TO GET THERE

There are three possible routes:

(1) Via the Old Andado Stock Route south-east from Alice Springs past Santa Teresa Aboriginal Community and Allambi Station (no services at both), is a formed and flat bladed road. It's regularly graded over its 320 km (198 miles) distance. At approximately 300km from Alice Springs is the turnoff to Mac Clarke Conservation Reserve.
(2) Via the Old South Road (the road to Chambers Pillars and Maryvale Station). It is approximately 310 kms (192 miles) and a more southerly route from Alice Springs, with a formed surface almost to Maryvale Station, after which it is flat bladed (see further details in *Territory 4WD Tracks* in Part One).
(3) From Kulgera on the Stuart Highway via Finke, it is 185kms (115 miles) of formed road surface to New Crown Station and then approximately 60kms (37 miles) of flat bladed road to Old Andado.

While these routes are 4WD recommended, conventional vehicles, with care, can be used, but always check road conditions first.

ACCOMMODATION
Bunkhouse - $20 single, $37 Dinner B&B; Camping is $7 per person. There are some shade shelters, pets allowed, dogs must be leashed.

SERVICES AND FACILITIES
Toilets and showers, station type meals for guests booked in only and an airfield. No fuel services. Cash only, and it's essential that you phone well before arrival, (08) 8956 0812.

RAINBOW VALLEY CONSERVATION PARK

2483ha (6133 acres)

LOCATION

97km (61 miles) south of Alice Springs, by road via the Stuart Highway.

CHARACTERISTICS

The major feature of this reserve is a valley with free-standing sandstone ridges and bluffs, that effuse rainbow-like bands of colour when touched by the early morning and late evening sunlight. The valley forms part of the James Range, where the north-west surrounding area is characterised by spinifex-clothed sandplains with a system of interconnecting claypans that enhance the landscape when filled with water. In the southern parts of the reserve, dissected sandstone hills and ridges add further interest with Aboriginal petroglyphs (rock engravings) and ochre paintings that dot the area. Desert oaks, ironwoods and, after the rains, wildflowers have a softening effect.

It is a delightful area that offers plenty of fascination for walkers, photographers, and for those who wish to enjoy some wilderness beauty and tranquillity.

GEOLOGY

The fine-grained quartzite layers have been inclined from their original horizontal beds, and millions of years of weathering and erosion have shaped the valley outline, rock faces and towers.

The varied colours are the result of water permeating through tiny pores in the sandstone and mixing with a range of iron oxides during earlier geological time scale periods, when rainfall was much higher. The dissolved oxides were drawn to the surface by the sun's heat, and effectively stained the surface layers, while iron deficient layers below were bleached a creamy-white. The dark red iron oxides, once percolated to the surface, formed a hard crust that is more erosion resistant, while the white sandstone below crumbles easily.

CONSERVATION

This is a particularly fragile area, which has been damaged by thoughtless drivers. Please stay on the access track. No fires are permitted outside barbecues provided, and extinguish fires before leaving.

Bring your own firewood (wood is scarce in the reserve and it is an offence, as in all reserves and parks, to remove or damage plants in any way). Pets are not allowed, take all your rubbish with you, and deeply bury all toilet waste.

HOW TO GET THERE

The turn-off to the reserve is 14km (9 miles) north of Stuarts Well on the Stuart Highway, where a flat bladed 22km (14 mile) track, with some deep sandy patches, takes you to the valley. It is 4WD recommended and vehicles are required to remain on this track and in the parking area only. The reserve is accessible year-round, with the cooler months being the most pleasant times to visit. *The Outback Experience* run 4WD day trips to Rainbow Valley and Chambers Pillar from Alice Springs, ph (08) 8953 2666. See also *Camel Outback Safaris* in *Stuarts Well* listing.

SERVICES AND FACILITIES

Facilities include wood BBQs, picnic area, pit toilets and camping area (fees apply). There is no drinking water.

RYAN WELL HISTORICAL RESERVE

2ha (5 acres)

LOCATION

Approximately 120km (75 miles) north of Alice Springs, on the Stuart Highway.

CHARACTERISTICS

Sunk by Mr Ryan in 1889, the well was one of several the South Australian Government sank along the track that followed the Overland Telegraph Line, to encourage settlement through what was then its Northern Territory. In 1914, the Glen Maggie sheep and cattle station was established around the Well, and the owner, Sam Nicker, charged a small fee for its use by drovers. The ruins of the homestead which replaced the family's original mud and wattle dwelling in 1918, are reminders of these tough pioneering days. The homestead also functioned as a telegraph office and store from 1921. Despite the station being sold and incorporated into the Aileron property in 1929, the store kept going until this building was finally abandoned in 1935. There are no facilities at the reserve.

Native Gap Conservation Reserve (11ha-27acres)is a scenic stopping place on the Stuart Highway, a few kilometres south of Ryans Well where travellers can appreciate a shady picnic area and Centralian scenery. It marks a gap in the Hann Range and has significance for Aboriginal People. Facilities include picnic, toilet and disabled amenities. Camping is allowed.

STUARTS WELL - ALICE SPRINGS CAMEL OUTBACK SAFARI

LOCATION

On the Stuart Highway, 90km (56 miles) south of Alice Springs.

CHARACTERISTICS

This man-made 'oasis' in the desert is where Noel Fullerton and his family keep their herd of 70 camels that provide the backbone for a range of Outback treks lasting up to two weeks. The *Camel Outback Safari* has been operating from this site for many years. It offers visitors the option of camel rides of varying duration, a place to picnic or merely to browse inside the large corrugated iron barn that has a shop, photograph-lined walls and roof, memorabilia of the past, and some interesting Aboriginal artifacts. In addition to safari work, the property has the only very selective camel breeding programme in Australia (same bloodlines), and the quality of the racing camels is such that the Fullertons have never lost the well-known premier *Camel Cup Race* in Alice Springs from the time they started it over two decades ago! And Arab countries have expressed much interest in the camels for racing purposes. It is a fascinating place to learn something about these animals, and equally interesting to talk with the Fullertons. Noel's daughter Michelle and her husband Crispin now run the business, although Noel has some involvement especially in the *Camel Safaris*.

CAMEL FACTS

The camels here are dromedaries (Camelus dromedarius), native of North Africa, Arabia and East Asia, commonly called Arabian, and have one hump, as distinct from their near relatives in Mongolia, the bactrian (Camelus bactrianus) with two humps. Like horses, there are varieties from heavier built draught beasts to light swift types bred for riding and racing. They have remarkable mechanisms designed to cope with their harsh desert habitat. The camel has the ability to use body fluids contained in tissue, and to recycle urine to prevent dehydration. This allows days without intake of water. The hump is a food store of fatty tissue that enables survival for lengthy periods without replenishment - in fact if times are hard the hump can literally disappear, so if you see a flat-topped camel you know he's quite hungry! They regulate their body temperature to adjust to outside conditions to prevent moisture loss. At night, heat is released and the coating of body hair acts as an insulator, and assists in temperature control by preventing sweating during the day.

It's interesting that the camel can be virtually dehydrated, drink 30 litres of water, and be quickly back to normal again. The secret is the elasticity of the corpuscles which, unlike humans, have the ability to expand and absorb under such conditions of stress. During sandstorms, adaptive features allow the nostrils to be sealed, while double lids and protective hair effectively seal the eyes.

Camels live for about 48 years, and certainly have distinct personalities. They are ruminants; cloven-hoofed, cud-chewing animals that regurgitate semi-digested food and grind away on it. Bull camels, particularly in the wild, can get nasty. An interesting human statistic for you to ponder over is that women are far keener on riding camels than men, in fact on the longer safari treks, over 90% of the riders are female.

CAMEL HISTORY

Between the 1860s and 1920s, camels and their 'Afghan' camel-masters played a vital development role in an Australian Outback of relentless heat and drought that exacted a terrible toll on traditional beasts of burden; horses, donkeys and bullocks.

Camels were first imported in the early 1840s. They were few, and used for show purposes in the southern states. John Horrocks from Adelaide imported some in 1840, but most perished on the ship. Burke and Wills were the first to use camels in an organised way for exploration, and Giles, Warburton and Gosse followed suit for their expeditions. Madigan's 1939 Simpson Desert crossing was the last important use of camels in Australian exploration.

Camels carried telegraph poles for the Overland Telegraph Line, hauled rock to build repeater stations, heaved sleepers for the railway line, carted minerals for mining companies, and wool for the graziers, and supplied stations with goods and mail. The thousands of kilometres of camel tracks, or camel 'pads' as they were known, created a distinctive network that linked the scattered settlements of the vast interior. Although often unsung, camels and camelmen are as legendary in the Outback as the explorers, cattlemen, drovers and miners.

Some early colonists and settlers in South Australia and Victoria had experience of the usefulness of camels in the development of arid regions, and this knowledge encouraged the first large shipment to Australia in 1860 for the Burke and Wills expedition. The 24 camels were purchased in Peshawar on the Afghanistan border, and along with three 'Afghan' camelmen, arrived in Melbourne on the steamship *Chinsurah*. Pastoralist Thomas Elder (later Sir Thomas, who founded the pastoral company in the 1860s that later became the multinational Elders IXL Group) and partners imported 124 camels and 31 donkeys. Thirty-one Afghans accompanied this shipment in 1865. Several varieties were brought; heavier beasts best suited to large loads from cooler mountain areas; riding and baggage breeds from the Karachi region; and swifter, riding camels from the western desert region of India. Elder established the first camel farm on the Beltana pastoral property, near Lake Torrens in South Australia, and the camel's superiority in the desert as a beast of burden assured success of the venture.

In the Territory, Afghans and their camel strings (the name given to the camel supply trains) worked mainly from the Oodnadatta railhead in South Australia to Alice Springs, where further strings travelling at 10km a day would supply settlements to the north, on a 6 monthly basis. Up to 40 camels comprised a string, and in their hey-day, 12,000 camels, many of which could carry 600kg of load each, were working the camel pads throughout the Australian Outback.

When the railway finally reached Alice Springs the train was called 'The Ghan' in honour of the Afghan cameleers.

Most Afghans had tribal associations with Afghanistan, even although some came from India. They were a nomadic people who adapted well to Australian conditions, and their wandering way was a probably reason for harmonious relationships with Aborigines. Afghans were certainly distinctive in their baggy clothing and turbans, and tended to live in 'Ghan towns' on the fringes of the main settlements, where they faithfully maintained their customs and religion. European attitudes towards them were at times ambivalent. Alice Springs commemorates the Afghans by a bronze statue situated in the railway station foyer, and the Cameleers' Memorial on the Council Lawns near the Todd Mall.

Sally Mahomet was one of the best-known Afghan camelmen, and before he died in 1984, his skills had been well and truly passed onto Australia's 'camel king', Noel Fullerton. By an ironic twist, the railway and motorised trucks which brought about the demise of camel strings worked in the reverse for Fullerton. He is an 'ex-truckie' from New South Wales, now turned camelman. While he is the reigning king, he was not the first to have this title. Frank Wallis, Alice Springs pioneer, storekeeper and forwarding agent, owned about 200 camels, which earned him the title in 1884.

With their period of usefulness over by the 1920s, many camels were left to wander free, and it is estimated that about 20,000 of these ruminants roam Central Australia today. This stock provides a source of camels to meet breeding, circus, zoo, tourist and export demands.

CAMEL RIDES AND TOURS

Short rides cost $4 adult, $3 child; half-hour $15 p.p, child $10; one hour rides, $25 adult, $15 child. Half-day rides including lunch - $55 adult, $35 child; one day rides including lunch, $75 adult, $55 child. Overnight and longer tours cost $110 per day ($90 child) which includes all meals and sleeping swag. The three day *Rainbow Valley Tour* is one of the most captivating safaris through a deeply evocative landscape.

SERVICES AND FACILITIES

It has a shop selling souvenirs, artifacts and snack/takeaway food type meals, soft drinks, teas and coffee. It's *open daily 7.30am-5pm*, credit cards accepted, ph (08) 8956 0925.

Next door to the Camel Outback Safari is **Jim's Place**, a roadhouse/pub that has accommodation. It's run by Jim Cotterill, formerly of Wallara Ranch. Jim Cotterill is one of those legendary Territorians, who with his late father, pioneered tourism in the Kings Canyon area. They established a ranch on land leased form Angus Downs Station in 1961 and cut a 100km (62 miles) track into the canyon by using an old Dodge weapon carrier. This vehicle dragged lengths of railway iron welded into a solid A-frame to gouge the way. Jack Cotterill was also associated with early tourist developments at Uluru and Palm Valley. The old Dodge is on display at Jim's Place, while inside is a fascinating pictorial history of tourism in Central Australia.

ACCOMMODATION

Accommodation includes cabins - $75 x 2; backpackers - $20 p.p. made up, $15 unmade; camping, powered sites - $15 x 2; unpowered sites $6 p.p. Sites are shaded, amenities excellent, pets allowed, dogs leashed.

There is a shop selling a range of food, including take-away and buffet style meals and bar. Ice, souvenirs and artifacts are available. Tourist information, picnic/BBQ/shaded area and showers for travellers ($2.50) are offered. Fuel includes LP, ULP, diesel, autogas, oil and camping gas. Full mechanical repairs are available at a garage next door. It has a swimming pool and spa.

It is *open daily 6am-10pm*, credit cards accepted, EFTPOS facility ph (08) 8956 0808.

TI TREE

Population 362

LOCATION

On the Stuart Highway, 193km (120 miles) north of Alice Springs.

CHARACTERISTICS

The township, situated close to the Pmara Jutunta Aboriginal settlement, consists of a modernised licensed roadhouse and general store/supermarket, police station, medical clinic, school, post office, art gallery, garage and a small park and recreation area. While the roadhouse has a pleasant beer garden with free range kangaroos, it is the full-sized coffin behind the bar that catches the eye. Territorians have a distinctive sense of humour and the owner says it's his spirit cabinet!

HISTORY

Ti Tree takes its name from the Melaleuca glomerata which grew around the creek and waterholes about 300m to the west of the present roadhouse site. Originally named Tea Tree Wells by Dr Woodruff in 1869, the name was changed in 1981. Explorer John McDouall Stuart was the first European in the area in 1861, and in 1888 the Overland Telegraph Line declared a 5 square mile area a reserve for a station. The township is built within this area, and the lonely grave of an Overland Telelgraph Line linesman lies opposite the roadhouse.

The region is homeland for the Anmatjera people, and some interesting rocks and potholes about 2km to the east of the township is where they used to grind their grain for a type of flour. In 1971, local Aborigines were granted the least of Ti Tree Cattle Station, which now sustains an Aboriginal population of about 320. The Pmara Jutunta Settlement has a modern school, and an excellent medical clinic which is also available to the local European population of about 60.

The wells and waterholes of Ti Tree guaranteed some future for the settlement. The water was regarded as the cleanest for 160km (100 miles) in either direction, and was a welcome spot for travellers and users of the north-south stock route, so it is not surprising that one of the first roadhouses on the 'Track' was built here.

ACCOMMODATION

Motel units - $65 double, $55 single.

Camping/Caravans - powered sites $15 x 2, unpowered sites $5 per person. Sites grassed and shaded. Pets allowed, dogs leashed.

SERVICES AND FACILITIES

The roadhouse has a store, bar (no take-away liquor sales), restaurant (good main serve for $10), beer garden, picnic/BBQ area, swimming pool (guests only), toilets for the disabled, and showers for travellers ($2). It sells ice, souvenirs, take-away food, and has a well-stocked store. Fuel services include LP, ULP, diesel and Autogas.

The roadhouse is *open daily 6.00am-10pm*, credit cards accepted, EFTPOS facility, ph (08) 8956 9741.

A nearby garage, undertakes a range of mechanical repairs, including tyres and recovery service. The town also has the *Aaki Gallery,* which has an excellent range of locally produced artifacts for sale. It is located next to the roadhouse.

TNORALA (GOSSE BLUFF) NATIONAL PARK

LOCATION
Approximately 150km (93 miles) directly west of Alice Springs.

CHARACTERISTICS
Gosse Bluff is an astro-geological feature; the scene of the Territory's biggest bang when a comet struck here 142 million years ago. It's one of the most significant and best documented comet impact geological structures in the world, and many of its landform features are highly significant to Aborigines. It was discovered in 1872 by Ernest Giles, who named it after Alice Springs telegraphist Harry Gosse, not the explorer William Gosse, as widely believed.

The 4km (2 miles) ring of rugged hills that rise some 200m (655 ft) above the plain is all that remains of the core of the original crater. The actual Bluff is an erosional remnant of the crater, and an estimated 2000m (6540 ft) of weathering and erosion since the impact, has removed visible traces of the outer rim which had a diameter of 22km (14 miles). Evidence for this comes mainly from satellite images which reveal a distinct halo effect, thought by scientists to show the extent of affected rock. Rings of differing vegetation (one of which is the grass tree, unique to this location in Central Australia), are surface indicators of re-arranged rock structures. Shatter cones, smaller scale structures characterised by cone-shaped fractures that result from extreme shock, are further evidence of a major impact here. From these shatter cones, scientists determined that the object was most probably a large comet which had a low density, consisted of an agglomerate of frozen carbon dioxide, ice and dust, and a high velocity (40km/sec-25 miles/sec). The impact force released energy equivalent to one million times that of the atomic bomb at Hiroshima. No extra-terrestrial material has been found; not surprising as with all that energy on impact, the comet would have vaporised.

The sandstone rock strata that form the inner rim were uplifted from their original bed (between 1000 and 3000m - 3270 and 9810 ft - below the present land surface), by the shock waves. Not only is it a scientific marvel, but also it's of great spiritual significance to Aborigines who call it Tnorala - *Father of the Mountains*. The feature is a registered sacred site and the Aboriginal and scientific interpretations of the Bluff are similar in that both have a celestial origin. Visitors are requested to walk only on designated tracks and to respect signage. Access within Tnorala is restricted in accordance with the wishes of the traditional owners - clans of the Western Arrernte people. A good view of the feature can be seen from the *Tylers Pass Trig Station*.

HOW TO GET THERE

By road, it is about 167 kms (104 miles) from Alice Springs via Larapinta Drive, about one hour from either Glen Helen Homestead or Hermannsburg. The road surface is variable and 4WD is recommended for the 10km drive into the park. A Mereenie Tour Pass, available from Glen Helen, Kings Canyon Resort or the Regional Tourism Association in Alice Springs is required to travel on this road.

FACILITIES

There is a picnic area, pit toilets, shade shelter with excellent interpretive information about the area. There are no BBQ facilities and fires are not permitted. Pets and camping are not allowed - the nearest camping is available at the *Redbank Gorge* (West MacDonnell National Park), 45 kms (28 miles) north-east of Tnorala.

ULURU - KATA TJUTA NATIONAL PARK

1325 sq.km. (822 sq miles)

LOCATION

On the arid sand plains, 450 kms (279 miles) south-west of Alice Springs by road.

CHARACTERISTICS

Australia's first Aboriginal National Park offers visitors insight into the unique cultural landscape of Anangu, part of which includes the stunning landform features of Uluru itself and Kata Tjuta (formerly named Ayers Rock and The Olgas respectively by non-Aboriginal Australians). For its rare blend of cultural and natural attributes, the Park is recognised internationally by its inclusion on the World Heritage Register of significant places.

Culturally, Uluru-Kata Tjuta National Park represents a landscape with spiritual and artistic associations with the natural world. From a natural perspective, the Park is captivating for the exceptional beauty of Uluru and Kata Tjuta, the on-going geological processes and combination of both natural and cultural elements.

Uluru is the world's greatest monolith and its haunting and humbling qualities and colour changes at sunrise and sunset, are legendary to the extent that it has become a national symbol: Uluru is to Australians what the Black Forest is to Germany or the Grand Canyon is to Americans. Approximately 44kms (27 miles) by road to the west of Uluru, is Kata Tjuta, which consists of a series of remarkable dome-shaped rock formations that constitute a dramatic visual contrast to Uluru.

The Park embraces the homelands of the traditional owners, the Pitjantjatjara and Yantunytjatjara people or Anangu, a number of whom reside permanently in the Mutiljulu Community in the Park. Uluru-Kata Tjuta National Park is jointly managed by

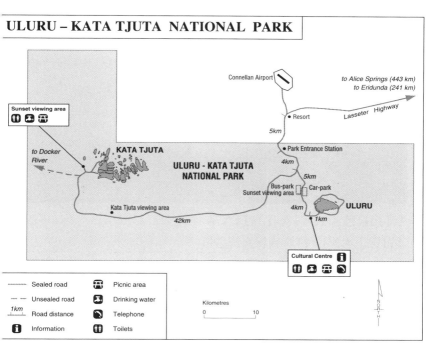

ULURU – KATA TJUTA NATIONAL PARK

Connellan Airport

to Alice Springs (443 km)
to Eridunda (241 km)

Lasseter Highway

Resort

5km

Sunset viewing area

to Docker River

KATA TJUTA

ULURU - KATA TJUTA NATIONAL PARK

Park Entrance Station

4km

5km

Bus-park   Car-park
Sunset viewing area

4km

ULURU

1km

Kata Tjuta viewing area

42km

Cultural Centre

	Legend	
——— Sealed road		Picnic area
– – Unsealed road		Drinking water
1km Road distance		Telephone
Information		Toilets

Kilometres
0   10

Anangu and Parks Australia, and it's interesting to reflect that this symbolic, spiritual heart of Australia is also where two cultures have come together in a positive way in what Anangu call, 'tjunguringkula waakaripai' - 'working together'.

Located just outside the Park's northern boundary is Yulara, the modern resort town purposely designed to service nearly 400,000 people who visit Uluru and Kata Tjuta each year, and in which Ayers Rock Resort Management Group operate most of the tourist facilities. As Yulara and the National Park are separate entities, details of how to get there, and services and facilities available (other than those listed within the Park), are outlined separately under *Yulara*.

ULURU - KATA TJUTA -
THE LAND OF ANANGU

From an Anangu perspective, Central Australia has been a part of their culture since the beginning of time. Archaeological evidence suggests that Aboriginal people have lived continuously in the Uluru area for at least 22,000 years. During this massive time scale, Aboriginal culture has evolved, with a complex belief system unmatched by any other society in the world (apart from other Aboriginal clans in Australia) for its enduring qualities.

NAMING

With the exception of inclusion in direct quotes elsewhere in the book, the word 'tribe' is not used. European society inherited the word from early studies of North-American Indians and peoples in Africa. The word has several meanings, none of which have ever fitted the social organisation and relationship to the land of any Aboriginal group in Australia. Instead, clan, group or band are used. For at least 22,000 years, the two great landform features have been named Uluru and Kata Tjuta respectively. Since the reinstatement of these areas to Anangu in 1985, the persistent use of European nomenclature, Ayers Rock and the Olgas is like renaming a person without his or her consent.

TJUKURPA
(Pronounced: chook-oor-pa)

Tjukurpa is the foundation of Anangu culture. It encapsulates the creation period, religious beliefs, laws and morality in a complex social system in which the totality of the landscape is an integral part. Tjukurpa also refers to time, and 'Dreamtime' or 'Dreaming' are inadequate attempts in the English language to explain a system of belief which perceives the past, present and future as interacting with each other in an eternally dynamic relationship which guide and affect Anangu in their everyday life.

  In practical terms, Tjukurpa also provides a framework for knowledge acquisition, for example, the understanding of relationships between people, plants and animals, and physical environment, how these relationships came to be, what they mean, and how they are to be maintained. This intimate environmental awareness has enabled Anangu, in an economic sense, to successfully overcome the constraints of the desert environment. Their traditional lands are in effect, large natural 'farms' and 'supermarkets', the various 'stocks' of which are harvested and selected respectively according to the season and managed in a sustainable way. Management practises such as controlled burning of vegetation promote new growth and wildlife, while the protection and maintenance of waterholes is a deliberate action to sustain life. Through their knowledge, and environmental manipulation, what could be said of Anangu is that they have developed a system of natural 'farming' practice not unlike a type of permaculture. This also allows a semi-sedentary life rather than a truly nomadic lifestyle as portrayed in much literature about desert Aborigines.

ABORIGINAL TJUKURPA OF THE CREATION PERIOD

In the beginning of time, the world was unformed and featureless. During the creation period, ancestral beings in the form of people, plants and animals travelled widely across the land and in a process of creation and destruction, gave shape and lifeforms which characterise the landscape today. The land is inhabited by many ancestral beings and their journeys and activities are recorded at sites linked by iwara (ancestral paths). In this way, Anangu lands are 'mapped' through events of Tjukurpa and are powerful sources of knowledge and identity.

Anangu are the direct descendants of these beings and are today custodians of their ancestral lands. The knowledge necessary to fulfil these responsibilities has been passed down from generation to generation in accordance with the Aboriginal law through ceremony, song, dance and art.

SOCIAL STRUCTURE, MORALITY AND LAW

The identity with the land and Tjukurpa shapes Anangu relationships with other people. The kinship system prescribes a range of proper behaviours within immediate family groups and with other relations, and governs rules for marriage. Family obligations also extend to the whole language group. Similarly, Tjukurpa provides Anangu with a system of belief and morality whose interpretation of what is right and wrong is determined by the Elders in the clan.

Tjukurpa establishes the rules used to govern Anangu society and management of the land. It dictates procedures for dealing with problems and penalties for breaking laws. The arrival of non-Aboriginal people has caused some modification and also adaptation of non-Aboriginal law to help enforce Tjukurpa, for example, sacred sites are protected under Commonwealth and Northern Territory legislation.

MAINTENANCE OF TJUKURPA

Tjukurpa is not written down but memorised, and it is a cultural obligation of Anangu to pass on this knowledge. Ceremonies play an important role in handing down this knowledge. Specific people or groups in the Anangu kinship system are assigned responsibility to maintain different sections or 'chapters' of Tjukurpa.

This delegation of responsibility may relate to a specific site or section of an ancestral path. There are many interrelated devices for remembering the assigned 'chapters', such as specific verses of inma (songs), site-related stories, ritual dances or rock art. Designs and paintings such as the dot painting of the Western Desert people, are other ways of recording aspects of Tjukurpa. These are often 'sacred', and use and creation of these designs is restricted to specific groups or individuals who have inherited or earned the rights to use them. Tjukurpa may also be recorded in physical forms such as ritual objects. Some objects are created for a specific ritual and then destroyed; others are very old and passed on from one generation to the next. Knowledge of their form and existence is restricted.

The **Cultural Centre** displays on Tjukurpa are recommended viewing. A useful way to seek further understanding of the complexities of Aboriginal culture is to read and reflect upon a selection of Anangu interpretive literature at a quiet spot in the surrounds of Uluru (but confine your spot to designated areas only).

ART

Anangu paintings are created for religious and ceremonial expression and for teaching and storytelling. They still create sand drawings and body paintings for these purposes, but have largely abandoned the use of rock paintings to teach and tell stories. Instead, a range of new materials, including acrylic paint on canvas are used. However, artists use the same symbols and meanings their ancestors developed. Examples of their ancient rock art can be viewed in several rock shelters along the *Mala and Mutitjula Walks*, while in the Cultural Centre, an impressive range of works using contemporary materials, but traditional symbolism, illustrate the adaptation of sand and rock paintings. Contemporary use of Anangu art, with traditional designs reflecting modern meanings has extended to a range of quality commercial products including T-shirts.

EUROPEAN ARRIVAL

In contrast to Anangu, European history in the area is relatively short but not without major impact on the traditional owners.

William Giles was the first European to sight Kata Tjuta while exploring near Kings Canyon in 1872, and named the highest dome 'Mt Olga'. In 1873, explorer William Gosse saw Uluru and named it Ayers Rock after the Chief Secretary of South Australia, Sir Henry Ayers. Giles, in a second expedition, arrived here two months after Gosse and his inspired description is worth recalling:

"it is formed of several vast and solid, huge and rounded blocks of bare red conglomerate stones of all kinds and sizes, mixed like plums in a pudding and set in vast rounded shapes upon the ground ... it displayed to our astonished eyes rounded minarets, giant cupolas and monstrous domes ...".

Comparing the two features he said Kata Tjuta was "more wonderful and grotesque", while Uluru was "more ancient and sublime".

A short period of competitive exploration followed for an evaluation of the area's pastoral potential. As the lands were deemed too harsh, Uluru and Kata Tjuta were included in the South West Reserve, gazetted as an Aboriginal Reserve in 1920. The effect of this was that few non-Aboriginal people visited Anangu lands until the 1930s, apart form some prospectors including Lasseter, missionaries, doggers (men who received a bounty from the Government for dingo scalps), adventurers and Native Welfare Patrol Officers. Anangu contact with doggers introduced them to European foods, implements, clothes and expectations concerning white Australian behaviour.

Although contacts with these groups were often far from friendly, it was not until the pastoralists attempted to use these lands for cattle grazing in the 1930s, that serious clashes between the cultures occurred. Conflict was fuelled by natural food shortages due to drought and the consequent competition for scarce resources. Police patrols became more frequent and after the shooting of an Anangu man at Uluru, increasing fear of police resulted in many Aboriginal people leaving the area. By 1940, the fully traditional pattern of Anangu land use had been severely disrupted. To counter the movement of Anangu into towns and because of an apparent concern that Aboriginal society was collapsing, the government accelerated attempts to 'assimilate' Anangu. This led to government funded settlements and missions. The assimilation policy, here as elsewhere in Australia, was a dismal failure - the strength of Tjukurpa withstood this attempt at cultural re-education.

In 1958, the Uluru-Kata Tjuta area was excised from the Reserve for purposes of a National Park. Bill Harney was appointed as the first ranger and showed considerable empathy for Anangu and did much to counter white intolerance. By 1959 the first motel lease had been granted and Connellan had built an airstrip at Uluru.

With tourism growing in the area, and increasing numbers of Anangu returning to Uluru during the 1960s, Anangu/visitor interaction worsened and tour operators applied pressure to the Native Welfare Branch to have the Anangu removed. In 1964 pastoral leases were revoked forcing large numbers of Anangu off these properties and so many gravitated to Uluru. As their traditional economy had been largely destroyed, many Anangu sustained themselves by selling artifacts to tourists.

The detrimental impact of tourism on the environment in the 1970s led to the construction of Yulara which opened in 1983. This was also the decade when the struggle by Anangu for the handback of their ancestral lands began. At this time, Anangu became increasingly alarmed at the desecration of sites by tourists and a protracted period of negotiation with the Commonwealth Government commenced. In 1973 it was accepted by government that the Park be managed by the Federal Parks and Wildlife Service with provision for an active role in management by Anangu.

However, it was not until 1979 that recognition of the existence of traditional owners was acknowledged by the government, and it remained until 1983 when serious negotiations for inalienable freehold title began. For the traditional owners of Uluru, Kata

Tjuta and surrounding lands, a significant milestone was achieved in 1985 when title to Anangu homeland was finally handed back. The land was immediately leased to the Australian National Parks and Wildlife Service (now Parks Australia) for 99 years to be managed jointly as a National Park.

In 1994, Uluru-Kata Tjuta National Park became only the second national park in the world to be listed as a cultural landscape. The World Heritage Council, gave international recognition of Tjukurpa as a religious philosophy linking Anangu to their traditional environment and Anangu culture as an integral part of the landscape.

THE GEOLOGICAL STORY

The makeup and evolution of Uluru and Kata Tjuta is explained differently by Anangu and non-Aboriginal scientists. This outline explains the features from a geological perspective.

The prominences of Uluru and Kata Tjuta are merely the tips of massive slabs of sedimentary rock which extend beneath the surface as far as five or six kilometres. Uluru measures 9.4 km (5.8 miles) in circumference, 3.6 (2 miles) in length, 2.4 km (1.5 miles) in width and 340 metres in height above the surrounding plain (863 metres a.s.l.). Uluru is composed of arkose - a course grained sandstone rich in felspar minerals. The sandy sediments, which hardened to form arkose, were eroded from huge mountains composed largely of granite.

Kata Tjuta consists of 36 domes covering an area of 22 sq.km (14 sq. miles), with the highest, Mt Olga, rising to 500 metres above the plain (1066 metres a.s.l.). In contrast to Uluru, it is composed of conglomerates - gravels consisting of pebbles, cobbles and boulders cemented together by sand and mud. Most of the gravel pieces are granite and basalt.

FORMATION

About 900 million years ago a depression formed in the earth's crust, now known as the Armadeus Basin, the southern margins of which lie Uluru and Kata Tjuta today. At times, the basin was a shallow sea, accumulating huge amounts of sediment over a 300 million year period. The older sedimentary beds in the basin were buckled and uplifted by tectonic forces about 550 m.y.a to form the Petermann Ranges. As these towering ranges were bare and lifeless (bacteria and algae excepted), the processes of weathering and erosion were relatively rapid. At this time, it must be remembered that the continental location was still north of the equator, so the tropical zone position of Central Australia meant high rainfall.

Rivers carried sediments from the eroding ranges to form massive fans of deposited rock debris on land and in the nearby sea. It is the remains of at least two of these vast alluvial fans formed on land that we see today as Uluru and Kata Tjuta. And in this outwash of material, the size of rock particles transported by running water decreased with distance. Kata Tjuta, being closer to the source of eroded rock, is made up of larger fragments, while finer graded material laid the basis for Uluru.

By about 500 m.y.a, another marine incursion laid down sediments which gradually covered the alluvial fans. These overlying sediments of sand and mud compressed and cemented the arkosic sand into arkose and the coarse gravels of Kata Tjuta into conglomerate. The sea retreated from the Amadeus Basin and between 400 and 300 m.y.a., a major period of uplift saw the creation of the Musgrave Ranges and an intensified period of tectonic activity on the northern margin of the basin in what geologists call the Alice Springs Orogeny (it also formed the MacDonnell Ranges). In this period of uplift, the region was raised above sea level and the horizontal layers of the Uluru arkose were folded and tilted 90 degrees to their present position. The Kata Tjuta conglomerate were inclined by only about 15 to 20 degrees from the horizontal. Geologically, these two features are called inselbergs.

External processes of weathering and erosion at Uluru and Kata Tjuta began to modify the prominences about 300 m.y.a. The sculpturing of Uluru is due to a number of processes and factors:

water and scouring effects of runoff, abrasion, moisture induced chemical erosion, tension in the rock and variation of hardness or resistance in the rock layers themselves.

At Kata Tjuta, erosional processes have exploited fractures in the rock sustained during uplift, thus forming canyons. Temperature range causes tension in the rocks which are split smoothly as a result. And as surface rocks are worn down the release of pressure produces fissures parallel to the rock surface. These can be seen on both landforms.

The flaky surface of Uluru results from the chemical decay of minerals, while the red coating of iron oxide (rust) masks the underlying, grey-coloured arkose.

The sunrise and sunset colour changes are not so much due to Uluru's geological makeup as the effects the earth's atmosphere has on the sun's rays. When the sun is low in the sky, the atmosphere acts like a giant prism, splitting the rays into a colour spectrum. As the red end of the spectrum dominates at these times, it is further enhanced by reflection from Uluru itself, the rock colouration and surrounding red sand plain.

The surrounding sand dunes have remained in their current position for 30,000 years, except for wind movement of looser sand on the crests. The Cultural Centre has detailed literature on the geology of the Park.

FLORA AND FAUNA

Most of the flora as outlined in the introduction to the Central Australian region is well represented in the park with a tendency of Desert Oak, Mulga and Spinifex to dominate. Similarly, the Park contains a considerable variety of wildlife. Within the Park there are 25 species of mammals, 178 species of birds, 72 species of reptiles and 5 introduced mammal species. And 416 species of plants have been identified. A free Ranger guided Botanical Tour is offered in some winter/spring months (enquire at the Cultural Centre) for those interested in flora.

INFORMATION: ULURU-KATA TJUTA CULTURAL CENTRE

Before exploring the Park visit the Cultural Centre first. It features a visual and sound depiction of Tjukurpa in which Anangu perceptions are strong themes. A second major display area has a focus on the history and how the Park is jointly managed by Anangu and Parks Australia.

Maruka Arts and Crafts, situated in the courtyard, displays and sells an extensive range of works in several mediums by artists from the Central and Western Desert areas. At times, artists may be seen at work. The *Ininti Store and Kiosk*, stocks a good range of souvenirs, books, videos and clothing, while the cafe offers a variety of light foods.

Other services include The Information Desk for Park literature, information on free guided tours, ranger activities, cultural events and multi-lingual services while The Tour Desk offers information about free guided tours at Uluru including a 1.5 hour Cultural Centre tour. Even if you do not take advantage of this offering, it's suggested that you allow at least 2 hours for a visit to the Cultural Centre.

There are picnic areas and toilets, including for disabled visitors, and the Centre has wheelchair access. Visitors are asked to respect the wishes of Anangu not to be photographed, and no photography or video recording is permitted at the Cultural Centre. It's *open daily, 7am-6.00pm (Nov-March)*, 7am-5.30pm (April-Oct) and entry is free with Park entry ticket. Credit cards accepted, EFTPOS facility, ph (08) 8956 3138.

PRACTICAL INFORMATION

Entry to the Park *costs $15 (valid for 5 days)*, children under 16 are free. No camping is permitted in the National Park (see *Accommodation* at Yulara); pets allowed in designated areas and must be leashed at all times and visitors are asked not to feed wildlife or to 'souvenir' rocks from Uluru or Kata Tjuta, and to walk or drive only on designated tracks and roads respectively.

GUIDED TOURS AND WALKS

Free Ranger guided tours are available (see under *Cultural Centre* and *Activities*).

Anangu Tours is a company owned by Pitjantjatjara and Yankumytjatjara people, and Anangu guides host tours covering their history, knowledge and lifestyle in their traditional homelands. Tours are: **Uluru Breakfast Tours** which includes a special breakfast at the Cultural Centre restaurant, discovery walk along *Liru Track* to Uluru, bush skills and ancient creation laws. Full tour including transfer from Yulara is $78 adults, $63 child, tour only $39 adult, $29 child; **Kuniya and Sunset Tour** is a cultural tour around the base of Uluru, tour only $39 adult, $29 child.

An *Anangu Culture Pass* offers a complete cultural experience at 15% discount - adult $120, child $95. For **Anangu Tour** bookings, contact Tour and Information Centre or Hotel Desks at Yulara.

Uluru Experience offer a blend of cultural and natural history in their tour offerings.

Uluru Walk Tour is a dawn time experience around the base of Uluru with breakfast included, while **Spirit of Uluru** is a vehicle-based exploration of the features around the base of the monolith. Cost for each tour is $69 adult, $54 child.

A **Kata Tjuta and Dunes Tour** includes insight into arid land ecosystems, a gorge walk and champagne sunset viewing. Costs are $51 adults, $41 child. Most of these tours are of over 3 hours duration.

Desert Tracks, owned and operated by Pitjantjatjara people, run longer duration tours (1-6 days) in their ancestral homelands. *Cave Hill* is a one day tour that includes rock art sites in the Musgrave Ranges, Mt Conner and Cave Hill. Costs are $260 adults, $170 child.

Pitjantjatjara Art Tour takes 3 days and includes Cave Hill and Ernabella to watch artists work in various mediums. Costs $790 adults, $520 child.

Walking Tours include Mt Woodroffe (1.5 days) and a 6 day camel walk with Aboriginal guides and expert cameleer.

ULURU

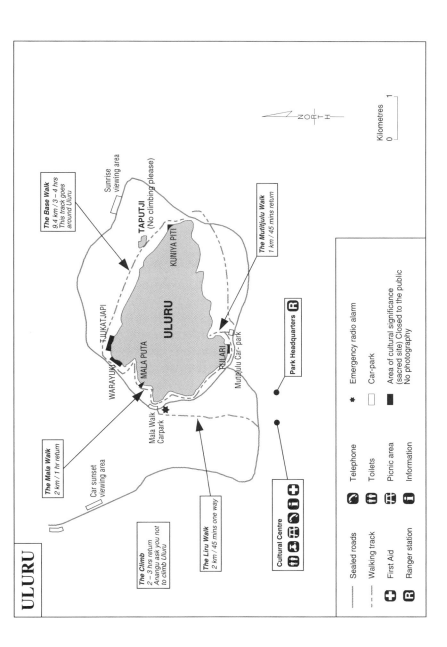

The Base Walk
9.4 km / 3 – 4 hrs
This track goes
around Uluru

Sunrise viewing area

TAPUTJI
(No climbing please)

KUNIYA PITI

TJUKATJAPI

WARAYUKI

ULURU

MALA PUTA

The Mutitjulu Walk
1 km / 45 mins return

Car sunset viewing area

Mala Walk Carpark

PULARI

Mutitjulu Car-park

The Mala Walk
2 km / 1 hr return

The Climb
2 – 3 hrs return
Anangu ask you not
to climb Uluru

The Liru Walk
2 km / 45 mins one way

Park Headquarters Ⓡ

Cultural Centre

* Emergency radio alarm
▫ Car-park
■ Area of cultural significance
(sacred site) Closed to the public
No photography

Kilometres
0   1

— Sealed roads
-- Walking track
✚ First Aid
Ⓡ Ranger station

☎ Telephone
🚻 Toilets
🏕 Picnic area
ℹ Information

N

V.I.P. offer personalised, chauffeured limousines, small executive coaches and 4WD tours of the National Park and Watarrka (Kings Canyon) from their Yulara base, ph 1800 806 412 (free call).

AAT Kings have a range of options from Sunrise, Climb and Base Tour, adults $74, child $37, and Kata Tjuta and Uluru Sunset Tour, adults $62, child $31, Valley of the Winds BBQ Tour which includes an afternoon walk through the domes, champagne and sunset, traditional Aussie BBQ rounded off with a guided tour of the night sky constellations, adults $95, child $48.

Uluru Motor Cycle Tours offers a very different experience and approach as you pillion ride on Harley Davidsons around the monolith. Costs from around $80 p.p.

Check with the Cultural Centre or Tours and Information Centre, Visitor Centre and hotel desks in Yulara for further details of all tours.

ACTIVITIES
Comfort and Safety Advice

For your comfort and safety, all visitors should be mindful of the following information:

 Be aware, Anangu asks visitors not to climb Uluru. If you decide to climb Uluru, don't overestimate your capability on this difficult and potentially dangerous ascent. It is a demanding climb and should only be attempted by those in top physical shape. Visitors with the following conditions should not climb; heart problems, high blood pressure, angina, asthma, vertigo and fear of heights. A number of deaths have resulted as a consequence of heart failure caused by over-exertion, while a number of plaques at the base of Uluru are sobering reminders of the deaths caused by falls.

• Wear suitable protection against the sun's rays.
• Keep fluid levels up.
• Children should be closely supervised on walks and climbs, and reckless behaviour on the climb is potentially life-threatening.
• Kata Tjuta is a maze of rock formations and it is easy to become disorientated. Do not walk off main tracks.
• A brochure, "For Your Comfort and Safety" is a free publication in several languages, that should be read by all visitors.

Around Uluru

Free ranger guided walks offered daily (8am, Oct-Apr; 10am, May-Sept), include the Mala Walk - a 1.5 hour walk outlining Anangu associations with Uluru in their culture and how the traditional owners and Park Australia Rangers are jointly looking after the Park. The route track is wheelchair accessible. Meet the ranger at the Mala Walk sign at the base of Uluru. There's also a free Botanical Tour. A range of other organised, guided tours is outlined under tours.

The *Mala* and *Mutitjulu Walks* may be self-guided. Obtain an excellent interpretive booklet from the Cultural Centre and follow its clear directions. Mutitjulu is a permanent waterhole on the southern side of Uluru. You can also walk around the base, but please respect signage and fenced off areas at sacred sites, or you can drive to various stopping places and do short walks to the base. A self-guided brochure is available for this circuit walk which takes 3-4 hours.

The *Pathway to the Summit* of Uluru is the *iwara* taken by ancestral Mala Men on their arrival at Uluru. Because this path is of great spiritual significance, Anangu rarely climb it. Although Anangu have given permission for visitors to climb to the summit, they would prefer that you respect this spiritual path and so not follow it. Also, Anangu have a duty of care determined by Tjukurpa, and injury or death on their land causes anguish. Make up your own mind. From base to summit, it is 1.6 km (1 mile); certain sections are very steep although there's a chain to help, and it can get cold and windy near and on the top. If you have any doubts, talk with the rangers.

Sunset Viewing

A viewing area is located about 6km (4 miles) from Uluru and 14 km (9 miles) south of Yulara and you won't miss it because of the crowds. Best advice is to get there early for the spectacular parade of Uluru's colours and the hype that goes with it. Check with the Cultural Centre for sunset times. Sunrise viewing can be just as startling with advantages of smaller crowds.

FACILITIES

At the Mala Walk carpark, there are toilets and emergency telephone.

KATA TJUTA

Kata Tjuta is located approximately 25 kms (16 miles) directly west of Uluru (by road approximately 44 kms; 27 miles, on a sealed surface). The dirt road west from Kata Tjuta leads to Kaltukatjara (Docker River), 180 kms (112 miles) away (permits required).

WALKS (SEE MAP)

There are two walking tracks. The *Walpa (Olga) Gorge Walk* (2km return) leads over conglomerate pavements of rock to the shady end of a gorge where there's a viewing platform. To the west, there are good views of the sand plains. It's an easy walking track which takes about 1 hour return. *Valley of the Winds Walk* (7km; 4.3 miles),

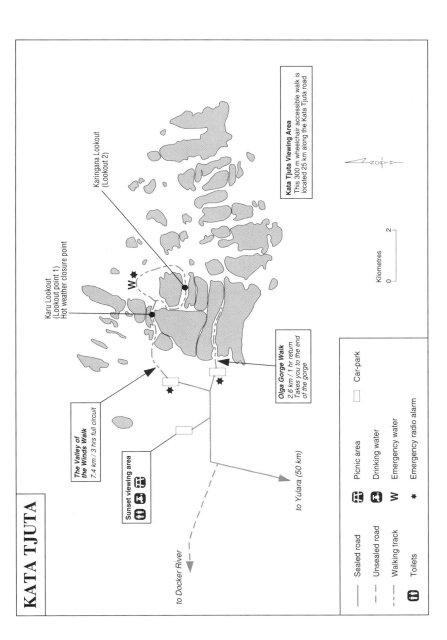

KATA TJUTA

Karu Lookout
(Lookout point 1)
Hot weather closure point

Karingana Lookout
(Lookout 2)

Kata Tjuta Viewing Area
This 300 m wheelchair accessible walk is located 25 km along the Kata Tjuta road

W

The Valley of the Winds Walk
7.4 km / 3 hrs full circuit

Sunset viewing area

Olga Gorge Walk
2.6 km / 1 hr return
Takes you to the end of the gorge

to Yulara (50 km)

to Docker River

Kilometres

0   2

——— Sealed road	⬜ Car-park
- - - Unsealed road	🅟 Picnic area
· · · Walking track	🚰 Drinking water
🚻 Toilets	W Emergency water
	✶ Emergency radio alarm

takes about 4 hours return and exposes some spectacular natural formations and views from two lookout points.

Be properly attired and carry plenty of drinking water (1 litre per hour). A number of heat stress cases on this walk each summer are due largely to inadequate preparation for this demanding walk.

FACILITIES

There's a sunset viewing area with toilets, picnic tables and water. At 26 kms (16 miles) along the Kata Tjuta road is a car park from where a 300 metre boardwalk across the dunes leads to the Kata Tjuta Dune Viewing Platform. It's a great spot for photography and views of the domes. Interpretive panels provide information about the surrounding environment. The track is wheelchair accessible. An excellent reference is *Uluru, Kata Tjuta and Watarrka* by Anne Kerle (pub. UNSW Press).

YULARA

CHARACTERISTICS

Located 20km (12 miles) from Uluru, this highly imaginative resort town was designed by one of Australia's leading architects, Philip Cox. The long, low development nestles comfortably within the swales of the region's sinuous sand dunes, and, with its subdued ochre-painted structures, blends easily into the landscape.

It was built of necessity. The rapid increase in the number of visitors to Uluru was causing environmental problems. The outcome in 1984 was a $160 million resort that incorporated elements unique in Australian design technology, while its scale and scope and fine attention to detail made it an attraction in itself.

The serpentine-form layout results from following the natural lines of the dunes and, to prevent 'dead' areas of activity or interest, the hotels were located at the extremities. Between these poles, magnets or attractions were placed, thus creating an even flow of movement and interest along its length. Of further interest

are the spaces, shapes and roofscapes, in particular the 68 spectacular sails designed to deflect the sun's heat. A lively village atmosphere results, complementing the natural wonders that spawned it.

The telephone area code is (08).

INFORMATION

The Visitor Centre (next door to Desert Gardens Hotel) features displays on Uluru and Kata Tjuta and elements of the cultural and natural landscape of the region. It's open daily 8.30am-5.00pm, ph 8957 7377.

The Tour and Information Centre, is centrally located and provides a facility for tour operators to sell direct to visitors. It also dispenses a general information service and sells videos and books. It's open daily 8.30am-8.30pm, ph 8956 2240. They also have desks in the hotels.

Uluru-Kata Tjuta National Park Cultural Centre (refer to *National Park Listing*).

TOURS, WALKS AND TALKS

For details of tours within the National Park, refer to Uluru-Kata Tjuta National Park. Bookings for *Anangu Tours* can be made at Yulara (Tour and Information Centre and Hotel Desks). Within Yulara, *The Garden Walk* is a free guided tour through the native flora of *Sails in the Desert Hotel* gardens, weekdays at 7.30am, meeting in the hotel lobby. *The Night Sky Show*, held at the observatory near the camping ground, provides an informative look at the stars of the southern skies. *It costs $21 adult, $16 child and first show starts at 8.30pm* - check with the visitor centre for further details. There are a number of lookout points and a walking/jogging track (see map).

Scenic Flights. Two helicopter companies offer very popular aerial experiences of Uluru and Kata Tjuta and beyond.

Ayers Rock Helicopters (ph 8956 2077), have 15 minute tours from around $75 p.p; 30 minute Uluru and Kata Tjuta tour $145 p.p.; and champagne Uluru and Kata Tjuta Sunset Tour around $155 p.p.

Professional Helicopter Services (ph 8956 2003) offer a Kata Tjuta tour, $100 p.p. and Uluru and Kata Tjuta and Lake Amadeus $220 p.p.

Rockayer (ph 8956 2345) offer fixed wing flights with a 30 minute Uluru and Kata Tjuta Tour around $65 p.p.

Air North (ph 8956 2093) offer flights to Kings Canyon, $220 p.p. and Uluru and Kata Tjuta around $65 p.p.

Frontier Camel Tours (ph 8956 2444) offer "Take a Camel to Sunrise or Sunset" tours ($65 p.p.) and also extended camel tours.

HOW TO GET THERE

See also under *Tours* in Alice Springs listing.

By air

Ansett and Qantas have daily flights from Alice Springs (connecting with other domestic ports) to Uluru, and the trip takes 45 minutes.

Kendall has regular flights to Conellan Airport from South Australia, and Air North has daily flights from Alice Springs.

By coach
Greyhound-Pioneer and McCaffertys have daily schedules.
By road
The Lasseter Highway is a sealed road, 244km (151 miles) from the Stuart Highway turn-off.

Local Transport
Sunworth Taxis, ph 8956 2152. They also offer return shuttles to Uluru - $20 p.p. and Kata Tjuta, $35 p.p.
Car Rentals: Avis, ph 8956 2266; Hertz, ph 8956 2177; Territory Rent-A-Car, ph 8956 2556.
AAT Kings operates an Airport to Resort Complimentary Shuttle Service for guests.

And there's a free shuttle bus which runs every 15 minutes between all accommodation places in late morning, early afternoons and evenings - check with Visitors Centre.

ACCOMMODATION
Yulara caters for all tastes and budgets in an accommodation range from campsites to highly rated hotels. Bookings are advised for all accommodation types, particularly in peak holiday periods. As all accommodation places are operated by Ayers Rock Resort Management, telephone 8956 2200 for enquiries.

Hotels
Sails in the Desert offers luxurious rooms from around $350 to $640 and all the services expected of a highly rated establishment.
The Desert Gardens Hotel also offers quality accommodation with rooms from around $290.
The Outback Pioneer Hotel and Lodge has rooms from $260; budget (cabin - maximum 4) from $120; dormitory from $20; bunkhouse Y.A.A. dormitory style from $18. All hotels have swimming pools and facilities for disabled guests

Apartments and Lodges
Emu Walk Apartments offer one bedroom apartments (maximum 4) from around $265 and two bedroom apartments (maximum 8) from $325. These represent good accommodation value in their central location.

The Outback Pioneer Hotel has Lodge style (see *hotels*).

Spinifex Lodge has share facilities with rooms from $105.

Camp Ground

Cabins from $95 (up to 4 people) with $10 extra p.p. (maximum 6). Powered sites around $16 p.p.; $10 extra persons. Campsites around $10 p.p.; children $5. Facilities and amenities are very good with swimming pool, kiosk, communal kitchen, laundry, games room and disabled facilities. There's little shade, and pets, provided they are leashed are allowed.

Ph, 8956 2055.

EATING OUT

For food finesse, *Sails in The Desert Hotel* offer four options catering generally for the top end of the market: Contemporary Australian food styles in the casual elegance of the *Kuniya Restaurant*; lighter, generally Asian style dishes, al fresco daytime dining experience at the poolside location of the *Rockpool Restaurant*; and a popular, less expensive option at *Winkiku* which has a relaxed cafe style catering for all meals from 6.00am.

Many consider their 'piece de resistance' to be *"Sounds of Silence"* - a memorable, tourism award winning dinner in the desert. Included is an Uluru sunset viewing, to the accompaniment of the digeridoo. Australian meats (kangaroo, emu, barramundi) and local bush salads are a menu feature, while after dessert, stories of the starry southern skies are told by an Uluru Experience astronomer. It *costs around $90 adult, $45 child* (not recommended for children under 10).

The White Gums Restaurant at the *Desert Gardens Hotel*, has a formal but relaxed dining atmosphere with Australian and modern cuisine styles offered.

At the *Outback Pioneer Hotel* their *Bough House Restaurant* has outback Australian theme surrounds and offers speciality buffet foods, seafood and roast meats.

The Pioneer BBQ and Bar features a self-cook BBQ style with good value meat packs including kangaroo and buffalo often on offer and a good choice of salads. In its casual outdoor setting, the atmosphere is enhanced by an Aussie entertainer.

The popular **Pioneer Takeaway Kitchen** also represents good value and serves all meals daily.

At the *Resort Centre*, **Gecko's Cafe** has continental style fare, specialising in pizzas, pasta and pastries, while **Quickbite**, **Ayers Rock Bakehouse** and **Ayers Rock Icecreamery** are further choices for meals or snacks.

NIGHTLIFE

Generally there's an Aboriginal dance, music and storytelling group performing at the *Amphitheatre* nightly. The cinema screens latest releases and for these and other entertainment, check with the Visitor Centre for details.

SERVICES AND FACILITIES

All services and facilities are available, credit cards accepted and EFTPOS facilities available. Most shops generally *open 9am to 9pm daily*. Apart from these already mentioned, there's a post office; police station; medical centre; supermarket; gift/souvenir shops; art and craft shops; beauty salon; travel agent; newsagent; ANZ Bank; Commonwealth Bank Agency at Post Office; foreign currency exchange at ANZ Bank; Hotels; one hour photo processing; vehicles - full services, repairs and all fuels; camping gas; childcare facility; multilingual guides (ph 8956 2240); church services (check with Visitors Centre); airport - at Uluru itself, (see under Uluru-Kata Tjuta National Park).

Radio Stations: ABC 99.7 FM; Radio 8HA can be heard on 100.5FM.

Recreational facilities include tennis courts, putting green, swimming pools, playground, walking/jogging tracks and lookout points.

WALLACE ROCKHOLE

Population 160

LOCATION

Approximately 120 kms (74 miles) south west of Alice Springs via
Larapinta Drive.

CHARACTERISTICS

The small Aboriginal settlement has a beautiful setting in the
scenic James Range and has a community store, health clinic,
school, art and crafts centre and Council Offices at its centre. The
Arrernte Community have won several awards, including the NT
Tidiest Town citation in 1995 and it's an ideal base for MacDonnell
Ranges region exploration. No permits are required, but alcohol is
prohibited. The small rockhole is located about one kilometre from
the township, but swimming is not permitted.

TOURS

The community offers highly recommended Aboriginal cultural tours,
one of which includes rock art. It lasts for an hour and costs $7 p.p.
The 3-4 hour **Bush Tucker Tour** costs $40 p.p and involves traditional
cooking of kangaroo tail among other interesting experiences to the
palate. This tour also includes rock art interpretation.

SERVICES AND FACILITIES

It has a well stocked general store, ice, snack foods and fuel (LP,
ULP, diesel) and undertakes minor vehicle repairs. The **Art and
Craft Centre** features a display and sales area of locally produced
works which are reasonably priced.

The camping ground has good amenities and offers on-site vans
around $30; self-contained cabins from $95; unpowered camp
sites $7; powered $8. Pets allowed, dogs leashed, open throughout
the year, ph (08) 8956 7993. Credit cards accepted.

The store *opens daily 9am-5pm* and for further information,
telephone Council Offices (08) 8956 7415.

WATARRKA NATIONAL PARK (KINGS CANYON)

722sq.km (448 sq.miles)

LOCATION

330km (205 miles) south-west of Alice Springs, near the western end of the George Gill Range.

CHARACTERISTICS

Watarrka National Park, features contrasting coloured canyon walls of a mighty cleft in the *George Gill Range*, dome-shaped buttresses on the plateau and a narrow, verdant valley climaxing in a large rockpool called the 'Garden of Eden'. No trip to Central Australia is complete without having experienced these dramatic features that are contained in a relatively compact area, and which can be seen via a walking track. Aboriginal art and a ranger station with excellent interpretative displays are complementary features.

HISTORY

The area is homeland for the Luritja people, who have three main living areas in the park. In association with the Parks and Wildlife Commission, they are involved with future development plans for the canyon.

In 1872, explorer Ernest Giles and his companion Samuel Carmichael were the first non-Aboriginals in the area when their expedition was forced to skirt Lake Amadeus while on its way to Mt Olga. They were attracted to this red sandstone range. Giles named the range after his brother-in-law, and wrote enthusiastically about the creek, which he named after the expedition's main financier, Fieldon King. His glowing reports brought the pastoralists, which not surprisingly upset local Aborigines, and a few skirmishes resulted.

The Canyon takes it name from the creek, but to the Aborigines the whole locality is known as Watarrka, after the Acacia ligulata, which

WATARRKA NATIONAL PARK

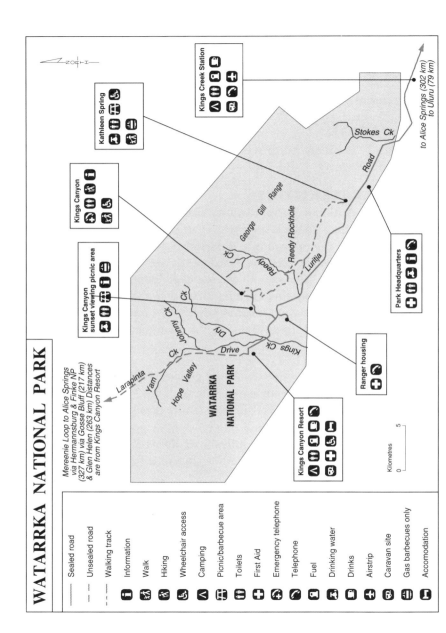

Mereenie Loop to Alice Springs
via Hermannsburg & Finke NP
(327 km) via Gosse Bluff (217 km)
& Glen Helen (263 km) Distances
are from Kings Canyon Resort

Kings Canyon sunset viewing picnic area

Kings Canyon

Kathleen Spring

Kings Creek Station

Park Headquarters

Ranger housing

Kings Canyon Resort

WATARRKA NATIONAL PARK

Larapinta

Yam Ck
Johnny Ck
Hope Valley
Dry Ck
Kings Ck
Kings Ck Drive

Reedy Ck
George Gill Range
Reedy Rockhole
Lurnja
Stokes Ck
Road

to Alice Springs (302 km)
to Uluru (79 km)

Kilometres
0   5

Sealed road
Unsealed road
Walking track

Information
Walk
Hiking
Wheelchair access
Camping
Picnic/barbecue area
Toilets
First Aid
Emergency telephone
Telephone
Fuel
Drinking water
Drinks
Airstrip
Caravan site
Gas barbecues only
Accomodation

grows in profusion, particularly at the beginning of the walking track. William Gosse came this way in 1873 and camped at Kings Creek before heading south to discover Uluru, curiously missed by Giles.

GEOLOGY

The evolutionary sequence of the canyon in Devonian Times (about 350-450 million years ago) was sedimentation (laying down of sands, silts and clays under a shallow estuary), sandstone rock formation, uplift of sandstone blocks by tectonic activity (great internal energy forces) and, according to one theory, an associated monumental splitting of the sandstone. Subsequent flood-waters of Kings Creek have, over millions of years, undercut the softer base sandstone, causing massive slabs to shear from the towering 100m high walls, thus widening the canyon.

The lower level rock consists of reddish-brown sandstone, silty sandstone, and red-green and white silt and claystone laid down about 440 million years ago, called Carmichael sandstone. Overlying this is a bed of highly permeable white quartz-rich rock known as Mereenie Sandstone, characterised by ripple and cross bedding marks from wave (water) movement and joints (fractures) from the uplift period. Traces of worm trails have been found, particularly on the plateau.

FEATURES

The distinctive red colouration of the south wall's almost vertical joint face, due to coatings of iron oxide, contrasts with the creamy colour of the equally awesome one kilometre length of the north wall.

Dome-shaped structures on the plateau result from sandstone blocks being eroded along their joints, the edges of which were rounded by further weathering processes. Keep to the arrow-directed track, as it is easy to get disorientated here.

You won't be disappointed by the 'Garden of Eden', a narrow gorge with native fig, gum and cycads lining the creek that flows into a triangular-shaped rockpool, before plunging over the edge into the canyon when the rains come. The unforgettable grandeur of the canyon unfolds at this point.

Flora and fauna characteristic of Central Australia are well represented. An extended walking track, foot-bridges and boardwalks now complete a round trail up to the plateau to the canyon rim and down into the 'Garden of Eden', across to the south wall, descent to the canyon floor, and back to the car park. It's a physically demanding walk - take something to drink, wear a hat, and have supportive footwear. The climb to the plateau is particularly steep. It's a beautiful wilderness area, where a thoughtlessly dropped sweet wrapping constitutes pollution.

The Luritja people offer a number of guided tours (check with the ranger station or resort) which give insights in local Aboriginal culture. And aerial views of the Canyon may be seen from helicopter flights ($80 p.p.) - for further details check at the resort. At the base of the range, a path leading to a rock pool is accessible for visitors confined to wheelchairs.

HOW TO GET THERE

From the Ernest Giles/Luritja Roads junction, it is a sealed road to the Canyon.

KINGS CANYON RESORT

Located 10kms from the Canyon on Luritja Road, the resort complex provides a full range of services and facilities including accommodation. Hotel rooms - standard from $224; deluxe from $227; budget $79 double; family rooms from $145; backpacker four share dormitory style $35 p.p. The caravan park has excellent amenities - powered sites $25 x 2; unpowered $10 p.p. Sites are shaded, no pets allowed.

The resort has a licensed restaurant which offers buffet style evening meals ($29). The **Desert Oaks** restaurant caters for all meals with dinner from $12.50 p.p.

Facilities include swimming pool and tennis courts and a sunset viewing area. The general store has a wide range of goods and foodstuffs, and fuel (LP, ULP, diesel, autogas), *open daily 7am-7pm*, EFTPOS facility and credit cards accepted. Telephone (08) 8956 7442.

Other Services and Facilities

A ranger station and visitor centre at the park entrance (about 20km [12 miles] from the canyon) have displays and literature. Facilities at the canyon include car park, walking track, interpretive information and toilets. At the day-use area, 700 metres from the car park, facilities include picnic area, gas barbecues, toilets and drinking water. There is no camping within the park except at the Resort. Fires within the park and collection of firewood are not permitted. Swimming in the rock pools is not permitted with the exception of the waterhole in the 'Garden of Eden'. A memorial stone cairn at the beginning of the walking track recognises the pioneering work of Jack Cotterill.

Kings Creek Station (*see separate listing*) offers good budget and camping accommodation 30 kms east of the National Park.

The Barkly Region

The Barkly Region extends from the desert, through tableland, to the Gulf of Carpentaria coastline. It's the transitional zone between arid Central Australia and the tropical Top End, and there's plenty of interest as the ochre landscape tones give way to a softer green. Renner Springs marks the geographical end to the semi-arid lands; around here is the southern limit of the Wet Season tropical rains.

Tennant Creek is the flourishing centre of this huge, sparsely populated region, which has an economy based on pastoral, mining and tourist activities. A large area around Tennant Creek is Warumungu homeland, while other Aboriginal clans live in the more isolated western and eastern margins.

Within its vast boundaries are some of the Territory's largest cattle stations, longest 'beef roads', fascinating bush pubs, historic stock-routes, gold mines and settlements, interesting flora and fauna, and some outstanding geological features. You can even sail at Tennant Creek, or if you're into fishing, Borroloola is the barramundi capital of the Gulf, and gateway to an idyllic, tropical island fishing retreat.

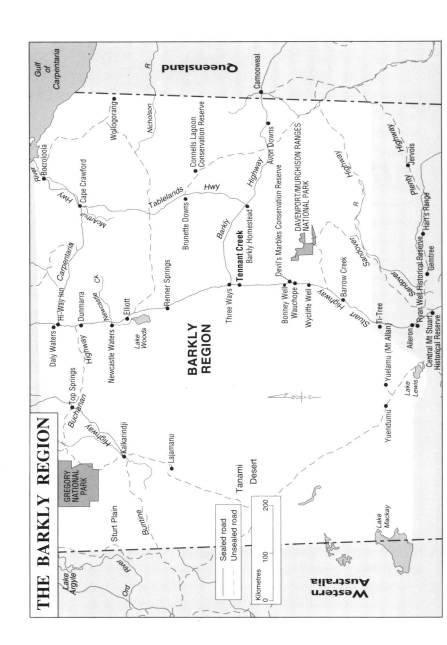

THE BARKLY REGION

Gulf of Carpentaria

Queensland

Western Australia

BARKLY REGION

Tanami Desert

Sturt Plain

GREGORY NATIONAL PARK

DAVENPORT/MURCHISON RANGES NATIONAL PARK

Connells Lagoon Conservation Reserve

Devil's Marbles Conservation Reserve

Ryan Well Historical Reserve

Central Mt Stuart Historical Reserve

Lake Argyle
Lake Mackay
Lake Lewis
Lake Woods

Ord River
McArthur River
Nicholson R
Sandover R

Borroloola
Wollogorang
Cape Crawford
Brunette Downs
Avon Downs
Camooweal
Renner Springs
Three Ways
Tennant Creek
Barkly Homestead
Bonney Well
Wauchope
Wycliffe Well
Barrow Creek
Ti-Tree
Aileron
Gemtree
Hart's Range
Jervois
Yuelamu (Mt Allan)
Yuendumu
Lajamanu
Kalkarindji
Top Springs
Daly Waters
Dunmarra
Newcastle Waters
Elliott

Carpentaria Hwy
Hi-Way Inn
Newcastle Ck
Tablelands Hwy
Barkly Highway
Stuart Highway
Buchanan Highway
Buntine
Plenty Highway
Sandover Highway

Sealed road
Unsealed road

Kilometres
0   100   200

N

CLIMATE

It has a definite Wet and Dry Season regime, with distinct
differences in temperature, rainfall and humidity between the
northern and southern areas. In the south, it's hotter in summer,
cooler in winter, and lower in humidity. On average, Tennant Creek
has 119 days over 35C (95F), 19 of which are over 40C (104F),
while winter is characterised by mainly warm days and some cold
nights. Generally, the further north you go, temperatures are less
extreme, while rainfall and humidity increase.

Tennant Creek	J	F	M	A	M	J	J	A	S	O	N	D	Ann Av.
Temperature: C													
Av. monthly max.	36	36	34	31	27	24	24	28	31	34	36	37	32
Av. monthly min.	25	24	23	20	16	12	11	14	17	21	23	25	19
Rainfall:													
Av. monthly mm.	105	106	67	16	9	9	9	3	11	23	36	65	459

Daly Waters	J	F	M	A	M	J	J	A	S	O	N	D	Ann Av.
Temperature: C													
Av. monthly max.	36	35	34	34	31	29	29	32	34	37	37	37	34
Av. monthly min.	23	23	22	19	15	12	11	13	16	20	23	23	18
Rainfall:													
Av. monthly mm.	161	156	119	22	6	6	2	2	5	22	59	103	663

LANDSCAPE

The Barkly Tableland dominates the landscape east of the Stuart
Highway, and gradually slopes until it merges west and south into
the vast semi-arid lands. It's nearly a perfect plain, almost free
from surface rocks with deep grey-brown soil clothed in tufted
Mitchell grass. Except for the creek lines, there are very few trees.
The tussocky grasses and extensive plain quickly attracted the
interest of cattlemen who saw it as ideal cattle breeding country,
best suited to produce young steer. Despite little permanent
surface water, the sinking of bores ensures that cattle remain king
on these grassy domains.

Of special interest is its geological makeup. While surrounding landscapes underwent massive geologic upheaval, it's extraordinary that the ancient rocks of the Barkly have remained virtually unchanged since Cambrian Times - 600 million years ago. It's one of the few places on earth where this occurs. During the Cambrian Period, the area sank, and under a shallow sea accumulated beds of shales and limestone. Later, two periods of slow uplift uniformly elevated the sea bed to about its present height. In the few places where the rocks are revealed, it is possible to see well-preserved remains of Cambrian Time marine species.

From the Barkly Highway, brown and grey termite mounds can be seen resembling tombstones; bleached grasses stretch to the horizon and shimmer under the Dry Season sun; willie willies distantly spiral columns of dust; and relentless heat produces unforgettable images.

> To the west, the sand ridges, sand plains and stone pavements of the Tanami Desert meet the tableland and merge into undulating semi-arid lands, broken only by some rocky outcrops - the best known being the *Devil's Marbles* and *The Pebbles*.

FLORA

Colourful flora abounds, and it's worth stopping for a closer look, particularly after the rains when spectacular windflower cover occurs in the more arid areas. Perennial grasses grow in clumps on the tableland - Curly and Mitchell mainly, with Panic, Kerosene, Blue and Love, lesser varieties. Spinifex or porcupine grass thrives in semi-arid areas. Distance gives the illusion of a complete grass cover - in fact, the clumps can be widely spaced with barren ground between. Other species are: mulla mullas which bloom fluffy mauve in the Dry Season; cassia shrubs, which are distinctive with their yellow flowers; mulga with its grey-green foliage, denser in the south but fading away north of Tennant Creek, its hard durable wood used by Aboriginal craftsmen;

lancewood, bauhinia or bean tree further north; native hibiscus which blooms all year and has five petalled pink flowers; the native pomegranate has creamy petals with silky filaments and produces apple shaped fruit; candelabra is a large acacia bush which has cylindrical yellow flowers and twisted seed pods. (When green pods are rubbed with water on your hands, the sodium produces a lather or 'bush soap').

Main eucalypts are snappy gum, yellow box, bloodwood, ironwood, woollybutt, stringybark and the coolabah (Banjo Paterson's favourite shade tree). Ghost and river red gums tend to line the sandy creek beds and red bud mallee is common in the Tanami. But most trees give little shade.

FAUNA

Cooler times of the day are best for wildlife observation. Larger animals include: red kangaroo (in lesser numbers now) on the treed, grassy plains - you'll need sharp eyes to spot them resting in the daytime heat; euro or wallaroo which mainly inhabit rocky outcrops; feral donkeys and horses, often in groups which can be a surprise encounter; dingo and of course, station cattle. Goulds goanna with an average length of nearly 1.3m is a most impressive reptile, and snakes, while present, are not really interested in meeting you.

Birdlife is plentiful - emu and bustard on the plains, while wedge-tailed eagle, with a 2m wing-span, black kite and brown falcon are some of the birds of prey. Waterholes attract a great range - whistler duck, heron, egret and ibis are some. Open wood and shrublands have honeyeater, finch, cockatoo and galahs.

Of the insects, termites (white ants) are most fascinating. They are large, whitish in colour, soft bodied, avoid sunlight, and build large clay mounds. The mound's outer shell is tough and durable. Inside it's full of softer, woody material arranged into galleries and chambers. The queen produces thousands of eggs, conveyed by workers to the nursery chambers, where high humidity levels are maintained to assist hatching. Termites forage and harvest organic matter, and while they play an important role in soil ecology, they are bad news for wooden buildings. Most of Northern Australia's early architecture was destroyed by them.

TOURING SUGGESTIONS

Take time along the Stuart Highway. There are plenty of historic spots, some coinciding with the Territory's best bush pubs that offer original Outback architecture and intriguing interiors - Barrow Creek, Wauchope and Daly Waters Pub should not be missed.

For 'off the beaten track' Outback experience, try the narrow-sealed, all-weather Carpentaria and Tablelands Highways or 'beef roads' (so named because of the huge roadtrains and the cattle they transport), which give conventional vehicle access across the Tableland to Borroloola and the Gulf of Carpentaria.

This route forms the Territory Tablelands Loop (see also *Introductory Section* under *Territory Tourism Drives, Heritage Trails and 4WD Explorer Tracks*).

There's much to offer the adventurous. The Carpentaria Highway from Borroloola takes you south-east to the historic Wollogorang Station with its Gulf beach camping. To the west of the Stuart Highway at Dunmarra, try the Buchanan Highway to the Tanami desert fringes at the Top Springs and Kalkarindji outposts (*The Overlanders Loop* route).

A novel way to experience the Barkly is by mail plane, for a day's flight with the 'aerial postman' to remote cattle stations and settlements. Seat availability depends on the amount of mail and freight, the first priority of operator Skyport Group. Check with their offices in Tennant Creek or Katherine, or ph (08) 8952 6666; costs from $200 per person.

PLACES AND ATTRACTIONS

ATTACK CREEK HISTORICAL RESERVE

0.2ha (0.5 acres)

LOCATION

On the Stuart Highway, 70km (43 miles) north of Tennant Creek.

HISTORY

Explorer John McDouall Stuart's first attempt at crossing the continent from the south ended here on June 25, 1860, when sickness forced him to return to Adelaide. There is some dispute about the role of Warumungu clansmen who were supposed to have forced his retreat. An inscribed plaque marks the event.

20km (12 miles) north is Banka Banka Homestead, one of the few station settlements close to the highway, characterised by an attractive tropical garden including banana palms and bougainvilleas. It was used by the army during WW II as a staging camp, the second night stop for troops from Alice Springs enroute to Larrimah railhead.

SERVICES AND FACILITIES

Table, shade, wood barbecue, camping allowed.

AVON DOWNS

LOCATION

On the Barkly Highway, approximately 60km (37 miles) from the Northern Territory/Queensland border.

CHARACTERISTICS

Homestead of the 3939 sq km (2363 sq miles) cattle property situated just off the highway, thus allowing a glimpse of a station settlement.

SERVICES AND FACILITIES

A police station next door is the only public service. A roadside rest area includes fireplace, table and shelter.

BARKLY HOMESTEAD

Population 15

LOCATION

At the junction of the Barkly and Tableland Highways, 211km (131 miles) east of Tennant Creek.

CHARACTERISTICS

The only roadhouse on the Northern Territory section of the Barkly Highway, is a modern structure, established by current hosts, Bob and Lynn Rose in 1984. It is a welcome 'watering hole' on the arid fringes of the Tableland where summer temperatures hit 45C (113F) and features a restaurant that offers traditional to exotic food in a comfortable atmosphere.

HISTORY

Although the homestead is recent, it is named indirectly after Henry Barkly, Governor of Victoria, when William Landsborough named the tablelands after him while searching for Burke and Wills, in 1861. The tablelands were discovered earlier by Ludwig Leichhardt in 1845, and crossed by explorer A.C. Gregory in 1856. Legendary cattleman and drover Nathaniel Buchanan opened up the area for settlement between 1877 and 1878, and by 1884 there were over 100,000 sheep on the Barkly. Sheep were short-lived when cattle were found to thrive better in the harsh heat conditions, and they have been dominant ever since. A police station was established at Anthony Lagoon (about 226km-140 miles north of Barkly Homestead) in 1895 to protect the stock routes. It closed in 1979.

The Barkly Highway was constructed during the Second World War with the assistance of United States finance.

ACCOMMODATION

Motel - $62 single, $72 double.

Camping - powered sites for caravans $18, other sites $4 per person. Dogs must be leashed.

SERVICES AND FACILITIES

A bar, restaurant, shop, accommodation and 'bush' swimming - dam with pontoon and pleasant surrounds. Meals from $10, take-away food, ice, souvenirs, camping gas, fuel (LP, ULP, diesel, autogas), oil, minor repairs and a towing service. Showers for travellers ($2). It has a 1.2km dirt, airstrip. Credit cards accepted and EFTPOS facility available. *Open daily 7am-midnight*, ph (08) 8964 4549.

BARROW CREEK

Population 12

LOCATION

284km (176 miles) north of Alice Springs, on the Stuart Highway.

CHARACTERISTICS

This tiny township nestles at the foot of a table-top range and consists of the oldest roadhouse on 'The Track', and the historic Barrow Creek Telegraph Station. If you're beginning to think that real Outback pubs are a myth, try 'The Barrow'. Its well-worn comfortable atmosphere reeks of history, beer and cattlemen - the sort of place Crocodile Dundee would meld into, except there's an inquisitive donkey to greet you instead of a croc!

The bar walls are a pictorial essay of mainly humorous artwork, strongly suggesting that the more isolated the pub, the more creative are the people who flourish around it. Its crowning glory is the wall of dollar notes of all denominations and currencies behind the bar, called the 'bush bank'. Patrons make sure they're never caught short of cash by simply signing a note and pinning it to the wall of 'The Creek Bank' and withdrawing it if necessary at a later date. According to 'bank manager' and publican, Les Pilton, the house always wins. No-one has claimed money yet without spending it at the bar first. The pub is an art gallery, museum, "theatre", community centre and living shrine, that can provide the casual caller with a memorable, even if fleeting, insight into an isolated Outback community.

HISTORY

The area was first explored by Stuart in 1860, and named after South Australian clergyman and politician John Henry Barrow. The *Telegraph Station*, built in 1872, was one of a series the Overland Telegraph Line needed at about 250km (155 miles) intervals to boost the signals along. The stone fortress-like structure was surrounded by a 200 sq km (124 sq miles) grazing reserve - in such remote locations, the operators had to be well protected from hostile Aborigines and virtually self-sufficient. But, in a surprise attack by Kaytej clansmen in 1874, linesman John Franks and station master, James Stapleton, were killed. The station is now preserved as a memorial to them, and their graves are close by. The station was used for communications during World War II, and the yellow house, built in the 1950s, was a post office and residence until the early 1980s. The station is open to visitors.

The hotel was built by Joe Kilgariff in 1930, and there's a store of amusing tales about the ringers, prospectors, telegraph linesmen and travellers who have passed through. About 40km (25 miles) to the north are the concrete slab remains of New Barrow, which during World War II was a large staging camp, the first night stop for troops travelling by army truck between the Larrimah and Alice Springs railheads.

EVENTS

The desert golf course is the venue for the 'Barrow Open' held in October. The Creek Races are run in August, and the annual cricket match between the 'Barrow Bottlers' and Ted Egan's 'Eroes' from Alice Springs, takes place in mid-September, if not too wet inside or out!

ACCOMMODATION

Hotel room - $25 single, $40 double, $50 triple; Family $60.

Camping - Caravans $7 for 2 persons, $3 extra for power. Tents $4 per person. Some grassy, shady sites. Pets allowed, dogs must be leashed.

SERVICES AND FACILITIES

A bar, dining room (good selection of home cooked meals), accommodation, shop, tourist information, swimming pool (guests only), shaded BBQ area, shade shelters for vehicles (bough sheds), 6-hole golf course, 1km airstrip, ramps for the disabled and showers for travellers ($3). Take-away food, ice, alcohol, fuel (LP, ULP, autogas, diesel), oil, camping gas, basic spares, tyres, tubes, tyre and minor mechanical repairs, towing service and souvenirs are all available.

Credit Cards are accepted. Opening hours 7am-11pm daily, ph (08) 8956 9753.

BONNEY WELL

LOCATION

On the west side of the Stuart Highway, 85km (53 miles) south of Tennant Creek.

CHARACTERISTICS

A National Trust administered site featuring one of the last remaining original water improvements on the Overland Telegraph Line Stock Route. Alfred Giles, who later overlanded cattle for his Springvale property near Katherine, began the first well here in 1879, to provide water for mobs of sheep being driven up from Alice Springs. Well sinkers, who were excavating the bank of Bonney Creek were instructed to stop, as rains had provided sufficient surface water for the sheep. The well was completed later by the Telegraph Department in 1844, further altered in 1892, and finally abandoned in 1936. Much of the

original solid stonework remains intact. Leading east of Bonny Well is the Kurundi/Epenarra Station Track which is the northern access route to Davenport/Murchison National Park (see separate listing).

SERVICES AND FACILITIES
Roads Department rest area with fireplace, table and shelter.

BORROLOOLA

Population 900

LOCATION
Situated on the McArthur River, 50km (31 miles) from the Gulf of Carpentaria, 389 km (241 miles) east of Daly Waters on the sealed Carpentaria Hwy.

CHARACTERISTICS
Borroloola, thought to mean 'place of the paperbarks', consists of timber, fibro and iron buildings scattered over a few square

kilometres, and serves the cattle and tourist industry. It is also an administrative centre with government offices. It has an Aboriginal population including the Mara, Yanyula and Garawa people. Borroloola's 're-discovery' is based on the river which teems with barramundi, hence the 'Barra Capital of the Gulf' tag. And, there are plenty of saltwater crocs. A laid-back atmosphere, colourful history, and stunning gulf, make Borroloola an extraordinary community in the Outback.

HISTORY

Explorer Ludwig Leichhardt crossed here in 1845 on his epic walk to Port Essington. Overlanders Cahill, Buchanan, the Duracks and MacDonalds used it as a drovers' camp in the 1880s, and the pub was built in 1885. It became a port too: supplies and materials for the Barkly Stations were shipped to the Gulf and landed at Borroloola, and its colourful history began as 'a wild and lawless outpost where everyone wore Colt revolvers'. Its early days were further described as 'a resort for all the scum of Northern Australia', with robberies, drunkenness, prostitution and sly grogging rackets rife among the mainly male population. It's not surprising that a police station was quickly established in late 1886!

The early town consisted of two hotels with general stores attached; two general stores with grog shanties attached; two butchers' shops; three saddlers' huts; a bakery, blacksmith, Chinese market garden and dairy farm. The permanent population of about 30 was often boosted to over 100 by drifters, and there were some conflicts between Europeans and Aborigines.

Borroloola began with a bang and seemed destined to end in a whimper - the victim of isolation, high settlement costs and slow pastoral development on the Barkly. For 50 or so years, it was a backwater. The few Europeans who remained had little contact with the outside world, and subsisted around the few dilapidated buildings left.

The police station continued to function, and there's a good story about one of its officers, Corporal Power, who was so bored with lonely outpost duties, that he asked the Carnegie Foundation in New York for a book or two to read. He got them alright - a whole classics library! The library became something of an institution, continued to acquire books until the 1930s, and nourished the mind of many a bushman. Outback raconteur and writer the late Bill Harney (the first Ranger at Ayers Rock) read most of them in gaol. He had plenty of time, five months in fact, while waiting for his appeal against cattle duffing (stealing) charges to be upheld. He was freed when the papers eventually arrived from Darwin.

It's the story of the last old white men that makes Borroloola a legendary place. Described as hermits and eccentrics, they cut biblical figures with their beards and bush staves as they hobbled around their Utopia. David Attenborough made a film about them in 1963. One, Roger Jose, arrived here in 1916, lived in an upturned corrugated iron water tank, and was widely read (he had read all the books in the library before it disappeared - the termites not only ate most of the books, but the building too!). He rarely left the town where he lived with his Aboriginal wife. He wore a heavy coat 'to keep out the hot air', and died here in 1963. He hated material things, saying *man's true wealth is the fewness of his wants* , while about Aborigines he said, *...No one could ever make converts of them. They had too strong a culture of their own, a profound attachment to nature that transcended the white man's materialistic creed*. Jack Mulholland, another 'hermit', lived in the old hotel until it crumbled away in the early 1960s, by which time the main street doubled as an airstrip.

There is not much left of the old town, but there is a wealth of stories about both its notorious past, and its legendary 'lotus eaters'.

ATTRACTIONS

The old *Police Station* is the oldest surviving example of such an outpost in the Northern Territory, and houses a interesting museum. A Heritage Trail starting at the museum includes restored buildings, pioneer grave sites and the McArthur River along its path.

Most visitors come for the barramundi - a large fish, highly prized for its fighting spirit and delicate taste. A guide to the best spots and lures is available in town, and the pub will give you plenty of good advice and information, as will other friendly locals.

OUTLYING ATTRACTIONS

These include curious "lost city" sandstone formations at *Caranbirini Conservation Reserve* which features a waterhole with plenty of native birds as well as some fascinating geological formations. It's located about 40kms (25 miles) southwest of Borroloola, accessible by conventional vehicle and walking trails.

Barranyi National Park encompasses a group of islands off shore from the McArthur River mouth. Collectively, they are called *The Sir Edward Pellew Group*. The *North Island* of this group belongs to the Barranyi people and parts of this idyllic tropical island are open to visitors. Access to some of its beautiful beaches, excellent fishing spots and pervading tranquillity of Paradise Bay is by boat only or by organised tour.

Paradise Fishing Tours have a comfortable base on the island and offer excellent accommodation in a package which also includes all meals, most transfers and guided fishing tours in a luxury cruiser (a range of fishing options available). Costs are $165 p.p. per night, reduced rates for children. Camping is another option, but you will need to be self-sufficient as facilities are limited. For further details, ph Mark and Jennifer Banlon, Paradise Fishing Tours 0145 199 084.

King Ash Bay (Batten Pt.) 25km (16 miles) north-east of Borroloola. A popular fishing and camping spot on the coast with a ramp facility and local fishing clubrooms.

TOURS

Most focus on the river, reef or gulf.

Croc Spot Tours - fishing charters, croc spotting, scenic river and gulf island camping charters, ph (08) 8975 8721.

Shore Flights - scenic flights, ph (08) 8975 8668.

EVENTS

The *'Barra Classic'* at Easter is a premier fishing competition; *Rodeo* in August; and the *District Show* is held mid year.

HOW TO GET THERE

By road

The narrow sealed all-weather Carpentaria Highway is about a five hour, 379km (234 miles) trip from the Stuart Highway at Daly Waters, and gives all year access. From the south, the Tablelands Highway gives similar conventional vehicle access over 391km (242 miles) from the Barkly Highway turn-off.

By air

Air North operates three flights per week from Katherine.

ACCOMMODATION

Borroloola Inn (hotel) - rooms from $45 per room, ph (08) 8975 8766. Borroloola Holiday Village - units from $92, economy single from $50, bunkhouses from $30, ph (08) 8975 8742.

McArthur River Caravan Park - budget rooms from $30; units from $65; powered sites from $15 x 2, camping sites $12 x 2. All sites grassed and dogs must be leashed, ph (08) 8975 8734.

SERVICES AND FACILITIES

The range is sufficient to satisfy most tourist needs, credit cards are accepted, and many have EFTPOS facilities. There's a supermarket, two general stores, pub, garages, fuel outlets (LP, ULP, diesel, aviation, camping gas), butcher, post office, police station, health clinic, church, art gallery and local government offices. Bank agencies are Westpac (Chicken Shop) and Commonwealth (Post Office and Bulk Discount).

Boating and fishing requirements, hire boats, souvenirs and Aboriginal artifacts are available. Three boat ramps, sealed airstrip, swimming pool (Borroloola Inn) are the main recreational facilities.

There is a choice of take-aways, and The Restaurant (Borroloola Inn) has main courses from $12.

Radio Stations: ABC 103.7 and 107.7 FM.

BRUNETTE DOWNS

Population 100

LOCATION
On the Tablelands Highway, 140km (87 miles) north of Barkly Homestead Roadhouse.

CHARACTERISTICS
This huge cattle station, owned by The Australian Agricultural Company, covers 12,250 sq km (7595 sq miles), making it the largest in the Northern Territory. It has 2,200km (1364 miles) of fencing, and runs 53,000 Santa Gertrudis cattle. The homestead settlement is town-like and clusters close to the Brunette Creek. While established in 1883, it's not the oldest or the largest, but its far-flung reputation, based on quality stock, characters and incidences, gives Brunette Downs a legendary status amongst cattlemen of the Outback.

EVENTS
The station hosts an annual event in mid-June that's being going since 1910 - The Brunette Downs Bush Races, featuring campdraft on Friday, racing Saturday and campdraft finals, rodeo and gymkhana on Sunday. It is held 20km away from the homestead and the 'Club' even has its own corrugated iron hall and bar. The 'locals' come from hundreds of kilometres away by plane or road, and a carnival atmosphere exists in the campsites near the track. Bush dances, BBQ and bar ensure lively evenings. Anyone is welcome, camping is free, and meals cost around $10 during the day, $20 for evening meals, with bar prices for drinks. The station is closed to visitors at all times. The race track area only is open to visitors during the event.

HOW TO GET THERE
By road, via the Barkly or Carpentaria Highways to the Tablelands Highway. It is sign-posted, and access is okay for conventional

vehicles. By air: an airstrip for light plane travellers is located at the western end of the race track, prior arrangement only for use of station airstrip. Ph (08) 8964 4522.

CAPE CRAWFORD

Population 6

LOCATION

At the junction of the Carpentaria and Tablelands Highways, 280km (174 miles) east of the Stuart Highway at Daly Waters, and 383km (237 miles) north of Barkly Homestead Roadhouse.

CHARACTERISTICS

Cape Crawford consists of a roadhouse only, intriguingly called Heartbreak Hotel. Many stories circulate as to how it got its name - the most likely seems that when being constructed in the 1980s, spasmodic supplies caused the builder to constantly exclaim in frustration to anyone who would listen *"... it breaks your bloody heart!"* And why is a place so far from the sea called a cape? It is thought that the land shape as the Tableland drops resembled a coastal feature to the Telegraph survey party, who named it after one of their officers. Lack of ocean was obviously immaterial!

ATTRACTIONS

Lost City Landforms of 500 million year old sandstones have been weathered into weirdly angled and shaped domes. They constitute an ancient city appearance. These are located in the Abner Range, about 70kms (43 miles) south-east of Cape Crawford. Access is by helicopter only during the dry season. The hotel offers helicopter tours, and tours to Bukalara Rock Formations - an extraordinary array of chasms that dissect the sandstone formations.

HOW TO GET THERE

By road, via the narrow sealed Carpentaria or Tablelands Highways. This all-weather road is suitable for conventional vehicles.

ACCOMMODATION

Rooms - single $60, double $70. **Camping** - powered sites $10, unpowered sites $5. Grassed sites, pets allowed, dogs leashed.

SERVICES AND FACILITIES

It offers good homestyle meals around $15 with BBQ Sundays ($10), take-away food, shop, bar, ice, camping gas, picnic area, showers for travellers ($2) and swimming pool (guests only). Vehicles services: fuel (LP, ULP, diesel), oil, tyres, tubes. Credit cards accepted, EFTPOS facilities available. Open 7am-11pm, ph (08) 8975 9928.

CONNELLS LAGOON CONSERVATION RESERVE

25,890ha (639,483 acres)

LOCATION

East of Brunette Downs Station. Turn off from the Carpentaria Highway just north of the station.

CHARACTERISTICS

An area set aside to preserve and protect the Mitchell grassland ecology from pressures of grazing. There are no facilities, or lagoon (except after rains). No animals are allowed.

HOW TO GET THERE

Access is via a formed road to this reserve.

DALY WATERS

Population 20

LOCATION

3km west of the Stuart Highway, 392km (243 miles) north of Tennant Creek, and 265km (164 miles) south of Katherine on the Stuart Highway.

CHARACTERISTICS

Tucked away from the hustle of the highway, and situated near a creek and large waterhole, this small township centres around a quaint, bougainvillea-draped pub and offers a rare blend of Australian bush and traditional architecture that should not be missed. In its tropical woodland setting, Daly Waters consists of the old pub, six houses, caravan park, the remains of a telegraph station, and Australia's first international airfield. It is surrounded by the nearly 4000 sq km (1520 sq miles) Kalala cattle station. Apart from the delight of finding an unspoilt (and plastic-free) Outback spot, it has quite a few historic surprises in store, too!

HISTORY

Explorer John McDouall Stuart's final expedition discovered a small creek which began "improving wonderfully", broadened, deepened, became "splendidly grassed", and was surrounded by ironwoods, lancewoods, bloodwoods and crimson-blossomed bauhinias. Stuart was obviously delighted with his May 23, 1862 find, and named the place after Sir Dominic Daly, the then Governor of South Australia. But words written here by Stuart also tell of the enormous physical and mental strain of the expedition, *"I feel this heavy work much more than I did the journey of last year; so much of it is beginning to tell upon me. I feel my capability of endurance beginning to give way..."*. There's a tree about 800m from the pub on which Stuart, or a member of his party, is said to have carved the initial 'S', and the large waterhole bears his name.

An overland telegraph repeater station was built here in 1872, and until the lines were joined near Dunmarra later that year, a pony express plugged the gap between Daly Waters and Tennant Creek. A West Australian expedition, led by Alexander Forrest to explore the Kimberley, might have perished in the desert had it not been for the telegraph line and Daly Waters. Striking north-east from the De Grey River on the west coast in 1879, the party failed to find a way through the precipitous Kimberley gorges, and dwindling rations forced Forrest to abandon attempts to trace the Ord River outlet. They struck east to the telegraph line, surviving on weaker horses, snakes and birds. When some members became ill about 160km (99 miles) from the line, Alexander Forrest and Arthur Hicks rode for two days and nights for help; found and followed the line to Daly Waters, where a rescue party was hastily organised. The point where Forrest found the line is commemorated today by an inscribed roadside cairn, approximately 50km (31 miles) north of the township.

Mr and Mrs Bill Pearce built the present pub in 1930. From the north they brought supplies of Maranboy Cypress Pine, known to be disliked by white ants, and built the pine and corrugated iron pub that architecturally remains unchanged today.

Daly Waters was eventually put on world maps by two Australian World War I fighter pilots, Hudson Fysh and P.J. McGuinness, who in 1922 purchased two war-surplus biplanes and began the Queensland and Northern Territory Aerial Services (Qantas). When Qantas started its first international service between Singapore and Brisbane in 1934, Daly Waters was the refuelling stop, and nearly all who travelled to Australia by air during the 1930s came via here. Pianist Arthur Rubenstein flew in from London in 1936 and coincidentally met violinist Bronislaw Huberman, who had arrived from Perth - a most unlikely meeting place for the two famous musicians who had not seen each other for 15 years. Many other well-known and titled people passed this way, as did the Australian pioneer aviators. These aviators didn't impress overland telegraph linesman Waldemar 'Wallaby' Holtze.

He loved the solitude of the Outback and complained that Daly Waters was too noisy. Kingsford Smith had just roared in with the first airmail for London and for a few months 'Wallaby' endured such mad fliers (as he called them) as Bert Hinkler, Amy Johnson, Jimmy Broadbent and Ray Parer. 'Wallaby' Holtze applied for, and was granted, a transfer to Tennant Creek in 1932. He didn't find much peace there either - the Tennant Creek gold rush had just begun!

  Bill Pearce's pub thrived under this unexpected aerial bonanza, which increased further with the development of internal air services. All of this happened well before the Stuart Highway was built! For a while Daly Waters was the major junction of these early air routes.

  The airport was an important United States and Australian Air Force base during World War II, mainly for the US Flying Fortress Bomber Squadrons, and after the Japanese bombing of Darwin in 1942, an RAAF hospital was established here. The 2000m runway is still used, mainly by light aircraft, while the hangar and staff quarters building are reminders of earlier, action-packed days. The old hanger now houses a fascinating aviation history display.

ATTRACTIONS

Daly Waters Pub. One of the Territory's best Outback pubs that has a 'bush bank', plenty of interesting nooks and crannies and memorabilia, a friendly kangaroo, loads of hospitality, and a sign over the bar which offers credit to any woman over 80 who is accompanied by her mother!

The Airfield and ***Stuart's Tree*** can be visited, but Stuart's Swamp, which teems with birdlife when full (pelicans, black cockatoos), is on private property.

Telegraph Station. The original wooden structure was destroyed by fire, and burnt foundation posts are all that remain. The usual stone construction for telegraph stations was not possible here because of lack of accessible rock.

EVENTS

The *Daly Waters Rodeo* runs for three days over the last weekend in September.

ACCOMMODATION

Air-conditioned rooms - $28 single, $38 double.

Camping/caravans - powered sites $10 two persons, unpowered $3 per person. Sites grassed and shaded, pets allowed - dogs must be leashed.

SERVICES AND FACILITIES

Most are centred around the pub and include a general store, bar, restaurant (meals from $14, 'beef and barra' BBQ each night in season), picnic/BBQ shaded area, swimming pool, 2000m airstrip, showers for travellers and facilities for disabled. Ice, take-away food and souvenirs are also available. Fuel (LP, ULP, diesel, aviation, oil and camping gas) is available and there are basic spares, tyres and tubes, and limited mechanical repairs for vehicles.

Credit cards accepted and EFTPOS facility available. *Open 7am-11pm*, ph (08) 8975 9927.

DALY WATERS JUNCTION - HI-WAY INN

Population 10

LOCATION

At the junction of the Stuart and Carpentaria Highways, 3km (1.8 miles) south of Daly Waters township turn-off, and 389km (241 miles) north of Tennant Creek.

CHARACTERISTICS

Often mistaken for Daly Waters (the historic township, 3km north and 3km west of the Stuart Highway from here), the Hi-Way Inn hotel/motel was built in 1974 to provide fuel, food and accommodation for passing travellers. Confusion comes from its closeness to Daly Waters; it's known by some locals as Carpentaria, while to others it's Daly Waters Junction, a 'suburb' of Daly Waters that is more conveniently located on the Stuart Highway.

ACCOMMODATION
Motel style - $47 single, $58 double, $68 triple.
Caravans/Camping - powered sites $14 x 2, unpowered $4 per person. Sites shaded, pets allowed - dogs must be leashed.

SERVICES AND FACILITIES
It has a shop, restaurant (seafood, grills), bar, tropical beer garden, picnic/BBQ area, swimming pool (for patrons), and showers for travellers. Take-away food, ice and souvenirs are available. Fuel includes LP, ULP, diesel, autogas and oil. For attractions see Daly Waters listing.

Credit cards accepted and EFTPOS facility, *open 7am-11pm daily*, nightbell for after hours fuel (fee), ph (08) 8975 9925.

DAVENPORT/MURCHINSON RANGES NATIONAL PARK

LOCATION
Approximately 75 kms (47 miles) south-east of Wauchope.

CHARACTERISTICS
This recently declared 1120 sq km (694 sq.miles) National Park protects a relatively unspoilt wilderness area important for its transitional zone (between the tropical Top End and arid centre) environmental qualities. The ranges have a quiet, timeless appeal and the area is a significant refuge for fauna, particularly water birds attracted to an extensive network of waterholes.

The Davenport Ranges mark the boundary between the lands of the Warunungu, Alyawarre and Kaytetye people who continue to have strong associations with the land.

DAVENPORT RANGE NATIONAL PARK

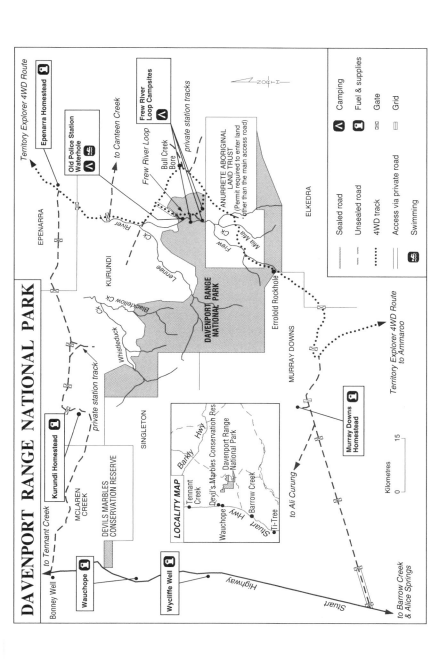

Territory Explorer 4WD Route

Epenarra Homestead

Old Police Station Waterhole

Frew River Loop Campsites

to Canteen Creek

private station tracks

Bull Creek Bore

ANURRETE ABORIGINAL LAND TRUST
(Permit required to enter land other than the main access road)

EPENARRA

Frew River

KURUNDI

Lennee Ck

ELKEDRA

Mia Mia Ck

Frew Ck

DAVENPORT RANGE NATIONAL PARK

Errolold Rockhole

Blackfellow Ck

MURRAY DOWNS

Whistleduck

SINGLETON

Territory Explorer 4WD Route to Ammaroo

Kurundi Homestead

private station track

MCLAREN CREEK

DEVILS MARBLES CONSERVATION RESERVE

Murray Downs Homestead

to Ali Curung

Bonney Well

to Tennant Creek

Wauchope

Wycliffe Well

Stuart Highway

to Barrow Creek & Alice Springs

LOCALITY MAP

Tennant Creek
Barkly Hwy
Devil's Marbles Conservation Res
Davenport Range National Park
Wauchope
Barrow Creek
Stuart Hwy
Ti-Tree

0   15
Kilometres

N

Legend

Sealed road
Unsealed road
4WD track
Access via private road

Camping
Fuel & supplies
Gate
Grid
Swimming

Mining activities, particularly Wolfram extraction at Hatches Creek and grazing were former European uses of the region.

FEATURES AND FACILITIES

The main attraction, apart from the wilderness, is the ***Old Police Station Waterhole*** - an extensive body of water where swimming is popular. There are only basic camping facilities at this site and along the Frew River Loop 4WD Track (see map).

The park is isolated and unstaffed. You must be well prepared and self-sufficient with supplies. Fuel is available at Kurundi, Epenarra and Murray Downs (see map).

ACCESS

A high clearance vehicle is essential, 4WD recommended. Old Police Station Waterhole is approximately 171 kms (106 miles) via the Kurundi/Epenarra Stations track which leads off the Stuart Hwy at Bonny Well, 90km (56 miles) south of Tennant Creek). Alternatively, it is 156 kms approximately (97 miles), via Taylors Creek Track (Murray Downs Station track), which heads east from the Stuart Hwy near Taylors Creek Crossing, 43 km (27 miles) north of Barrow Creek. 4WD is essential.

This loop track forms part of a Territory Explorer 4WD route, and the round trip is about 327 km (203 miles).

Remember to advise authorities beforehand of your travel plans in this area and don't forget to advise of your return. The area is subject to frequent flooding between December and March. Always check local road and weather conditions - phone police at Ali Curung (08) 8964 1959.

DEVIL'S MARBLES CONSERVATION RESERVE

1828ha (4515 acres)

LOCATION

On both sides of the Stuart Highway, 87km (54 miles) south of Tennant Creek.

CHARACTERISTICS

An extensive rocky outcrop scattered across a wide, shallow valley features a collection of gigantic granite boulders, some of which perch precariously on top of one another. It has an aura reminiscent of Stonehenge, and is a sacred site of the Warumungu, who believe that the Rainbow Serpent laid them. They are a photographer's delight.

GEOLOGY

The 'marbles' were formed from an original granite mass. As it cooled and uplifted slowly, the mass developed three main sets of joint planes (cracks) at right angles to each other, breaking the granite into three to seven metre rectangular blocks. Erosion along the joints associated with flaking away of thin slabs from the surface, widened and rounded the corners to their present shapes. Where the surrounding granite has worn away, these boulders are left, one upon the other.

FLORA AND FAUNA

Ghost gums cling to some boulders, and spinifex is the main ground cover. Pygmy spiny- tailed goannas frequent crevices; the larger sand goanna prefer spinifex. On the underside of over-hanging boulders, fairy martin mud nests may be found; painted and zebra finch are numerous.

CONSERVATION

It is a fragile, arid environment. You can help preservation by keeping vehicles to existing roads, and taking your litter away with you. Fires should be lit only in places provided, and wood must not be collected in the reserve as trees are sparse, and decomposition of fallen branches is an important part of the food chain for birds and reptiles. Defacing the 'marbles' in any way is an offence, and incurrs a fine.

FACILITIES

Information signs along a short walk. Wood bbqs, picnic area, and basic toilet. Camping is allowed. For supplies, Wauchope is 9km (6 miles) south.

DUNMARRA

Population 12

LOCATION

On the Stuart Highway, 350km (217 miles) north of Tennant Creek, and 44km (27 miles) south of Daly Waters.

CHARACTERISTICS

Roadhouse, pub, store and restaurant, the Shell Wayside Inn, is a convenient stop after the dry stretch from Elliott. The original pub, built by drover Noel Healey in the 1930s, was replaced in 1971 by the present structure. Opposite are remnants of one of the original telegraph poles, and an area of the former Dunmarra Cattle Station was a wartime RAAF base. An interesting historic marker about 20km (12 miles) south, commemorates not only the Overland Telegraph Line construction, but is also near the spot where the wires were joined in 1872. The Buchanan Highway turn-off to Top Springs is 8km (5 miles) north of Dunmarra.

ACCOMMODATION

Motel units - $35 single, $40 double, extra person $5. **Caravans/Camping** - powered sites $7 couple; unpowered sites $2.50 per person. Pets allowed - dogs must be leashed.

SERVICES AND FACILITIES

It has a bar, shop, restaurant, accommodation, camping and shaded barbecue area. Take-away food, ice, fuel (LP, ULP, LPG, diesel), tyre and minor mechanical repairs are available. Credit cards accepted and EFTPOS facilities provided, open 6am-11pm, ph (08) 8975 9922.

ELLIOTT

Population 600

LOCATION

Approximately half-way between Alice Springs and Darwin on the Stuart Highway - 790km (490 miles) north of Alice Springs, and 735km (456 miles) south of Darwin.

CHARACTERISTICS

Elliott is a small, friendly regional service centre and cattle town. Services include a hotel/motel, camping grounds, supermarket, dining rooms, vehicle services, police station, post office, medical centre, airstrip, school, and various local government offices. It's an attractive settlement, set in an open woodland landscape, and surrounded by the 4000 sq km (1520 sq miles) *Newcastle Waters Cattle Station*.

It had its origins during World War II, when it functioned as a staging camp for troops on the move between Darwin and Alice Springs. The name is after Captain Elliott from Adelaide, the officer in charge of the wartime camp, and its development was assisted by both the decline of Newcastle Waters township, and its more convenient location on the Stuart Highway. It got a boost when the Junction Hotel licence at Newcastle Waters was transferred to *Jimmy Munckton's Elliott Hotel* in 1962, and the pub today is a good place to meet the locals, and like the town, it is unpretentious.

ATTRACTIONS
The nearby historic droving township of Newcastle Waters is worth visiting (see separate listing). Visitors should be aware that nearby Lake Woods is on private property and, contrary to information in many publications, it is not available for public use of any kind. The town has a grassed golf course (visitors most welcome), mini golf course and heritage walking trail. For information check with caravan parks and hotel.

ACCOMMODATION
Elliott Hotel - cabins $45 double, $30 single. Hotel has shaded BBQ area, pool (guests only), ph (08) 8969 2069.
Halfway Caravan Park - camping/caravan sites $13 for powered site, $6.50 extra person; unpowered sites $7; rooms from $40. Pets allowed, pool, ph (08) 8969 2025.

SERVICES AND FACILITIES
There are well-stocked supermarkets (Halfway Caravan Park), and Mobil Service Station; Bank Agencies are ANZ (Mobil Service Station), Commonwealth (Midland Caravan Park); Licensed

dining room meals at the Hotel and Mobil Service Station (from $6). Take-aways from Mobil; All fuels (LP, ULP, diesel, autogas and camping gas) are available; Medical services are available at the health clinic; ice; Aboriginal artifacts; showers for travellers.

Major credit cards are widely accepted and EFTPOS facilities are available.

KALKARINDJI

Population including Daguragu - 500

LOCATION

On the northern fringe of the Tanami Desert on the Buntine Highway, 460km (285 miles) south-west of Katherine.

CHARACTERISTICS

Set among low hills, plains of spinifex and stunted eucalypt, Kalkarindji (formerly Wave Hill) basically services the Daguragu Aboriginal settlement and local cattle stations.

HISTORY

Daguragu, 8km (5 miles) from Kalkarindji and originally called Wattie Creek, is significant in the Aboriginal Lands Rights Movement, being the site of the first grant of land ownership to an Aboriginal group. Led by Mr Vincent Lingiari in 1966, 200 Aboriginal stockmen and their families protested about their poor conditions on Wave Hill Station, and later demanded ownership of their traditional land. Because Wave Hill's Wattie Creek was sacred land - the main place of Guringi Dreaming and site of sacred totem paintings - the issue evolved into the first land rights claim. The Whitlam Labour Government granted the Guringi people a pastoral lease in 1975, on 3200 sq km (1984 sq miles) of the Wave Hill property. Then in 1986, they were formally granted ownership. Land rights pioneer Vincent Lingiari died in 1988. Daguragu is an Aboriginal settlement where tourists are not allowed.

HOW TO GET THERE

Best access for conventional vehicles is from Katherine during the Dry Season, via the sealed (mainly narrow) Victoria Highway and Buntine Highway (formerly Delamere Road). From the Stuart Highway (turn-off near Dunmarra), the Buchanan Highway is compacted gravel - with care, suitable for conventional vehicles. The Buchanan Highway from Halls Creek is gravel; reasonable after grading (generally twice a year) but can become corrugated - 4WD recommended. During the Wet Season (between December and early March), it is 4WD only, as floods at creeks and rivers can occur on both sides of Kalkaringi.

ACCOMMODATION

Camping - powered sites from $10, unpowered $5. Sites grassed and shaded. Pets allowed - dogs must be leashed.

SERVICES AND FACILITIES

It has a service station, supermarket and caravan park as one enterprise - open 8am-6pm weekdays, weekends 9am-5pm. Ph (08) 8975 0788. There is also a police station ph (08) 8975 0790, and a health clinic and council offices. Other facilities include airstrip, and showers for travellers ($2). Services include take-away food, ice, fuel (LP, ULP, diesel), oil, camping gas, minor mechanical and tyre repairs (Daguragu - check with Council first), tyres and tubes.

Credit cards accepted, EFTPOS facility at the store.

LAJAMANU

LOCATION

In the Tanami Desert, 104km (65 miles) south of Kalkarindji on the Lajamanu Road.

CHARACTERISTICS

Lajamanu is an Aboriginal settlement with transit services only for tourists. It has a well- stocked store ranging from foodstuffs to hardware, fuel (LP, ULP, diesel), mechanical repairs and some spares. An Aboriginal Arts Centre has a range of local works for sale. The store and service station is *open 8am-5pm weekdays, 8am-12noon Saturday and is closed on Sunday* (Fuel by prior arrangement outside these hours is subject to fee).

Credit cards are accepted and there is an EFTPOS facility, ph (08) 8975 0644.

NEWCASTLE WATERS

Population 10

LOCATION

3km (2 miles) west of the Stuart Highway, 24km (15 miles) north of Elliott.

CHARACTERISTICS

This old droving township, situated at the intersection of the Murranji and Barkly stock routes, and by the intermittent waters of Newcastle Creek, features historic buildings including the Junction Hotel, and a recent National Trust acquisition, George Man Fong's House, now known as Jones' Store. Interspersed are old houses occupied by Newcastle Waters Station employees. The 1988 opening of the Drovers' Memorial Park, historic trail and Jones' Store, with its memorabilia, is the first preservation and commemoration stage of Newcastle Waters' legendary droving heritage.

  At the beginning of The Last Great Cattle Drive from here (the Northern Territory's major Bicentennial event in 1988), it must have been gratifying for the oldest living drover, 95-year-old Tommy Williams, to see the place much as it was in his hey-day. The ersatz 'traditional' buildings now appearing in the Territory are sad reminders of how much of Australia's Outback architectural heritage has been lost. At Newcastle Waters, as elsewhere, the National Trust, along with other local groups, has done a magnificent job in ensuring the preservation of, and making available for public appreciation, this significant architectural and historic site.

> At this stage, the township has no facilities or services, and visitors are asked to respect private station roads and property.

HISTORY

Explorer Stuart was the first non-Aboriginal in the area in 1861, and he named the stretches of water after the Duke of Newcastle who was Secretary of State for the Colonies. The waters are known locally as Longreach Waterhole, and lie between the old town and Lake Woods to the south. The thick, savage scrub and dry stony plains proved too much of a barrier for the party, and concern for his men and supplies led Stuart to abandon any further movement north on this expedition.

The settlement developed primarily as a droving town in two distinct phases. In the first, between 1919 and 1930, it was a depot for construction gangs working on watering facilities for the east-west stock route. When government bores provided reliable water points after 1930, the second phase began, which saw the establishment of stores and the hotel. Apart from the police station, the fledgling township relied entirely on stock routes and their users for its livelihood.

The Junction Hotel, so named because of its location at the meeting place of two of the world's longest stock routes, has been described as *"seeing more good-natured fights and non-malicious brawling than any other pub on the Track"*. In its hey-day, it is also claimed the place saw about one fight per gallon of beer! It is not surprising, when the most common drinks taken in excess were beer and rum with a 'Rankin Bomb' being a popular mix - an 8oz glass filled almost with neat rum and topped off with port to sweeten it!

It did not cost Newcastle Waters storekeeper Jack Sargent much to build the 'Drovers Pub' in 1932. Old windmill blades found abandoned at stock route bores provided materials, while those who owed him money at the store "wiped their slates clean" with their labour. It certainly had plenty of atmosphere with its galvanised iron walls, iron bars on the windows, and hitching rail outside for the horses. Busiest times were at the beginning of the Wet Season when up to 14 droving plants camped here, and with no cattle to look after, the men had plenty of time for drinking. Max Schober, who ran the pub between 1935 and 1956, was as colourful as he was enterprising - he would travel for hundreds of kilometres, first by wagon, then in later years by motor vehicles, to meet the drovers with stores and food supplies. His successor, Dutch-born Oscar Schank, loved to prepare exotic food and despaired when his culinary delights were spurned. "All they want," he said, "is steak and eggs mate, always steak and bloody eggs!"

By the early 1960s, the widespread movement of cattle by motorised road trains, the construction of 'beef road' networks, one of which by-passed the Murranji stock route, and its location off the Stuart Highway, meant the end of both drover and pub. Oscar sold the licence, which was transferred to Jimmy Munckton's new establishment at Elliott in 1962, and the pub reverted to a store and bottle shop for the cattle station, until it finally closed in 1975.

The main part of Jones' store was built in 1935, and run by Arnold Jones from 1936 until 1949 as a store and butchery. In the late 1950s and early 1960s, George Man Fong, when he wasn't out on trips as a Boss Drover, worked from the premises as a saddler during his occupancy of the store. Architecturally, the store represents a traditional style common in the Territory; having had many owners and roles it has been adapted to meet each new need. Its construction of mud-brick walls, large bush timbers, corrugated iron and bamboo slatting that has withstood a harsh environment, along with its important function in the town's community life, highlight the building's significance. The house next to the pub was built in 1942 as a telegraph repeater station for World War II communications, and is now a private residence.

The large group of buildings away to the left is the homestead complex of the 4000 sq km (1520 sq miles) Newcastle Waters Cattle Station, first leased by Dr Browne from London in 1883, and established by the mid-1880s. Today, it runs between thirty and forty-five thousand cattle, mainly Santa Gertrudis, Brahman and some Charolais breeds.

In more recent times, the town was close to decay and used by itinerant Aboriginal families and station workers for housing, but never with any permanency. 1983 saw Newcastle Waters station bring about a revival by housing married staff in the town. You can wander through the old settlement, store and pub, and along the short, information posted, heritage trail and small park where there are monuments of the legendary drovers.

The Murranji Stock Route

Victoria River properties received their cattle via Top Springs along the Murranji Track, which took its Aboriginal name from the desert frog that was capable of living for long periods underground without water. It was the shortest route to the Eastern States from the Victoria River region; 234km (145 miles), in comparison with an extra 644km (399 miles) that the northern route through Katherine and the Roper River area entailed. The Murranji, opened in 1886, tapped into the pastoral lands of legendary owners and overlanders, Kilfoyle, Bradshaw, Buchanan, MacDonald and Durack, and between 50,000 and 70,000 cattle were brought down this track each year, reaching a peak of 77,000 in 1951.

It was the toughest track of them all: limited water until the bores went in; witchwood scrub with spiked branches that could spear stock, horse and rider; and a horror stretch of limestone country, called 'drummy' ground, that reverberated under the hooves and caused cattle to take fright and stampede. All this contributed to the route's deadly reputation. A 'Rankin Bomb' at the Junction Pub was clearly understandable after the Murranji!

HOW TO GET THERE

From the Stuart Highway, access is by a 3km sealed road.

DROVERS AND DROVING

The explorers first made known the pastoral potential of the Outback, but it was the overlander and drover who filled these huge spaces with cattle and sheep, often with epic treks that lasted many months, covered hundreds of kilometres and broke open new land. There were considerable profits to be made from these animals, and wealthy pastoralists and financiers in New South Wales, Victoria and South Australia eagerly snapped up land options in the Territory and Kimberley.

The only way to stock these frontier lands was to overland livestock from the Southern and Eastern states. Once established, the stations were the source of a steady supply of cattle droved along a network of stock routes that criss-crossed the continent to the southern railheads and markets.

The linchpin of this whole operation was the drover, a nomadic horseman who for nearly 100 years 'punched' the cattle across the vast, often arid, tracts of the Outback. In the late 1800s, they became *a symbol of the young nation's spirit; their stoicism, sardonic humour, mateship and restlessness expressed in folklore and balladry gave them legendary status and laid the basis of character traits much revered and regarded as typically Australian today.*

Droving cattle long distances was a well-ordered operation. A drove of 1500 cattle would require eight to ten men, a cook and horse-tailer (the man who tended the horses at the stock camp). Gear (food, water, general equipment and personal belongings) would either be carried by pack-horse, or in a sturdy wagon pulled by horse teams, and driven by the cook. Usually, there were about eight saddle-horses per man, and at least forty night horses. The leader was called a Boss Drover and 'ringers' were expert stockmen, so named for their ability to circle the herd at night to quieten them, and the term is quite distinct from the southern meaning - the fastest sheep shearer in the shed. A 'jackaroo' is an apprentice stockman who acquires his skills on the station, and the team of drovers was called 'a plant'.

Drovers operated in stages, moving the cattle about 12km (7 miles) a day (for sheep it was about 10) along nearly one kilometre wide designated stock routes. When a plant was passing through their property, station owners rode by to make sure their land was not being eaten out by some 'grass pirates'. Journeys were undertaken during the Dry Season, and for water they depended on natural surface supplies, until permanent bores at regular intervals along the routes were sunk

It took great skill to control the cattle, many of which would not have been mustered for two years, and so could be wild and unsettled. The drovers' greatest fear was the sudden rush or stampede, and a few lost their lives in this terrifying way. Night watches were kept; the horses for this were carefully selected for their dark colour and ability to see well and move unobtrusively at night so as not to disturb the cattle. Drovers got to know each individual beast, helped by the fact that cattle adopted set positions in the herd.

Drovers were expert stockmen, horsemen and bushmen, and almost Aboriginal-like in their intimate knowledge of the land. They were independent, courageous and had to cope mentally and physically with the loneliness and rigours of the vast empty spaces.

The harsh environment had an important bearing on their attitude towards life. Drought, heat, floods, and stampedes shaped fatalistic outlooks expressed in their dry and often sardonic humour. They were thinking men too, and many carried books in their saddlebags including histories and philosophical works, which were read and discussed during the long waiting hours. Many wrote poetry. The drover was distinguishable by his generally long, lean frame, weather-beaten hat, flannel shirt, moleskin trousers, and riding boots. Beef or mutton, damper (unleavened bread) and billy tea was the staple diet, and the latter are a popular legacy with Australians today.

King of the drovers was Nat (Bluey) Buchanan, "legendary for his sense of locality and skill in uncharted country", and there were others; Tommy Williams, Charlie Swan (he drove cattle for 60 years from Queensland to the Kimberley), Les Griffiths, Matt Savage, Clarrie Pankhurst, and John Hagen, to name a few. Drinking and droving did not go together, and it's hardly surprising that at the end of long hazardous droves, many 'cut' their wages at the nearest pub. Banjo Paterson's words *"...the drover's life has pleasures the townsfolk never know..."* provide some insight into the strong attachment they had to the bush, and the story of drovers, droving and stock routes is well worth reading in Keith Willey's book *The Drovers*.

RENNER SPRINGS

Population 18

LOCATION
On the Stuart Highway, 158km (98 miles) north of Tennant Creek.

CHARACTERISTICS
It is a well-weathered wayside inn (hotel/motel) that has a rough and ready charm about it, and is surrounded by the 5062 sq km (3138 sq miles) Helen Springs Cattle Station. The roadhouse offers comfortable accommodation, good value homestyle food (3 course meal from $16.50) and home baked bread. It also has a small collection of historic objects.

The building itself is a museum piece. Basically, it's an old army hut, hauled from Banka Banka Station in 1949, where it was used to quarter troops during the war. The construction reflects the resourcefulness of immediate post-war roadhouse builders, who faced short supplies of materials, and Renner Springs is one of the few buildings of this period left along the Stuart. Higher rainfall here marks a climatic change reflected in the vegetation, which becomes lush and green. At the turn-off to Helen Springs on the eastern side of the Stuart Highway, there is an amethyst and smoky quartz fossicking area.

HISTORY

The freshwater springs nearby were named after Dr Renner, an Overland Telegraph Line engineer, but today water at the roadhouse is from a bore. The first 'roadhouse' consisted of three tents (one a dining room, one a kitchen, and one a house) pitched by proprietors Jack and Dorothy Doyle before they converted the army hut in 1952.

A prominent feature of the plains to the east of the highway and 4km (2.5 miles) south, is a flat-topped mesa called Lubra's Lookout (Lubra = Aboriginal Woman). In the Dreamtime it is thought that the plains were a significant meeting place for Aboriginal clans who came from hundreds of kilometres away; the local women sat on the lookout to report arrivals to their men below.

ACCOMMODATION

Hotel/Motel style units - single $50, double $55.
Camping/caravans - powered sites $12 for 2 persons, other sites $4 per person. All sites grassed and shaded, and there are barbecue facilities. Pets allowed - dogs must be leashed.

SERVICES AND FACILITIES

It has a shop, bar, dining room, camping ground, airstrip, and showers for travellers. Take-away food, ice, souvenirs, fuel (LP, ULP, LPG, diesel), oil, basic spares, qualified motor mechanic, tyres, tubes and repairs, towing service, camping gas, are all available, with aviation fuel on request.

Credit cards accepted, and EFTPOS facilities available. *Open daily 6am-11pm* ph (08)8964 4505.

TENNANT CREEK

Population 4000

LOCATION

On the Stuart Highway, 507km (314 miles) north of Alice Springs, and 675km (419 miles) south of Katherine.

CHARACTERISTICS

Situated in the centre of the Territory between Alice Springs and Katherine, this modern, progressive town with an attractive, wide, tree-lined main street, serves mining, cattle and tourist industries, and has all the facilities and comforts of the city. It is also the centre for the Warumungu people who, along with Walpiri, Warlmanpa, Alyawarra and Kaytej Aborigines, refer to Tennant Creek as Jurnkurakurr after a significant Dreaming Place.

Tennant Creek's past as a Telegraph Station outpost and tough goldrush town is the stuff of Outback legend; the remnants of this era can be seen at the old mine sites which dot the rocky outcrop landscape. Its colourful mining history, fascinating geology, and modern tourist facilities, make a few days' stay a rewarding interlude between the Central Australian Region and The Top End.

HISTORY

Stuart discovered the slow-moving creek, 11km (7 miles) north of the present town site, in 1860, and named it after South Australian pastoralist, John Tennant. The Overland Telegraph Line repeater station was built beside it in 1872. Legend has it that the town stands where it does today because that's where the beer cart broke down. Rather than manhandle beer and building materials for the intended hotel back to the creek, everyone simply moved camp! There is the story too, that the establishment of a government reserve around the Telegraph Station prevented any commercial development here. In fact, the pub and shops were built on the present site because it was closest to the goldfields; miners didn't want to walk 10km from the creek each day! Water

TENNANT CREEK AND REGION

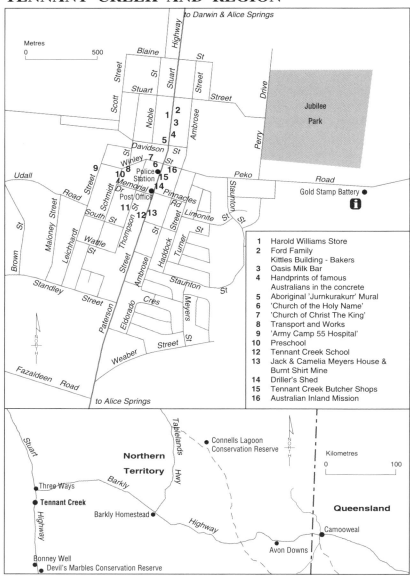

Metres
0   500

to Darwin & Alice Springs

Highway

Blaine   St

Scott Street

Stuart   St   Stuart Street   Ambrose Street   Street

Noble   1 2
         3
         4
         5

Davidson   St

Winley   7
9   8 6   16
10   Police Station   15
Schmidt Street   Memorial Dr   14
Post Office   Pinnacles Rd
11   12 13   Limonite
South   St   St

Udall

Road

Maloney Street

Leichhardt

Brown St

Standley   Street
Street

Wattle St

Thompson St

Haddock Street   Turner   St

Ambrose

Paterson   Eldorado   Cres   Staunton   St
Meyers St

Weaber   Street

Fazaldeen   Road

to Alice Springs

Peko   Road

Staunton St

Gold Stamp Battery ●

ℹ

Jubilee
Park

Perry Drive

1   Harold Williams Store
2   Ford Family
    Kittles Building - Bakers
3   Oasis Milk Bar
4   Handprints of famous
    Australians in the concrete
5   Aboriginal 'Jurnkurakurr' Mural
6   'Church of the Holy Name'
7   'Church of Christ The King'
8   Transport and Works
9   'Army Camp 55 Hospital'
10 Preschool
12 Tennant Creek School
13 Jack & Camelia Meyers House &
    Burnt Shirt Mine
14 Driller's Shed
15 Tennant Creek Butcher Shops
16 Australian Inland Mission

Stuart

Northern
Territory

Tablelands Hwy

Connells Lagoon
Conservation Reserve ●

Three Ways ●

● Tennant Creek

Barkly

Barkly Homestead ●

Highway

Avon Downs ●

Queensland

Camooweal ●

Kilometres
0   100

Bonney Well ●
● Devil's Marbles Conservation Reserve

Highway

had to be carted from the creek as bore water was too salty. The high cost of water (50 cents for a 40 gallon drum) led many miners to believe that it was cheaper to drink beer, a habit that was hard for them to break when water supply systems improved!

Gold discoveries in 1932, and the boom town conditions that briefly followed, put Tennant Creek on the map. It became the site of the last major goldrush in Australia. More than 100 separate mines were in operation before World War II - most were shallow and small with only 22 producing more than 1000oz (31kg) of gold. The first mines, some with names reflecting the optimism of the 'gougers' (miners were called gougers as they used a 'hammer and tap' method to gouge their way through the granite), included Great Northern, Shamrock, Peter Pan, Rising Sun, Pinnacles, Nobles Nob, Weabers Find, Peko and Eldorado. Eldorado produced 175,000gr of fine gold between 1932 and 1958. The great Peko Wallsend Mining Company had humble beginnings here when Joe Kaczinski and Bill Bohning pegged Peko Mine (named after Joe's dog) in 1933.

Tennant Creek was in danger of becoming a ghost town after the goldrush, but sizeable copper deposits breathed new life into the town during the 1950s. There is still plenty of mining - gold, copper and bismuth - in the area, and a few of the goldrush miners sometimes relive the 'old days' at the local pubs.

Tennant Creek's major mining company, Normanby Gold, has the White Devil Mine, one of Australia's highest grade gold producers.

GEOLOGY

Tennant Creek is situated on an area known as the Warramunga Geosyncline. This consists of a considerable thickness of inter-bedded sandstones and siltstones which were originally laid down under a shallow sea. Over millions of years, much upheaval and change has occurred and scattered within these sediments are iron-rich horizons and intrusive and extrusive quartz porphyries (dark, purplish red igneous rock with small felspar crystals). Ironstones, consisting of black to metallic grey magnetite and haematite in fine-grained sedimentary rocks are widespread on the surface. They offer mineralogical interest as they may contain fine specks of gold, bluish-green copper, or veins of red jasper, cross-cutting white quartz and black haematite.

ATTRACTIONS

The Tennant Creek Regional Tourist Association is located at Battery Hill, along the Peko Road, 1.5km east of the town centre and offers excellent local information and up-front service and bookings. *Open Monday-Friday, 9am-5pm and Saturday 9am-12noon*, ph (08) 8962 3388.

Bill Allen Lookout is one of the best places for views and orientation. Located 2km east along Peko Road.

National Trust Museum, built in 1942 as a wartime Army Hospital, is one of a number of historic buildings, and houses an interesting display of early day reminders. Located in Schmidt Street, open weekdays.

Church of Christ The King. This Catholic church has certainly been places. Built in Pine Creek in 1904, dismantled in 1935, trucked to Tennant Creek, washed overboard by floodwaters near Daly Waters, and finally re-erected in Windley Street. It's no wonder that the corrugated iron and timber structure is called the 'longest Church in Australia'! It has historic building classification.

Airport Memorial. The engine of a DH914 aircraft, which crashed at the present Goldfields Hotel site in 1929, is on display at the Airport Terminal, and also recognises the work of the early pioneers.

Telegraph Station. Established in 1872, this stone structure is now a museum, where visitors are welcome. Located by the creek, 12km (7 miles) north of the town.

Isolated Graves. Near the Telegraph Station at what is known as the Seven Mile, are two graves; one of Tom Nugent, who was supposed to have been a member of 'The Ragged Thirteen' - a notorious band of cattle duffers (thieves) who ranged the Territory in the early days. The other grave, to the south, is that of

Overland Telegraph Station telegraphist Archibald Cameron, who died around 1918.

The Pebbles. A geological formation consisting of rounded boulders scattered in heaps across a large area and is also a significant Aboriginal Sacred Site. They have resulted from the weathering of a 1700 million-year-old intruded granite mass (similar in formation process to Devil's Marbles). Their makeup is an unusual mixture of minerals - circular pink felspar crystals surrounded by blades of black biotite, outcrops of porphyry (similar to granite but with distinctive bluish quarts fragments) and various types of felspar. The evening sun enriches the natural granite tones to produce magnificent colours for photographers. Ghost gums, spinifex and rock wallabies complement this outstanding geological feature. Camping is allowed, but there are no facilities. Located 11km (7 miles) north on the Stuart Highway, then left onto a dirt road (suitable for conventional vehicles - but check with the Information Centre regarding accessibility) for 6km (4 miles).

Mary Ann Dam. This delightful recreational reserve features a man-made lake, where you can enjoy swimming, sailing and boating (non-powered only), but there are no boat hire outlets. Facilities include boat ramp, pontoon, bbq, picnic and toilet, making it an ideal family leisure stop. For the energetic, there's a bicycle track connection to the town, and bush walking tracks in the nearby Honeymoon Ranges (bicycles can be hired in Tennant Creek). Located 6km (4 miles) north of the town.

Purkiss Reserve Travellers' Rest Area. Located on the corner of Ambrose and Peko Roads, this reserve has shade, bbq, playground equipment, swimming pool, and toilets.

Battery Hill, home of the Tennant Creek Gold Stamp Battery. Here gold-bearing haematite-quartz ores from local claims were crushed for small miners in the first stage of extracting the fine grain gold. Flushing processes complete the task. The battery was originally built in 1939, and during the day you may watch it in action, making it one of the few such working museums in existence. There are also various displays - historic artifacts and the former battery site and buildings. Shaded bbq area and toilet facilities are available. Tour times - *9.30am and 5pm daily. Costs are $12 adult, $6 child, $24 family.* Located 1.2km (0.7 miles) along Peko Road.

Nobles Nob Mine. Actual mining in this huge open cut mine stopped in 1985. It was one of the richest gold mines, producing $65m worth of fine gold. It was discovered in 1934 by Jack Noble and William Weaber. When the main pillar collapsed in 1967, it was converted to an open cut operation, and at its maximum size, the mine measured 910ft long, 480ft wide and 270ft deep. It is located 16km (10 miles) east on the Peko Road.

Burnt Shirt Mine. So named when co-founder Bluey McIlroy accidentally scorched himself when burning off nearby spinifex. Access is by conducted tour only. Check with the Battery Hill Information Centre.

Fossicking. The Moonlight Rock Hole locality, north of Warrego mine, is available for gold fossickers. Check with the Information Centre for details.

Riding. Trail riding at Kraut Downs is available by appointment only. Check with the Information Centre for details.

TOURS

Norm's Gold and Scenic Tours incorporate Battery Hill tours as well as The Devils Marbles and Burnt Shirt Mine among a range of daily, informative tours. *Costs from $15 p.p.* represents excellent value, ph 0418 891 711

Battery Hill Mine Tour includes viewing of modern, underground operations with working machinery and sound and lighting effects a feature. Tours *11am daily, $12 adult, child $6, family $24.* Theres also a ghost mine tour at night - check with the Information Centre.

The Jumo Horse Centre offers trail rides and Cattle Drives *from $25 p.p.* Phone (08) 8962 2783 for details.

Dot 6 Mine Tours offer a journey into the past with night tours and billy tea and bush yarns around a camp fire. *Costs - $15 adults*. Ph (08) 8962 2168.

EVENTS

Races - St Patrick's Day; Tennant Creek Race Day in May. Renner Springs Races are held here over Easter weekend - also include camp-draft (Good Friday), *Rodeo and horse events* on Sunday. Tennant Creek also features a show (July), *Go-Kart Grand Prix* (May), and a *Golf Open* (June).

HOW TO GET THERE

By coach: Greyhound-Pioneer Australia and McCafferty's run daily services between Alice Springs and Darwin. Coaches stop at the Tennant Creek Transit Centre.
By air: Airnorth operates daily flights.

ACCOMMODATION

There are 4 motels, 1 hotel/motel, self-contained apartments, a youth hostel, and 2 caravan/camping parks. The telephone area code is (08).

Goldfields Hotel/Motel, Paterson Street, ph 8962 2030 with rooms from $55.

Bluestone Motor Inn, Paterson Street, ph 8962 2617 - pool, disabled facilities from $85 double and rooms only from $62.

Eldorado Motor Lodge, Paterson Street, ph 8962 2402 - pool and rooms from $89 double, $73 room only.

Safari Lodge, Davidson Street, ph 8962 2207 - rooms from $62 single and $72 double, bunkhouse section from $12 p.p.

Desert Sands Apartments, Paterson Street, ph 8962 1346 from $55.

Youth Hostel, Leichhardt Street, ph 8962 2719 - $12 per person.

Outback Caravan Park, Peko Road, ph 8962 2459 - cabins from $50 for 2; - pool and spa. No dogs. Sites from $12 x 2 persons unpowered; $16 powered.

Tennant Creek Caravan Park, Paterson Street, ph 8962 2325 - cabins from $40 for 2; powered sites $15 for 2; unpowered $12; bunkhouse from $20 p.p. - pool, pets allowed, dogs leashed.
Bush Camping, Jumo Horse and Training Centre, ph 8962 2783. $6 p.p., no powered sites, group discounts.

EATING OUT
The Dolly Pot Inn, Davidson Street, is one of the Territory's most highly regarded restaurants (main course from $13).

Others offer reasonably priced meals - *Bluestone*, *Eldorado*, *Goldfields* and the *Hotel* (all in Paterson Street).

The Memorial Club, Memorial Drive, and *Sportsman Club*, cnr Ambrose and Stuart Sts, give further choice.

Rocky's Pizza, *Mr Perry's* and *Barkly Bakehouse* offer take-away.

SERVICES AND FACILITIES
The wide range includes all vehicle needs and all fuels. Hire vehicles (Budget, Barkly, Hertz).

There is a full range of shopping services: chemist; banks - Westpac (auto teller), ANZ Branches, Commonwealth Agency (PO); medical - hospital, clinic, visiting dentist and chiropractor; churches - Anglican, Catholic (both Windley Street), Uniting, Aboriginal Inland Mission (both Paterson Street).

Credit cards are widely accepted; EFTPOS facility.

Local radio station call sign and frequency - 8TC 684 (ABC).

Emergency Road Service, ph (08) 8962 2468 - AH (08)8962 2312 (Wyatt Motors).

RECREATIONAL FACILITIES
Swimming pool, Purkiss Reserve; golf course; bowls; squash; tennis; speedway; cycling tracks.

THE TANAMI DESERT

CHARACTERISTICS

An advertisement that appeared in the Alice Springs paper a few years ago stated: *For sale. One rain gauge. Two years old. Never used. As is, where is. Apply Mongrel Downs Station.* Mongrel Downs, before it was abandoned, was within a hundred kilometres of Rabbit Flat, and the advertisement gives some idea of what the climate is like.

It's a 160,000 sq.km. (100,000 sq. miles) semi-arid region with average rainfalls peaking at about 140mm in January, dropping to below 10mm between July and August, with yearly totals between 300 and 900mm. Rainfall is erratic, and high evaporation rates leave little surface water. Average maximum temperatures are just over 40C (109F) in November and December at Rabbit Flat, while the average temperature in December and January is 39C (106F)! Between June and August, average minimum temperatures are as low as 10C (50F) at Rabbit Flat, so nights can get cold, and sometimes freezing.

The landscape is characterised by: gently undulating sand plains, the dominant feature; sand dunes, occur in many places with major dune fields about 60km (37 miles) south of Rabbit Flat, vary in colour from yellow to red, and in height; ranges, rises and rocky outcrops are generally low reflecting the degree of degradation of the ancient Precambrian granites and sandstones by erosion over millions of years; salt and freshwater lakes tend to be found in the central and south-western parts of the desert, the former often appearing as dried-out salt lakes, while freshwater form in depressions such as Lake Surprise near Rabbit Flat, or in claypans and river floodouts.

Other features are distinct low depressions of drainage systems which collect and divert rainfall without forming channels, particularly around Rabbit Flat, and provide a habitat for termites (*Nasutitermes triodiae*), whose red mounds are dominant landscape features. Limestone outcrops and Eucalyptus-lined creek beds complete the landscape picture.

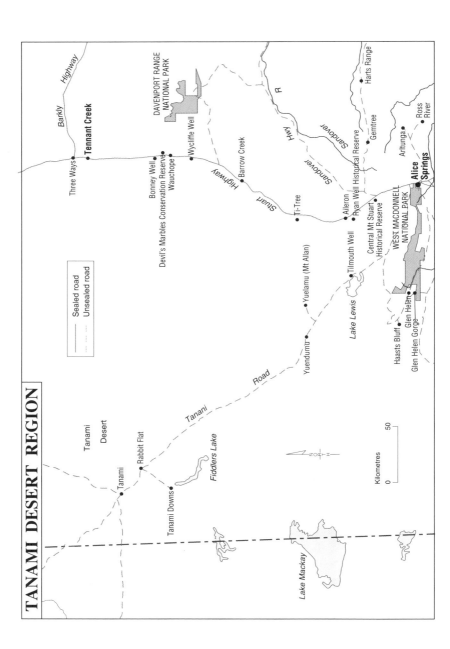

TANAMI DESERT REGION

Sealed road
Unsealed road

Barkly Highway

Tennant Creek

Three Ways

DAVENPORT RANGE NATIONAL PARK

Bonney Well

Wycliffe Well

Devil's Marbles Conservation Reserve

Wauchope

Barrow Creek

Stuart Highway

R

Sandover Hwy

Ti-Tree

Sandover

Harts Range

Gemtree

Ross River

Aileron

Ryan Well Historical Reserve

Arltunga

Alice Springs

Tilmouth Well

Central Mt Stuart Historical Reserve

WEST MACDONNELL NATIONAL PARK

Lake Lewis

Yuelamu (Mt Allan)

Haasts Bluff

Glen Helen

Glen Helen Gorge

Yuendumu

Road

Tanami

Tanami Desert

Rabbit Flat

Fiddlers Lake

Tanami

Tanami Downs

Kilometres

0   50

Lake Mackay

FLORA AND FAUNA

Spinifex, grasses, shrubs (acacia, grevillia, mulga, witchwood) and trees, particularly along watercourses (river red gum, coolabah, melaleuca) give the landscape further interest. The surprisingly abundant flora of the desert is due to the closeness of its northern part to the sub-tropics, and so is an interface between sub-tropical and semi-arid plants.

The Tanami hosts a fascinating array of wildlife, deemed so important that 37,529 sq km (14,261 sq miles) was protected by Wildlife Sanctuary status in 1964.

It's also been subjected to a number of wildlife studies in recent years, that have revealed some of its biologically unique and pristine characteristics. Facts from studies show a rich wildlife occurrence; 2 species of fish; 17 amphibians; 90 reptiles; 188 birds; and 41 mammals. Five new species were found for the Northern Territory - the lesser hairy-footed dunnart, skinks and frog. Greater bilby, spectacled hare-wallaby and northern nailtail wallaby are common in some areas, as well as the rabbit-sized Rufous hair-wallaby, known to the Walpiri people as the Mala - once widespread throughout much of semi-arid Australia.

The Tanami also seems to be a biological paradox - while appearing to be a refuge for species once more widespread in Australia, there's also the extinction of about 58% of medium sized mammals in an area relatively free of European pressures. This constitutes a loss to conservationists and the Walpiri, whose culture incorporates these animals in song, dance, dreaming tracks and dreaming sites.

The current theory, according to D.F. Gibson of the Conservation Commission Research Division, is that fires (or lack of them) may have been the cause. With the decrease in traditional Aboriginal hunting methods, which is directly related to the increase in European occupation in the last 50 years, came the decrease in the number of small, controlled, patchwork burning activities. Naturally sparked fires from lightning could now spread for hundreds of kilometres, instead of being checked by limited plant growth - large animals, being more mobile, could escape, medium sized ones were either killed or died because of lack of food. This consequence emphasises how arid and semi-arid regions can become ecological disaster zones if fires are not controlled - that is one reason why the Conservation Commission is providing more gas barbecues in parks and reserves that are more susceptible to fire damage, and why it is important to conform to regulations regarding fires in the open.

TANAMI DESERT HISTORY
This little-known region mirrored the trends of European development in the Territory - exploration, then mining, followed by attempts at pastoral activities.

Traditionally, the Tanami is homeland for the Walpiri people, with neighbouring Walmanpa to the north-east, Alyawarra and Kayetj to the south-east, Kurintji to the north, and Pintupi to the south-west. In recent times, Land Rights claims led to the granting of 90,000 sq km (34,200 sq miles) of the Tanami, including the Wildlife Sanctuary, as freehold title to the Walpiri Aboriginal people.

Explorer A.C Gregory and his expedition members were probably the first Europeans to see the Tanami when, in 1855-56, they reached an area near Lajamanu. Other explorers tended to skirt the desert. The first crossing is attributed to Nat Buchanan in 1896. Thorough explorations were made in 1900 by Alan Davidson, who discovered gold at The Granites in the same year, and Michael Terry in the 1920s and 1930s.

Pastoral development, with the exception of Suplejack and Tanami Downs Stations (both within 100km [62 miles] of Rabbit Flat), was never a great success in the central areas. The abandoned Granites and Mt Doreen Stations are reminders of the hardships.

The Tanami and The Granites are both old gold mining sites discovered by British prospector, Alan Davidson, in 1900. Between

1910 and 1911, there were about 200 men working in the Tanami fields. However, the heat, severe water shortages, and little returns saw most miners leave after 1911. Spasmodic workings at both sites continued into more recent times, and by 1961 the fields had yielded over 12,000oz.

Today, mining companies have agreements with Aboriginal land owners to mine gold at The Granites site. These mine sites are not open to tourists.

THE TANAMI ROAD

(See also section on *Territory Tourism Drives, Trails and 4WD Tracks* in Introductory Section). Better known as the Tanami Track, the road begins west from the Stuart Highway, 20 kms (12 miles) north of Alice Springs. At this point there are signs indicating that its over 700 kms (434 miles) to the Western Australia border and that conventional vehicles are not suitable west of Tanami. The first 128 kms (79 miles) is sealed, after which it's formed, then flat bladed with some gravel stretches to Rabbit Flat. Beyond Rabbit Flat, a 4WD vehicle is definitely needed on a mainly flat bladed road characterised by sand buildups in the middle interspersed with rocky outcrops.

The road finds increasing appeal for those wishing to get off the beaten track. And it offers an adventurous route to Halls Creek in the Kimberley region of Western Australia, or part of an interesting loop road incorporating the Lajamanu Road (turnoff to the north, just west of Tanami) through the Aboriginal settlements of Lajamanu and Kalkarindji to Top Springs and the Victoria Highway.

Best time to travel is during the winter months and always check road conditions and fuel availability before leaving. A permit to travel on this road which traverses Aboriginal land is not required and note that Rabbit Flat Roadhouse is closed on Tuesday, Wednesday and Thursday of each week. Water at some bores along the route is undrinkable.

SETTLEMENTS ALONG THE TANAMI ROAD

These are sequentially outlined.

TILMOUTH WELL

Population 5

Location

It is located 169 km (105 miles) from the Stuart Highway, and consists of a relatively new roadhouse complex which rightfully adds new meaning to its 'Oasis on the Tanami' claim.

Characteristics

It's pleasantly sited by the wide, red-river gum lined Napperby Creek on the 5442 sq.km. Napperby Pastoral Lease. It's also a working cattle station and visitors are offered tours or may take advantage of a self-drive station pass.

There's plenty of wildlife in this timeless spot, and walks allow experiences of the bush, space and tranquillity. Other activities include golf (9 hole course), swimming, picnicking and clay shooting. The Wirmbrandt Gallery features Aboriginal art from the surrounding communities.

Accommodation

Includes **airconditioned cabins** $65 per double; camping $5 per person. A Tilmouth package includes dinner, B&B, $135 double.

Services and Facilities

Include a shop selling a range of general goods, licensed restaurant (mains from $14) take-away food, artifacts, fuel (LP, ULP, diesel), oil, basic spares for vehicles. Facilities include swimming pool, lawns, BBQ, Clay shooting range (guns supplied), desert golf course (hire clubs). *Open daily 7am-9pm*, Credit cards accepted and EFTPOS facilities. Ph (08)8956 8777.

YUELAMU (Mt Allan)

Populaton 180

Location

It is an Aboriginal settlement, located 31 kms (19 miles) north of the Tanami Road from the turnoff, approximately 63 kms (39 miles) north-west of Tilmouth Well.

Characteristics

If you have time, it's worth a visit for its friendly community atmosphere, Aboriginal art created by local Walpiri and Walmanpa artists, and opportunities for genuine, cross-cultural experiences.

The community welcomes day-time visitors to the township where in the hilly terrain surrounds, are many sacred sites. The community own and run over 2000 cattle on the former 2,200 sq.km. Mt Allan Station.

Services and Facilities

Services include an elaborately stocked community store which also houses a good representation of local artworks. The store offers takeaway food, fuel (LP, ULP, diesel) and a full range of foodstuffs. Its *open daily 8am-11am, 2pm-5pm weekdays; 8am-12noon weekends*, and is a good source of information, ph (08) 8956 4050. There's also a school and health clinic. A permit to visit is not required, but visitors are asked to advise the Administrator of their arrival at the first building in the settlement. No alcohol is permitted and the access road is suitable for conventional vehicles.

YUENDUMU

Population 1100

Location

It is another Aboriginal community situated approximately 107 kms (66 miles) north-west of Tilmouth Well.

Characteristics

The community has a world wide reputation for the artworks painted by the Warlukurlangu school of artists and travellers are welcome at their gallery. And a visit may coincide with the time when the artists are at work. Best advice is to check with the store as opening times are variable.

Yuendumu is also noted for its colourful sports and cultural festival held each year during the long weekend in August, for Aboriginal communities in the Tanami Region. The Yuendumu Festival is among the longest running event of its type in the Territory and attracts a large influx. Visitors are welcome and no permits are required to visit the town at this time or other times during the year.

Services and Facilities

Include two stores, art gallery, police station, administrative offices, school and the highly sophisticated Tanami Network - a satellite TV network which permits TV conferences linking Yuendumu to major cities in Australia and overseas. The Yuendumu Store offers a full range of goods and foodstuffs, artworks, takeaway food and fuel (LP, ULP, diesel), Credit Cards accepted, EFTPOS facility, *open daily 8am-5pm weekdays, 9am-12noon weekends*, ph. (08) 8956 4006.

The Yuendumu Mining Store is smaller with necessary supplies and fuel. Opening times are similar to Yuendumu Store weekdays, but opens afternoons at weekends, ph. (08) 8956 4040. No alcohol is permitted and as yet, there is no accommodation for travellers. A permit is required if visits are after dark.

RABBIT FLAT

Population 2

Location

It is located 307 kms (190 miles) north-west of Yuendumu, and 122 kms (76 miles) east of the Western Australia Border.

Characteristics

One of the most remote Outback pubs in Australia consists of a small cluster of fortress-like buildings, the largest of which is a concrete and corrugated iron structure that functions as a store, cafe and bar, and is the second to last fuel stop before Halls Creek in Western Australia, 488km (302 miles) away.

Services and Facilities

Basic services are available only on Friday, Saturday, Sunday and Monday. On Tuesday, Wednesday and Thursday, the roadhouse is completely closed. In view of this partial closure, intending travellers should check availability of services prior to leaving.

Accommodation

With the determination and spirit reminiscent of the early pioneers, Bruce and Jacqui Ferrands established the roadhouse here in 1969. They ran a weather station and sent off daily reports to the Meteorological Department. In 1975, Rabbit Flat was headline news when the settlement's population doubled overnight - Jacqui gave birth to twins, helped by Bruce who followed radio instructions from the Royal Flying Doctor Service. The Ferrands continue to run the roadhouse.

Accommodation is **camping only**, ($2 p.p.) with basic facilities and no powered sites. Services and facilities include a bar, a shop selling basic goods, ice and take-away food. Fuel services include LP, ULP, diesel and oil. It's cash only, *open 7am-10pm* on Fri, Sat, Sun and Mon only, ph (08) 8956 8744.

From Rabbit Flat it is 45 kms (28 miles) to Tanami (place name only - no services or facilities). Approximately 2km west of Tanami is the turnoff to the Lajamanu Road from where it is 240 kms (149 miles) to Lajamanu and 344 kms (213 miles) to Kalkarindji on an unformed, flat bladed sand road surface (4WD recommended). From Kalkarindji, the Buntine Highway (formed road) leads North- east to Top Springs and Victoria Highway, a distance of 336 kms (208 miles).

THREE WAYS

Population 25

LOCATION

Located 25km (15.5 miles) north of Tennant Creek, at the junction of the Stuart and Barkly Highways.

CHARACTERISTICS

A roadhouse, motel, road train 'mecca', and hitchhiker 'get stuck' point, located at the Territory's major intersection in the heart of heat, scrub and dust country. It was originally established in the

1950s and rebuilt in 1974. A large stone cairn commemorates the founder of the Royal Flying Doctor Service, Rev John Flynn.

ACCOMMODATION

Motel - $50 double, $45 single; Dongas (cabins) - $20 x single.
Camping - powered sites $15; unpowered $5. Sites are shaded, grassed, pets allowed, dogs on leash.

SERVICES AND FACILITIES

It has a shop, bar, licensed restaurant (meals from $8), tourist information, picnic/bbq area, accommodation, and swimming pool. Take-away food, ice, souvenirs, fuel (LP, ULP, diesel, autogas and camping gas), oil, basic spares, and showers for travellers ($2) are available.

Open daily 6am-midnight. Credit cards accepted, EFTPOS facility, ph (08)8962 2744.

TOP SPRINGS

Population 8

LOCATION

At the junction of the Buchanan Highway and Buntine Road (formerly Delamere Road), 289km (179 miles) south-west of Katherine.

CHARACTERISTICS

Top Springs consists of the aptly named Wanda Inn, that offers some real Outback hospitality and reaffirms the Territorian liking for a beer or two. Apart from the increasing tourist trade, it serves the surrounding cattle stations including the huge Victoria Downs property (12,359 sq km-4696 sq miles), Dungowan (4456 sq km-1693 sq miles), Montejini (3142 sq km-1194 sq miles), Killarney (2839 sq km-1079 sq miles), and the road train 'truckies'.

The historic Murranji stock route, along which overlanders skirted the Tanami Desert in their westward cattle trek to the Victoria River and Kimberley regions, passes close to Top Springs.

HOW TO GET THERE

From the Victoria Highway near Timber Creek, the Victoria River Downs Road is compacted gravel - with care, suitable for conventional vehicles during the Dry Season, but check conditions at Timber Creek. For other routes, see *Kalkarindji* listing.

ACCOMMODATION

3 **motel units** - $57 single; $67 double; $77 family; Room $30 single, $40 double.

Camping $4, grassed and shaded sites. Pets allowed; dogs must be leashed.

SERVICES AND FACILITIES

The Wanda Inn has a bar, restaurant (meals from $9), accommodation, general store, picnic/bbq/shaded area, swimming pool, showers for travellers ($2), and disabled persons facilities. Take-away food, ice, souvenirs, artifacts, fuel (LP, ULP, diesel), oil, basic spares, minor mechanical and tyre repairs, tyres, tubes, and limited towing service are available. Credit Cards are accepted and EFTPOS facilities available.

Open daily from 6am, ph (08) 8975 0767.

VICTORIA RIVER DOWNS (VRD)

LOCATION

On the Buchanan Highway 102 kms (63 miles), east of Top Springs.

CHARACTERISTICS

The huge pastoral holdings of Northern Australia are much revered in Australian folklore for their size, colourful history and often dramatic attempts made by owners to control them. For this type of legendary status, none exceed VRD or The Big Run. In its heyday, it sprawled over a massive 41,000 sq.km. area (25,420 sq.

miles). Today it is still huge by any standards at nearly 12,000 sq.km. (around 3 million acres), the second largest in the Territory after Brunette Downs.

It occupies one of the finest pastoral regions in Australia - the black soil plains of the vast Victoria River Basin which support a cover of sweet, cattle-palatable native grasses. VRD runs around 85,000 Brahman cattle, most of which are shipped live to feedlots in Malaysia, Indonesia and The Philippines from ports at Darwin and Wyndham.

Today, this progressive pastoral enterprise forms part of the Heytesbury group of companies under the stewardship of Janet Holmes aCourt.

FEATURES

The road passes right by the homestead and township-like cluster of station buildings, home to a permanent population of around 60. Also based here is Heli-muster - a company which does contract helicopter mustering across the Top End and parks 20 or so choppers by the airstrip.

While there are no tourist facilities, visitors are welcome to patronise the station store - a good place for genuine stockmans wear or for a good read - to purchase a copy of *The Big Run* by J. Machin which captures the essence of VRDs long history.

From VRD, the Buchanan Highway continues north-east for 110 kms (68 miles) to join the Victoria Highway. This is a beautiful scenic drive with the spectacular *Jasper Gorge* (approx. 60 kms - 37 miles - from VRD), a top spot for camping and walking. It borders *Gregory National Park* (listed under Top End Region).

The Buchanan Highway (named after a legendary drover - see *Newcastle Waters* listing) forms one of the Northern Territory Heritage Trails - *The Overlanders Loop* (see under *Tourist Drives, Heritage Trails and 4WD Explorer Tracks* in the Introductory Section).

The road is a formed gravel surface, suitable for conventional vehicles during the dry season (with care), but watch out for road-trains on this beef highway.

WAUCHOPE

Population 6

LOCATION

113km (70 miles) south of Tennant Creek, on the Stuart Highway.

CHARACTERISTICS

Pronounced 'walk up', this bougainvillea-draped hotel invitingly hugs the highway, exudes character, and is a branch of the 'bush bank'. Owner Bob Richard thinks it was named after one of the Overland Telegraph Line surveyors, and it celebrated 50 years as a pub in June 1988. Apart from the usual roadhouse services, the hotel offers comfortable accommodation and good country-style food.

HISTORY

It began as a Post Office and Store, serving miners from the rich Wauchope and Hatches Creek wolfram fields, discovered in 1914. Prior to War World II, there were about 200 Chinese helping at the diggings, a few of whom began a soft drink factory here as well. Imminence of war stimulated demand for the tungsten ore which was used to harden steel. They brought it out by camel, then dray, and finally by truck load, slaking their thirst at Wauchope before the long haul east. Soft drink was not the stuff of miners in the searing heat, and in 1938, the Post Office and Store became a rather lively pub.

   Like most of the old pubs of 'The Track', Wauchope stories are as rich in imagination as they are in truth - it's even said that the pub changed hands in 1946 as the result of a poker game. As the Devils Marbles landform features are only 9kms north of Wauchope, you can hire bicycles from the pub ($15 per day) for a novel and leisurely way of enjoying the local landscape.

ACCOMMODATION

Motel - single $25, double $55-$65; bunk rooms $20 p.p.; Backpacker $12 p.p.

Camping/caravans - powered sites $5 p.p.; tent sites $4. All sites grassed. Dogs must be leashed.

SERVICES AND FACILITIES

There's a bar, shop, dining room (meals from $11), bbq, accommodation, a 1.2km airstrip, and showers for travellers cost $2. Take-away food, ice, souvenirs, fuel (LP, ULP, diesel), aviation fuel by prior arrangement, camping gas, tyres and tubes are available. There is also a tennis court and a zoo (camels, kangaroos, emus).

Credit cards accepted and EFTPOS facilities. *Open 6am-11pm*, ph (08) 8964 1963.

WOLLOGORANG - GULF WILDERNESS LODGE

Population under 10

LOCATION

On the Great Top Road, 257km (159 miles) south-east of Borroloola in the NT and 228km (141 miles) north-west of Burketown in Queensland.

CHARACTERISTICS

The station's licensed lodge not only offers supplies and accommodation, but also superb fishing, and a taste of real-life on a cattle run. This 'Gulf Gateway to the Territory' straddles the Northern Territory/Queensland Border, and covers 6912 sq km (2700 sq miles), including about 80km (50 miles) of beautiful, sandy beach frontage onto the Gulf of Carpentaria. Paul Zlotkowski, who owns and manages the station, will tell you where the fish bite best, and he doesn't need much of a cue to talk about one of his favourite subjects - local history. Wollogorang is a weather station, and temperatures between December and March can reach 45C (113F); coldest is down to 7C (45F) in June/July.

HISTORY

The station was established in 1881 by Chisholm, who came from a property near Goulburn (NSW), and is the longest continually settled cattle station in the Northern Territory; other properties were settled before this but were later abandoned. The ruins of the original homestead hut can be seen; the existing homestead, built in 1926, was extensively renovated in 1984.

When established, its situation near Settlement Creek was on the only road into the Territory from Queensland that guaranteed water. Since the Creek was presumed to be on the Queensland/South Australian Border (in the early days, what is now known as the Territory was part of the South Australian colony - an area South Australia later abandoned), the employees of drovers bringing cattle to the West demanded 'the settlement' of their wages as they entered the Northern Territory - hence the name of the creek. Once they were outside Queensland and the jurisdiction of its courts, they could not force employers to pay their wages.

In August, 1886, Carruthers completed the task of surveying the Northern Territory/Queensland Border, and in 1986, a small group of surveyors from Queensland, Northern Territory and South Australia met on the coast and celebrated the centenary of Carruthers' great work by replacing his original, final post with a concrete one with an inscribed plaque.

Near Seigals Creek is a small Aboriginal settlement - the Waanyi Garawa People, some of whose artifacts and paintings are for sale at the roadhouse.

ATTRACTIONS

You can visit the survey post on the coast, but 4WD is necessary, or fish and camp on the unspoilt Gulf beaches - many visitors spend a week or so here, it costs $20 per day per car. Swimming is not advised. Special fishing and hunting safari type tours can be arranged to meet your requirements.

HOW TO GET THERE

The road from Borroloola is a good, formed gravel surface, as is the road from Burketown. The road is suitable for conventional vehicles and trailers or vans, but care is needed. Check road conditions.

By air, a weekly service from Tennant Creek by Chartair's Barkly mail plane, is an interesting alternative.

ACCOMMODATION

Motel type, air-conditioned - $80 double; $50 single.
Camping - $7 p.p. per night. All sites grassed and pets are allowed - dogs leashed.

SERVICES AND FACILITIES

The lodge has accommodation, bar, dining room (large station type meals from $10), general store, aerodrome, picnic/bbq area, tourist information, and showers for travellers. Take-away food, ice, fuel (LP, ULP, diesel), oil, aviation fuel, basic spares, minor repairs, tyres, tubes, towing service, are available. Artifacts and souvenirs are also for sale. All Credit Cards and EFTPOS accepted. *Open daily*, ph (08) 8975 9944.

WYCLIFFE WELL

Population 15

LOCATION

On the Stuart Highway, 131 km (81 miles) south of Tennant Creek.

CHARACTERISTICS

It consists of a surprisingly well-stocked store, and recently modernised pre-war roadhouse, motel and caravan park. It's a beer connoisseur's delight, too - Irwan Farkas reckons he has the largest selection of foreign beers in Australia (300 types). You can even watch local Warumungu craftsmen making artifacts, which can be bought. A large windmill and a 10 acre, man-made lake are features of the surrounds. Boating, bird-watching and fishing or watching regular UFO visits at night are among activities offered. A few kilometres away is Ali Curung Aboriginal settlement, with a population of around 400.

In the early days, Wycliffe Well was a watering hole for the stock route, and during the war, vegetables and fruit were grown and flown out daily to supply the troop camps along The Stuart Highway.

ACCOMMODATION

Motel - $75 double, $60 single and family $85. Cabins from $40, on-site vans from $35, house from $60 single and $90 family. Grassed **camping sites** $13 x 2, powered sites $17 x 2, and large indoor swimming pool ($2). Pets allowed on leash.

SERVICES AND FACILITIES

It has a licensed restaurant (Hungarian Goulash specialty), shop, motel units, pool (guests only), 300 seat auditorium, take-away food, ice, liquor, artifacts, souvenirs, fuel (LP, ULP, diesel, autogas), oil, range of spares, mechanical repairs, tyres and tubes, and towing service. Tourist information, showers for travellers ($2), shaded picnic/bbq area, are available.

Credit cards accepted and EFTPOS facilities available. *Open 6.30am-9pm daily*, ph (08) 8964 1966.

The Top End

CHARACTERISTICS

The main features which unify the Top End are climate and the luxuriant greenness it spawns during the Wet. Stretching from Larrimah in the south, the Top End encompasses vast woodland and savannah tracts, escarpment and plateau, and flood plain before meeting long, lazy beaches on its northern, eastern and western boundaries.

Darwin is the thriving heart of a huge hinterland whose life-blood is cattle on the sprawling runs, tropical agriculture, mining, defence establishments, port and trade links to Asia, and tourism based on the wonders and delights of a number of National Parks including Kakadu, Litchfield and Nitmmuluk (Katherine Gorge). Cosmopolitan Darwin, tropical beaches and islands, turquoise waters, mystical Arnhem Land, crocodiles, and hunting and fishing, all give a unique colour and flavour to a region that's more like another country than a part of a fledgling mainland Australian state.

CLIMATE

The Top End has a tropical monsoon climate which means two distinct seasons: The Wet or Green from November to March; The Dry from May until September, with April and October

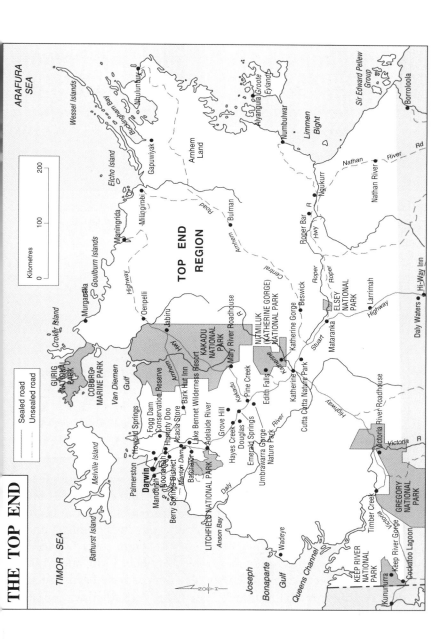

THE TOP END

TIMOR SEA

ARAFURA SEA

Bathurst Island

Melville Island

Joseph Bonaparte Gulf

Queens Channel

Anson Bay

Darwin

Palmerston

Mandorah

Noonamah

Berry Springs District

Howard Springs

Fogg Dam Conservation Reserve

Humpty Doo

Acacia Store

Manton Dam

Batchelor

LITCHFIELD NATIONAL PARK

Lake Bennet Wilderness Resort

Bark Hut Inn

Adelaide River

Grove Hill

Hayes Creek

Douglas

Emerald Springs

Umbrawarra Gorge Nature Park

Kakadu River

Daly River

Pine Creek

Edith Falls

KAKADU NATIONAL PARK

Mary River Roadhouse

Jabiru

Oenpelli

Cooinda

GURIG NATIONAL PARK

COBURG MARINE PARK

Van Diemen Gulf

Croker Island

Murganella

Goulburn Islands

Maningrida

Milingimbi

Gapuwiyak

Elcho Island

Wessel Islands

Buckingham Bay

Maluluntuny

TOP END REGION

Arnhem Land

Arnhem Highway

Central Arnhem Road

Arnhem Highway

Bulman

Numbulwar

Ayangula Groote Eylandt

Limmen Bight

Sir Edward Pellew Group

Borroloola

Nathan

Nathan River

Nathan River Rd

Ngukurr

Roper Bar

Roper Hwy

Roper River

Beswick

Katherine Gorge

NITMILUK (KATHERINE GORGE) NATIONAL PARK

Katherine

Cutta Cutta Nature Park

Stuart Highway

Mataranka

ELSEY NATIONAL PARK

Larrimah

Hi-Way Inn

Daly Waters

Victoria River Roadhouse

Victoria R

GREGORY NATIONAL PARK

Timber Creek

Victoria River

KEEP RIVER NATIONAL PARK

Keep River Gorge

Cockatoo Lagoon

Kununurra

Wadeye

Kilometres

0   100   200

Sealed road

Unsealed road

Darwin	J	F	M	A	M	J	J	A	S	O	N	D	Ann.Av
Temperature:													
Av. monthly Max	32	31	32	33	30	30	30	31	32	33	33	33	32
Av. monthly Min	25	25	24	24	22	20	19	21	23	25	25	25	23
Rainfall:													
Av. monthly mm	409	353	316	99	17	2	1	6	18	72	142	224	1659
Relative Humidity:													
Av 9am	81	83	83	75	67	63	63	68	71	70	73	76	73
Av 3pm	69	71	67	52	42	38	38	41	47	52	58	64	53
Sunshine Hours:													
Average	5.6	5.9	6.6	8.7	9.5	9.9	10.1	10.2	9.8	9.4	8.4	7.2	8.4
Thunder Days:													
Average	15	11	11	4	0	0	0	0	1	5	12	15	74
Katherine	J	F	M	A	M	J	J	A	S	O	N	D	Ann.Av
Temperature:													
Av. monthly Max	35	34	34	34	32	30	30	32	35	37	38	36	34
Av. monthly Min	24	24	23	21	17	14	13	16	20	24	25	24	21
Rainfall:													
Av. monthly mm	234	214	166	33	5	2	1	0	7	31	86	193	972
Relative Humidity:													
Av 9am	77	81	76	64	58	55	52	51	51	55	61	70	63
Av 3pm	53	55	49	36	34	31	27	25	24	26	33	43	36
Thunder Days: Av	3	3	2	0	0	0	0	0	0	1	3	4	16

transitional months. The Wet Season coincides with the highest temperatures, humidity and rainfall. It's hot and oppressive, and locals describe it as the `suicide season'. Torrential rains can begin from November (the real rains generally start in December) and continue to March, dumping on average 1659mm (over five feet) of water on the land. Sometimes tropical cyclones form, and while damage has been severe when populated areas have been struck, their occurrences are fortunately infrequent. At Katherine, rainfall is less than Darwin, but temperatures are higher.

The Dry Season is characterised by lower temperatures and humidity, but don't be misled by the 'cooler months' description - it can still be hot, but evenings are pleasant and humidity is much lower. Sunshine hours are high in Darwin, even during the Wet Season.

Lightning and thunderstorms in late October and November herald the build-up to The Wet. At this time, unstable and moisture-laden equatorial air masses begin to dominate. Thunder storms during the build-up are impressive for towering cloud formations (up to 20km high) and dramatic lightning displays (in December, between 10,000 and 20,000 flashes have been recorded within an 80km range of Darwin). When the moist equatorial air retreats northward in March and April, the rains diminish, and south-easterly winds follow, spinning off the great high pressure systems now dominating the continent. The Dry Season begins.

Climate statistics for Darwin and Katherine highlight monthly characteristics.

LANDSCAPE

The mainly flat to undulating landscape is interrupted by a belt of broken rocky country that ranges north-eastward from the Victoria River region to the great sandstone massif of the Arnhem Land escarpment. The escarpment and the vast spread of the gorge-cut plateau it backs, is the dominant and most scenic landform feature in the region, best seen at Kakadu. The sweep of coastal floodplain provides contrast, while shallow seas, reefs, long sandy beaches, and mudflats, characterise the coast. The Roper and Katherine-Daly drainage systems, rising from limestone springs, are the only rivers that permanently flow along their entire length; others may dry up beyond the tidewater marks. Whereas landform lines are sharply delineated in Central Australia they are subdued in the Top End by the relentless cover of tropical savannah woodland. Before the land bakes and dries in the rainless days of winter, the mantle of softer, lush-green landscape tones dominate.

FLORA AND FAUNA

Tropical eucalypt woodland covers 85% of the flat to undulating landform of the Top End. It is dominated by the Darwin woolly-butt (*Eucalyptus miniata*) and the Darwin stringybark (*E. tetrodonta*); their canopies are sufficiently spaced to enable plenty of sunlight to the understorey of shrubs and grasses. Often, the landscape has a more open savannah character. Ironwood (*Erythrophleum chlorostachys*), smooth-stemmed bloodwood (*E. bleeseri*), the attractive salmon gum (*E. alba*) are other eucalypts. Smaller species are billygoat plum, also known as a vitamin C tree (*Terminalia ferdinandiana*), green plum or wild mango (*Buchanania obovata*), sand palm (*Livistona humilis*), and acacias. Tall spear grass (*Sorghum intrans*) flourishes during the Wet season.

Representative plant species of the low-lying areas, floodplains, escarpment and plateau are highlighted under *Kakadu National Park*. Wildlife representative of the Top End is also outlined under *Kakadu National Park*.

CROCODILES

Of the two species found in northern tropical waters, the estuarine (salt-water or 'saltie') crocodile (*Crocodylus porosus*) is definitely the most dangerous to man (attacks in recent years have resulted in a few deaths). The smaller, freshwater type (*Crocodylus johnstoni*) is considered relatively harmless unless provoked. Both types demand utmost respect! Crocodiles in a way are living dinosaurs - the last remaining members of the class Archosauria, the ruling reptiles of the Mesozoic era (between 70 and 200 million years ago) that have changed little since roaming with their Tyrannosaurus rex and Brontosaurus relatives.

Crocodiles are now totally protected. Prior to 1971, they were shot for skins, and numbers declined dramatically. Since 1971, numbers have increased, as has their size.

Estuarine Crocodile Facts:

The name salt-water crocodile is a misnomer - they do inhabit tidal rivers and inland freshwater billabongs and lagoons. (See map of distribution).

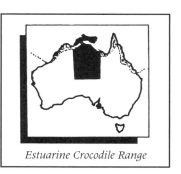
Estuarine Crocodile Range

Size - males can grow to 6m (19ft), most large ones are around 4m. Males mature at about 3-4m, at an estimated age of 16 years. Females rarely exceed 4m, and may nest at 2-3m, around an age of 10 years. They live to about 100 years.

Appearance - apart from their large size as adults, crocodiles are distinguishable by their broad snouts, but small crocodiles may be difficult to recognise at a distance.

Food - young feed on small animals (crabs, prawns, fish, occasional snakes and mammals); adults on a range including larger mammals and man! Prey behaviour may well be observed before attacks. Large males can reach speeds of 40km/h in water, and can stay submerged for up to 2 hours. Smaller crocs are 'slower' underwater, and submerged time span is less. A third eyelid assists better underwater vision, while a flap seals the nostrils. Very large males can lunge with awesome speed from the water to take a buffalo drinking at the edge, drag, roll, and drown it, in what has been described as 'the death roll'. Once locked, the jaws exert a pressure of 5 tonnes per sq cm. A fleshy valve at the back of the throat prevents the crocodile from drowning. On land, smaller crocodiles can reach speeds up to 20km/h (12 mph) over short 20m (65 ft) distances, while larger ones are much slower. But they rarely move too far away from water, preferring to bask on mud-banks where their 'slides' may be seen.

Breeding - nesting occurs in the Wet season. A large mound of vegetation and soil is built. About 50 eggs are laid, covered and guarded by the female. Crocodiles are particularly aggressive at this time. The hatchlings squeak for assistance when they are ready to emerge at the end of the 90-day incubation period. Only a small number survive to become mature adults.

Freshwater Crocodile Facts:
Mainly found in freshwater habitats, and unique to Australia.
Size - males may reach 3m (9 ft); females rarely exceed 2m (6 ft) in length.
Appearance - a narrow snout and a row of 4 large scales at the base of the head, are the distinctive features.
Food - mainly insects, spiders, fish, frogs, lizards and birds.
Breeding - nest during Dry season by excavating a hole in the sand, where about 12 eggs are laid. A 65-90 day incubation period allows the young to hatch before the onset of the Wet. Other features include its ability to rise 'on all fours' and run fast over short distances. A sensory organ in the head makes it instinctively

snap, so 'attacks' on air mattresses and the like in some locations are probably a reflex action. Behaviour is not entirely predictable, and best advice is to give them plenty of space and respect.

Be 'Crocodile Wise':
People and crocodiles can 'co-exist' if a few simple rules are followed.
• Observe the warning signs. Absence of a warning sign does not mean the area is safe.
• Seek local or expert advice about crocodiles before swimming, camping, fishing or boating.
• There is a potential danger anywhere salt-water crocodiles occur. If there is any doubt, do not swim, canoe, or use small boats in estuaries, tidal rivers, deep pools, or mangrove shores.
• Do not paddle, clean fish, prepare food, or camp at the water's edge. Fill a bucket with water and do your chores at least 50m away. Returning daily or regularly to the same spot at the water's edge is dangerous.
• Do not lean over the edge of a boat, or stand on logs overhanging water and exercise care when fishing from banks.
• Dispose of food scraps, fish offal and other wastes properly, and away from your camp site.

PROTECT YOURSELF
In the tropics, it's essential to wear a hat, advisable to use sun-cream, and always carry sufficient water, even on short walks. Confine strenuous activities to the 'cooler' parts of the day. Face nets and insect repellents are useful bushfly and mosquito deterrents. Mosquitoes, in particular, can be a nuisance, and nets are advised for campers. Water from billabongs must be boiled before drinking. Clothing ideally should be light, cotton material, which 'breathes' better in the humid conditions.

FISHING

The Top End and fishing are synonymous, and there's plenty of scope for this popular recreational activity. Australia's premier native sport fish is the legendary fighting barramundi, a superb table fish as well.

Estuarine crocodiles (all year) and box jellyfish (between October and May), are dangers associated with fishing. Tidal range in Darwin can be 8m (26ft) leaving boat ramps high and dry on spring lows! Tide charts are essential. Darwin Harbour has 3 artificial reefs - sunken ships called fish aggregate devices (FAD), designed to attract fish. Another FAD is at Lee Point. For regulations and bag limits refer to the *Practical Information Section* in Part One. Special bag limits apply for barramundi fishing in the Mary River system. Many Fishing Tour specialists operate out of Darwin and other locations - check places listings.

The following fishing guide is a sample of the main fish species found in these northern tropical waters.

FISHING TABLE		
Type	**Location and Characteristics**	**Best Times of Year**
Barramundi or Perch	Coastal and inland waters (rivers, lagoons). Arnhem Highway-Kakadu Region. Darwin Harbour arms, Roper and Daly Rivers are good locations. Succulent table fish.	All year but 'pre' and 'post' Wet is ideal.
Bream	Same as for Mangrove Jack.	All Year.
Black Jewfish	One of the biggest reef fish. Can exceed 50kg but schools 5- 15kg is most common. Deep holes in river mouths, rock ledges and rocky headlands and sunken wrecks.	All Year.
Queenfish	Rocky headlands, exposed reefs at creek and river mouths. Islands, Darwin Harbour, Gurig Peninsula.	All Year.

Spanish Mackerel	As for the Queenfish but also inhabits waters above shallow reefs next to deeper waters.	June, July, August.
Longtail Tuna	Inshore Waters.	June, July, August.
Giant Trevally	Shallow reefs and strong tidal flow areas. Vernon Islands -good location.	Most of the year.
Barracuda	Shallow reefs but not in great numbers.	Most of the year.
Threadfin Salmon	Similar location to barramundi.	All year but prior to Wet is best.
Sailfish and Marlin	Deeper waters off the coast. Arnhem Land coast.	All Year.
Golden Snapper and Fingermark Beam	Shallow inshore and estuarine reefs. Sometimes found in deeper waters. Fine table fish. Generally 2-5 kgs but up to 10kgs.	All year.
Saddle Tail Snapper Called red fish.	Inshore/offshore reefs. Fine table fish 1-2kg. All Year. Red Emperor Deeper reefs. 3-5kg but up to 10kgs. Fine eating	All Year.
Rock Cod	Wide ranging, non-schooling reef dwellers.	All Year.
Coral Trout	As for rock cod but a better table fish.	All Year.
Moonfish	Inshore reefs and estuaries. Schools of 1-2kg common.	All Year.
Mangrove Jack	Shallow estuarine reefs, rockbars, mangroves and tidal rivers.	All Year.

HUNTING

Wild buffalo, boar, banteng cattle, wild goats and sambar deer may be hunted via licensed safari operators in some areas of tropical wilderness country. Trophy and non-trophy is offered for the experienced and novice hunter, mainly in the Cobourg Peninsula and Arnhem Land regions. Contact **Davidsons Arnhemland Safaris** for details of their hunting prices and safari locations, ph (08) 8927 5240.

TOURING SUGGESTIONS

While Kakadu is a must, try to spend a few days there and explore some of the attractions on the way - a round trip from Pine Creek is well worth considering, as is a flight over the floodplains and escarpment.

Many of the Top Ends extraordinary natural and cultural attractions are more accessible via the designation of a number of tourist drives, some of which are fascinating loop roads. Refer to Territory Drives, Trails and 4WD Tracks in Part One for the range of features these various routes offer.

PLACES AND ATTRACTIONS

ADELAIDE RIVER

Population 280

LOCATION

On the Stuart Highway, 110km (68 miles) south of Darwin.

CHARACTERISTICS

A colourful township on a river of the same name, is noted for its wartime history and proximity to the picturesque Daly River area.

Apart from a tourist function, the township serves surrounding cattle properties and gold mines. A fascinating wartime role, local scenic river and wildlife features, and some down to earth Territorian hospitality at the Adelaide River Inn, merit a visit to the town. The Adelaide Inn is home of Charlie, the buffalo star of the popular films, Crocodile Dundee I and II.

HISTORY

The Kungarakan were the first people in the area. European discovery, and naming of the river, was by two crew members of HM Survey ship *Beagle* in 1849. The name honours the then Dowager Queen, Queen Adelaide. The Overland Telegraph Line construction in 1870, laid the basis for permanent European settlement when a depot was established. The taking up of pastoral leases and the extension of the North Australia Railway Line in the 1880s, consolidated its economic base, and the railway station and bridge were built in 1888-89.

Because of the township's strategic position and railway, it was the centre of much military activity during World War II. A major armaments depot was established at nearby Snake Creek, the buildings of which still remain. Partly for their own protection, Aboriginal people were moved out of areas to the north during the war, and placed in camps at Adelaide River and other more southerly locations. They contributed to the war effort in many ways; tending the extensive army fruit and vegetable gardens, handling ammunition, driving army vehicles, and stripping down engines for re-conditioning. Today, the old army depot and cemetery are reminders of the war on mainland Australia.

ATTRACTIONS

Adelaide River World War Two Cemetery. Australia's largest war cemetery has the graves of those who were killed in the Darwin bombing raids of 1942, in a well-maintained, lawn and garden setting. The graves include 434 servicemen and 54 civilians killed in the first of a number of bombing raids on Darwin. Opposite the War Cemetery is the **Fresh Food Kiosk**, which is well worth a visit and its Barra and Chips are highly recommended.

Railway Station. Now a National Trust property, this restored station was the only one on the North Australian Line that had a refreshment room for passengers. Also known as the '77 mile', the station is a fine example of railway architecture in isolated regions.

The catering in the 1930s was interesting. At a time of no refrigeration, Mrs Eve Sack who ran the refreshment rooms, was a lateral thinker, and enterprising as well when the red meat supplies ran low. She recalls, *"... We'd give them roast fowl then plenty of goats - call it mutton - nobody knew it was goat- they all liked it!"*

  Indirectly, she was responsible for the township's first liquor licence. While her premises had a licence only to serve grog half an hour either side of the train being in the station, she managed to get one that allowed all travellers to imbibe - with the help of the local constabulary. The policeman, rather thirsty after a patrol, was understandably annoyed when refused a drink; a full licence soon followed! Beer came in bottles, four dozen to a box, packed in straw, and covered with wet hessian to keep them cool. At the end of World War II, a full hotel licence was granted, and accommodation was provided at the rear of the building. The Licensees decided to purchase a large army hut located in the railway yard, and the Fawcetts used this as the basis of the 'new' pub in 1951 - this building remains as the present Adelaide River Inn.

Railway Bridge. Also built in 1888-89, it was the largest on the North Australian Line, and even doubled as a road bridge when the low level one was under water during the Wet.

Snake Creek Arsenal. It was established in 1942 as an armaments depot and large wartime military camp. The basic structures, although deteriorating, remain intact, and visitors are allowed. Keys are available from the police station.

Robin Falls. Located approximately 15km (9 miles) south on the Old Darwin to Katherine Road, the 12m (39 ft) falls are at their best during the Wet season. Interesting rock formations, gorge and tropical vegetation, make it a popular picnicking spot, but there is about a 10 minute walk into the falls. Continuation on this road leads to the Daly River attractions (see separate listing).

EVENTS

The Adelaide River Show, Rodeo, Campdraft and Gymkhana is a colourful, action-packed event held in early June. Later in June, the annual Country Race Meeting is held. For dates contact the Adelaide River Inn.

ACCOMMODATION

Adelaide River Inn has rooms - single $45, double $55. The Inns BP Caravan Park has powered sites $12, unpowered sites $3 pp. Sites grassed, shaded; pets allowed on leash. The Inn is open 6am-11pm daily, ph (08) 8976 7047 for both establishments.

Mount Bundy Station is located 4kms east of the Adelaide River Railway Station, along Haynes Road. The 570 sq.km. Mount Bundy property offers excellent en-suite farmstay accommodation in the homestead (B&B $120) and single and share accommodation in cottage and stockmans quarters (from $32). Areas of shady riverside lawns are available for campers and caravaners. Other features include bush and river setting, fishing and billabong swimming. It's open daily, ph (08) 8976 7009.

SERVICES AND FACILITIES

The township has most basic services including two small supermarkets; post office; takeaway food outlets; good value meals at the Adelaide Inn (sunset buffet nightly $12.50; sunrise breakfast $8.50); three service stations (all fuels), vehicle repairs (Shell Autoport, Mobil); Church (Catholic); health centre; and police station. Souvenirs are widely available an authentic didgeridoos can be purchased at the Inn.

Credit cards are widely accepted and EFTPOS facilities are available.

ARNHEM HIGHWAY - KAKADU REGION

CHARACTERISTICS

The superb all-season, sealed, and sometimes elevated, Arnhem Highway is the gateway to the Territory's fastest growing tourist destination: World Heritage listed *Kakadu National Park*. This route forms part of the Natures Way Tourist Drive where along the way, there are many worthwhile places to visit including a number of Parks and Wildlife Commission reserves and parks, and good fishing spots. Although the Wet Season restricts access to some places, travel to most attractions and all commercial establishments in the region including Kakadu, is possible at this time of year. To protect new tropical agricultural enterprises in the Humpty Doo district, a fruit quarantine station is located 23kms from the Stuart Highway turnoff and all vehicles are checked.

SWIMMING

Be mindful that estuarine crocodiles lurk in billabongs, rivers and coastal areas, while freshwater crocs may inhabit the pools of the escarpment and gorge country. Respect the crocodile warning signs and Parks advice. Theres no absolute guarantee of safe swimming in natural waters anywhere in the region. While it is common for people to swim in the pools at *Twin Falls*, *Jim Jim Falls*, *Gunlom and Barramundi Gorge* at Kakadu, and at *Leaning Tree Lagoon*, it is at the swimmers' own risk. Parks Australia advice for Kakadu is simple: **No swimming anywhere in natural waterways**.

TOURING SUGGESTIONS

For the independent traveller, a round trip beginning either at Pine Creek via the Kakadu Highway, or the Arnhem Highway, avoids back-tracking. Budget several days if you can - once you have read through the range of attractions, it will be appreciated that a day trip to Kakadu gives only a cursory insight. *Fogg Dam* for birdlife is highly recommended while in Kakadu, at least the *Yellow Water cruise*, and visits to art sites and escarpment and waterfalls in the south of the park should be undertaken. If possible, take a half hour flight over floodplain, lowland and Arnhem Land - it's good value at around $60 per person.

Extended touring via Arnhem Land to the *Cobourg Peninsula* (Gurig National Park) is another option, but there is a limit on vehicle numbers allowed to enter Arnhem Land each week, so you may need to make early application for permits.

For places listed along the Arnhem Highway, refer to *Top End* map.

PLACES AND ATTRACTIONS
HUMPTY DOO

The town (population approximately 8000), located 6km east of the Stuart Highway, is mainly a service centre for Darwin's rapidly growing rural-urban fringe and has most services available in its commercial centre. The derivation of the name remains a subject of much conjecture among locals, but the town's origins were based on a rice growing project initiated in 1956 using water stored by the nearby Fogg Dam. Rice was first grown here in the 1890s to supply the large number of Chinese mine workers. While the abandonment of the scheme in the early 1960s depressed the town's growth, expansion of rural small-holdings, tropical agriculture and tourism have injected new life.

The world's largest crocodile replica leaves no doubt that you are entering croc country, while the Humpty Doo Hotel exudes plenty of Territorian character - the walls are lined with interesting memorabilia, including a set of buffalo horns measuring 178cm (5'10) between the tips. The hotel offers meals and accommodation, ph(08) 8988 1372.

Not to be missed is *The Barra Shack,* where Waldo and Sue Bayley run a home-based barramundi fish skin leather craft cottage industry. They make ladies' shoes, bags and wallets among an extraordinary range of leather products as well as polished buffalo horns. They offer free tea or coffee, and you can be photographed feeding Darwin, their pet buffalo. A buffalo and barramundi BBQ meal is available ($15, minimum 6 persons). You will need to make an appointment. It's located at 41 Acacia Road, open daily 7am to 6pm, credit cards accepted, EFTPOS facility, ph (08) 8988 1258.

FOGG DAM CONSERVATION RESERVE

The 1569ha (3875 acres) reserve is located 10kms (6 miles) north of the Arnhem Highway, 30km (19 miles) from the Stuart Highway turnoff.

The reserve features a low dam that provides a refuge and breeding ground for large numbers of water birds, including magpie geese, ducks, herons, egrets, ibis, brolgas, and the rainbow pitta. During the Dry season, the permanent water attracts birds from the dried billabongs to the east, and sunrise and sunset are the most spectacular times for viewing this abundant and diverse wildlife.

The dam was built in the 1950s to regulate water for an ambitious, but short-lived, rice growing project. Its failure was due to management, bird, buffalo and insect problems. The magpie geese even became adept at intercepting the aerial-sown seeds before they reached the ground!

An all-weather sealed road makes it accessible for all vehicles and facilities include picnic tables and toilets, and good bird watching and boardwalks through forests in the reserve. Camping, fishing, boating and pets are not permitted and estuarine crocodiles prevent swimming.

BEATRICE HILL - WINDOW ON THE WETLANDS VISITOR CENTRE

A few kilometres east of the turnoff to Fogg Dam, the Arnhem Highway skirts vast tracts of the Top End wetlands. The conservation value of these wetlands and the complex relationship existing between the fauna and their habitats is recognised by the recent establishment of a magnificent interpretive centre, located at Beatrice Hill, one of the highest points on the Adelaide River floodplains. It provides panoramic views over a region of great contrasts and offers a fascinating insight into wetland ecological processes through a range of displays, some of which are interactive. The top floor of the centre is also a great spot for early morning and later afternoon views and to witness spectacular lightning storms in the build up to the Wet Season.

Apart from natural interpretive displays, the centre provides detailed coverage of local Aboriginal and European history of the region. To the Limilngan-Wulna people, Beatrice Hill is known as Lidawi, the three hills of which represent the Turtle Creation called Lulak. Beatrice Hill takes its name from the HMAS *Beatrice* which surveyed the Adelaide River in 1864.

Entry to the centre is free, open daily 7.30am - 7.30pm and I recommend it as an introduction to the Parks and Wildlife Commission Parks en route to Kakadu National Park. The Centre is run by the NT Parks and Wildlife Commission, ph (08) 8988 8188. Just before the centre, water buffalo and prolific birdlife of the Marrakai Wetlands can be observed.

DJUKBINJ NATIONAL PARK

Declared in 1997, the 55,000 ha (135,850 acres) Djukbinj National Park (pronounced Jook-binge) incorporates a number of former conservation reserves (Escape Cliffs Historical Reserve, Cape Hotham Forest and Conservation Reserve and parts of Marrakai Conservation Reserve) under one title and administered jointly by the Parks and Wildlife Commission and the Limilngan-Wulna Aboriginal Corporation. The park's name Djukbinj refers to King Brown Creation Time and the creation time trails criss-crossing the region.

The park also encapsulates elements of significant European History, where Escape Cliffs is the site of the first British attempts at settlement in the Northern Territory. Also in this pristine coastal area, are stands of rare palms in a mosaic pattern of wetland, coastal, estuarine and other habitats.

Currently the park has limited facilities and access is by 4WD to some areas only. Access is limited also by seasonal rains. For further details, contact the Parks and Wildlife Commission at Beatrice Hill Visitor Centre, ph (08) 8988 8188.

ADELAIDE RIVER CROSSING

Adelaide River Crossing is the base for a number of adventure cruises aboard the shallow drafted vessels, Adelaide River Queen and Kakadu Spirit. The most popular 1.5 hour *Jumping Crocodile Cruise* takes you in the comfort of upper viewing decks into wide, grey-green waterways of the Adelaide system where huge crocodiles may be seen in their natural habitat. The creatures are encouraged to leap dramatically from the waters for prey, etching unforgettable impressions of their awesome power.

Crocodiles are not the only attraction. The river cruises expose all the natural character of the floodplains, including prolific wildlife and best advice is to ensure that you have plenty of film to capture these moments. Cruises cost $26 adults, child $15 and operate several times daily. At the Pavilion, facilities include a range of foods, souvenirs and crocodile related products as well as comfortable lounge facilities. Credit cards accepted, ph (08) 8988 8144 for further details.

LEANING TREE LAGOON NATURE PARK

Located approximately 10kms (6 miles) east of Adelaide River on the Arnhem Highway, the 101 hectare (249 acre) park features a large, isolated freshwater lagoon that is a refuge for water birds during the Dry Season, and a popular spot for picnickers and campers. Technically, its a shallow, perched (raised) billabong that is regularly checked for estuarine crocodiles by Parks and Wildlife Commission Officers.

The lagoon offers good bird watching opportunities with species such as Green Pygmy Geese concentrating there during the Dry Season.

A track leading from the Highway provides conventional vehicle access. There are limited facilities. Camping is allowed in designated areas, but fishing is not permitted.

CORROBOREE PARK TAVERN

A further 10kms from Leaning Tree Lagoon is a licensed road house which has an attractive setting and offers a range of services to travellers. Features include a bushwalking trail and an albino buffalo in an enclosure. Accommodation offered includes rooms from $47.50 to $52.50; powered sites $15 and camping sites $5 pp. Other services and facilities are a bar, bistro style meals, takeaway food, ice, souvenirs, artifacts and all fuels and swimming pool. It's open daily from 6.00am, EFTPOS facility, ph (08) 8978 8920.

TERMITE MOUNDS

Five kilometres east of Corroboree Park Tavern are some fine examples of cathedral termite mounds. A boardwalk and interpretive signage provide insights into the huge creations of these tiny creatures, and an opportunity to photograph these wonderful natural sculptures. For further details of termites, refer to the description contained in the introduction to the Barkly Region.

MARY RIVER NATIONAL PARK

At the time of writing, areas designated as Shady Camp Reserve, Wildman River Reserve and Mary River Crossing Reserve are in the process of being incorporated into the proposed Mary River National Park. This park protects a range of diverse environments of the Mary River Floodplain, accessible from the Arnhem Highway via Point Stuart Road (see map - *Arnhem Highway* - Places and Attractions). It is characterised by freshwater billabongs, paperbark and monsoon forests and provides visitors with excellent year round opportunities for wildlife observation, fishing, bushwalking and photography.

Features

Mary River Crossing Reserve is adjacent to the Arnhem Highway, 3km before the Bark Hut Inn. A picnic area, toilets and boat ramp make this an ideal site to access the Mary River system and take walks on the surrounding hills. Camping is not permitted. North Rockhole is a popular access point to the channels of the Mary River. Signs of early Aboriginal occupation can be found throughout the area in the form of grindstones and middens. A boat ramp and campground are located here.

Couzens Lookout offers exceptions views of the Mary River. It is only a short walk to the vantage point where stunning sunsets may be viewed. Barramundi fishing is popular.

Brian Creek Monsoon Forest is easily accessible and situated only a couple of kilometres from the Wildman Resort access road. Such diverse patches of rainforest and associated wildlife contrast strongly with the surrounding woodlands.

Shady Camp is a popular fishing venue with boat ramp, picnic area, toilet facilities and a good access road. Camping is permitted, however privately owned facilities are also available adjacent to the park.

Facilities

Apart from those provided by the Parks and Wildlife Commission (see indicated on map), the *Wildman River Wilderness Lodge* offers a range of privately operated facilities. Accommodation includes cabins with share facilities (Dry Season only) and luxury style safari fabric cabins. Cabins cost from $95 and dinner B&B packages are available from $125 pp with concessions for children. The lodge also offers powered camping sites ($15) and unpowered sites ($10). Other facilities at the Lodge include pool and spa, pool entertainment area, small shop selling a limited range of goods. The Lodge is base for some highly recommended nature-based adventure tours. It is *open all year*, credit cards accepted, ph (08) 8978 8912.

Most areas of the park are accessible to all vehicles except during the Wet Season (November to April) when flooding may cause road closure.

THE BARK HUT INN

Located 2 km east of the Mary River Boat Ramp, the long, low roadside inn is an architectural replica of the original Annaburroo Station homestead, established in 1918. The stout bush timber construction, and array of historical artifacts and hunting trophies hanging from the inside walls, gives the inn a well-worn welcoming character, despite its recent establishment around 1975. It is a popular pub on the way to Kakadu, where a wildlife enclosure which includes buffalo, pigs, kangaroos, wallabies and emus, adds further interest.

The Inn offers good value accommodation - demountables (similar to cabins) $35 double, $22 single; all powered camping sites $14 x 2, unpowered $4 pp. All sites are shaded. Services and facilities include a well-stocked general store, bar, all meals (around $12 for evening meals), takeaway food, ice, souvenirs, large picnic/BBQ/shaded area and all fuels except autogas. Its *open daily from 6.00am*, credit cards accepted, EFTPOS facility, ph (08) 8978 8988.

KAKADU NATIONAL PARK

19,000 sq km (7220 sq miles)

LOCATION

Encompassing the catchments of the Alligator Rivers, 220km (136 miles) east of Darwin.

CHARACTERISTICS

Kakadu National Park, included on the United Nations' World Heritage List and Wetlands of International Importance Register, is not only one of the most spectacular, but also one of the most popular parks in Australia. Dissected plateau, rugged sandstone escarpment, and outliers (isolated rock outcrops), gorges and waterfalls, lowland savannah and woodland, vast floodplain tracts, grey-green rivers and sparkling billabongs, provide a basis for diverse vegetation and prolific wildlife. Apart from the magnificent scenery and busy billabong birdlife and crocodiles, an Aboriginal presence of at least 50,000 years has left a priceless heritage of rock art, the scale and scope of which is regarded by some as being as great as, and older than, the Palaeolithic art sites of France and Spain. It is also one of only 17 parks recognised internationally for its Cultural landscape attributes.

Within the park, the township of Jabiru, Frontier Kakadu Village, Gagudju Lodge Cooinda and Border Stores, are establishments that provide a wide range of tourist services (these places are separately listed).

Because of the yearly rhythms of Wet, Dry and transitional seasons, marked landscape changes occur - to appreciate this you need at least a Wet or green season visit as well. Don't expect a lush tropical jungle brimming with wildlife as you drive in during the height of the Dry season. At this time, the landscape from the Southern Pine Creek entrance is a dusty-brown. But the billabongs and shaded gorges, not seen from the main access road, are verdant and teem with wildlife.

To appreciate the park's massive 200km (124 miles) north-south by 100km (62 miles) east-west dimensions, as well as its rich biological, escarpment and cultural features, a few days' stay is necessary. Some express disappointment with Kakadu - hardly surprising when they only visit a billabong and an art site on a day trip from Darwin!

Some of the most startling landscape features are Jim Jim and Twin Falls, Barramundi Gorge and Gunlom (Waterfall Creek), all to the south. Here, the isolated pools, while containing freshwater crocodiles, are mainly free of `salties', but it pays to check at Park Headquarters. In addition to land based exploration and boat trips, a half-hour scenic flight over the park offers exciting unparalleled viewing.

HISTORY

Aboriginal people first set foot on the Australian continent at a time when sea levels were much lower, and a partial land bridge provided a link to Asia. The first Australians have left their traces in some 5000 archaeological sites throughout the park. These include 20,000-year-old edge-ground stone axes (one of the earliest records of stone grinding technology in the world) and paintings on the walls of rock over-hang shelters.

There is sufficient evidence that Aborigines have lived in Kakadu for at least 50,000 years. About 300 descendants of the original clans live in Kakadu today, and many are involved in various facets of the park's operation.

Kakadu is a phonetic rendering of Gagadju, the name of one of the traditional owners of the land. It's thought a European mis-heard the name, wrote down Kakadu, and it has stuck ever since. British explorer and navigator Phillip King charted Van Diemen Gulf in 1818, noted the large river estuaries, and named the Alligator Rivers after one of the ships. Today the park is home to many Aboriginal people who prefer their culture to be called Bining/Mungguy.

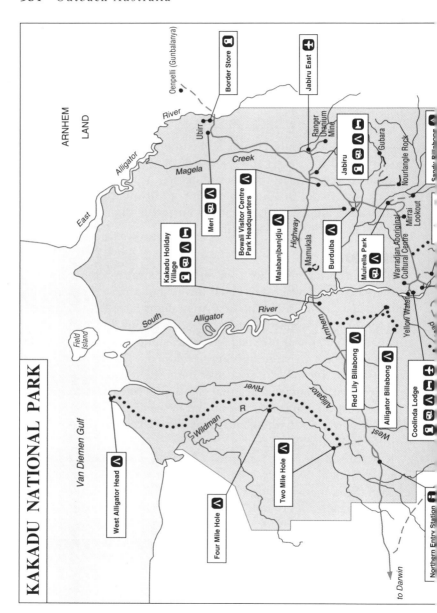

KAKADU NATIONAL PARK

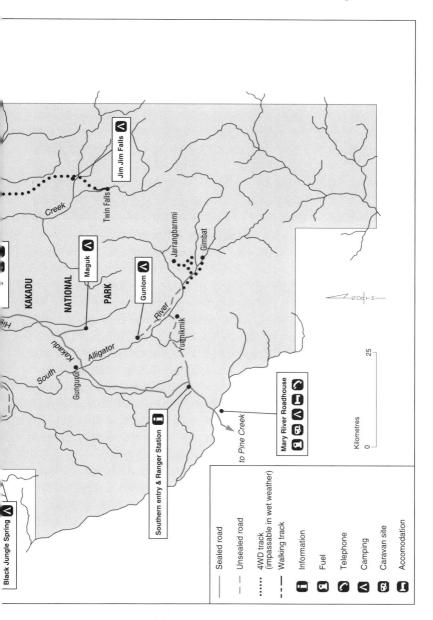

Jim Jim Falls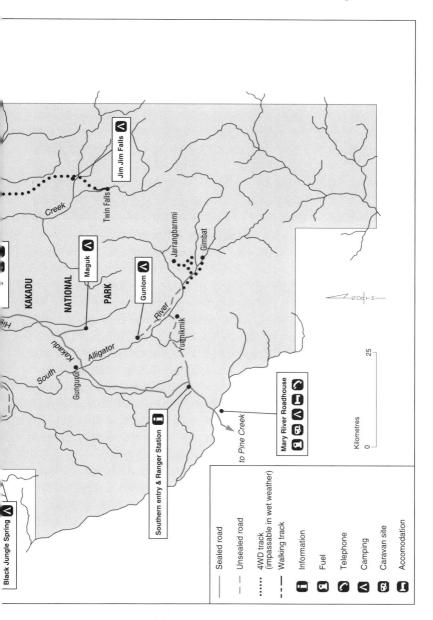

Twin Falls

Creek

Jarrangbarnmi

Gimbat

Maguk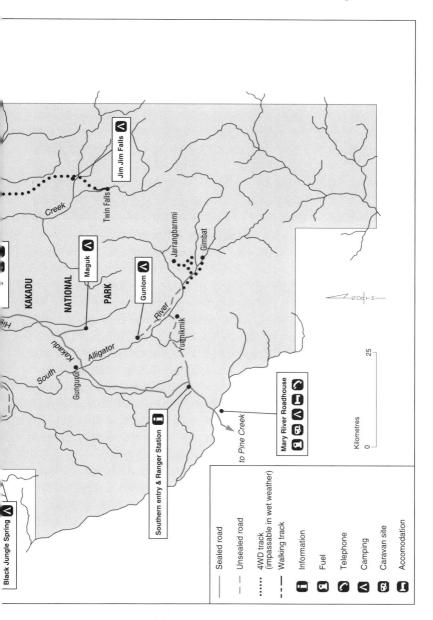

KAKADU

NATIONAL

PARK

Gunlom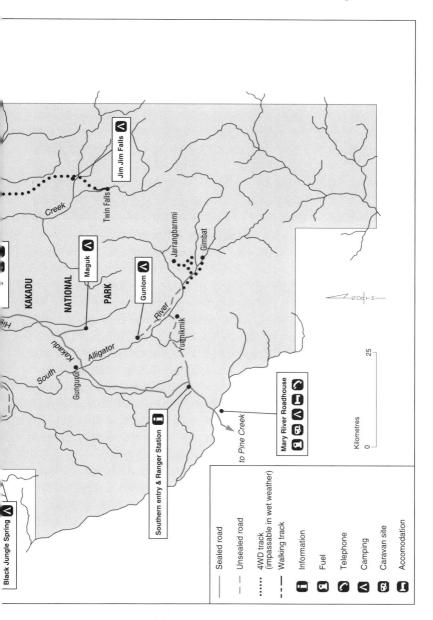

River

Yurmikmik

South   Alligator

Kakadu

Gungurul

Hills

Southern entry & Ranger Station

to Pine Creek

Mary River Roadhouse

Black Jungle Spring

Kilometres

0   25

Sealed road
Unsealed road
4WD track
(impassable in wet weather)
Walking track
Information
Fuel
Telephone
Camping
Caravan site
Accomodation

Several British attempts to establish settlements on the coast (Cobourg Peninsula) between 1824 and 1840 failed, but their major legacy remains today - the buffalo. The buffalos' days are numbered because of the environmental damage they cause. From 50 or so set free with the abandonment of the Cobourg Peninsula settlements in the 1840s, their numbers increased to around 175,000 in the Top End by the 1970s. Only a few hundred remain today in Kakadu as they have been removed under the Brucellosis and Tuberculosis eradication campaign. Cattle stations were established in the 1880s, but distance and disease brought about the demise of many a decade later. Pastoralist and drover, Paddy Cahill, held original leases here and at Oenpelli, and also hunted buffalo in the 1890s. The East Alligator River crossing is named after him.

Explorer Ludwig Leichhardt came this way in 1844 on his long trek from the east, met friendly Aboriginal clans, reported an abundance of buffalo, and discovered some of the rock art sites.

Four major mining leases were granted before Aboriginal land rights and the park establishment. One area has been rehabilitated, and the operating Ranger Uranium Mine produces 3000 tonnes of uranium oxide (yellow cake). Its operation within the park, along with the development of the Jabiluka mineral lease, is a continuing contentious issue for environmentalists and politicians. Today, Kakadu is owned in both traditional and contemporary law by Aborigines and leased to Parks Australia. The Gagadju Association represents Aboriginal interests, and they work closely with Parks Australia in the management and planning of Kakadu. Aboriginal people are willing to share some of their knowledge and understanding of the land in the hope that visitors will learn to appreciate the importance of Kakadu, and share responsibility for its protection.

LANDSCAPES

While the tidal flats, floodplains and lowlands each have their unique wilderness qualities, the soaring craggy escarpment is the park's most outstanding geological feature. It varies from vertical cliffs to stepped rocky outcrops, rises to 300m (984ft) above the lowlands, ranges for 500km (310 miles) and marks the edge of the Arnhem Land Plateau. Outliers (isolated rock outcrops), such as Ubirr are remnants of former plateau edges - in fact, it is thought that the escarpment is retreating at a rate of 1m (3 ft) every 1000 years.

The rock is quartz sandstone, horizontally bedded over older granites and formed by sand deposits under a shallow sea about 2,000 million years ago. Consolidation and probably slow uplift created this vast sandstone block criss-crossed with joint planes (fractures). Aeons of weathering and the action of running water have deeply dissected the plateau along these joint lines, leaving impressive gorges, and fragmenting the escarpment rock into huge angular blocks, some of which perch precariously one on top of the other. The awe-inspiring, weirdly weathered shapes of the escarpment are further highlighted by the suffusion of soft, golden colours in the late afternoon sun.

During the Wet season, massive volumes of water pour from the plateau, and spectacular waterfalls thunder over the edge. The intricate river systems swell and not only inundate the floodplains, but also link and lend life to the various Kakadu landscapes.

FLORA

Over 1000 plant species find a niche in Kakadu.

Tidal Flats: 22 mangrove varieties, pandanus, acacia and eugenic rainforest, while samphire, sedges and grasses grow on the mud flats.

Floodplains: Annual grasses, sedges; swamp paperbarks, freshwater mangroves fringe billabongs. Red lotus lilies float on, while yellow flowering lilies grow near billabongs. On higher ground grow acacias, pandanus and ficus (fig).

Lowlands: They are characterised by closed forest pockets, open woodlands and grassland with local variations due to soil, water and micro-climatic differences. Eucalyptus miniata (Darwin woollybutt) and E. tetrodonta (stringybark) dominate. Others include ghost gums, banyan, grevilleas and acacias.

Escarpment/Plateau: Rainforests in gorges and shady areas include Allosyncarpia ternata, cottonwood, mosses, ferns and orchids. On the plateau are heaths, spinifex and grasses.

FAUNA

There are at least 60 mammal, 280 bird, 115 reptile, 25 frog, 55 fish, and approximately 10,000 insect species. Buffalo, pig, horse, cattle, cats and dogs are feral species. During the Dry season, the lagoons and billabongs, creeks and rivers magically reappear as the plains drain and dry, thus concentrating wildlife. Early morning is the best time to see and photograph birdlife as this is prime feeding time. Birdlife represents one-third of all Australia's types, and the vast flocks of magpie geese around the billabongs are a fascinating and photogenic sight. King of this domain is the awesome estuarine crocodile.

A sample of wildlife in the Park is as follows:

Tidal Flats: Boobies, cormorants, curlews, greenshanks, herons, ospreys, oyster catchers, plovers, rails, sand pipers, egrets, mangrove robins, and warblers, are some birds. Estuarine crocodiles, dugongs, turtles and snakes.

Floodplains: Burdekin duck, magpie and pygmy geese, pelicans, ibis, pied and white-faced herons, egrets, jabiru (stork), lotus bird, honey eaters, king fishers, sea eagles, letterwing kite, yellow chat and brolgas. Agile wallaby, dingo, crocodile, water python, feral animals, reptiles and frogs. Silver barramundi or giant perch, ox-eye herring, fork-tailed catfish and mullet are some freshwater species of interest to fishermen.

Lowlands: Wedge-tail eagle, sparrow hawk, black and whistling kite, honey and bee eater, friar bird, flycatcher, finches, cuckoo shrike, parrot, cockatoo, pheasant concal, and quail, with bustard and emu rarer. Termite hills, dingo, bandicoot, kangaroo, hare wallaby, euro, quoll (native cat), snakes and smaller reptiles.

Escarpment/Plateau: In rainforest areas jungle fowl, rainbow pittas, Torres Strait and banded pigeons, white-lined honey eater are to be found. On the plateau, chestnut quilled rock pigeon and white-throated grass wren live. Animals include goanna, bat, flying fox, agile wallaby in the rainforest with the narbalek, short-eared rock wallaby, echidna and snakes elsewhere.

INFORMATION

The Park Visitor Centre (Bowali) ph (08) 8938 1120, on Kakadu Highway, is open daily 8am-5pm, and has a wealth of information and displays about the Park. Enquiries and bookings for tours can be made at the *Jabiru Tourist Centre*, ph (08) 8979 2548; from *Kakadu Air*, ph (08) 8979 2411; *Gagudju Crocodile Hotel*; *Gagudju Lodge Cooinda*; *Frontier Kakadu Village*; and *Frontier Lodge and Caravan Park*, Jabiru.

Entry fees to the Park are $15 per adult, children under 16 are free. It is advisable to check with Rangers about camp fees and access to more isolated regions within the Park.

ATTRACTIONS

Yellow Water. As the billabong contracts during the Dry season in some years, the concentrated nutrients produce an algae which gives the waters a distinct yellow tinge. A two-hour boat trip where you can spot crocodiles at close range and observe an incredible array of birdlife in a paperbark, mangrove fringed billabong, is a must. See *Cooinda* listing for details. Facilities include toilet and boat ramp. Fishing is allowed, but no camping.

Warradjan Aboriginal Cultural Centre. The Centre showcases the culture of Bininj/Mungguy people in captivating fashion via a range of sound and visual display techniques. The circular design of the centre represents a Warradjan (pig-nosed turtle), an important totemic being. The centre also features a video room and gallery that sells a good range of local arts and crafts and gifts. Its open daily 9am-5pm and is highly recommended viewing.

Rock Art Sites. Three major sites are open to visitors during daylight hours (closed at night): *Anbangbang* and *Nanguluwur* Galleries at Nourlangie and *Ubirr* (Obiri Rock). Aboriginal art reflects much deeper spiritual and cultural relationships with the natural environment than the outwardly simplistic drawings of animals, beings and objects suggest. Artists evolved highly stylised symbols among others, designed mainly to communicate traditional cultural beliefs. Paintings are not an idea of the moment but rather a honed down record of essential aspects of their culture, the precise meaning of which is generally obscure to non-Aborigines. All art has strong links to the past and some sites are sacred because of the special knowledge they contain.

Other Aboriginal art forms, such as bark and sand paintings, also represent similar links with the past, and contemporary works follow the tradition of significant messages being economically conveyed. Historically, environmental differences throughout the Territory and Kimberley have spawned a wealth of subject and artistic styles, while further evolution and complexity is seen in the works of present-day artists.

Periods of the various styles and motifs provide a useful basis for art appreciation in Kakadu. The early period (more than 20,000 years ago) features object imprints; animals such as the Thylacine

(Tasmanian Tiger) at Ubirr represent a Naturalistic Period (up to 20,000 years ago); Stylisation and Symbolism is typical of 15,000 years ago and characterised by animals, humans, weapons and mythological figures, while the intricate 'X-ray' depictions which show the internal organs and skeletons of barramundi, crocodile and 'Lightning Man', introduce a Realism period. The last 1000 years saw the evolution of more decorative 'X-ray' subjects, while contact with Macassans (people from the Indonesian Island of Sulawesi) and Europeans, produced depictions of boats, buffalo, horses and guns. Apart from their intrinsic value to Aborigines, the subject matter offers a fascinating window on past environmental conditions and human activities.

Rock Art Conservation. To protect the ancient rock art, visitors are asked to observe two simple rules: Do not touch painted surfaces or interfere with sites in any way, and follow directional signs by keeping to marked paths and walking trails.

Ubirr Art Site. The main gallery contains some of the best examples of Rock Art in Australia, while another rock overhang has a series of paintings including a Warrior frieze. A loop walking track provides access designed for wheelchairs too. The outlier shapes add landscape interest, and a walk to the lookout gives sweeping views across lowland and plain. Facilities include a carpark, picnic, drinking water, toilets including for the disabled, interpretative display and brochures (it's wise to get one at park headquarters first). Ranger guided tours during the Dry Season. Open 2pm-sunset (December 1 to May 31); 8.30am-sunset other times.

Other things of interest in the *Ubirr-East Alligator River Area* include a day-use area (toilets, boat ramp, fishing), Bardedjilildji and Manngarre short walks, Cahill's Crossing to Arnhemland (a permit is required to enter Arnhemland so please obey signs at causeway), Border Store (see separate listing), Youth Hostel, Merl camping ground and visitor centre. The road to the area is sealed but becomes flooded in the Wet Season when it is often impassible or restricted to 4WD vehicles with high clearance.

Nourlangie Rock Art Site. The Anbangbang Shelter has been a home for Aborigines for at least 20,000 years and archaeological evidence points to more frequent usage during the last 6000 years, when environmental change brought a more hospitable climate and abundant food resources. The gallery, smaller in scope than Ubirr, has some magnificent figures including 'Lightning Man'. An interesting nature trail to a lookout leads from the gallery.

Nanguluwur Gallery is another art site on the northern side of Nourlangie Rock (Burrung-gui). An interesting 3-4km walk (about 1.5-2 hours return) leads to the gallery which has creation beings, hand stencils and a ship of the contact art period.

Facilities include car park, access tracks to main art galleries suitable for wheelchairs, interpretative displays, walks and lookouts, picnic and toilet, including for the disabled. There's a good sealed road to the site.

Jim Jim Falls. Located in the southern part of the park via a 4WD only track, the falls plunge dramatically 200m (654 ft) from the escarpment edge. While little or no water falls during the Dry, awesome volumes provide spectacular viewing from the air during the Wet season. Rugged escarpment scenery, deep plunge pool, freshwater crocodiles, sandy beaches, exhilarating walk to the plateau, and fine camping, make it one of the scenic highlights of the park. Facilities include pit toilets, walks and camping area.

Twin Falls. Located 10km (6 miles) south of Jim Jim via a 4WD track which includes fording Jim Jim Creek. Extreme care is needed with this crossing. Most visitors take the 'easiest' route to the falls - via a series of short swims and rock scrambles up the gorge, but it's definitely for the fit and energetic, and some find an air mattress helpful. But, freshwater crocodiles are present, and

you take this route at your own risk. The other alternative is by a rugged walk and climb.

Not only does water cascade down in two places, but ferns and other greenery give the stepped waterfall face a hanging garden appearance. A fine natural pool, sandy verges, and pockets of rainforest, make it an idyllic spot. Freshwater crocodiles and a walk to the top add further interest. There are no facilities and camping is not allowed. 4WD tours to Jim Jim and Twin Falls are available.

Maguk (Barramundi Gorge). A delightful walk along the rainforest-lined series of pools, rapids, and beaches of the gorge, leads to a large main waterhole. There is plenty of birdlife and freshwater crocs in this verdant spot. Camping is allowed - pit toilets are the only facility. Located in the southern part of Kakadu, access is via a 10km (6 miles) 4WD track from the Kakadu Highway.

Gunlom (Waterfall Creek). One of the locations for the film *Crocodile Dundee*, Gunlom features a 100m (327 ft) waterfall, a huge, deep pandanus and paperbark fringed pool, sandy beaches, large flat rocks to meditate or sun-bathe on, freshwater crocodiles and surrounding energetic bush walks. It has all camping amenities but no powered sites. (Access is suitable for conventional vehicles and caravans during the Dry Season, but check road conditions first).

FISHING AND BOATING

All fishing in the park is by hand line or rod using lures only. Cast nets, live bait, traps, spear guns and crab pots are not permitted. These items may be left at Park HQ for safe keeping. Upstream areas are closed for fishing, but check with rangers where fishing is allowed and regulations, as these are subject to change. Territory bag limits apply.

Be aware of crocodile dangers when fishing, and you could be placing yourself and others at risk if you clean fish or leave food waste near water. People in boats should keep away from both species of crocodiles and not harass them.

The East Alligator River is within the park, but please note that the eastern or left bank (when facing upstream) is Arnhem Land (Aboriginal Land) and boats are not allowed to land on this bank. Boating downstream in this tidal river is hazardous - mud bars can span up to 90% of the river channel at low tide; there is no drinkable water downstream of the crossing, and some of the largest crocodiles in Kakadu inhabit the waters. The Visitor Information map details fishing areas and boat ramp locations.

WALKING TRAILS AND LOOKOUTS

A number of short and extended tracks provide access to different park habitats. Information on these is available in brochures, Park Information Centre, and on signs along the tracks. Wear a hat and take ample water (billabong water, unless boiled, is unsuitable for drinking). Lookout spots throughout allow excellent landscape viewing. Check with Rangers first if you plan longer walks.

PARK PROTECTION AND HAZARDS

Remember that all natural and cultural features in the Park are protected. Don't provoke wildlife. Hunting and firearms are not allowed in the park, and because of bushfire risk, all campfires are best confined to the fireplaces provided. The cutting of live vegetation is prohibited.

Drive carefully - roads are dusty, and horses and other animals on roads, particularly at night, pose a danger. At times areas of the Park may be closed for feral animal eradication purposes - a major reason why visits to remote parts should be checked with rangers first.

Obey crocodile warning signs and be mindful of their presence. Do not 'souvenir' croc warning signs - such action could result in the deaths of other visitors. Buy a replica sign instead, available from souvenir shops and Park HQ. Keep children away from the edges of all natural waterways.

TOURS

A number of tours within the park, including 4WD, are available through *Gagudju Crocodile Hotel*, *Gagudju Lodge Cooinda*, *Frontier Kakadu Village* and *Jabiru East Airport* (see also under separate listings). Parks Australia offer guided walks and talks in the Dry season.

HOW TO GET THERE

A number of tour operators and large coach companies offer day and extended tours from Darwin. *Kakadu Air* has regular services into Jabiru East from Darwin.

If you fly in, 4WD hire allows independence - if you are not used to these vehicles, Territory Rent-a-car (Cooinda and Crocodile Hotel) will give you instruction for their 4WDs, but you need to book well in advance. Within the park, roads and tracks (some 4WD) provide conventional vehicle access to the main attractions.

For budget travellers, backpackers, independent travellers and bushwalkers, *The Blue Banana* is a bus company with a difference. It provides a jump-on, jump-off service which includes the Kakadu Region, Litchfield Park and Katherine areas among others in the Top End Region. For details and costs of this very flexible service, ph (08) 8945 6800.

By road, the all-weather Arnhem Highway provides year round access to Frontier Kakadu Village and Jabiru, while the Kakadu Highway provides similar road conditions from Pine Creek to Jabiru.

PARK ACCOMMODATION

Apart from commercial establishments (see separate listings) and Youth Hostel (see *Border Store* listing), there are four *Parks Australia* camping sites which have showers, flushing toilets, disabled facilities, hot water and drinking water: **Gunlom, Mardugal, Muirella Park** and **Merl (Mel)**. Along with Malabanbandju, these camping sites are suitable for caravans. All campsites, with the exception of Mardugal, are subject to closure during the Wet season.

More isolated designated camping areas are: **Two and Four Mile Holes** on the Wildman River (the latter is 4WD and has no facilities, Two Mile has pit toilets). **Burdulba, Sandy Billabong, Jim Jim Billabong** and **Alligator Billabong** have pit toilets only, while on the Old Darwin Road, **Black Jungle Creek Springs** and **South Alligator River Crossing** have no facilities. These Parks Australia sites have no power, and permits are required for camping outside designated camp grounds.

FACILITIES

Jabiru township and other commercial establishments have a wide range of services that are detailed following the Kakadu listing. Boat ramps (concrete) are located at the South Alligator River/Kakadu Highway Bridge, the East Alligator River, Muirella Park, Mardugal and Yellow Water.

ALL SEASONS FRONTIER KAKADU VILLAGE

Located in the South Alligator Area of the Park, the tourist complex has a rainforest and billabong setting and extensive grassed areas that offer a retreat quality for all types of visitors. And you don't have to be a guest to enjoy the facilities that the village offers.

Accommodation includes **motel** style rooms from $168 double, and **camping** - powered sites $14 x2; unpowered $10. Sites are grassed and shaded. The resort has a shop, bar, licensed restaurant and cafe, takeaway food, ice, artifacts, souvenirs and all fuels except autogas. Recreational facilities include picnic/BBQ areas, rainforest walking track, tennis courts and swimming pool. By arrangement, management can attend to tour requirements within the national park.

It's *open daily*, credit cards accepted, EFTPOS facility, ph (08) 8979 0166.

JABIRU

Population 1800

CHARACTERISTICS

Jabiru is a modern, compact mining town, attractively designed to service the nearby Ranger Uranium Mine, located on a lease before the national park was proclaimed. While it continues to serve mining interests of Energy Resources Australia including the development of the Jabiluka mineral concession, it has assumed an important tourist function in providing services to the Kakadu visitor.

The spirit of Jabiruvians is epitomised in the Jabiru Wind Festival, held in early September, which celebrates the regions cultural diversity and finds expression in live music, dance, artworks, clothing and fine foods.

ATTRACTIONS

Gagudju Crocodile Hotel. A 250m long, 30m wide, crocodile-shaped and coloured two-storeyed hotel, where guests enter through the jaws, sleep and dine in the belly and head, may seem rather bizarre, but this is what the *Gagudju Association* have built. Outwardly, the unique design may appear trendy - in fact the Ginga or giant crocodile is a spirit ancestor of the Gagudju people, and a highly respected totemic figure. From this perspective, the symbolism embodied in the design is appropriate. The reptilian theme dominates the 110 room complex. The circular car parking areas represent crocodile eggs; gaping jaws complete with teeth herald visitors, while ventilation units are housed within the slatted yellow eyes. The head section contains foyer, shops, restaurants and bars. All guest rooms are located within the belly section overlooking an internal courtyard. The shaded pool and barbecue in the courtyard represent the heart, the walkway the spine, and the flowing billabong is the croc's alimentary canal. A lushly landscaped courtyard and a paving representation of an X-ray bark painting complete an innovative internal design.

   Facilities include bars, restaurant (specialties are barramundi, crocodile and buffalo), gallery and swimming pool. It is a tour-booking agent, and also runs conducted tours of the hotel according to demand.

Aboriginal Art
The *Ochre Gallery* in the Crocodile Hotel features an impressive range of paintings and crafts by local artists.

TOURS
Ranger Uranium Mine; conducted tours of the mine depart from Jabiru East Airport. Telephone (08) 8979 2411 for tour times, or book through Gagudju Crocodile Hotel or Kakadu Air at Jabiru East.
Kakadu Air: Scenic half-hour and hour flights over the floodplains, escarpment and Arnhem Land are highly recommended for an exhilarating, wider perspective of landscape and wildlife. Costs around $60 per half hour, ph (08) 8979 2411.
   A number of other tours with an adventure, natural and cultural focus are available. Some examples are: *Guluyambi Cruises* ph (08) 8979 2411, is a cultural exploration of the East Alligator River; *Lord of Kakadu Tours*, ph (08) 8979 2970 offers specialised tours to Jim Jim and Twin Falls and Arnhem Land, while *Kakadu Gorge and Waterfall Tours* ph (08) 8979 0111 specialise in exciting 4WD excursions to remote attractions. *Kakadu Fishing Tours*, ph (08) 8979 2025 have a number of fishing options. *Magela Cultural and Heritage Tours* offer unique insights in their 4WD exploration of Kakadu and Arnhem Land, ph (08) 8979 2422.

For further details of tours, contact the *Jabiru Tourist Centre* ph (08) 8979 2548, located at the Travel Agency in the town centre.

ACCOMMODATION

Gagudju Crocodile Hotel: rooms from $210 double,
ph (08) 8979 2800.

All Seasons Frontier Lodge and Caravan Park: superb amenities are offered at this establishment. Self-contained cabins cost $165 per night; Lodge rooms from $95 shared facilities. There are also facilities for disabled guests. Powered sites $25 x 2; unpowered campsites $9 p.p. Sites are grassed and shaded. Facilities include swimming pool and restaurant and kiosk, ph (08) 8979 2422.

SERVICES AND FACILITIES

Jabiru dispenses a wide range of services with credit cards widely accepted and EFTPOS facilities available at a number of establishments. There is a police station, council offices, post office, medical centre, supermarket, newsagent, craft shops, eateries and restaurants, chemist, bank (Westpac), hair salon,

clothing outlets, full vehicle services and all fuels, church, bakery, tourist centre and travel agency. Recreational facilities include a 9 hole golf course, sports and social club, and public swimming pool and water slide. Hire vehicles (Territory Rent-a-car) Crocodile Hotel, and a busy airport (Jabiru East) are among other services and facilities offered.

GAGUDJU LODGE COOINDA

Located approximately 60kms (37 miles) south-west of Jabiru, the resort, rests comfortably admidst massive mango trees and fragrant frangipanni near one of Kakadus most popular attractions, *Yellow Waters Billabong*. It features comfortable accommodation - lodge style rooms $147 per double, backpacker $25 p.p.; camping - powered sites $10 p.p.; unpowered $8 p.p. Sites are grassed and shaded. There are accommodation and tour concessions for *Youth Hostel Association Members*.

The Lodge runs 6 *Yellow Waters Boat Tours* daily; $27 for 2 hour tour and $23 for 1.5 hour tour (children half-price). These tours offer intimate viewing of a billabong where diverse birdlife and crocodiles can be seen at close, safe range. Kakadu Gorge and Waterfall Tours can be booked here, $120 p.p. and Kakadu Air offer scenic flights from the Cooinda airstrip.

Other services and facilities include a spacious bar, restaurant (all meals) in informal mode, or at their a la carte restaurant, takeaway food, ice, mini- supermarket, artifacts, souvenirs, tourist information, vehicle services (all fuels except autogas) and emergency repairs only, and swimming pool. There are good walking tracks in the area and in close proximity is the *Warradjan Cultural Centre*.

The Lodge is *open daily from 6.00am*, credit cards accepted, EFTPOS facility, ph (08) 8979 0145.

BORDER STORE

The store is located near Ubirr, approximately 40kms (25 miles) north-east of Jabiru and as the name suggests, it is also adjacent to the East Alligator River which marks the National Parks eastern boundary. The store is operated by the Gagadju Association and sells groceries, drinks, snack-foods, souvenirs, artifacts and fuel (diesel and ULP). You can make bookings for the Guluyambi boat cruises. The store is at the centre of major activity areas, including Ubirr art sites, Cahills crossing on the East Alligator River, interesting Ranger guided walks and talks during the Dry Season and gateway to Oenpelli and Arnhem Land. An open day at Oenpelli in early August each year gives an insight into these lands.

The store *opens daily*, although access on the all-sealed road may be restricted due to flooding during the Wet Season. For further information, ph (08) 8979 2474.

KAKADU HOSTEL

Located behind Border Store is the hostel, which despite its proximity, has no affiliation with the store. It offers comfortable budget accommodation with air-conditioned dormitory and fan-cooled double rooms for $15 p.p. It has a well equipped self-catering kitchen and provides a base for exploration of this sector of the National Park. For details, ph (08) 8979 2232.

MARY RIVER ROADHOUSE

A colonial-style roadhouse of recent vintage is located by the Mary River on the Kakadu Highway, 60kms (37 miles) north east of Pine Creek and provides a range of services for travellers entering Kakadu National Park via the southern route.

It offers motel rooms, $65 double; single rooms $25 and camp sites $5 p.p. Other services and facilities include bar, meals, takeaway food, limited range of groceries, ice, souvenirs and all fuels except autogas. The roadhouse *opens daily, 7am-11pm*, credit cards accepted, EFTPOS facility, ph (08) 8975 4564.

ARNHEM LAND

Population approximately 13,000

LOCATION

The region stretches east from the East Alligator River to the Gulf of Carpentaria and includes Nhulunbuy.

CHARACTERISTICS

A huge area of dissected plateau country, first proclaimed a reserve in the 1930s, is now owned by Aboriginal people who live in a number of scattered communities. The region has a rich heritage of art sites, some of which surpass even the Kakadu galleries in age, scope and style. Artists of the oldest continuing culture in the world have left their traces, particularly in some cave and rock overhang sites near Oenpelli. A permit is required to enter Arnhem Land, and the only way to view the art sites is by organised tour.

HISTORY

Navigator Matthew Flinders named the region in 1803 after one of the two ships of a Dutch expedition led by Jan Carstensz, who discovered this coast in 1623. More recent evidence suggests Indonesians, Malaccans and Portuguese visited the region at earlier dates. Overland explorer Leichhardt (1845) and surveyor David Lindsay (1883) were early Europeans to cross Arnhem Land. Pearling in the late 19th century, cattle stations, mission stations, and more recently uranium mining in 1980 (Narbarlek was mined out in one season and rehabilitated) were the main European activities.

ATTRACTIONS

Fascinating Aboriginal art sites, escarpment and plateau scenery, prolific birdlife, rivers and shaded, forested gorges, and an insight into a totally different way of life are the main features offered by Arnhem Land tour operator, ***Davidsons Arnhemland Safaris***. From their base camp near Mt Borradaile, 47km (29 miles) north-east of Oenpelli, Max and Phillipa Davidson conduct small group tours which include one art site featuring a huge Rainbow Serpent painted on a 20 feet high cave ceiling, while other sites have hand stencils, macassan praus and European figures. And, while much is undocumented, some paintings are thought to be over 60,000-years-old. Max demonstrates the abundance of the natural 'supermarket' (medicinal plants, bush tucker) and talks about Aboriginal relationships with the environment. Barramundi fishing adds further excitement to what is one of the most enlightening and stunning tours in the Territory. The Davidsons have won eight major tourism awards including the 1997 Australian award for Heritage and Culture, since 1994. Facilities at the camp include large tents, beds and linen, hot and cold showers, toilets, enclosed eating area and an airstrip. The *cost is $300 a day per person*, and includes accommodation, meals, all tours and permits. *Air transfers extra,* tours can be tailor-made to meet specific interests. For further details ph (08) 8927 5240.

Umorrduk Aboriginal Safaris also have a cultural, rock art focus, ph (08) 8941 3882.

HOW TO GET THERE

For those travelling overland to Gurig National Park, only 15 vehicles a week are permitted, and it's booked up well ahead. Oenpelli is a closed community, so no facilities or services are available, and travellers are not allowed to enter (emergencies, as in all closed Aboriginal communities, excepted). Basically, entry to Western Arnhem Land is by organised tour only.

EAST ARNHEM LAND - NHULUNBUY

POPULATION

Of the approximate 13,000 people in Arnhem Land, 4000 live in the Nhulunbuy area to the east, on the Gove Peninsula, located 650km (403 miles) east of Darwin.

CHARACTERISTICS

Australia's most remote tropical frontier town is a modern, vibrant mining and resort centre, set amongst lush bush and woodlands on the coast where the Gulf of Carpentaria meets the Arafura Sea. The 96,000 sq km (37,056 sq miles) of Arnhem Land separate Nhulunbuy from the rest of the Territory, while the only road connection is to Katherine, over 700km (440 miles) away via a 4WD track that is inaccessible at times during the year. This remoteness means that it is relatively untouched by large scale tourism, thus allowing visitors to merge comfortably into the local scene, rather than just being a tourist. Most goods come by sea to the deep water harbour, and visitors arrive by air.

The attractively laid-out town centre offers a full range of services and facilities, and accommodation provides a good base from which to explore the area's attractions. Endless white sandy beaches, an excellent variety of fishing, superb sailing waters and landfall for round-the-world sailors, extensive sporting facilities including a highly rated golf course, a rich Aboriginal heritage and culture, plenty of interesting scenery and wildlife including colourful birds, salt-water crocodiles and buffalo, are some of the town's features. In fact, it's not unusual for a buffalo or two to check out what's happening on the golf course, or in town - one was even found enjoying the waters of the pub's swimming pool one night.

 The balmy, tropical climate and young average age of the town's inhabitants, most of whom work at the massive bauxite mine, have fostered possibly Australia's most sports-crazy place, and outdoor oriented life style. There are over 33 sporting organisations, and many locals indulge in quite a few different sports each week. Visitors are quite welcome to join in too. The Surf Lifesaving Club tower is not for checking sharks, it's for spotting crocodiles! To a large extent, sun, sea and sand sum up this amazing tropical paradise that provides a fine environment for adventure and relaxation.

HISTORY

The prominent landform around which the town is built is Mt Saunders, called Nhulunbuy (meaning roughly 'hill by the sea') by Aboriginal people, which gives the town its name, while the peninsula is named after an Australian airman, William Gove, who was killed in the area during World War II.

On a human occupation time scale, the European presence is a mere blink when compared with the 50,000 year or more occupancy by Aboriginal people. The art work of their ancient culture can be seen at Yirrkala, the name of the most significant clan living here today. Macassan beche de mer (sea slug) and trepang (sea cucumber) fishermen were regular visitors from Indonesia as early as the 16th century, and this contact is shown in some Aboriginal words and art designs. Europeans and Aborigines work closely and amicably here today, and cross-cultural experience opportunities for tourists are a highlight of a visit to this area of Arnhem Land.

Navigator Matthew Flinders explored the coastline in 1803, and it's probable that Portuguese and Dutch mariners were much earlier explorers of the coastal region. Flinders noted the red coastal cliffs which were later discovered to be bauxite - the ore from which aluminium is derived.

During World War II, an RAAF airstrip was constructed on and out of bauxite, but it was not until the early 1950s that it was recognised. The town began with the mine in 1971 (construction started in 1969). While essentially established to service the mine, alumina plant and port, the climate and natural attractions encouraged tourism as an important secondary function.

LAND OWNERSHIP

The area is part of Arnhem Land owned by Aboriginal people. Unless you are driving overland from Katherine, no permits are required to enter Nhulunbuy. However, if you travel overland independently out of Nhulunbuy, eg, up the coast, a *'recreational permit'*, easily and instantly obtained from the *Northern Land*

Council Office in town, is required. Tour operators arrange permits for organised expeditions. If in doubt, check with the Land Council, ph (08) 8987 2602 or Yirrkala (08) 8987 3433.

ATTRACTIONS

Climate. Because it's surrounded by water, gentle breezes have a pleasant modifying effect on temperatures, so it's not as hot or humid as other Top End places. Inland, it can be hotter. Temperatures average around 26C (79F), 18-20C (64-68F) at night (June, July), rising in average to 32C (90F) in November and December, the hottest months.

Natural Features. Sweeping beachscapes, aquamarine waters, inland waterways, billabongs and rock pools, and patches of tropical rainforest, offer much to naturalists, adventurers and walkers.

Wildlife. Large salt-water crocodiles inhabit coastal and inland waters. Buffalo range freely, while the occasional king red kangaroo may be seen. Perentie, frill-necked lizards, king brown and python snakes are around, as are dingoes. Birdlife includes blue-winged kingfisher, a range of parrots including the colourful red-shouldered lorikeet, honeybirds, white-breasted sea eagles, terns and falcons. Whilst wildlife is prolific, sightings during daylight hours are a bonus. You'll see plenty of birds, and if you are quietly observant, it's amazing what may be seen in the bush.

Fishing. Gove Peninsula offers first rate fishing. Reef fish include coral trout, cod, red emperor, sweet-lip and schnapper. Surface fish range from the fighting tuna to barracuda, queen fish, trevally and shark. In the rivers are barramundi, bream and mangrove jack. Out in the Gulf, October to May are ideal months only because June, July and August are subject to the uncomfortable south-east prevailing winds (SE Tradewinds), but the fish still bite! Charter boats are available, and reasonably priced one-day fishing trips can be negotiated with private boat owners.

Bauxite Mine. Nabalco Pty Ltd operate the open cut mine where huge 85 tonne capacity trucks haul the ore to a crusher. Once reduced, the ore is transported by a 3-tiered 17.5km (10 miles) conveyor belt system (one of the world's largest) - one to feed the alumina plant, the other two belts for direct bulk export from the deep water port at Melville Bay. The harbour here is also a safe haven for yachts. Overburden (waste rock) is used to rehabilitate area mines in the 250 million tonne reserve. About 5 million tonnes of ore are mined, producing 1 million tonnes of alumina annually, and 2 million tonnes of bauxite are exported directly.

Yirrkala. A former mission is now a major Aboriginal centre, best known for the Yirrkala people's struggle to win title, in contemporary Australian law, to their traditional lands. It houses Australias most important Aboriginal Art Museum containing works of historic and spiritual significance. Aboriginal art, representative of Arnhem Land, is on display. Some artifacts may be purchased here, ph (08) 8987 1701.

Nambara Arts and Crafts. This gallery also displays a range of artworks which, like Yirrkala, epitomise the power and depth of Aboriginal culture. Nambara can arrange a didgeridoo playing demonstration by the man who makes these ancient musical instruments for the Australian Aboriginal band Yothu Yindi who live on the Gove Peninsula. Outings may be arranged for insights into Aboriginal culture. For further details, ph (08) 8987 2811.

Golf Course. A 9-hole course attracts golfers from all over Australia for the various tournaments held there. Visitors are welcome, ph (08) 8987 3191.

Swimming. People do swim, but with caution, as there are salt-water crocodiles in all these tropical waters, and stingers in the Wet season. Check with the locals about the 'safer' spots.

TOURS

A number of tours are available. ***Birds, Bees and Things*** is an ecotour of Aboriginal culture and wildlife, ph (08) 8987 1814.

For fishing safaris and charters, contact ***Gove Diving and Fishing Charters*** (08) 8987 3445; ***Walkabout Lodge Charters*** (08) 8987 1777; ***Lady Sariah Charters*** (08) 8987 2832; ***MV Iron Lady*** ph 070 581 726. Diving and snorkelling charters in beautiful coral coasts can be arranged.

For scenic flights, contact ***Air Frontier*** (08) 8987 1833; ***Laynhapuy Aviation***, ph (08) 8987 3155; ***MAF*** (08) 8987 2777 or ***NTAS*** ph (08) 8987 1770.

The Nabalco Mine offers a free 4 hour tour of the mine on Friday mornings. Bookings essential ph (08) 8987 5345.

EVENTS

Gove Game Fishing Classic (sailfish and marlin) is held during the third week in November.

HOW TO GET THERE

By Road

Access to Arnhem Land via the Central Arnhem Road is monitored by Aboriginal owners and permits must be obtained from the Northern Land Council. Allow at least two to four weeks for processing. The turnoff from the Stuart Highway is approximately 60kms (37 miles) south of Katherine. Information about the often rough 4WD track should be obtained from police before attempting the 700km (434 mile) journey. Fuel is available at Bulman (about the half-way point) but check before leaving. There are many creek crossings and while it can be a good run during the Dry Season, do not exceed 80kmph and expect the unexpected! This route is for well-equipped, experienced drivers and most users, sensibly travel in 4WD convoys. There are designated camping spots en-route.

By Air

Qantas and *Ansett Australia* have regular flights (over 26 flights weekly from Darwin and Cairns). Some visit by light aircraft. There's an airport shuttle bus service for air travellers.

ACCOMMODATION

All rooms are air-conditioned and all establishments accept credit cards and with the exception of Hideaway, all have EFTPOS facilities.

The Walkabout Lodge has a superb beach front location and offers rooms ranging from $126 - $157.50 per night. Facilities include swimming pool, bars, a la carte restaurant (excellent seafood meals in particular) and Conference facilities. Ph (08) 8987 1777.

Gove Peninsula Motel has a tropical garden setting close to the town centre and offers self-contained rooms - single $99.75, double $110.25, twin share $120.75. Facilities include swimming pool and BBQ area, ph (08) 8987 0700.

Hideaway Guest House has rooms from $55 and is located near Gove Airport, ph (08) 8987 3933.

CAMPING

There are no camping grounds, but bush camping areas are designated outside the town. There are no amenities at these sites.

EATING OUT

The town has good restaurants with a range of food styles available. The *Walkabout Lodge*, *Arnhem Club*, *Yacht Club* and *Country Golf Club* are excellent venues. The *Chok Stix Cafe* is the place to enjoy a wide selection of Chinese and Asian dishes. The *Arnhem Club* also hosts a Sunday movie night.

SERVICES AND FACILITIES

A full range includes police station, post office, hospital, medical services, supermarkets, restaurants and eateries, chemist, banks (Westpac and Commonwealth Bank Agency - Post Office), a number of specialty shops, churches (Assemblies of God, Catholic,

Uniting, Jehovah Witnesses), take-away food, full vehicle services and fuel (LP, ULP, diesel), hire vehicles, sporting goods (including fishing), charter boats and yachts. Conference facilities are available at the Walkabout Lodge.

Credit cards widely accepted, EFTPOS.

RECREATIONAL

Public swimming pool, golf course, bowls, tennis and squash courts and hire bicycles are a few. Visitors are welcome to use facilities at the sports clubs, in particular the Gove Yacht Club.

BATCHELOR - LITCHFIELD NATIONAL PARK

The turnoff from the Stuart Highway to Batchelor, 90kms (56 miles) south of Darwin, offers a rewarding loop road exploration of the pristine beauty of Litchfield National Park - a park which complements the attributes of Kakadu. A number of routes are possible via Batchelor without too much back-tracking. The main features of the park can be visited in an extensive loop road which can take you north to Darwin via Tumbling Waters and Berry Springs. Alternatively, you can head south via the Southern Access Track (4WD only) to Daly River, then east to the Stuart Highway via the Daly River Road, (see map - Litchfield National Park).

The region is also rewarding for its early history, and a number of unusual attractions and activities in and around Batchelor.

BATCHELOR

Population 680

Located 14 kms (9 miles) west of the Stuart Highway on Batchelor Road, the towns relatively unspoilt, lush-green woodland setting is largely due to the environmentally sensitive town plan and construction of 1952, in which the removal of trees was kept to a minimum. And there's plenty of colourful birdlife, including an extraordinary range of parrots, so much so, that Jacki Hargreaves calls her restaurant at the *Rum Jungle Hotel*, **Birdies**.

The Overland Telegraph Line and The Track (Stuart Highway), experimental agriculture, railway development, war-time air bases and old mine sites give a great sense of history to the district. Apart from continuing mining operations (gold, lead and zinc) and a large export beef and buffalo abattoir, as well a major education functions, Batchelor is the gateway to Litchfield National Park.

A unique Aboriginal Teacher Training College and the Top End Aerial Sports Association (parachuting and gliding) based at the airport, add to the town's variety of activities. All basic services and facilities to meet tourist needs are available in the town.

History

The Overland Telegraph Line and subsequent track spawned a few pubs in the region during the 1870s, one of which, *The Rum Jungle* (located in the vicinity of the mine site), was a popular stopover for travellers. The derivation of Rum Jungle, like that of Tennant Creek, is typically Territorian. A horse and dray loaded with supplies broke down on the rough track tipping off a barrel of rum. The teamsters set up camp where the wheel and the barrel rolled off and drank the lot in the jungle-like forest!

As early as the 1880s, coffee, rubber and tobacco were grown for a short time, and a site a few kilometres south of Rum Jungle was selected for an experimental farm in 1911. The farm's object was to prove that specialised crops were viable in the tropics - in its first year of operation the pumpkin story pointed to a successful venture. It was supposed to have measured 1.3m (4 ft) in height, 1.6m (5 ft) in diameter, and 4.5m (14 ft) in circumference! Despite what appears to be the fairytale pumpkin, insects, climate and management problems saw the scheme abandoned after a few years. The site was named Batchelor in 1912 after South Australian politician, Egerton Batchelor.

A legacy of a large World War II Allied air base, attacked in 1942 by Japanese bombers, is an old airstrip where General Douglas

McArthur landed en route to important meetings. Army installations and other wartime relics lie scattered in the bush.

  The discovery of uranium and the subsequent development of an open-cut mine in the early 1950s, gave the town its first solid economic base. The population rose to nearly 700, but with the mine's closure in 1971, Batchelor struggled to survive. An abattoir established in 1972, the Woodcutters lead, tin and zinc mine, gold mining and more recently tourism, promise a bright future.

Attractions

Wartime Relics. Airfield and army installations.

Karlstein Castle. A miniature, detailed replica of a Bohemian castle is a major eye-catcher, located on a rocky outcrop in front of the police station.

Batchelor Recreation Lake. Sometimes called Rum Jungle Lake, this large spring-fed tract of water is a popular spot for boating (non-powered only), sailing, canoeing, swimming and picnicking. Located 5km (3 miles) from town, with a sealed road to the Lake.

Rum Jungle Mine Site. Uranium ore bodies were discovered by Jack White in 1949. The mining project began in 1952 and Batchelor was established as a town for miners in 1954, with the official opening of the mine. The actual mine ceased in 1963 as the remaining ore was uneconomic to treat. The treatment plant closed eight years later when the stockpiled ore had been processed. The area has been rehabilitated, but visits are by organised tour only, through Caravillage. There's a fossicking locality nearby.

Aerial Sports Association. Based at Batchelor Airport, parachute and gliding clubs have weekend instructional flights, including tandem free-fall parachuting from the airport, ph (08) 8976 0036. Scenic flights are available, ph (08) 8976 0023, while for gliding experience ph 018 920 510.

Batchelor Butterfly Farm. The Territory's only butterfly farm features 9 colourful native species housed in a rainforest enclosure, complemented also by a large, walk through bird enclosure. Owner Christopher Horne conducts informative tours through the butterfly house (open 9.30am-4.45pm) and adjacent facilities include static displays, gift shop, childrens play area and a BYO restaurant/cafe (open 9am-9pm). The Farm opens daily is located in Meneling Road (behind the Ampol Service Station), entry fees $7 adult, $5.50 senior citizens, $3.50 children, ph (08) 8976 0199.

Accommodation

Rum Jungle Motor Inn - motel rooms $78 single, $98 double; $108 triple. Rooms designed for disabled guests, swimming pool, restaurant (bistro style meals), credit cards accepted, EFTPOS, open daily, ph (08) 8976 0123.

Batchelor Caravillage - cabins $78; powered camp sites $20 x 2; unpowered $8 p.p. Sites shaded, grassed, no pets allowed. Facilities include BBQ, kiosk, swimming pool. Open daily, credit cards accepted, ph (08) 8976 0166.

Services and Facilities

Batchelor has a hotel (Rum Jungle Inn), general store, supermarket, health centre, police station, post office, garage (full range repairs), service station (all fuels), churches (Catholic, Uniting, Seventh Day Adventist), bank agencies (Westpac at Caravillage, Commonwealth at Post Office), restaurants (Rum Jungle Inn - excellent meals from $9) and Butterfly Farm, takeaway food outlet, travel agent, newsagent, and Parks and Wildlife Offices and Council Offices. Recreational facilities are located at airport (sky diving, gliding, scenic flights), Cultural Centre, public swimming pool, bowls and tennis centre. Shops open daily, credit cards widely accepted and EFTPOS facilities widespread.

LITCHFIELD NATIONAL PARK

Only two hours drive from Darwin, this 146,118ha National Park includes spectacular waterfalls, patches of rainforest, intriguing magnetic termite mounds, massive sandstone formations and 4WD tracks. Swimming in specified areas, photography, wildlife observation and bushwalks (ranging from a 20 minute stroll to extended wilderness walks), are popular activities at Litchfield. Camping is permitted in designated areas. Most campgrounds are managed by Campground Services and fees apply. These should be placed in honesty boxes provided. There are no powered sites in the park and caravans are restricted to Wangi Falls.

Landscape

Litchfield National Park's rugged *Tabletop and Tableland Ranges* were created by an uplifting of the earth's crust millions of years ago. It is composed of highly fractured, rain permeable rock deposits. Wet season rain is absorbed into the upper rock layers and then released throughout the year, resulting in the park's waterfalls flowing throughout the dry season when there is no rain.

  The Tabletop Range is perhaps the park's most important landform. The waterfalls, originating from watercourses at the top of this plateau, have worn through the escarpment to form cliff faces with deep, amphitheatre-like rock pools at their base. The park's main access road has been specially designed to allow visitors to appreciate the diverse landforms and other natural features of the area. The road incorporates long sweeping curves and carefully-placed gradients which open up the best possible view of the surrounding countryside. The road heads west in a wide loop from Batchelor, passing *Florence Falls* then climbs into the escarpment and heads south-west across the plateau before descending over the eastern edge to other waterfall attractions.

Flora and Fauna

The vast majority of Litchfield National Park consists of open woodland dominated by Woollybut and Stringybark Eucalyptus

LITCHFIELD NATIONAL PARK

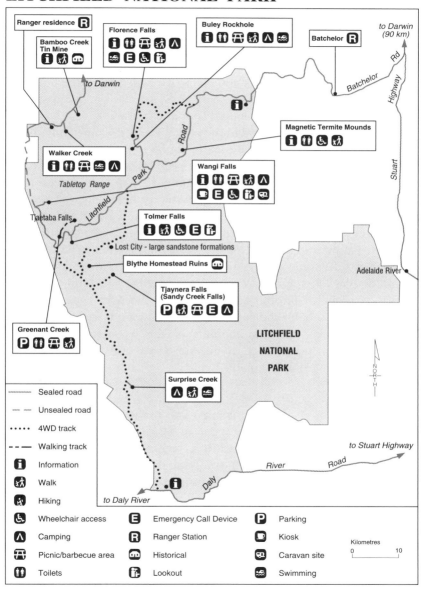

Ranger residence **R**

Bamboo Creek Tin Mine

Florence Falls

Buley Rockhole

Batchelor **R**

to Darwin (90 km)

to Darwin

Road

Batchelor Highway

Magnetic Termite Mounds

Walker Creek

Tabletop Range

Park

Litchfield

Wangi Falls

Stuart Highway

Tjaetaba Falls

Tolmer Falls

Lost City - large sandstone formations

Blythe Homestead Ruins

Adelaide River

Tjaynera Falls (Sandy Creek Falls)

LITCHFIELD

NATIONAL

PARK

Greenant Creek

Surprise Creek

NORTH

to Stuart Highway

River Road

Daly

to Daly River

Legend		
——— Sealed road		
– – – Unsealed road		
•••• 4WD track		
– – Walking track		

Information
Walk
Hiking

Wheelchair access	Emergency Call Device	Parking
Camping	Ranger Station	Kiosk
Picnic/barbecue area	Historical	Caravan site
Toilets	Lookout	Swimming

Kilometres
0   10

trees. Beneath these are a mid-stratum of Sand Palm, Banksia, Cycads and a variety of Acacias and Grevilleas.

Monsoon rainforest patches thrive in the deep, narrow gorges and the species most common in these areas include Carpentaria Palm, Carillia Wood, Wild Nutmeg, Tuckeroo, Native Lasiandra and a variety of vines, ferns and epiphytes which cover the boggy floor of the forest. These monsoon forest species provide a year round supply of brightly coloured fruit and berries.

The largest native mammal in the park is the Antilopine Wallaroo which is similar to the Red Kangaroo found in more arid regions.

The Dingo, the dog thought to have been brought into Australia by Aboriginal people thousands of years ago, can also be seen in the park. Smaller mammals are nocturnal in habit but can often be seen around the campsites at night. Those that are most commonly spotted include the Northern Quail, the Northern Brown Bandicoot and the Northern Brushtail Possum. The Ghost Bat, Australias only carnivorous bat, the Orange Horseshow Bat and the Black Flying Fox are among many of the bats found in the Park. A range of birdlife have also made the park their home. Termites also inhabit the park visibly, their mounds including the huge castle-like cathedral mounds of the woodland termites, arboreal nests found high up in the trees and the magnetic mounds of the black soil plains.

FEATURES
Wangi Falls. This is the most popular falls in the park and includes a large, permanent natural pool at its base providing good swimming opportunities. Facilities include a kiosk, camping ground, grassed picnic area and walking trails.

Florence Falls. Offers a superb natural pool for swimming, along with established walking trails for those who are interested in exploring the surrounding forest. The area offers two campgrounds, one of them accessible to conventional vehicles, and the other suitable only for visitors with 4WD vehicles.

Tolmer Falls. Spills into a large deep pool at the end of a narrow gorge. A loop walking track and lookout platform provides spectacular views of the gorge and surrounding sandstone formations. The gorge and plunge pools have been declared a protection zone to assist the conservation of vulnerable bat species.

Blyth Homestead. One of the park's historical features, Blyth Homestead is a relic of a bygone pastoral era. The earth-floor structure of saplings and corrugated iron was built in 1929 by the Sargeant Family who lived there until 1964 and used it as a base from which they conducted their pastoral operations.

The Lost City. This is one of the park's most fascinating natural landmarks and consists of a large collection of unusual sandstone pillars which are the result of weathering of the Tabletop Range. Provides excellent photographic opportunities.

Tjaynera Falls (Sandy Creek). Accessible by 4WD vehicles via a track leading from the main park road, these falls are sometimes described as the best of Litchfield's waterfalls. Parking, picnic and camping areas are located away from the falls and a 1.7 km walking track provides access to the pool.

BUSHWALKING
The scenic terrain, and permanent water make the park an ideal location for bushwalking. Best advice is to inform Rangers of your intended route and time of return, and for extended walks, take detailed maps.

CROCODILES
The Australian Freshwater Crocodile is common in the upstream section of many Top End rivers and streams, including those in Litchfield National Park. The freshie is usually regarded as harmless to man, but may become aggressive when protecting nest sites, so large individuals are removed from areas used for swimming. The Estuarine Crocodile is rarely found in the park's smaller freshwater streams, but removed if detected in the park.

Visitors should only enter the water in areas designated for swimming and should not swim in the Finniss or Reynolds Rivers as they are inhabited by the Estuarine Crocodile.

CONSERVATION

Please help to keep this area in its wilderness state. Collect firewood before arriving at your campsite and only light fires in the places provided. Guns and traps are prohibited. Pets are not permitted.

HOW TO GET THERE

Situated near the town of Batchelor, 100km south-west of Darwin, the park is accessible either by gravel road via the Cox Peninsula Road or sealed road via Batchelor. The loop road through the park has a good formed surface suitable for conventional vehicles but access to some features requires a 4WD. The park is open all year, but check road conditions particularly during the Wet Season when flooding may temporarily restrict access into the Park. 4WD tracks are closed for the duration of the Wet Season. Also, some swimming areas can become unsafe after heavy rain and may be closed.

For budget and independent travellers, *The Blue Banana Bus Company* offers an alternative way of visiting the park (see details under *Kakadu National Park - How to Get There*).

TOURS

Reynolds River Safari and Wetland Cruises. From a base located between Cascade and Wangi Falls, *Grahams Park*, offers 3 daily tours which include a cattle station visit and wetland cruises. The tours are recommended for their ecotourism qualities and cost $27 p.p. ($75 family). Also offered are helicopter flights over the park; $75 for 25 minutes, $45 for 15 minutes.

Camping is available at Grahams Place $5 p.p. (free if you take a cruise). The base is on privately owned land adjacent to the Park. For details, ph (08) 8978 2345.

Other Tours. A number of Darwin based tour operators include the Park in their tours, including *Northern Territory Adventure Tours*, ph 1800 063 838; *Australian Outback Expeditions*, ph 1800 891 190; *Discovery Ecotours* ph 1800 801 208 and *Northern Territory Gateway* ph 1800 813 288.

SERVICES AND FACILITIES

The Litchfield National Park map included, illustrates facilities in the park. The *Wangi Falls Kiosk* is open daily and sells food, drinks, ice and groceries, ph (08) 8978 2861. Privately owned *Pethericks Rainforest* located near Walkers Creek, lies adjacent to the National Park and offers camping facilities (fees apply). Near Wangi Falls, *Grahams Park* offers camping, tours and helicopter flights from a base adjacent to the park (see under *Tours*). If you access the park via Berry Springs in the north, near the Finniss River crossing is one of the most laidback and colourful outback shops - the *Finnis River Store*.

B A T H U R S T   A N D   M E L V I L L E   I S L A N D S   (T I W I   I S L A N D S)

Population 2500

LOCATION

Off the mainland coast, about 80km (49 miles) north of Darwin.

CHARACTERISTICS

Two islands separated from the mainland by the Clarence and Dundas Straits are themselves divided by the very narrow Apsley Strait. Together they cover an area of 8000 sq km (3040 sq miles), and Melville is the second largest island so near the Australian coast after Tasmania. Relatively flat, mangrove-lined rivers, indented coastline, rocky shorelines and long white sandy beaches fringed by she-oaks, are some of the landscape features. Colourful birdlife, and an abundance of marine life including estuarine crocodiles, add interest.

The Islands are owned by the Tiwi people, whose contact with mainland Aborigines was limited until about the late 1800s. The Tiwis, meaning 'people'; 'we, the people', are outgoing and relatively confident, and have a culture that differs in significant ways from mainland Aborigines. This confidence and proximity to Darwin in recent times is reflected in the Nguiu community, which has a well-developed range of commercial activities. Of interest is the Tiwi Design screen printing workshop, Tiwi pottery and wood carving, Bima Wear clothing and Tiwi Pima Art Centre. Nguiu is the main centre with a population of 1200 administered by the Tiwi Land Council. Milikapiti and Pularumpi are the two main communities on Melville, with a population of around 300 in each. In conjunction with the Northern Territory Government, the Tiwi people have established a forestry enterprise which will be a major supplier of Caribbean Pine to the mainland.

Visits and accommodation are by packaged tours, and each offers an opportunity to meet Tiwi people and experience something of their dynamic culture. Permits are required to enter.

HISTORY

The first authenticated sighting of the islands by Europeans was by the Dutch in the early 1600s. Great Britain established a presence on Melville Island in 1824 at Fort Dundas (near where Pularumpi is today) in order to counter growing Dutch interest in the area. Captain Bremer of the Royal Navy was empowered to set up a military settlement, but tropical diseases, poor relations with the Tiwi, and isolation, all contributed to its failure and abandonment in 1829. This was the first European attempt at settling the North Australian coast, and very little remains of it today. Phillip Parker King landed on and named the islands in 1818. Bathurst was named after Earl Bathurst, Secretary of State for the colonies. King found the Tiwi knew some Portuguese words, suggesting earlier exploration and contact with these Europeans.

Macassan fishermen were the only other known overseas visitors, and contact led to trade in some areas with the Tiwi - in fact with the steel blade axes, the Tiwi were able to forego traditional bark canoes and build dugout ones.

Nguiu began as a Catholic Mission in 1911, and mission activities have had a strong influence on the lives of the Tiwi. During World War II the first ever Japanese bullets on Australian soil came from a strafing raid on February 19, 1942, the same raid that bombed Darwin. A Tiwi captured the first Japanese prisoner, a pilot who crash-landed on Melville.

In the early 1980s, the advent of tourism and other enterprises added another dimension to both Tiwi culture and European understanding.

ATTRACTIONS

Tiwi Culture. Meeting Tiwi people and visiting their creative workshops at Nguiu gives an appreciation of the values and customs of the community. This is enhanced by a visit to the Milikapiti community and a Tiwi pukamani burial ground featuring tall, elaborately carved and decorated totems.

Fishing. The local coast offers some fine fishing, including barramundi, mackerel, trevally, threadfin salmon, tuna, marlin and sailfish. These are some of the 17 species regularly caught. Huge tides characterise coastal waters.

Turacumbie. Lush tropical vegetation, a waterfall with a large pool suitable for swimming, is located in the centre of Melville Island. While there are large estaurine crocodiles around the islands, they don't frequent this pool.

HOW TO GET THERE

Only through an organised tour (See under *Tours*).

Independent boat or yacht owners should check with the Tiwi Land Council in Darwin, ph (08) 8981 4898 for details of permits, regulations and areas where fishing is not permitted.

Independent private aircraft visitors using the gravel airstrip at Nguiu must make prior arrangements with the tour operators, and have permits.

ACCOMMODATION AND TOURS

Tiwi Tours - Offer a one day tour of Bathurst Island which includes return airfares from Darwin, morning tea and lunch, and entry permit fees. It costs $260 p.p and is available weekdays only. Special interest tours are negotiable, ph (08) 8981 5115.

Barra Base Lodge - Lodge-style rooms, swimming pool, bar and dining room with a wide verandah and basic shop, is the base for guided fishing trips to some of the Territory's best spots. Wet Season fishing is a delight before and after storm cloudscapes (you don't fish during the storm!). Minimum of 2 days, costs around $500 per day including lodge accommodation, fishing guides, return air fares to Darwin, meals and fishing gear. It's located on the western side of Bathurst at Port Hurd, ph (08) 8978 3987.

SERVICES AND FACILITIES

Nguiu has a store for those things you have forgotten. Barra Base sells basic items from its store, and except for the special licensed bar at Barra Lodge, no alcohol is permitted on the Islands. Credit cards accepted, EFTPOS facility available.

CUTTA CUTTA CAVES NATURE PARK

1499ha (3702 acres)

LOCATION

West of the Stuart Highway, 30km (19 miles) south of Katherine.

CHARACTERISTICS

The park protects two aspects of a typical karst or limestone landscape; a series of limestone caves with classic stalactite and stalagmite formations, and weirdly weathered pillar formations of

limestone on the surface called tower karsts. Other characteristics of karst country are evident on the surface, namely the sink holes (doline or swallow-hole), conical depressions in the limestone. Geologically, the Tindal limestone was formed some 500 million years ago and this type of tropical karst landscape is limited to only a few locations in Northern Australia.

The caves consist of a series of caverns connected by narrow passages and two caves are now open to visitors. The park continues to be important to the Jawoyn people. The geology of the area is well explained by rangers who conduct a number of tours daily. A number of tour operators in Katherine include the caves in their tour offerings.

FLORA AND FAUNA

Most of the area is open woodland dominated by Eucalyptus (*E.foelscheana*; *E.tectifica* and *E.confertiflora*) with tall grasses (*Themeda triandra*, *Sehima nervosum* and *Sorghum ssp.*) small leaf bauhinia are also evident. Clusters of tropical rainforest/vine thickets in the area are thought to be the remains of an inland fringe of rainforest which once predominated in Northern Australia. The most notable of this remnant species is the native fig (*Ficus virens var, dasycarpa*) with their bizarre tangle of root systems into the limestone.

There's a rich variety of wildlife. The brown tree snake is often seen coiled upon cave ledges (they are not considered dangerous but should not be disturbed). Five species of cave-dwelling bats occur in the dark cavern recesses. These include the Ghost Bat and the Orange Horseshoe-bat both considered to be rare. Two rare species of blind shrimp inhabit the warm pool waters in the caves.

Rock wallabies and prolific birdlife (over 170 species recorded in the park including the Hooded Parrot and Gouldian Finch) add further natural interest to the area.

SERVICES AND FACILITIES
There's a tropical woodland walking track. Ranger guided tours operate several times daily in the season. The park has a kiosk and visitor centre.

Guided tours cost $8 adult, $4 child and the park is open from 8.30am-4.30pm daily. An all weather road provides easy access from the Stuart Highway and *opening times during the Wet Season may vary because of flooding*. For further details ph (08) 8972 1940.

DALY RIVER

Population 450 (township and environs)

LOCATION
On the Daly River crossing, 112km (69miles) west from the Stuart Highway via the turn-off near Hayes Creek and approximately the same distance from Adelaide River.

CHARACTERISTICS
Daly River is a dispersed settlement with the Daly River Inn and Police Station located by the Daly River crossing. The main body of the commercial and cultural functions is clustered at the Nauiyu Nambiyn Community a few kilometres downstream from the crossing. Elsewhere, establishments catering for visitors are widely scattered, their distances apart enhanced by circuitous road systems. Nevertheless, this tourist loop route exposes visitors to a beautiful, lush and tropical environment - an idyllic spot to go bush for a few days and where the tranquil river, barramundi fishing, crocodiles and some fine natural camping sites are the main attractions.

Because of the scattered nature of Daly Rivers main tourist establishments (Perrys on the Daly; Daly Mango Farm and Woolianna Tourist Park), these are separately outlined under attractions.

HISTORY

The river was named after Sir Dominick Daly, Governor of South Australia (1862-1868) by Explorer Stuart in 1862, and the later settlement took its name from that source.

A short-lived copper mining venture in the 1880s brought a sharp clash between cultures when three miners were murdered by Aborigines in 1884. White retaliation was ruthless. The Jesuit missions established in 1886 provided a buffer between the races, and today Aborigines run the old mission through their Naniyi Nambiyu Council. The Mango Farm Safari Camp occupies part of the former mission property, including historic ruins and huge old mango trees planted by the Jesuits.

A few agricultural ventures were attempted in the region - sugar cane in the early 1880s; peanuts between the 1920s and 1950s, and even dairying in 1915 - all with little lasting success. Pastoral runs established in the 1880s are the most enduring agricultural activity. Mrs Nancy Polishuk has written a detailed account of the local history, entitled *Life on the Daly River*.

ATTRACTIONS

Daly River Nature Park. The 60ha (148 acres) reserve preserves a scenic area at the lowest Daly River crossing point. Barramundi fishing and boating activities are popular. It has picnic facilities, and camping is allowed.

Perrys on the Daly. The 1000 acre (400 hectare) property is base for a tourist venture which offers homestay packages, camping, barramundi fishing safaris and guided day fishing trips. Its located on the Daly River and offers visitors a range of flexible options as to activites and accomodation styles. Homestay and fishing safari packages can be tailored to suit, and prices for 7 day safaries can be provided on application.

Services and facilities available include; boat hire, fishing tackle, marine services, gift shop, basic provisions including gas and ice, bush golf course, bush walking trails, crocodile spotting, swimming pool, boat ramp and a range of accomodation all in a beautiful, secluded river frontage setting. Its open daily (restricted access during the wet season), credit cards accepted. Ph (08) 8978 2452

Daly River Mango Farm. Also located on the river, the 814 acre (326 hectare) cattle and mango orchard property offers guided fishing trips, boat hire and river cruises and accommodation.
   Cabins are available from $55, units from $115 and campsites cost $7 p.p unpowered, $3 extra for town power. Sites are secluded and have tranquil, tropical settings. Facilities include a swimming pool, mini store, restaurant and all meals if required. Part of the property contains ruins of the old Jesuit mission, one of three established between 1886 and 1891. The hearth, chimney and concrete relics are all that remain. The farm is open daily (restricted access at times during the wet season), access roads suitable for conventional vehicles, located north of the community, credit cards accepted. Ph (08) 8978 2464

Woolianna Tourist Park. The park offers another idyllic tropical spot by the river and another good base for experiencing the attractions of the region. Activites include guided barra fishing, scenic river trips, bush walking, wildlife spotting or simply relaxing using the swimming pool facility.
   Accomodation includes cottages and camping - powered sites $20 - x2; unpowered $18 x2. Meals can be provided. Facilities and services include hire boats, boat ramp, most boat needs, kiosk and mango products from the orchard. No pets are allowed, and it closes during the wet season. Credit cards accepted. Ph (08) 8978 2478

HOW TO GET THERE
Some sealed roads and good gravel surfaces allow conventional vehicle access during the dry season. The location of the main establishments in the district are generally well signposted.

SERVICES AND FACILITIES

Daly River has a hotel (Daly River Inn) which offers meals, accomodation including camping and a police station located at the river crossing. To the north of the crossing the Nauiya Nambiyu Community has a Catholic Church, small supermarket (open Monday - Friday 9am - 5pm; Saturday 9am-Noon; Sunday 5pm-6pm), Commonwealth Bank Agency (post office), Merrepen Arts Centre (Aboriginal arts and crafts), service station (ULP and diesel), camping gas and airstrip, council offices and health centre. The Merpeena Arts Festival is held in August and features work of the local Aboriginal artists. About 4 km north of the community along the Woolianna Road is the Eagle View general store.

DARWIN CITY

Population 73,000

LOCATION

Astride Beagle Gulf Peninsula, on Australia's northern coast, 1482km (918 miles) north of Alice Springs.

CHARACTERISTICS

Darwin is an attractive tropical city with a distinct cosmopolitan flavour. Forty seven or so nationalities reside here. The cultural mix, torrid climate, tropical coastline, experience of man-made and natural disasters, hard-drinking frontier-town reputation, proximity to Asia and great distance from anywhere in Australia, are the basic ingredients that give Darwin flair, colour, and an easy-going and harmonious life-style.

The dominant population centre in the Territory is also the capital city of an embryo state, and Australia's 'newest' city by virtue of an almost complete reconstruction after being flattened by *Cyclone Tracy* in 1974. The relaxed city enjoys one of the highest daily sunshine hours in Australia, even during the Wet season when some of the most beautiful cloudscapes, sunsets and lightning displays highlight the many sparkling white buildings and luxuriant vegetation.

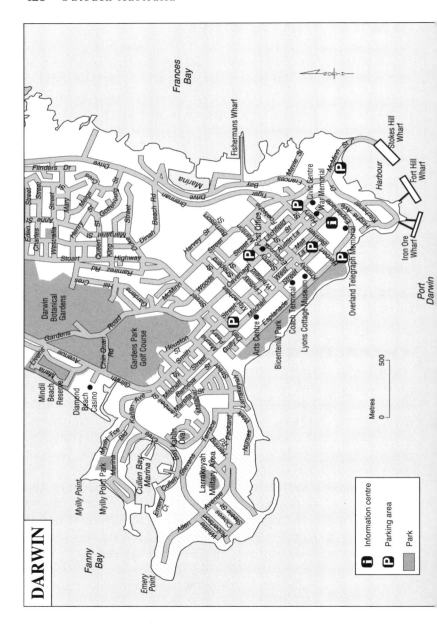

DARWIN

Frances
Bay

Fishermans Wharf

Stokes Hill
Wharf

Harbour

Fort Hill
Wharf

Iron Ore
Wharf

Port
Darwin

Overland Telegraph Memorial

War Memorial

Civic Centre

Post Office

Lyons Cottage Museum

Coabt Terminal

Bicentennial Park

Arts Centre

Esplanade

Darwin Botanical Gardens

Gardens Park Golf Course

Mindil Beach Reserve

Diamond Beach Casino

Cullen Bay Marina

Larrakeyah Military Area

Myilly Point Park

Myilly Point

Fanny Bay

Emery Point

Flinders Dr

Marina Drive

Brennan Drive

Beach Rd

Metres

0   500

ℹ Information centre

🅿 Parking area

Park

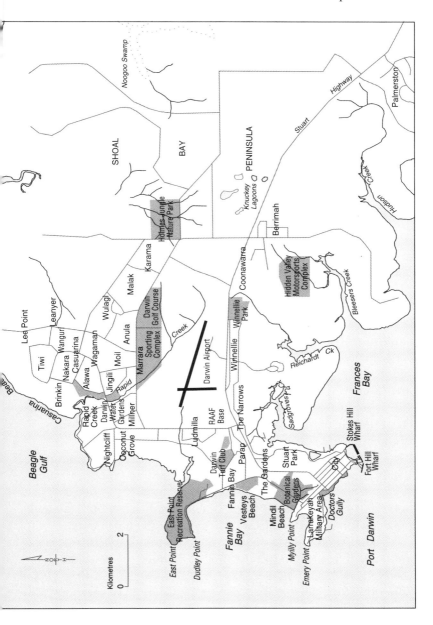

CITY CENTRE

A geographical paradox of the city centre site is that you have to drive south to enter it. It's a modern, but mellow centre with huge shady trees in the squares surrounding the hub of it all, *Smith Street Mall*. The variety of shops, plazas, cultural mix, lush-green palms and the bougainvillea-splashed 'Vic' walls, is a delight for first-time visitors. Early morning is an ideal visiting time; it's cooler, good for photography, and pleasant for walking. The Mall has plenty of atmosphere, and a favourite activity is people-watching from the outdoor table settings.

HISTORY

The present sites of Government House and Stokes Hill were the Aboriginal camping grounds of the first occupiers of the peninsula area, the Larrakeyah people. In 1839, Captain J.C. Wickham and John Lort Stokes of the HMS *Beagle* were the first authenticated European discoverers of Port Darwin, and Stokes named it after his friend, the famous naturalist Charles Darwin. No attempt at settlement was made until 1869, when the South Australian Government despatched Surveyor-General Goyder to map out a settlement. It was an instant settlement too - Goyder's party numbered 135! The street pattern was laid out; streets were named after surveyors in the group, and with remarkable foresight, the Esplanade was designated as a public reserve. The embryo town was officially named Palmerston, after the British Prime Minister of the time, but was popularly called Darwin.

The building of Government House in 1870, the completion of the Overland Telegraph Line in 1872, the first newspaper *Northern Territory Times* in 1873, and a town council in 1874, all reflected an optimistic outlook for the town, despite the harsh hinterland and previous ill-fated attempts at settlement on the north coast.

The population in 1874 of about 600 Europeans and 180 Chinese and Malays, rose rapidly at the time of the Pine Creek Goldrush of the 80s and 90s, to 4898 in 1891, but dropped to less than 1000 when the gold petered out. Pearling began in 1884, and the first motor car crossing from Adelaide to Darwin was in 1908 by Dutton and Aunger. In 1911, the name was officially changed to Darwin at which time the population was 944, and already the basis of its cosmopolitan character today was in evidence.

During World War II the port was an important naval base, and the Japanese bombing of Darwin on February 19, 1942, interestingly parallelled the attack on Pearl Harbour the year before. Non-essential civilians, women and children were evacuated from Darwin in 1941, but the suddenness and ferocity of the first attack curiously caught everyone by surprise. Recent evidence suggests that over 1000 people were killed rather than the 243 as officially stated. Altogether the city was bombed over 60 times in 1942, with massive structural damage resulting. Many of those killed are buried at Adelaide River.

The war highlighted Darwin's strategic position, and its defence role in the post-war years has been one of its major functions. Improved communications and facilities, important mineral discoveries (uranium at Rum Jungle in the 50s), increasing trade drawn from its huge pastoral hinterland sustain growth, while more recent mineral finds have been a further catalyst to expansion.

Cyclone Tracy struck on Christmas Day in 1974, wrought a level of destruction that saw few buildings left standing, and 66 people killed. Temporarily quelled by the magnitude of the disaster, the indomitable spirit of Territorians brought about a remarkably rapid return to normal functions. And some time later, a bright, vibrant, modern, tropical city emerged and added large scale tourism to its range of other functions.

INFORMATION

The telephone area code for Darwin is (08).

The Darwin Regional Tourism Association operate *The Tourist Information Centre* located at Beagle House, 38 Mitchell Street. Good up front advice is offered, all bookings undertaken and the centre has a wealth of literature about Darwin and outlying tourist regions. Parks and Wildlife Commission material is available and the centre has an information booth at the airport. Its open Monday - Friday 8.30 am - 6pm; Saturday 9am - 3pm; Sunday 10am - 3pm. Ph 8981 4300

The National Trust located in the Myilly Point Heritage Precinct at Burnett Place, functions from a pre-World War II house and apart from being the Trusts Headquaters, the centre offers excellent heritage information including historic walk maps and has a quality gift shop. It's open 10am - 3pm weekdays, admission is free, Ph 8981 2848.

The Northern Territory Government Bookshop in Smith Street is a useful source of more specialised information about the Territory. It's open weekdays.

Publications and Maps. APN Publications distribute a well - produced, handy sized booklet - *This Week in Darwin* - which comes out monthly and contains a range of useful information including a well designed map of Darwin (this colour map is also available free in A3 format).

The Regional Tourism Association also produce a useful introductory booklet covering Darwin City and outlying attractions. Both these regular publications are free.

ATTRACTIONS
Historic Buildings and Sites
In and around the City centre and Esplanade area are examples of Darwin's architectural heritage and historic sites, all within easy strolling reach from the city centre. Historic walks maps can be obtained from the National Trust or Tourist Information Centre.

In Smith Street Mall, *The Victorian Hotel*, affectionately known as the Vic, was built in 1890 and is one of Darwin's major survivors having withstood WWII bombing and Cyclone Tracy.

On the corner of the Mall and Bennett Street only the colonade from the original 1893 *Commercial Bank Building* was retained when it was rebuilt in 1981.

Continuing along Smith Street are the wall remains of the *Old Town Hall*, built during the 1880's and flattened by Cyclone Tracy.

Today the wall provides a dramatic backdrop for outdoor theatrical performances.

Browns Mart, on the corner of Smith and Harry Chan streets is a stone structure with a romantic past. Now a small, well patronised theatre, it was first intended as a mining exchange, later became a fruit and vegetable market and is supposed to have been first, a police station then a brothel.

Further along Harry Chan Street, in the Civic Centre Square is **The Tree of Knowledge**, an ancient banyam tree (Ficus virens), a species much revered by Buddists as the tree of knowledge. Its great spread and softening effect makes it a famous Darwin City landmark.

A little further to the north on the corner of Bennett and Woods Streets is a **Chinese Temple**. The first temple built on this site in 1887 was virtually destroyed by Cyclone Tracy. The new temple serves Darwin's Chinese Community and may be visited.

On the corner of Smith Street and the Esplanade is **Christ Church Cathedral**. The original church was built in 1902 and destroyed by Cyclone Tracy. The new, modern building, constructed in 1975, used parts of the ruins of the original.

Virtually opposite are **The Tunnels** - a network of WW II oil storage tanks. Tunnel no. 5 is open to the public and also houses some fascinating photographic displays of Darwin during the war years. And on the opposite corner to the Cathedral stands **The Old Courthouse and Police Station**. It was built in 1884 for the South Australian Government and its classic style reflects South Australian architectural influence. The courthouse joined the police station with a cell block at the back. The navy used the building from the WWII period until 1974 when it was damaged by the cyclone. It is now used as Government offices. Close by is a plaque noting the site of the original Telegraph Station.

Across the road from here is *The Survivors Lookout* - a covered interpretive display area which recaptures Darwin during the WW II period. The lookout, with views over the wharf precinct, has steps leading down to this area.

Further along the Esplanade is *Government House*, also known as The Residency and house of the seven gables. It was built in 1879 as a stone and timber replacement for the original timber building destroyed by the ravages of white ants. The gardens and gables give the residency a colonial appearance. It is closed to the public but you can get good views from the Esplanade.

The interesting, modern design of *N.T. Parliament House* can be seen tucked away in Parliament Square, between Smith Street and the Esplanade. Tours are available and often there are displays in the foyer area.

The Hotel Darwin occupies the site of Darwin's original hotel, *The Palmerston,* at its corner of Herbert Street and Esplanade location heading north west. The current, still functional pub, was built in the 1940's.

Continuing along the Esplanade to Knuckey Street are two old buildings, both located in Knuckey Street. *The Old Admiralty House* is a tropical - style structure, built in 1927 to house North Australia's naval commander. It survived Cyclone Tracy and now has a gallery / cafe function.

On the opposite corner is the porcellanite stone heritage structure of *BAT House* (Lyons Cottage), built in 1925 to house staff from the British and Australia Telegraph Company. After WW II it became the residence of Darwin's Mayor, John Lyons. It now functions as an historical museum under the management of Museums and Art Galleries N.T.

Nearby on the corner of Mitchell and Knuckey Streets is the **Old Wesleyan Church**. This prefabricated building was erected in 1889 and features a steel framed structure with cyclone-resistant corner ties. The original church building of 1887 was destroyed by a cyclone. It's the oldest church building in the Territory.

Myilly Point Precinct

At the Northern extremity of Smith Street, in Burnett Place, is a significant enclave of four heritage houses, designed by Government architect B.C.G. Burnett and built in 1938-39 for high ranking government officers. The houses were specially designed for tropical conditions and the leafy, Myilly Point location chosen, had fine views and caught tempering sea breezes. In particular, Audit House / Giese Residence is a fine example of tropical architecture. Burnett House functions as an art gallery and coffee garden while one of the residences houses the National Trust (see under *Information*). All four houses are now on the Register of the National Estate.

At the point itself is the relatively new **Cullen Bay Marina**, an upmarket residential area featuring modern apartments, restaurants and shops and marina.

Fannie Bay Gaol

Located along East Point Drive, it functioned as Darwin's main gaol until 1979. The oldest part of the complex was built in 1883, the infirmary was constructed in 1885, and the gallows, a replica of England's notorious Newgate Gallows, were established in 1952 for the Territory's last hanging. You can wander around the gaol and capture the oppressive atmosphere. It also features good displays covering Cyclone Tracy and transport history. It's *open daily 10am - 5pm and admission is free*, ph 8999 8290.

Museum and Art Gallery of the Northern Territory

This museum and art gallery has outstanding South-east Asian and Oceania anthropological galleries while in the natural history section you can see Sweetheart - a 5.1 metre stuffed crocodile which died after being captured for unsociable behaviour in the Finnis River, south of Darwin. One of the gallery's many highlights is the superb exhibition of Aboriginal Art, imaginatively displayed in spacious surrounds. It features works of artists from Arnhem Land and carvings and bark paintings from the Tiwi Islands. There's a very good section on Cyclone Tracy and other galleries house maritime displays, crafts, and modern art.

Facilities include an amphitheatre, museum shop, facilities for disabled visitors, education unit and an excellent cafe where you can eat outdoors overlooking extensive gardens, which are dotted with exhibits down to the waters of Fannie Bay. It's located in Conacher Street, Fannie Bay, *open weekdays, 9am - 5pm, weekends 10 am - 5pm, admission is free*, ph 8999 8201.

Australian Aviation Heritage Centre
Located on the Stuart Highway, 10kms from the city centre, the purpose built museum showcases the Territorys aviation history. Aircraft on display include a massive Boeing B52 Bomber, one of only two on display outside the U.S.A, a B25 Mitchell Bomber, Mirage and Sabre Jet fighters, a Mk VIII Spitfire replica and wreckage of a Japanese Zero fighter. There are many informative and eye catching displays and guided tours are conducted several times daily by staff. Facilities include a souvenir shop, refreshments and facilities for disabled visitors. Its *open daily 9am - 5pm, admission - $8 adults, $5 - pensioners and students, $4 children, $20 family*. Ph 8947 2145.

Wharf Precinct
An imaginative revitalisation scheme has turned the old Stokes Wharf area into an attractive precinct for visitors and locals. At the end of the wharf, an old warehouse has been transformed into a friendly arcade with shops and restaurants - great spots for outside waterfront eating.

The entrance to the precinct is the location of ***Indo Pacific Marine*** - a marine education and environment centre that has received many tourism awards for excellence in eco-tourism. It features a spectacular living marine environment with coral reef ecosystems successfully transplanted from the sea on display. There are over 30 marine displays including a variety of species and marine naturalists give informative talks about local marine life and complex ecosystems. They also conduct tours (see under *Tours*). Facilities include an educational centre, cafe and gift shop. Its *open daily 10am - 5pm, $12 adult, $4 children*. Ph 8981 1294.

Also housed in the same building is ***The Australian Pearling Exhibition*** which, by various displays, depicts the story of pearls and pearling in Northern Australia. It's *open daily 10am - 5pm, $6 adults, child $3, family $15*. Ph 8941 2177.

Aquascene

One of Darwin's most famous attractions features fish feeding at Doctors Gully, (access near corner Daly Street and Esplanade). Everyday at high tide, hundreds of fish from the sea congregate to be hand fed. Milkfish, catfish, mullet, bream, batfish and rock cod are some of the delightful free-loaders. Visitors can feed them bread (supplied) from a submerged ramp. *Open daily only at feeding times* which vary according to the tides. *Cost; adults $4.50, children $2.50*. Ph 8981 7837

Crocodylus Park

The park is a wildlife research and education centre which provides a fascinating insight into crocodile behaviour via live displays and a museum. You can watch these reptiles being fed and even hold a small one. The concept of the centre and approach by crocodile expert, Dr Grahame Webb and his staff, is unique in a facility which also features other Australian and exotic wildlife. It's *open daily 9am - 5pm, feeding and tour times 10am, 12noon, and 2pm generally, admission adults $15, pensioners $12, children $7.50*, located Mc Millans Road, Berrimah. Ph 8947 2510

Parks and Reserves

The *Charles Darwin National Park*, located 2kms from the city centre, protects coastal flats along with woodlands and waterways and relics of WW II, namely military storage facilities. It has picnic areas, lookout with great views across the harbour to the city and walking tracks. It was proclaimed in 1998.

The *Botanic Gardens* feature a wide variety of native and exotic trees, shrubs and flowering plants along many shady walking paths. Water fountains, plant evolutionary playground, lawns and BBQ facilities make it a popular strolling and picnicking spot. It's located just north of the city centre and is *open daily*.

East Point Reserve, located on East Point Road, is a 200 hectare park occupying much of a small promontory north of Fannie Bay. It protects craggy coastal cliffs, mangrove patches, and in it semi - natural woodland state, it is home to over 2000 wallabies, best seen early morning or evening when they come out to graze. The reserve also features man-made *Lake Alexander*, constructed to provide safe, salt water swimming and water-based activities.

At the northern end of the lake a boardwalk leads to mangroves. At the point are a number of WW II gun emplacements along with *The East Point Military Museum*, which houses war time memorabilia and has a number of old army vehicles. It's *open daily*. Facilities include a bicycle / walking path, lookouts with stunning views, picnic areas and BBQs and toilets.

The Casuarina Coastal Reserve is a semi-natural area of coastline, notable for pockets of rainforest, WW II gun emplacements, picnic area and an area set aside for nude bathing. Access is via Trower Road and Lee Point Road, Casuarina.

Holmes Jungle Nature Park protects a 250 hectare area of mainly wet monsoon rainforest to the northeast of the city. Some elevated walkways give access to the jungle environment - a representative remnant patch - typical of vegetation which once dominated much of the Darwin region. There are picnic facilities and access is via Vanderlin Drive, Karama.

 For outlying Darwin attractions refer to *Outer Darwin Region* listing.

TOURS

There's a huge variety offered, with a focus on the Kakadu region for extended tours. All activities including safari hunting, Aboriginal culture tours, sailing, cruising, fishing and diving are catered for. Good advice is given by the *Tourist Information Centre* and they undertake bookings. A good consultant is **Northern Gateway**, ph 1800 813 288.

Some sample tours and costs are:

City sights tours are offered by **Darwin Day Tours**. It includes history and main attractions (museums, Fannie Bay Gaol, East Point, fish feeding, gardens and historic buildings) and costs $29 adults, $17 child for the 5 hour tour, ph 8981 8696.

The Tour Tub offers a similar style of tour for $16 adult, $8 child, ph 8981 5233.

A Coral Reef by night tour by **Indo Pacific Marine** is an unusual but fascinating nocturnal experience which also includes a seafood dinner. It costs $45 adult, $25 child, ph 8981 1294. Indo Pacific also offer a Coral Coasts and Caves Tour, 4.5 hours, costs $75 adult, $35 child.

Darwin Pearl Lugger Cruises offer informative and nostalgic harbour cruises aboard Australia's last working pearl lugger. It costs $35 adult, $15 child for a two hour cruise, ph 8983 2892.

Extended Tours included **Arnhem Airs Mailplane** flight to remote Arnhem Land spots where you can meet the locals. It costs $250 p.p for the 4 hour scenic flight, ph 1800 089 113.

AAT Kings, Kakadu in a Day costs $129 adult, $65 child, ph 1800 334 009.

Coo-ee Tours offer Litchfield National Park day tour costs; $89 adult, $70 child, ph 1800 670 007.
Billy Can Tours offer 2 day Kakadu trips from $260 adult $225 child, ph 1800 813 484.

Aboriginal cultural tours are offered by *Davidsons Arnhem Land Safaris*, costs $750 p.p with air component for the day tour, ph 8927 5240.
Peppi Tours offer a 10 hour tour to the Peppimenarti Community at the Daly River. It includes an air flight and costs $314 p.p., ph 8981 1633.
Tiwi Tours Bathurst Island one day tour costs $240 adult, $190 child, ph 8981 5115.

EVENTS

In keeping with its laid-back tropical image, Darwin hosts a few zany events.

June

The *Top End Campdraft and Rodeo* is a 3 day event offering Australia's richest campdraft prize, an expo of bush skills and loads of country music. It's held in early June at Robbie Robbins Reserve.

July

Top End Country Music Festival in early July at Robbie Robbins Reserve.
The *Salt Water Peoples Festival* is a fun-filled cultural event held at East Point to Cullen Bay in mid July.
The *Royal Darwin Show* is held in late July.

August

The *Darwin Cup Carnival*, July / August is the high point of the Territory's racing calendar with the cup run in early August.

The *Darwin Fringe Festival* showcases the best local performing and visual arts in a spectacular program of theatre, dance, poetry and music. It's held in early August.

The *Darwin Beer Can Regatta* is Darwin's answer to Alice Springs Henley on Todd. The boats constructed from beer cans have to be seen to be believed in this charity race held at Mindil Beach in early August.

The *Darwin Rodeo and Country Music Show* is held in mid August.

September
The *Darwin Festival* celebrates the multicultural makeup of Darwin in this event which features a grand parade.

October
The *Wharf Precinct Food and Wine Festival* is held in October.

HOW TO GET THERE

By air: Ansett Australia and Qantas operate a number of daily services to Darwin from other Australian cities.

By coach: Greyhound Pioneer and McCaffertys operate daily interstate services.

LOCAL TRANSPORT

Buses: There's an excellent public transport system serving the city area, and connecting with suburbs including Palmerston, ph 8924 7666 for information. The privately run *Tour Tub Bus Company* offers a convenient, jump-on-jump-off service around the city area. For details of its routes, ph 8981 5233

Taxis: Theres a good taxi service - main city taxi ranks are at the end of Smith Street Mall; in front of Woolworths in Knuckey St and at the top end of Smith Street Mall by Bennett street. Phone numbers are: 131 008; 8932 5577; 8947 3000; 8981 2222; 8981 8777.

Hire Vehicles: Territory Rent-a-Car, ph 8924 0000 offer good value service. Others are Delta ph 131 390; Nifty ph 8981 2999; Avis ph 8981 9922; Hertz ph 1800 891 112; Thrifty ph 8924 0000; Cheapa ph 8981 8400; Budget ph 1800 805 627 and Brits ph 1800 331 454. Hire bicycles are often available from backpacker accomodation places.

SHOPPING

Darwin offers an exciting range of things to take home, partly due to its tropical and multicultural influences in the variety of clothing and artifacts available, as well as different artistic forms of expression by local Aboriginal Artists.

Good outlets for Aboriginal Art include *The Raintree Fine Art Gallery* which has a good selection of Tiwi totems, Arnhem Land paintings, carvings, pottery, fine arts including screen prints from the Tiwi Islands, didjeridoos as well as works from Central Desert artists. It is Aboriginal owned and operated and located at 20 Knuckey Street.

Framed - The Darwin Gallery, located at 55 Stuart Highway, Stuart Park, is another quality gallery for Aboriginal Art. Both galleries *open daily*. **Indigenous Creations**, located in Smith Street Mall, is also worth visiting.

Darwin's markets, in particular *Mindil Beach*, *Parap* and *Night* markets are good places for Asian style clothing, scarfs and t-shirts. For traditional Aussie outback clothing, the **N.T General Store** is worth visiting at its 42 Cavenagh St location. The **Wharf Precinct** offers further interesting shopping and pearls. And for another interesting reminder of Darwin, you can take home the world's largest bottle of beer, *The Darwin Stubby*.

MARKETS

The Darwin market scene is vibrant with none more popular than *Mindil Beach Sunset Market*. It has become a Darwin institution and features over 200 arts and crafts stalls, wonderful foods, particularly Asian styles at over 50 food stalls, plenty of entertainment including the natural wonders of sunset over Fannie Bay. It is held Thursday evenings 5pm - 10pm, May to October, and Sunday nights 4pm - 9pm, June to September.

The Nightcliff Market is held every Sunday, 8am - 2pm and is a mix of food, crafts and recycled goods at its Nightcliff Shopping Centre venue.

The *Parap Market* is held every Saturday from 8am - 2pm and features a great variety of stalls. Its located at the Parap Shopping centre.

Other markets are held at *Rapid Creek* each Sunday; *Palmerston* each Friday, 5.30pm - 9.30pm and the *Night Markets* in the Mitchell Street precinct has assumed a character of its own. It operates every night 5pm - 11pm.

ACCOMMODATION

Darwin offers accommodation styles to suit all tastes and budgets from international class hotels and resorts to budget motels and hostels. For campers, the only disappointing feature is the distance of good parks from the city centre. Because of the large number of accommodation places only a representative sample is included. Many have swimming pools and restaurants, particularly the more expensive establishments. Rates are quoted for peak season; rates are generally lower November - March.

Premier Class:
The MGM Grand Darwin, rooms for $210 - $840. Ph 8943 8888.
The Beaufort, rooms from $305 - $441. Ph 8980 0800.
Holiday Inn Park offers suites from $195 - $370. Ph 8943 4333.
The All Seasons Premier Central Hotel has rates from $226 - $251. Ph 8944 9000.
Marrakai Apartments from $242. Ph 8982 3711.
Rydges Plaza $165 - $205. Ph 8982 0000.
Cullen Bay Apartments, rates from $200 - $231. Ph 8981 7999.
The Novotel Atrium has rates from $190 - $260. Ph 8941 0755.

Most have facilities for disabled guests and prime waterfront locations.

Medium Range:
Coconut Grove Holiday Apartments, rates from $59 - $128.
Ph 8985 0500.
Darwin Travel Lodge, rooms from $142. Ph 8981 5388.
Mirambeena Tourist Resort, rooms from $120 - $207. Ph 8946 0111.
Primavera Hotel, apartments from $137. Ph 8981 7771.
Top End Hotel, rates from $110 - $136. Ph 8981 6511.
Casablanca Motel, rooms from $90. Ph 8981 2163.
Palms Motel, rates from $75 - $100. Ph 8981 4188.

Budget:
Park Lodge, $45 - $52. Ph 8981 5692.
Ross Smith Guest House, rooms $30 - $35. Ph 8981 8457.
Parkview Homestay, $75. Ph 8927 0606.
Value Inn, $67. Ph 8981 4733.
Robyns Nest, $75. Ph 8927 7400.
Phoenix Motel $85. Ph 8985 4144.
Banyam View Lodge (Y.W.C.A) from $30 - $50. Ph 8981 8644.
Capricornia Hotel, $75 - $100. Ph 8981 4055.
Hotel Darwin, $75 - $95. Ph 8981 9211.
Asti Motel, $90 - $105. Ph 8981 8200.
The Highway Motel (YMCA offers good accomodation).
Ph 8947 0979

Hostels:
Darwin City Y.H.A, dormitory beds, $18. Ph 8981 3995.
Melaleuca Lodge $15 - $17. Ph 8941 3395.
Frogshollow Backpackers, has dormitory beds $16; double rooms
$35 - $44 with breakfast included. Ph 8941 2600.
Globetrotters Hostel, has dormitory beds $16; double rooms $44
(breakfast and evening meals are included). Ph 1800 800 798.
Fawlty Towers, dormitory beds, $16, double room $40 (breakfast
included). Ph 1800 068 886.
   Most hostels are centrally located and facilities are generally
good.

Camping:
See also *Camping* in Outer Darwin Region listing.
  Costs listed are for two persons.
Shady Glen Caravan Park, is the closest to the city at Winnellie;
powered sites $19, tent site $8 p.p, on site vans $46. Sites shaded,
swimming pool, shop, pets allowed. Ph 8984 3330.
The Overlander Caravan Park, at Berrimah has on site vans and
caravan and tent sites. Ph 8984 3025.
Malak Caravan Park and ***KOA Caravan Park*** are located near the
airport and provide for caravans only. Ph 8927 3500 and 8927 2651
respectively.
Lee Point Resort, 15 kms north of the city, has powered sites $18,
unpowered $15 and cabins $60. No pets allowed, swimming pool
and shop. Ph 8945 0535.

EATING OUT

Darwin is the Gourmet Capital of Northern Australia. One of
Darwin's most understated attributes is the quality and diversity of
its numerous cafes, and restaurants and the lush, tropical surrounds
of al fresco dining styles at a number of establishments. Competition
is fierce and accordingly, most establishments offer good value.
  Cheapest eating out is at the markets (Mindil beach market is
famous for its Asian food) and at eateries in the Mitchell Street
precinct. ***The RAOB Club***, Stuart Park, offers good meals for under
$10. ***Sizzlers*** in Mitchell Street, with all you can eat options, is also
popular. There are numerous small cafes in and around Smith
Street Mall offering breakfast and lunch, and a number of take
away places. Plaza's off the Mall often reveal gourmet delights,
and reflect, as elsewhere in Darwin, the cosmopolitan character of
the city's population.

Restaurants:
Lindsay Street Cafe has an enviable reputation and a varied
contempory Australian menu edge. It has a tropical garden setting.
Ph 8981 8631.

Christos in the Wharf precinct, is a good *seafood* restaurant and has a Mediterranean menu influence. It's medium priced. Ph 8981 8658.

The Brasserie at the Beaufort offers superb dining and a varied menu including *Territorian meats*. Ph 8980 0880.

Tree Tops at the Mirambeena Resort has superb blends of *Asian and European influences* in its dishes. Ph 8946 0213.

The Swiss Restaurant has a traditional *Swiss cuisine*, Ph 8981 5079.

Good *Asian restaurants* include:

The Thai Garden, Ph 8981 8168;

Darwin Thai Cafe in Mitchell Street, Ph 8981 1989.

The Hanuman Thai Restaurant, 28 Mitchell Street is an excellent establishment. Ph 8941 3500.

At Casuarina, *Ming Court* offers you all you can eat seafood and Chinese Buffet, Ph 8927 6600.

Aya Teppanyaki Reef and Beef Restaurant at the Phoenix Motel, Nightcliff is a good Japanese restaurant. Ph 8985 4144.

The Waterhole Restaurant at the Darwin Central Hotel features South east Asian dishes and bistro style grills. Ph 8944 9000.

For *Italian fare* *Cafe Bella* is a popular place. Ph 8948 2773.

The Bay Seafood Cafe at Cullen Bay Marina Precinct boasts the best *fish and chips* in town. Ph 8981 8789.

Shennanigans Irish Pub in Mitchell Street serves *traditional Irish foods*. Ph 89812100.

The Hogs Breath Cafe in Smith Street Mall, serves a mix of *American and Australian grills*. Ph 8941 3333.

NIGHT LIFE

Darwin is just as lively at night. There are many pubs, clubs and theme bars and discos which offer a variety of live entertainment. One of Darwin's more unusual pastimes is Crab Racing at the Jabiru Bar, Novotel Atrium, every Friday at 6.30pm. The casino is a one stop night entertainment venue, and Darwin offers much for more sophisticated tastes in areas of theatre, film and concert performances. The Mindil Beach and Nite Markets in Mitchell Street add further variety to night time activity. For details of most up to date night life and entertainment in pubs and clubs, consult the liftout section of Friday's edition of the Northern Territory News.

Theatre

The Darwin Theatre Company offers a variety of performances. Ph 8981 8424.

The Darwin Entertainment Centre at 93 Mitchell Street has 2 theatres (a large playhouse and studio theatre) and hosts performances ranging from plays, rock operas to classical concerts. Ph 8981 1222.

The Old Browns Mart is another Venue for theatre performances.

Cinema

There are a few cinema complexes in and around the city. The local film society run rather unusual *Deckchair Cinema*, an alternative film experience under the stars. It has *outdoor screeenings Wednesday - Sunday nights (April - October)* at its near Wharf precinct location (behind Stokes Hill Power Station). Ph 8981 0700.

SERVICES AND FACILITIES

As one would expect, there's a full range of services offered from the City Centre and the huge air-conditioned suburban Casuarina Shopping Square and other shopping complexes at Palmerston, Karama, Fannie Bay, Nightcliff, Parap and Rapid Creek. Many shops open 7 days. Most church denominations are represented - St Mary Star of the Sea, 90 Smith St, Catholic, Anglican, Apostolic, Greek Orthodox, Baptist, Uniting, Salvation Army.

RECREATIONAL ACTIVITIES

Cycling

A very good system of coastal cycle tracks and easy terrain around the city area make cycling a popular activity. Bicycles may be hired from the Youth Hostel Association. Ph 8981 6344.

Golf

The Darwin Golf Club welcomes visitors on its 18 hole course at Marrara, Ph 8927 1322. The Palmerston Golf and Country Club has a good course. Ph 8932 1324. The Gardens Park Golf Links (near the Botanic Gardens) is a 9 hole public course. Ph 8981 6365.

Rock Climbing

At *Doctors Gully*, the *Rock Climbing Gymnasium* offers indoor and outdoor climbing in and around an old World War II oil storage chamber. *Costs; $14 with all gear supplied*, instruction given, *open Monday - Friday 3.30pm - 9.30pm, weekends 10am - 9.30pm*. Ph 8941 0747.

Other activities and facilities include public swimming pools and aquatic centres, tennis and squash courts, diving and fishing, bowls, ten pin bowling, horse racing, a speedway and a number of sporting clubs.

OUTER DARWIN REGION

Population aproximately 29,000

Within easy reach of Darwin city, the outer Darwin region harbours many surprises in its incident-filled landscape. It features a variety of worthwhile attractions including nature parks, scattered historic settlements, places to stay and a proliferation of small holdings growing a range of exotic fruits and plants from bananas and mangoes to orchids. Despite the horticultural diversity, much of the land remains in its tropical state, home to a great variety of wildlife.

PALMERSTON

Located 20 kms (12 miles) south-east of Darwin city, Palmerston is a new town, gazetted in 1980, and designed to become a self-sufficient city despite its closeness to Darwin. The establishment of extensive retail and office space in the centre will eventually be capable of providing 9000 jobs, thus ensuring its independence. It is one of the few examples in Australia of a new town developed

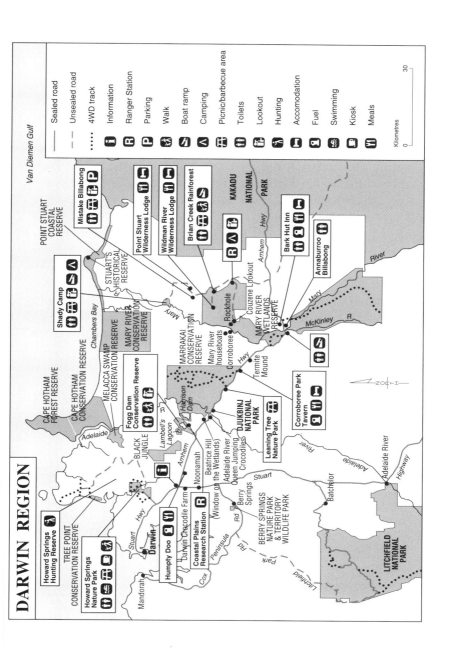

DARWIN REGION

Van Diemen Gulf

on a virgin site, a factor which has allowed planners to apply contemporary town planning ideas without any existing constraints.

The most noticeable **feature** is the road layout pattern for the suburbs; roads are curved to avoid the traffic intersection problems common with traditional grid patterns. Each of the suburbs so far developed (12 are planned) has a primary school that is also a neighbourhood community centre, while high schools double as district community centres. Residents have access to the facilities out of school hours, thus fostering stronger ties. Dominating the town centre is the 35m (115 ft) high water tower that is cyclone-proof, and has a capacity of 3000 tonnes, while the huge dishes of the Earth Satellite Tracking Station provide an interesting backdrop.

The town was named after Henry Temple, the third Viscount Palmerston (1784-1865) and British Prime Minister, after whom the original settlement at Darwin was also named. It's well worth visiting for its novel approaches to urban development, and for its shopping and recreational facilities.

Palmerston has a wide range of **services and facilities**, including good restaurants. *The Palms Caravan Park* is located 3kms from the town centre on the Stuart Highway. It's the only **accommodation** in Palmerston and has cabins from $68; on-site vans from $38; powered sites $18x2, unpowered $16x2. Facilities include shop, swimming pools, grassed sites, shaded, dogs allowed, credit cards accepted, EFTPOS facility, ph (08) 8932 2891.

HOWARD SPRINGS

Its located 34km (21 miles) south of Darwin, on and around the Stuart Highway in a scattered settlement pattern. The *Howard Springs Nature Park* is its prime feature of interest. Also, there's the Territory's only *Hunting Reserve* (water birds) nearby, and a road from Howard Springs leads to the remote *Gunn Point* fishing spot on the coast.

A number of caravan/camping parks make it a useful base for Darwin and environs exploration. All major services, including a tavern, are conveniently located here. Howard Springs takes its name from the river which honours the work of Frederick Howard, a naval officer who spent much time in the late 1860s mapping the north coast.

The Howard Springs Nature Park offers the closest and most attractive public fresh water swimming pool to Darwin. With its beautiful, clear, spring-fed waters surrounded by monsoon rainforest, it's a very popular spot - even more so when the box jellyfish prohibit beach swimming around Darwin during the Wet Season.

In the waters, numbers of barramundi and longtom may be seen, while the backdrop of rainforest species of red ash, white cedar and camphorwood, among others, host a large variety of birds. In fact, 125 species of birds and over 50 reptile types have been recorded here. Other wildlife include agile wallabies, flying foxes, and the occasional echidna and bandicoot. A walking track through the forest helps identify flora, and you can walk to the source of the waters.

The area now used for swimming was originally established as a water supply, partly to service Vestey's meatworks. During World War II, the weir was built to boost the capacity, and at this time it became a popular recreation area with its huge shady trees, landscaped lawns, facilities, and all year round swimming.

Facilities include picnic, wood barbecues, toilets, kiosk and ranger office. It is a day-use park, open 8am-8pm. Pets are not allowed.

The Howard Springs Hunting Reserve is located next to the Nature Park, and this area of floodplain and swamp near the Howard River mouth is the Territory's first duck and goose hunting reserve. A permit is required, and hunters need to check the declared season dates (enquire at Police Station or Parks and Wildlife Commission about permits, regulations, and season). Cleaning areas are provided, and shooters should be aware that this area is the home of the salt-water crocodile. Access off the Gunn Point Road is suitable for conventional vehicles during the hunting season.

Gunn Point is an isolated fishing, boating, camping and beachcombing spot on the coast located approximately 55km (34 miles) north of Howard Springs. Fishing is the major interest for most, while some visitors are content with beachcombing for shells. There's a boat launching ramp, but watch out for crocodiles, and because of the great variation in tides, it's advisable to have a tide table. Access is along the mainly formed, gravel, Gunn Point Road.

Howard Springs has a good range of **services and facilities** including a good hotel. **Accommodation** includes *Darwin Boomerang Motel and Caravan Park* with rooms from $60-85 and campsites. It's located on Virginia Road, ph (08) 8983 1202; *La Escondida Homestead* offers excellent B&B style, rooms from $100-$150, ph (08) 8988 1598; *Howards Springs Caravan Park* has on-site vans from $30-$60 and camping sites, ph (08) 8983 1169.

NOONAMAH

A further 44km (27 miles) south of Darwin on the Stuart Highway is the small settlement of Noonamah, consisting of a hotel and store/service station.

The township's origins were during World War II when the RAAF built a series of fighter airstrips serviced by army field depots here. The cluster arrangement of airstrips, supply depot, road and railway at this point was an ideal target for the Japanese, and it was attacked by a squadron of heavy bombers during WWII. The airstrips remain in remarkably good condition today, situated parallel to the highway.

The main **attraction** is the *Darwin Crocodile Farm*, located 5km (3 miles) north of Noonamah. The farm is Australia's first and largest. On display is a large selection of salt and freshwater crocs; a good opportunity to see them from a close, safe range. This is home for about 15,000 crocodiles which are commercially 'harvested' for their meat and skins - so it's primarily a business operation which tourists can visit. Staff give fascinating guided tours, and a visit is a very good way to learn something about these creatures before going to areas inhabited by crocodiles - for children it's one way to instil respect!

Facilities include picnic area and children's play area, kiosk, toilets. *Open daily 10am-4pm, costs $9.50 adult, $5 child*, feeding times 2pm, ph (08) 8988 1450.

ACACIA STORE AND MANTON DAM

Approximately 20 kms (12 miles) south of Noonamah on the Stuart Highway is Acacia Store (supermarket, all fuels) and caravan park. Ph (08) 8988 1055. The scenic *Manton Dam* is located approximately 7 kms (4 miles) south of *Acacia Store*. It is a popular recreational spot (picnicking, swimming, fishing and watersports) particularly during the wet season. The dam was constructed in 1940 to augment water supply to Darwin. Facilities include boat ramp, picnic area, wood BBQ and toilets.

BERRY SPRINGS DISTRICT

The district boasts a number of attractions in its location to the west of the Stuart Highway on the Cox Peninsula Road turnoff just south of Noonamah.

Territory Wildlife Park. It features a fascinating and, in many ways, unique open-range wildlife park that has on show bird, marsupial and reptile species representative of both arid and tropical zones. The Park has walkways through aviaries, a nocturnal house, an aquarium that allows underwater viewing of fish and other aquatic life via an acrylic tunnel underneath, while a special window allows a close-up view of a salt-water crocodile in its enclosure.

There are three ways to get around the exhibits, which all branch off the Park's 4km ring road. You can either walk, catch the shuttle train, or do a little of both.

A family favourite is the Kangaroos and Friends exhibit, which is all about close encounters, and provides opportunities for visitors to talk to keepers and have their questions answered. People can now mingle with free roaming Agile Wallabies, Antilopine

Wallaroos, Red Kangaroos and Emus. They can also watch stately Kori Bustards, and discover for themselves if the spikes of the Echidna are as lethal as they look.

Facilities include kiosk, displays and picnic areas. Entry fees are $12 adult, $6 child, family $30 with concessions for groups and pensioners. It's *open daily (Christmas excepted) 8.30am - 4pm*, ph (08) 8988 7200.

Berry Springs Nature Park. It features a delightful series of spring-fed pools surrounded by tall paperbarks, pandanus and carpentaria palms. A waterfall of warm thermal water, safe swimming, and plenty of birdlife (rainbow lorikeet, red-winged parrot, blue-faced honeyeater, blue-winged kookaburra are a few) add to the area's charm as a picnic spot for the family.

Facilities include picnic, wood barbecues, toilets, and walking tracks. A visitor centre has interesting displays explaining the area's history and ecology. It is a *day-use park only, open 8am - 6.30pm* and pets are not allowed.

Blackmore River Conservation Reserve. Also known as *Tumbling Waters*, the 547ha (1351 acres) reserve encompasses a 15km (9 miles) section of the river, and protects riverine and estuarine mangrove ecosystems. When gazetted in 1984, it became the first area to offer any protection to the mangrove communities of the Darwin Harbour and its tributaries. The presence of salt-water crocodiles prevents swimming. The low level crossing called 'Tumbling Waters' is the local name for the reserve area.

There are no facilities at the reserve. Picnicking and fishing are the main activities, and camping is popular. It's located approximately 10km (6 miles) south-east of Berry Springs.

Southport. The ruins of Southport lie a few kilometres to the north of Tumbling Waters.

Southport was one of four towns optimistically laid out by Surveyor-General Goyder in 1869, as part of an overall plan by the

South Australian Government to colonise its newly acquired north coast. It was hoped that townships, if laid out, would encourage settlers, thus providing a basis for the region's mineral and agricultural development. The South Australian Government had high hopes of good economic returns, and Goyder had not forgotten Fred Litchfield's find of a little gold in the Finniss River in 1865. In the 1880s, Southport was used to service railway construction crews. It was a sizeable shanty town, established during the gold rush days of the 1870s (small local finds but mainly a stopover and supply port for those heading to the Pine Creek diggings). At one time it had four pubs and 10 stores. Southport was soon abandoned when the railway bypassed it, leaving Goyder's second town merely marked 'ruins' on the map today.

Darwin River Dam. Located 17km (10 miles) south of Berry Springs, the dam's 260,000 million litre capacity augments Darwin's water supply. Picnic area with toilets and a lookout are facilities provided.

Two other worthwhile attractions in the area are *The Majestic Orchid Farm* and *Southport Exotic Fruit Farm*. The Orchid Farm is Australia's largest cut orchid flower producer and the property offers tours, cut flowers and trail rides. At the entrance to the farm is a separate commercial establishment - the licensed Litchfield Tavern which also has good food at its restaurant. Next door is the Trading Post and Service Station. Also in the vicinity is an arena where rodeos are held once a month. For details about the orchid farm, ph (08) 8988 6008. The Southport Fruit Farm runs tours and offers an amazing range of tropical fruits grown on the property. It's located just off the old Bynoe Road, south of Berry Springs, (08) 89 88 6248. The orchid farm is located on the Darwin River Dam Road.

Accommodation in the district is offered by *The Lakes Resort and Caravan Park*, located in Doris Road (just off the Cox Peninsula Road, 9kms (6 miles) from the Stuart Highway. It has ensuite cabins - deluxe $75 twinshare; standard $60 twinshare; powered sites $18x2, unpowered $15x2.

The park is built around two lakes - one natural and one man-made, and these provide for a range of water-based activities (water and jet skiing, canoeing and paddle boats). There's a waterslide and plunge pool, shop, restaurant and electric BBQs. All sites grassed, shaded, dogs allowed (must be leashed) and this one-stop holiday destination *opens all year*, ph (08) 8988 6277.

MANDORAH

Mandorah is a popular beach and fishing spot located on the north-east point of Cox Peninsula, 8 kms (5 miles) across the water from Darwin city. It features stretches of lonely sandy beaches, good fishing and good spots for bush beach camping. Crocodiles make swimming risky. Rock fishing for salmon and barramundi; bottom fish include bream, snapper, flathead and parrot fish to name some. Many fish from the jetty. The beaches are ideal for walking and you may spot some curiously-coiled shellfish - these are fossilised ammanoids, millions of years old. Of landscape interest, if you drive via the Cox Peninsula Road, are the distinctive magnetic anthills, so named because of their north-south orientation.

Services and facilities include a hotel, restaurant, supermarket / general store and service station (all fuels). Theres a jetty, boat ramp and airfield.

Accomodation is only provided by the *Mandorah Beach Hotel*, rooms $65, camping $5 per site, $5 extra for power. The hotel has a swimming pool, BBQ, sells fishing requirements and offers all meals. Ph (08) 8978 5044.

You can get there by the *Mandorah Jet Shuttle* boat which costs $15 return and departs from the *Cullen Bay Marina*, Darwin. Ph (08) 8981 7600 for times. By road, its 110 kilometres (68 miles) from Darwin via Berry Springs and Cox Peninsula Road. The road is now fully sealed to Mandorah.

DOUGLAS DALY REGION

The Region, located approximately 30kms (19 miles) south of Hayes Creek, includes Douglas Hot Springs (Tjuwaliyn) and Butterfly Gorge Nature Parks, Oolloo Crossing and two privately owned establishments - Douglas Daly Park and Lukies Farm. The focus is on some beautiful scenery and natural features including wildlife along glorious stretches of the Douglas and Daly Rivers. The route to these highly recommended attractions constitutes a most rewarding diversion off the Stuart Highway.

FEATURES

Fenton Airstrip. The WWII airstrip which is still operational at times has relics of the war period including the remains of a crashed aircraft. Interpretive signage enhance insights into WWII history in the locality. It's located just before the turnoff to Douglas Hot Springs.

Douglas Hot Springs Nature Park. Situated on the Douglas River, the park features thermal pools which create an oasis effect in the surrounding dry woodlands. The waters attract a variety of wildlife such as Northern Quolls, Northern Bandicoots and Antilopine Wallaroos and Agile Wallabies. Birdlife is as colourful as it is prolific.

The main activities are walking, swimming and camping. Before entering the thermal pools, check the temperature. Do not bathe in the hot springs themselves as the water temperatures can exceed 60 degrees C. Swimming is best in the cooler pools some 200 metres upstream and downstream from the hot springs.

Facilities include a large camping area with pit toilets, BBQs, picnic table and water. A camping fee of $1 p.p. or $3 family, should be deposited into the honesty box. Access is suitable for all vehicles on a formed gravel road from the turnoff to the springs.

Butteryfly Gorge National Park. A rough corrugated, 17km (10 miles) track leads from the Springs to Butterfly Gorge. The access road is 4WD only. The park features towering, sheer rock faces of a gorge edged by dense forest thickets and rocky spinifex country. There are also a series of large deep rock pools and some small waterfalls. A swim across the main pool and through the narrows of the gorge gives access to the upper pool. With a little climbing and swimming, a most beautiful gorge is revealed. For the energetic, climbing the rock faces exposes further idyllic landscapes. The park takes its name from the large numbers of common crow butterflies which find a haven in the cool gorge. A comfortable 10 minutes walk from the carpark leads to the gorge. There are no facilities and camping is not permitted.

Douglas Daly Park. The privately owned tourist enterprise, located a few kilometres south of the turnoff to the nature parks, offers a tranquil bush retreat and features which include natural thermal pools and cascades, good swimming and fishing. As in the whole region, the natural beauty is accentuated by the variety of wildlife.

The park has accommodation - basic air-conditioned rooms from $20 p.p and camping $5 p.p. for powered or unpowered secluded sites. No pets are allowed.

There's a swimming pool, restaurant (all meals and takeaways; main course around $12, steaks and seafood with a buffalo roast on Sunday), bar, wood BBQs, general store and fuel (LP, ULP, diesel, camping gas). It's open daily, credit cards accepted, EFTPOS facility, ph (08) 8978 2479.

Lukies Farm. Also run by the proprietors of Douglas Daly Park, nearby Lukies Farm provides bush camping on the Daly - an ideal spot for those who wish to find space and peace. There are good spots for fishing (Barramundi and Black Bream) and fishing requirements can be obtained from the General Store at Douglas Daly Park.

Oolloo Crossing. South from Douglas Daly Park, a gravel road (suitable with care for conventional vehicles), is a pleasant scenic drive to the crossing.

HOW TO GET THERE

The easiest route is via the all sealed road to Douglas Daly Park, turnoff approximately 6kms (4 miles) north of Hayes Creek, from where its about 40kms (18 miles) to Douglas Daly Park. From Adelaide River, the Old Stuart Highway scenic route to the region is a contrast to the Stuart Highway.

Access is restricted at times during the Wet Season to some attractions in the Douglas Daly region. Butterfly Gorge closes during this time, but the Douglas Daly Park is open all year.

Visitors should be wary of swimming in the Daly River in particular, because of the possible presence of estuarine crocodiles. Pets are not permitted in the nature parks.

EMERALD SPRINGS

Population 8

LOCATION

On the Stuart Highway, 22km (13 miles) north of Pine Creek, and 198km (122 miles) south of Darwin.

CHARACTERISTICS

An old roadhouse, pub and motel are set amongst tropical vegetation and bougainvillea. This is a comfortable stop along 'The Track'. The Springs, after which it was partly named, have dried up. Fossickers still occasionally probe nearby localities in the hope of finding precious minerals which gave the settlement its first name. Gold is the main objective of rock hounds today. The proprietors of the roadhouse will tell you where the fossicking areas are, and how to get to Douglas Hot Springs.

The original roadhouse structure, an old tin shed built in the 1930s, still stands, and the current building was constructed after

World War II. Mining activities in the area, including Pine Creek, during the 1930s and increased traffic along 'The Track', provide enough custom to warrant a roadhouse.

ACCOMMODATION

Motel - demountable units (shared facilities) - single $18, double $35; self-contained units - $65.

Camping/caravans - powered sites $8, unpowered $5; tent sites $4.

SERVICES AND FACILITIES

The roadhouse has a bar with homestyle meals from $8 (excellent steak sandwiches), take-away food, shop, ice, souvenirs, picnic/BBQ area, and showers for travellers. Fuel - LP, diesel, ULP, autogas, oil and camping gas. Credit cards accepted and EFTPOS facility, open daily, ph (08) 8978 2320.

GROVE HILL

Population 12

LOCATION

On the old North-South Road (former Stuart Hwy) approximately 20kms (12 miles) north-east of Hayes Creek.

CHARACTERISTICS

Grove Hill features the *Grove Hill Heritage Hotel* which exudes all the character of a past age. The museum houses much memorabilia giving an insight into the locality's mining, railway and World War II history. It is on the National Register of Significant heritage buildings, the hotel was established in 1934 during a mining boom at a time when the main Darwin Road ran past its doors. It was built out of recycled materials from the mines and railway by the Lucy family. The fact that the original structure is little changed from the time it was built, adds to its intrinsic charm.

The hotel is complemented by the fascinating character of proprietor Jan Hills, a self-confessed eccentric who has a pet buffalo and will cheerfully talk about the local history. However, before you start asking questions, check out the many interpretive displays and the museum at the hotel first.

The old Stuart Highway on which it is located, forms part of the *Northern Goldfields Heritage Loop Route*, which begins just north of Hayes Creek and takes you to Pine Creek (see also under *Territory Drives, Trails and 4WD Tracks* in Part One). At a time when authentic outback pubs are a very few in number, travelling along this route is richly rewarded by the flavour of this historic architectural gem, which continues to dispense all the services and hospitality of a traditional country pub.

Apart from its history, the area is noted for some wonderful birdlife and another memorable experience is dining out under a million stars at the pub.

HOW TO GET THERE

From the turnoff it is approximately 6kms (4 miles) north of Hayes Creek. The road is sealed for 11kms (7 miles) after which it is a good formed gravel surface for 9kms (6 miles) to Grove Hill, and is suitable for conventional vehicles and caravans.

SERVICES AND FACILITIES

The hotel offers excellent traditional homestyle meals - country roasts and corned beef and damper in particular. There's a garden and you can eat outside.

Accommodation includes air-conditioned rooms $44 double, a do-it-yourself cottage style suitable for backpackers (costs on application) and camping $5 p.p. There's also a spa for guests. It's *open daily*, credit cards accepted, EFTPOS facility, ph (08) 8978 2489.

GURIG NATIONAL PARK AND COBOURG MARINE PARK

220,700ha (545,129 acres) and 22,900ha (56,563 acres) respectively.

LOCATION

On the Cobourg Peninsula, 200km (124 miles) north-east of Darwin at the second most northerly geographic point of mainland Australia, after Cape York Peninsula.

CHARACTERISTICS

The Parks beyond Kakadu encompass a vast area of virgin, mainly inaccessible wilderness, and the protected marine foreshore and coral reefs are the emphasised natural features. On the United Nations Wetlands of International Importance Register, especially as a migratory waterfowl habitat, these little-known parks also feature magnificent bays and beaches, prolific marine and wildlife, and offer excellent hunting and fishing. A rich Aboriginal presence, relics of the Macassan trading era and the forlorn ruins of early attempts at European settlement are Gurig's cultural attributes. So significant are these early relics in Gurig that they have been placed on the National Estate Register.

The traditional owners, an amalgam of clans called the Iwaidja people, number about 40, many of whom live near the Black Point settlement, where some are involved in tourist services. A few choose to live semi-traditionally in the park. The Gurig people also work closely with the Parks and Wildlife Commission in the joint management of the park, and an Agalda Clan Elder is chairman of the management committee.

Permits to enter are required, and access by land via Arnhem Land is very restricted. Only fifteen groups or vehicles are allowed at the park's camping ground at any one time. Early applications are necessary as peak times are already heavily booked for the next two years. Most visitors fly in from Darwin. Black Point, a tiny settlement with a population of about twenty-eight, consists of a ranger station and visitors centre, store, jetty and a few houses.

HISTORY

Early European navigators included the Dutch in 1636, Abel Tasman in 1644, Matthew Flinders in 1803 and Phillip King, who in 1818 named Port Essington after a Royal Navy Admiral. The second attempt at establishing a permanent settlement on the north coast was at Raffles Bay on the Cobourg Peninsula (about 65km [40 miles] north-east of the Victoria Settlement site). While relationships with Aborigines were much better than at Fort Dundas (Melville Island), the Fort Wellington settlement established in 1827 failed commercially and was abandoned two years later.

Yet another attempt was made in 1838, when Victoria Settlement was built at Port Essington. Suspicion of French intent in the area was a major reason for the Colonial Office's decision; others included a base for Asian trade. The site was described as *the friendly hand of Australia stretched out towards the north...*, but before it too was abandoned in 1849, it was a 'friendly hand' for Ludwig Leichhardt, who ended his overland journey here from near Brisbane in 1845. Apart from the buildings the British abandoned, there are the descendants of their cattle, buffalo, pig, deer and horses, which still roam wild over Cobourg, with buffalo spread right across the Top End.

Macassans were earlier visitors; trepang collecting and pearl gathering mainly. In 1906, trepangers were prohibited from visiting the north coast. Other early European activities included timber mills, pastoralism and pearling, the latter still continuing today.

FLORA AND FAUNA

Tropical eucalypt forest, mainly Darwin stringybark and woolly-butt, covers the undulating landscape, with enclaves of monsoon rainforest, swamp paperbark and mangroves in the wetter areas.

Gurig is the first southern hemisphere stopover in spring for thousands of migratory birds, a reason for its United Nations listing in 1974. Brolgas and jabiru delightfully grace the wetlands and margins. The coastal waters have salt-water crocodiles, dugong (sea cow), turtles, and a great variety of fish. The park is inhabited by banteng cattle from Bali, sambar deer from India, buffalo from Java, ponies from Timor, pig (Javanese boar) from Java, all of which were imported by the British at Victoria Settlement. Dingo and wallaby are the main large indigenous species.

CONSERVATION
The parks have a preferred marine and coastal focus which means the interior, apart from licensed hunting safaris, is closed. Strict controls on numbers of vehicles entering the parks is to maintain environmental quality. Driving is strictly on designated roads only. No pets are allowed.

INFORMATION
Rangers at *Black Point* are knowledgeable about the area, and are more than willing to help, ph (08) 8979 0244.

ATTRACTIONS
Victoria Settlement Ruins. Extensive and some surprisingly well-preserved ruins of a British garrison town, established by Captain J.G. Bremer in 1838, lie in the bush. Up to 300 lived here at its peak, including a significant military element. Remnants include: powder magazine (half-buried); stone chimneys and walls; lime kiln; walls of a hospital kitchen; and foundations of other buildings. A cemetery is a reminder of the extreme hardships here. And, to commemorate the 150 year anniversary of the 'Red Coat' Garrison town, a visitor centre incorporating a small museum was opened at Black Point in 1988.

 Facilities include picnic area, toilets, and an interpretive walking track. A pamphlet available at the visitors centre details the history, and identifies particular ruins. There is no water, so take adequate fluids with you. Access is by boat only.

 Independent boat users should advise the ranger before leaving. It's a full day trip, and you should provision yourself accordingly.

Fishing. The waters offer superb all year round fishing, and most listed in the fishing guide frequent these waters. Sandy Island No 2 is a sacred site and no landings are permitted.

Hunting. Guided trophy hunting of Banteng cattle and Sambar deer is available. Contact Davidson Arnhem Land Safaris, ph (08) 8927 5240.

Marine Park. All foreshores and reefs have marine park designation. Beautiful sandy white beaches are ideal for walking and beachcombing for some fabulous shells. Coral reefs, tropical fish, turtles, and oyster beds add fascination. People do swim, but sharks and salt-water crocodiles make it dangerous, as do box jellyfish during the earlier and later parts of the year.

HOW TO GET THERE

By road: It's approximately 500km (310 miles) and 9 hours driving time from Darwin. The surprisingly good, but 4WD track only between the East Alligator River and Gurig has some rough patches, and is closed during the Wet season (between November and early April generally). Permits and bookings are required, available from the Northern Territory Parks and Wildlife Commission.

By air: Northern Air Charter offers day trip charters in a single engine, five seater plane - costs $410/aircraft, ph (08) 8945 5444

By boat: You can cruise in independently, provided you have permits.

ACCOMMODATION

Parks and Wildlife Commission: a small camping area nestles under a large stand of casuarinas, and has showers, toilets, picnic and BBQ facilities. The use of generators at night is not permitted. *Gurig Park*, between Black Point and Smith Point, has beach huts (sleep 6) available for rent (around $135 per day) and tent sites for

$10 per person. Bookings can be made at Gurig Park Store, ph (08) 8979 0262.

Seven Spirit Bay Resort: a wilderness retreat hotel - $350 per person twinshare plus air charter transfer costs from Darwin, ph (08) 8979 0277. They can also arrange fishing safaris.

SERVICES AND FACILITIES

At Black Point and nearby, there's a ranger station and visitor centre that houses an interesting historic section. The Gurig Store sells basic items and foodstuffs, fuel (ULP, diesel, marine fuel), camping gas, ice. There's an airstrip (near Smith Point), jetty and launching ramp. The store accepts credit cards and has EFTPOS.

HAYES CREEK

Population approximately 15

LOCATION

On the Stuart Highway, 140km (87 miles) north of Katherine, and 170km (105 miles) south of Darwin.

CHARACTERISTICS

Hayes Creek consists of a roadhouse which is a convenient stop along the highway. Not too far away in the bush, are major gold mining operations with a work force of about 100 men who live in camps near the mineral sites. The owners of the popular Hayes Creek Wayside Inn, will cheerfully tell you about the local and outlying scenic attractions.

ATTRACTIONS

The turn-off to the Douglas Hot Springs and Butterfly Gorge Nature Parks is 7km (4 miles) to the north of Hayes Creek. It is also the turn-off to the secluded and scenic Daly River area. To the east is Grove Hill - an extraordinary heritage hotel on the Goldfields Loop Road (see separate listing).

ACCOMMODATION

Motel rooms available (prices on application). The caravan park has powered sites, $15x2, camp sites $5 p.p., pets allowed, dogs leashed.

SERVICES AND FACILITIES

It has a bar, outside dining area (main course $8-$14), shop, takeaway and snack foods, ice, souvenirs, post office agency, picnic area and swimming pool (patrons only) and all fuels. Credit cards accepted, EFTPOS, *open daily*, 6am-11pm, ph (08) 8978 2430.

KATHERINE

Population approximately 11,000

LOCATION

320km (200 miles) south of Darwin, on the Stuart Highway.

CHARACTERISTICS

Katherine, best known for its famous nearby gorge, is a lively, rapidly growing town that in itself has much to offer visitors. From its river-side and tropical woodland setting, the third largest centre in the Northern Territory is the hub of a huge agricultural region ranging from torrid cattle country to local specialised farms which produce fruit and vegetable crops. It serves a hinterland some 700kms (434 miles) in extent from the centre.

The magnificent Katherine Gorge has given it a major tourist function, while the construction of Australia's largest Air Force Base to accommodate the front-line fighter squadrons at Tindal has boosted the population considerably. As a result, the town boasts all the comforts and facilities of a modern, small city. A strong sense of history and a range of scenic spots add interest to the town.

For the road traveller, it's also the place where you turn off west to the Victoria River and the Kimberley Regions. Even if you are

KATHERINE – TOWN AND AREA

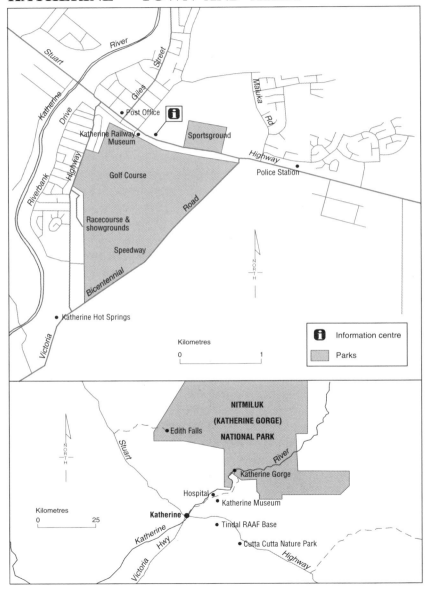

River

Stuart

Giles Street

Katherine Drive

• Post Office

ℹ

Katherine Railway • Museum

Sportsground

Maluka Rd

Highway

Highway

Riverbank

Golf Course

Road

Police Station

Racecourse & showgrounds

Speedway

NORTH

Bicentennial

• Katherine Hot Springs

Victoria

Kilometres
0   1

ℹ Information centre

☐ Parks

NITMILUK
(KATHERINE GORGE)
NATIONAL PARK

Stuart

• Edith Falls

River

• Katherine Gorge

Hospital •

• Katherine Museum

NORTH

Kilometres
0   25

Katherine •

• Tindal RAAF Base

Katherine Hwy

• Cutta Cutta Nature Park

Victoria Hwy

Highway

not planning a round trip of Australia, a visit to the Eastern Kimberley of Bungle Bungle fame, via the sealed Victoria Highway, is highly recommended.

HISTORY

The land around Katherine is most closely associated with people of the Dagoman and Jawoyn; the latter occupying areas north and north-west from the high level bridge, along the Edith and Cullen Rivers towards Pine Creek, and eastwards along the Stuart Highway to Beswick and beyond. The traditional Dagoman lands stretch south from the Low Level Weir.

While the river was named by explorer Stuart on July 4, 1862, after Katherine, the daughter of James Chambers, who was a major patron of the expedition, the first known European here was Leichhardt in 1844. 'The' Katherine was the first permanent waters found north on the trek through Central Australia, and 'The' emphasises the river's importance. Pronunciation is Kath-rhyne!

The Overland Telegraph Line construction gave substance to the original settlement site at Knotts Crossing - a tiny enclave of European civilisation and node for the gradual growth of pastoral and mining pursuits. The first pastoral lease in the Territory was at Springvale Homestead in the 1870s, the establishment of which was forerunner to increased overlander activity, and the laying down of firm foundations for a viable cattle industry that continues today.

With the railway came the town's second site, but the first official one was at Emungalan on the west bank of the river. Surveyed and gazetted as a town site in 1917 in anticipation of the railway, the railway bridge opened in 1926, and then attracted the settlement on the current town site. Little remains of Emungalan today.

During World War II, numerous airstrips were built between Katherine and Birdum, and RAAF and Army personnel were stationed in the area. The original construction of Tindal known as Carsons Airfield, was started in 1942 by a US Engineer Regiment, and completed by the Victorian Country Roads Board by 1944. Although designed for B24 Liberator sized bombers, the airfield was never used operationally and was renamed Tindal after Wing Commander A.R. Tindal, CO No 2 Squadron based in Darwin in 1941. He was killed in action in 1942 during the first Japanese air-raid on Darwin. Katherine was attacked by Japanese bombers during the war.

In recent times, Katherine's growth has been stimulated by its function as a regional base for construction (roads and Tindal), regional administration, agricultural and pastoral service centre, and tourism associated with the Katherine Gorge and other natural attractions.

And recent bold horticultural enterprises include some of Australia's largest mango plantations and market gardens and even a dairy farm, where the cows produce milk in air-conditioned comfort. Prior to its establishment, fresh milk to these parts of Northern Australia came via the worlds longest milk-run - via roadtrain from near Cairns, a distance of over 1800 kms (over 1000 miles).

TOURIST INFORMATION
The *Katherine Region Tourist Association* has an excellent Visitors Centre, located at the southern entrance to the town. Open Mon-Fri 8.45am-5pm, Sat 9.30am-2.30pm, ph (08) 8972 2650.

The *BP Roadhouse* and *Travel North* headquarters (almost opposite the Visitors Centre) offers information and takes tour bookings, ph (08) 8972 1044.

The *Parks and Wildlife Commission* has an office in Giles Street, open weekdays, which offers a large selection of publications.

ATTRACTIONS
Museum and Historical Park. Located on the original airport site in the former terminal building, the museum houses a fine visual display that takes you through Katherine's colourful past. Inventor of a peanut harvester, collector of relic machinery, pig and peanut farmer, are a few of the things Wally Christie has done since

arriving here in 1946. He's often at the museum, and is fascinating to talk with. The restored Gypsy Moth belonging to the Territory's first flying doctor, Dr Clyde Fenton, can be seen here, along with all the medical instruments of the time (while the Rev John Flynn flew, he was not a pilot). Open 10am-4pm weekdays, 2-5pm Saturday and Sunday, located in Giles Street (opposite hospital), ph (08) 8972 3945.

School of The Air. You can watch the action as teachers contact students for lessons via the radio. Visits are very entertaining and informative in the worlds largest classroom which covers a staggering 800,000 sq.km. (nearly 500,000 sq.miles) area of the Outback. It's open Mon-Fri, April-October, tours at 9,10,11am and 1,2pm. Costs $4 adult, $2 children. It's located in Giles Street, ph (08) 8972 1833.

Knotts Crossing. This is the original Katherine site where the modern town had its beginnings as a tiny bush settlement that consisted of a 'pub', store, police station and telegraph station. It was named after an early settler. The old pub, called the 'Sportsman Arms and Pioneer Cash Store', is situated at the top of the river bank. The Northern Times Newspaper described it in the year of its establishment, 1888, as *The Sportsman is well fitted with all the requisites of a first class country hotel where the comfort of visitors is studied*. Jeannie Gunn crossed here in a punt (now at the museum) whilst on her way to Elsey Station, in 1902.

The original Overland Telegraph Pylons are located across the river, and the one on this side can be seen about 1.5km from the crossing turn-off on Gorge Road. Access to Knotts Crossing is from a left hand turn-off just past the hospital. It's an interesting historic spot where you can picnic, fish, or swim. The old pub is not open to the public.

Katherine Railway Station. Along with the railway extension from Pine Creek, it was completed in 1926 to service the cattle industry

- meat company interests such as Vesteys were keen to transport live cattle for processing in Darwin. It was headquarters for the North Australian Railways during the war, and the track was called 'The Never Never Line'. An interesting display of railway memorabilia is now housed here, and the story of the North Australian Railway is well related in J. Y. Harvey's book *The Never Never Line*. It's a National Trust property. It's open 11am-1pm weekdays (April-October) and located in Railway Terrace.

O'Keeffe Residence. A fine example of some traditional Territorian architecture. It was built from bush poles, clad in corrugated iron and asbestos with fly-wired walls for maximum ventilation, for use by Army Engineers as an Officers' Mess during the war. Following the war, it was named after one of a number of its tenants, Sister Olive O'Keeffe. It has been restored by the National Trust, located on Riverbank Drive, opposite Campbell Terrace and is open to the public.

Heritage Trail. The Katherine branch of the National Trust have devised a heritage trail which identifies 10 sites and features of historic interest. The self-guide brochures are available from information centres and the National Trust office in the Old Railway Station.

Aboriginal Artifacts. The Katherine Art Gallery, offers a good selection of paintings and art and craft works by mainly local artists.

NT Rare Rocks. Offers an interesting selection that will please collectors, located at 1809 Zimin Drive.

Katherine Low Level Nature Park. Maintained by the Parks and Wildlife Commission, this 1104ha (256 acres) scenic tract of the river is a popular picnicking, fishing and swimming spot. Swimming is safe during the Dry season, but care must be taken in the Wet when floods make it hazardous. Always check the swimming safety sign, as during this time the river can rise at a rate of 3m (9 ft) per hour! The old Katherine River road causeway, pleasant grassed woodlands, gas barbecues, picnic and toilet facilities make it an ideal destination for families. Flora in the park is diverse. Common species include greybox (Eucalyptus tectifica), white-leafed bloodwood (E. foelscheana), red-flowering kurrajong (Brachyciton paradoxum), wild kapok (Cochlospernum fraseri), paperbarks (Melaleuca ssp) and fresh water mangrove (Barringtonia acutangula).

Barramundi, black and bony bream, rifle fish, garfish and catfish inhabit the waters. Fishing is allowed. Sometimes freshwater crocodiles and tortoises may be seen. On the land, agile wallabies are common; flying foxes (fruit bats) and brush-tail possum are nocturnal. There's plenty of birdlife - over 120 species have been recorded in the park. Camping is not allowed, and dogs must be leashed. Location is south-west of the town centre, via the Victoria Highway to the Low Level turn-off.

OUTLYING ATTRACTIONS

Nitmiluk (Katherine Gorge) National Park. See separate listing following Katherine.

Springvale Homestead. Claimed to be the oldest original station homestead in the Territory, the property now functions as a low key tourist resort from its attractive 81ha (200 acres) Katherine riverside setting. It features the well-preserved and still functional stone homestead, and some original outbuildings constructed in 1879; a waterlily-covered billabong that's home for some freshwater crocodiles; huge shady trees; and newer buildings.

Springvale Station was established in 1878, and stretched from Pine Creek to Mataranka. It was one of the earliest settled in the Territory, and the first livestock, 12,000 sheep and 3000 cattle, arrived after an epic drove from Adelaide that lasted nearly 20 months. Alfred Giles directed the mammoth operation. The stock were broken into smaller manageable mobs in a successful operation that involved 40 men. Giles, along with his wife, Mary, managed the station for owner Dr W.J. Browne for many years. While much is made of Jeannie Gunn's 13 months at Elsey Station, there were many other women, such as Mary Giles, who endured unsung, married lifetimes in the Outback of the 1880s at places like Springvale.

Sheep were not very successful, and a succession of land uses were attempted here, even a peanut farm in the 1920s. A fascinating guided walking tour around the property covers such things as station life, history, flora and fauna. The historical focus of this tour is complemented by the river cruises run by Travel North. A booklet on the *History of Springvale* by Peter Forrest makes interesting reading and is available at the Homestead.

The homestead offers budget accommodation and camping. Contact the homestead for cost details. Facilities at the homestead include an open bar, eating area, restaurant, shop, takeaway food, artifacts, BBQs and swimming pool. Generally there's live country and western music in the bar area during the season. Trail rides operate from the homestead (see under *Tours* in Katherine listing). Night time crocodile-spotting tours depart from here every evening, May-October. It's open daily, credit cards accepted, EFTPOS, located 8kms (5 miles) south-west of the town on the Shadforth Road, ph (08) 8972 1044.

Flora River Nature Park. Opened in 1998, the 1874 ha (4629 acres) park protects 25 kms of the Flora River environment and features tufa formations (soft porous sedimentary rock weathered by warm waters), waterfalls and cascades. Activities include walks along designated trails, boating, canoeing, fishing, swimming and camping in an unspoilt, natural landscape. Facilities include pit toilets, camping area, picnic tables, drinking water, disabled access and BBQs. It's located approximately 120kms (75 miles) south-west of Katherine; the turnoff from the Victoria Highway, is approximately 75 kms (47 miles) from Katherine, from where it's 43 kms (27 miles) to the park. The access road is suitable for conventional vehicles. Access may be restricted during the Wet Season. Fees are payable in honesty boxes for camping.

Manyallaluk. The former 3000 sq.km. Eva Valley Cattle Station is now owned by Jawoyn and Mayali Aboriginal people who run the Manyallaluk property as one of the most vibrant Aboriginal Tourism enterprises in the Northern Territory. In its remote location - the property abuts the eastern edge of Nitmiluk National Park - approximately 100kms (62 miles) by road from Katherine, visitors are encouraged to participate in Aboriginal activities from painting to spear throwing. It is this hands-on involvement and interaction with Aboriginal people that affords a memorable cross-cultural experience. Testimony to the quality of their cultural tours and community-based activities is reflected in a number of prestigious Tourism Awards received by Manyallaluk including Brolga Awards.

A number of revered artists reside at the community and their works are available for purchase. In fact, the community has an impressive array of works on display. Day tours afford unique insights into the culture of these people and cost $65 p.p. with transfers from Katherine available. Tours take you into rock art sites located in some beautiful, unspoilt country - an experience which evokes deeper landscape appreciation.

Facilities at the community include a well-stocked store, fuel (diesel only), excellent camping amenities, wood BBQs, beautiful natural spring drinking water and natural swimming holes all in an expansive, natural parkland setting. Camping costs $5 p.p. No alcohol is permitted. Credit cards accepted, it's open daily, no permits required and the road is suitable for conventional vehicles and trailers from May-October. To get there, take the Central Arnhem Road, turnoff 52kms (32 miles) south of Katherine from the Stuart Highway. The first 15kms (9 miles) is sealed to the turnoff to Manyallaluk after which it is 35kms (22 miles) of good, formed road. For further details, ph (08) 8975 4727. About 14kms

(9 miles) beyond the turnoff to Manyallaluk, on the sealed Central Arnhem Road is *Barunga* which hosts a lively Aboriginal Sports and Cultural Festival (see under *Events*).

TOURS

A wide range are offered. Contact Travel North (08) 8972 1044 (the Regions major tour operator) or the Visitor centre for advice. The following is only a sample of what is available.

Katherine Scenic Flights offer Outback Mail Run flights on Tuesdays, Thursdays and Fridays but seat availability depends on freight and mail. Costs are $240 p.p. ph, (08) 8972 2552.

Brumby Tracks Tours, ph (08) 8972 1425 offer an interesting Stockmans Breakfast and Drovers Tour from around $45 p.p.

Ironwood Station Adventure Tours, ph 0411 694 335, provide a working cattle station experience. Full day tour, $90 p.p.

Campbells Trail Rides operate out of Springvale Homestead; costs $20 p.p. ph (08) 8972 1355.

Far Out Adventures offer a range of tours including Aboriginal culture, 4WD, river cruises and wilderness canoeing, ph (08) 8972 2552.

EVENTS

Show and Rodeo in July; *Katherine River Canoe Marathon* in June; *The Flying Fox Festival* in late August, early September is an arts and culture event; *The Barunga Cultural and Sports Festival*, held at the Barunga Community, 80kms (50miles) south of Katherine (see reference under *Manyallaluk* in Outlying Attractions) is when Top End Aboriginal Communities compete in a range of sports. There are cultural activities, and artworks on sale. Bands entertain at night, camping facilities available and all are welcome for the mid-June weekend event.

HOW TO GET THERE

By coach: McCafferty's and Greyhound-Pioneer operate daily services from Alice Springs and Darwin.

By air: There are regular flights from Alice Springs and Darwin.

ACCOMMODATION

Katherine boasts some first-rate motel/resort type accommodation. A range of good, budget accommodation is available too. Many have swimming pools, most have air-conditioning and newer ones have facilities for the disabled. A representative sample is as follows:

Hotels and Motels

All Seasons Frontier Katherine, has double rooms from $130, ph (08) 8972 1744.

Knotts Crossing Resort offers rooms from $75-$146, ph (08) 8972 2511.

The Paraway Motel, rooms from $72-$110, ph (08) 8972 2644.

Pine Tree Motel, rooms from $79-$103, ph (08) 8972 2533.

Beagle Motor Inn, rooms from $60-$90, ph (08) 8972 3998.

Maud Creek Guesthouse has rooms from $70-$85,
ph (08) 89711814 and B&B style.

Kookaburra Backpackers Lodge offers dormitory beds from $12 p.p. ph (08) 8971 0257.

Palm Court Backpackers has dormitory beds from $12-$14 p.p., ph (08) 8972 2722.

Springvale Homestead (see under *Outlying Attractions*).

Knotts Crossing Resort, Beagle Motor Inn and All Seasons Frontier have facilities for disabled guests.

Camping

Katherine Low Level Caravan Park has powered sites $18x2, unpowered $14x2, ph (08) 8972 3962.

Riverview Caravan Park has cabins from $45-$80 and campsites $17x2 powered, ph (08) 8972 1011.

Redgum Caravan Park also has cabins priced from $65-$95 and campsites, $17x2 powered, ph (08)8972 2239.

Shady Lane Caravan Park has powered sites $14x2, unpowered $6 p.p., cabins $50 and bunkhouse $35x2, ph (08)8972 3259.

All Seasons Frontier offer powered sites with ensuite $20, site only $8 p.p., ph (08) 8972 1744.

Knotts Crossing Resort has powered sites $18 with ensuite, unpowered $14x2, ph (08) 8972 2511. Springvale Homstead (see under *Attractions*) has camping facilities.

Pets
Most accommodation places don't allow pets. Dogs can be boarded at *Waggin Kennels*, 10km from town on the Gorge Road. A vet immunisation certificate is essential. Ph (08) 8971 0699.

EATING OUT
While there's the predictable range of take-away food, Katherine does have a good selection of restaurants. Some good examples of these are:

Regent Court Chinese specialises in *Szechuan cuisine*, ph (08) 8971 1555.

Mekhong Thai Cafe offers authentic *Thai food*, ph (08) 8972 3170.

Knotts Crossing Resort - *Katies Bistro* has an enviable reputation for good food, ph (08) 8972 2511.

Crossways Hotel offers reasonable pub fare with entertainment as well, ph (08) 8972 1022. Also offering budget good quality family meals is *Pedros Bistro*, Katherine RSL, ph (08) 8972 1250.

The All Seasons Frontier - *Seasons Restaurant* offers a memorable dining out experience in relaxed surrounds, ph (08) 8972 1744.

The Steakhouse on Third is a carnivores delight, ph (08) 8972 1909. Another place worthy of consideration is *The Walkabout Restaurant*, Katherine Country Club, ph (08) 8972 1276.

Others include the *Cafe on First*, and the *Olympic Cafe* which specialises in *Greek and Italian* food.

SERVICES AND FACILITIES
Katherine has a full range of shopping and specialist services including medical, Police Station, Post office, supermarkets, full vehicle services and all fuels, banks (ANZ, Westpac,

Commonwealth, all with auto tellers). Specialist shops, galleries, eateries and restaurants. Many shops open 7 days. Credit cards are widely accepted, EFTPOS facilities.

Hire Vehicles, *Territory Rent-a-car* and *Thrifty* at Travel North ph (08) 8972 1044, *Hertz* and *Delta Car Rental* at Knotts Crossing Resort, ph (08) 8972 2511]

Churches: Anglican, Baptist, Catholic, Lutheran, Assembly of God, and Salvation Army.

Knotts Crossing Resort has convention facilities. Recreational facilities include a golf course, swimming pool, horse riding, tennis, squash, canoeing (hire canoes Shady Lane Caravan Park), boat ramp, fishing and cinema.

KATHERINE GORGE SECTOR - NITMILUK NATIONAL PARK

180,352ha (445,469 acres)

LOCATION
32km (19 miles) north-east of Katherine, via the Katherine Gorge Road.

CHARACTERISTICS
This huge park protects spectacular gorge and escarpment country, where the permanently flowing Katherine River has carved 13 deep canyons through the Arnhem Land Plateau sandstone.

The variety of landscapes include plateau, escarpment, gorges and valley floors, while the ruggedness of the terrain is heightened by the regular, rectangular dissection pattern slashed by the Katherine and Edith Rivers. During the Wet Season, the full fury of the Katherine is awesome, when the gorge fills and becomes a thundering torrent of brown water, many metres above its normal tranquil level.

GEOLOGY

The base rock is around 2,300 million-years-old. Folding and lifting, and associated volcanic activity, formed the bed on which the massive sandstone block rests. This block which forms the plateau and escarpment, evolved after millions of years of sedimentation. Volcanic intrusions, and deposition of gravels and sands, have produced an array of geological structures made more complex by later uplift. Amazingly, the Katherine Gorge was formed just 25 million years ago, by the river that exploited the rectangular lines of weakness in the great sandstone blocks. From the air the evolution of the gorge is easily understood, and the Visitors Centre has excellent models explaining the gorge origin, the time frame of geological events, and various rock samples.

GORGE FEATURES

Sheer rock faces up to 75m high contrast with the swirled surrealistic patterns deeply engraved into the gorge's hard stone floor. The canyon walls reveal fascinating histories from the geological to Aboriginal engravings and paintings etched on some smoothed rock faces. Most visitors take the 2-hour trip through the first two spectacular gorges, where there's a short, but easily manageable, walk between them. Mosses and ferns cascade down wetter parts of the rugged red bluffs; Livistona palms, pandanus, silver paperbark and freshwater mangroves line or climb the cliffs. Caves are home to bats, and places where fairy martin build mud nests under the overhangs. Aquatic life includes freshwater crocodiles, long-necked tortoises and fish. Other gorges are well worthwhile visiting, on 4 and 8 hour tours, but walking between them is often more demanding.

  In the picnic area near the boat ramps and jetty, the birdlife is colourful; friar birds, red-winged parrots, black cockatoos, grey bower birds, whistling and black kites, blue-faced (and very cheeky) honeyeaters and blue winged kookaburras, are common. Wallabies and goannas add interest to this area.

Vegetation here includes salmon gum, northern ironwood, Darwin woolly-butt and a few boab trees. Much of the park area vegetation is medium to open eucalypt woodlands with acacias and grasses.

For thousands of years the Park has been the traditional lands of the Jawoyn people who have resumed ownership of much of the Park area. The park is jointly managed by the Jawoyn and the Parks and Wildlife Commission.

TOURS AND ACTIVITIES

Boat tours operated by Travel North depart daily on a regular basis all week from the jetty. Costs are $28 adult for 2 hour trip; $41 for 4 hour and $71 for 8 hour cruise. There are concessions for children. Helicopter scenic rides cost $65 for 12 minute viewing of 6-8 gorges; $100 for 24 minutes covering 13 gorges. Bookings at the Gorge Caravan Park Kiosk or Travel North in Katherine, ph (08) 8972 1044.

WALKS

There are a number of walking tracks of varying lengths, and many involve overnight camping. The longest is the 76km (47 miles) one to Edith Falls. Check with the visitor centre for details before departing on the walk and obtain the walking maps available.

BUSH CAMPING

This is permitted and best advice is to check with Rangers about sites and facilities first of all. You must inform rangers and register with them before camping in the wilderness area of the park.

BOATS AND CANOES

Restrictions apply for the use of private boats in the gorge. Contact the visitor centre for advice and information. Canoes may be hired on a half-day and full day basis from the jetty.

FISHING AND SWIMMING

Fishing is permitted using hand-held rod or line. Many visitors swim, but some areas are very deep (over 27m).

HOW TO GET THERE

By car, it is a 32km (19 miles) sealed road from Katherine. BP Roadhouse (Travel North) operate daily bus services from Katherine ($16 return, $9 one way). Gorge Tours booked from Katherine generally include coach transfer.

ACCOMMODATION

Katherine Gorge Caravan Park has powered and unpowered sites, $7.50 per adult, $3.50 child. Shaded sites. Pets not allowed.

SERVICES AND FACILITIES

The Caravan Park has a general store/kiosk, take-away food, ice, souvenirs, telephone, fuel (super, diesel, camping gas), tourist information and tour bookings. *Open all year, 7am-7pm*. Credit cards accepted, ph (08) 8972 1253.

The **Ranger Station Visitor Centre** is an excellent starting point and offers displays, park literature, an extensive array of gifts and souvenir items, video screenings, and very good up-front advice. During the Dry Season, there are talks by Rangers at the centre. Other ranger guided activities are offered from time to time. For further information, telephone the centre on (08) 8972 1886.

PICNIC FACILITIES

Treed, grassy banks, and flats have tables, toilets, showers, water, and wood barbecues.

EDITH FALLS SECTOR - NITMILUK NATIONAL PARK

LOCATION

Located at the north-western extremity of Nitmiluk (Katherine Gorge) National Park. Access is via the Edith Falls Road; turnoff from the Stuart Highway 40km (25 miles) north of Katherine.

CHARACTERISTICS

The main attractions of the area are the waterfalls from the Edith River cascading over the Arnhem Land escarpment edge, and the large, deep plunge pool fringed by tropical vegetation and pandanus palms. Walkers taking the track to the top of the escarpment will be rewarded by some magnificent scenery, including numerous smaller pools and rapids. Generally there is plenty of birdlife, and wallabies may be seen too. Although it is a half-hour climb, the effort is well worthwhile.

The Falls were named after Lady Edith, wife of the Governor of South Australia from 1864 to 1873, Sir James Fergusson.

HOW TO GET THERE

The 20 km (12 mile) road into the Falls is sealed. A 76km (47 miles) walk along a track from Katherine Gorge is an alternate, more energetic way into the Falls area. It's for experienced bush walkers only, and the rangers at the Katherine Gorge Visitor Centre must be notified first.

SERVICES AND FACILITIES

Picnic, BBQ (please collect your own firewood before entering the park) and toilet and shower facilities are provided. Camping is allowed. People swim here despite freshwater crocodiles.

KEEP RIVER NATIONAL PARK

59,700ha (147,459 acres)

LOCATION

On the Victoria Highway, 468km (290 miles) west of Katherine, and 50km (31 miles) east of Kununurra, Western Australia. The Western Australian State border defines the park's western boundary.

CHARACTERISTICS

Noted for its striking ancient sandstone formations, and fascinating but complex geological structures, the Park also has some superb Aboriginal art sites. It's a geologists' delight, with evidence of glacial and marine deposits and volcanic activity imprinted in the exposed rock formations. Streams have sandy beds during the Dry season in this isolated, wilderness area, characterised too by enormous baobab and known as bottle trees (Adansonia gregorii) on the open plains and rocky ridges.

  The park is crossed by the Auvergne Stock Route, an old cattle track to the Kimberley, about 5km (3 miles) north of the Victoria Highway. Keep River is well worth visiting for its tropical savannah lands, and some spectacular escarpment and plateau landscapes.

LANDFORMS

Several distinctive landform types characterise the park. Cambridge Gulf lowlands and plains occupy a significant area of the park in the northern and central areas. The Keep River sweeps through the centre, cutting a gorge through the sandstone, before striking north and meandering into Joseph Bonaparte Gulf. The plains are broken by uplands and dissected plateaux of cross-bedded quartz sandstones and conglomerates of the Palaeozoic Era (between 250 and 500 million years ago).

  The south-eastern area is dominated by Victoria River plateau terrain, with older sediments and volcanic rocks forming gently folded, undulating landscapes. Mesas and benches up to 300m above the plains, like the plateaux, are mainly composed of siltstone and sandstone, and add extraordinary colour and variety. The Halls Creek Ridge geological formations in mainly the southern part, are distinctive for low parallel ridges of metamorphic rock, while igneous (volcanic) rocks also form ridges and plateau-like formations, but with weathered domes and resistant rearing outcrops. The variety of landform features make bushwalking and photographic activities most rewarding. An excellent Department of Mines and Energy booklet entitled *Geology of Keep River National Park* gives detailed information. It's available from the Mines and Energy Department in Darwin.

FLORA AND FAUNA

Many species of plantlife have been identified, the most widespread being eucalypts (bloodwoods and stringy-barks); banksias and grevilleas are others on the lowlands. Freshwater mangroves and pandanus border the waterways and soaks. Tall tropical perennial grasses grow on the lowlands, while more undulating and rocky slopes support spinifex.

There's a range of birdlife and reptiles. Short-eared rock-wallaby, white-quilled rock pigeon and sandstone shrike-thrush find a home in the rocky, dissected terrain.

ATTRACTIONS

Geology and landforms. Remarkable formations softened by the light vegetation cover are enhanced by sunrises and sunsets.

Aboriginal Art Sites. The area is Miriwung and Gadjerong homelands, and a 10-minute walking track from the car park leads to the Nganalam art site.

Keep River Gorge. For over thousands of years, the Keep River has exploited a fault in the sandstone, and has eroded a deep, 4km long gorge. The floor provides pleasant walking conditions, and interest is added by the Aboriginal paintings at intervals along its walls.

BUSHWALKING

There are seven marked walking trails in the park ranging from 10 minute walks to 2.5 hours. Take plenty of drinking water, and for extended walks, it is advisable to have the 1:1,000,000 No 4766 *Keep River Topographic Map*. Advise the ranger before setting off. It's hot here - the mean yearly temperature is 30C (86F), and the hottest months, October and November have an average maximum of 37C (99F). The days are usually longer in the Wet than in the Dry.

CONSERVATION

Please be mindful of fire risks. Vehicles must keep to designated roads only. Art sites, as with all natural elements in the park, are fully protected and must not be interfered with. Pets are not allowed.

HOW TO GET THERE

Entry to the park is 3km (2 miles) east of the NT/WA border, on the northern side of the Victoria Highway. Within the park, a formed gravel road provides conventional vehicle access, but roads may be temporarily closed during the Wet Season.

SERVICES AND FACILITIES

A ranger station (residence only) is located at the semi-permanent waters of Cockatoo Lagoon, near the park entrance. Information is available here. There are two campgrounds: *Gurrandalng* (15 km from the main road) and *Jarrnarm* (28km in from the main road). The latter has water available and drinking water is also available along the entrance road, 4km in from the main road.

During the Dry season - June to September - a ranger conducts campfire talks. For dates and times, enquire at the park, or contact the Parks and Wildlife Commissions office in Katherine on (08) 8973 8888.

LAKE BENNETT WILDERNESS RESORT

LOCATION

7km (4 miles) east of the Stuart Highway turn-off, 86km (53 miles) south of Darwin. The access road to the resort is sealed.

CHARACTERISTICS

The resort covers over 446ha (1101 acres) of tropical wilderness, including an 81ha (200 acres) man-made lake that is ideal for a range of water-based activities, including safe swimming, wind surfing, canoeing, sailing, and fishing (barramundi, black bream, freshwater prawns). Abundant birdlife (jabiru, spoonbill, sea eagles, pelican, among many others), bush walks and pleasant foreshores, add interest. The resort caters for families, groups, conferences and special events.

ACCOMMODATION

One and two bedroom **luxury bungalows** in private, lakeshore settings and studios cost from $110 per night.

Motel rooms from $89.

Camp-o-tels $15 p.p./$40 family.

Powered caravan sites $20 x 2; campsites $7 p.p./ $15 family. All sites shaded and grassed, no pets allowed.

SERVICES AND FACILITIES

The resort has a general store, bottle shop, take-away food, ice, artifacts, camping gas, picnic/BBQ/shaded areas, information, water-based activity hire equipment. No powered boats are allowed. It has a licensed bistro (meals including BBQ style from $8) and golf driving range. A courtesy pickup from the Stuart Highway is available.

It's *open daily, sunrise to sunset*, credit cards accepted, EFTPOS facility, ph (08) 8976 0256.

LARRIMAH

Population 15

LOCATION

On the Stuart Highway, 502km (311 miles) south of Darwin.

CHARACTERISTICS

The former North Australia Railway terminus township consists of three establishments: the historic *Larrimah Hotel;* the S*hell Roadhouse;* the *Green Park Tourist complex;* and some scattered old houses, in an open tropical woodland setting. It is well worth an overnight stay for its character, fascinating wartime history, and a nearby ghost town.

HISTORY

The original settlement was at Birdum (about 5km away), established in the 1880s by settlers on Birdum Creek. It had a population of between 20 and 30, and reached its peak during the war when the Birdum Hotel became HQ for the US Army Forces. After the war, the town effectively moved to Larrimah, mainly due to flooding and proximity to the Stuart Highway.

Larrimah was originally known as DOMF Siding, but was re-named Larrimah by the army in 1941 - Larrimah is an Aboriginal word meaning where one encounters another. During the war it was a staging camp for troops, a major supply base, and was part of the 'Drawback Line' (a line across Northern Australia where the country would have been defended from any Japanese invasion). About 10km (6 miles) to the north, the RAAF established Gorrie Airfield, which was highly secretive and serviced aircraft. It was here that some top level Pacific Theatre wartime decisions were made by Supreme Allied Commander, US General Douglas MacArthur. The longest airstrip in the Southern Hemisphere is now disused, and derelict aircraft are vivid reminders of the wartime action.

After the war, the 1920s vintage Birdum Hotel was moved to Larrimah, while the rest of Birdum was abandoned. The railway closed in 1976; a victim of lack of maintenance funds after Cyclone Tracy, de-stocking of cattle stations, and a mining slump. The Larrimah terminus is now the Shell Roadhouse. An old post office and Overland Telegraph Station remains are near the hotel.

ATTRACTIONS
Historic
The old *Gorrie Airstrip* and WWII aircraft remains, and old police station/museum. *Birdum Ghost Town*, the old post office, repeater station and railway terminus.

The Larrimah Hotel is an old bush pub which is full of character, humour and wartime memorabilia.

The **Green Park Tourist Complex** has a 4m salt-water crocodile, a number of freshwater crocodiles, and a pet buffalo on display.

Another interesting attraction is the **Larrimah Irish Ashes** - a cricket weekend, near March 17 each year.

ACCOMMODATION

Larrimah Wayside Inn (Hotel) - motel rooms $25 single, $30 double, $38 family. Camping - powered sites $10, unpowered $8; tent only $3 p.p. Pets allowed, dogs leashed. Open daily 7am-11pm, ph (08) 8975 9931.

Green Park Tourist Complex - cabins $25 double; family units $75; Camping powered sites $14 two persons, unpowered $4 per person. Swimming pool (guests only), Shell garage facilities. Pets allowed, dogs leashed. Open daily 7am-9pm, ph (08) 8975 9937.

Top of the Town Van Park - cabins, $25 double; family units $75; camping - powered sites $14 x 2, unpowered $4 p.p.. Swimming pool (patrons only), BP garage facilities. Pets allowed under control. Open daily 7am-11pm, ph (08) 8975 9932.

SERVICES AND FACILITIES

All establishments accept credit cards and have EFTPOS facilities. **Green Park** and **Top of the Town Van Park** have general stores, take-away food, ice, souvenirs, vehicle services (all fuels, some spares, minor repairs, tyres and tubes), Post office agency (Green Park), showers for travellers and picnic/BBQ/shaded area (Green Park has a delightful spot). For eating out, the hotel and Green Park offer good value meals from $10.

MATARANKA

Population 150

LOCATION

On the Stuart Highway, 104km (64 miles) south of Katherine.

CHARACTERISTICS

An old pub, heat and dust, and a few colourful locals, give plenty of character to a township that blends comfortably into its tropical bushland setting. Capital of the Never Never (when you reach this country you never, never want to leave), Mataranka is a small cattle and service town where the population drops dramatically during the Wet, and soars in the busy cattle and tourist season of the Dry. The nearby old Elsey Station was, in 1902, the setting for Jeannie Gunn's famous Australian outback story *We of the Never-Never* in which, as one of the very few white women in this harsh cattle country, she vividly recounts her experiences of remote station life. A varied and fascinating history, as well as the natural delights of nearby **Mataranka Thermal Pool**, make a stay in the area a must.

HISTORY

According to Aboriginal folklore, a wild wind swept across the region and created in its passage Mataranka, Bitter Springs and the thermal springs. The main descendants of the early Aborigines today are the Mungarai people.

The earliest Europeans in the region were Leichhardt in 1845, and Stuart in 1862. Both explored the Roper River region, while A.C. Gregory found and named Elsey Creek in 1856, after a young surgeon and naturalist attached to his party. The Overland Telegraph Line construction crews survived a massive Wet in 1872, and Warloch Ponds was named after a horse belonging to Alfred Giles (of Springvale Homestead fame) - it had an uncanny ability to find water, and twice saved the lives of men.

Elsey Station was established in 1881 by Abraham Wallace on a 6000 sq km (2280 sq miles) lease which encompassed Mataranka,

then known as Bitter Springs. Melbourne-born Aeneas Gunn was appointed manager of Elsey Station in 1901 and, along with his bride Jeannie, took up the post the following year. Aeneas contracted malaria and died in 1903. Jeannie then managed the station for a short time before returning to Melbourne where she wrote her story. The film *We of the Never Never* was filmed here in 1981, and a replica of the old homestead used for the set is located at Mataranka Homestead.

A division of The Elsey in 1916 saw the formation of Mataranka Station, the homestead of which is now the tourist resort centre. Dr Gilruth, the then Administrator under South Australian Government direction, started the short-lived Mataranka Horse and Sheep Experimental Station. Dingoes, climate and spear-grass were the main reasons for its failure, and by 1919 the area had reverted to cattle.

The railway line came through in the 1920s, and about the same time the township was officially gazetted and named. The name derivation is obscure: because of Dr Gilruth's New Zealand connections, some think it is a Maori name; others say it is Aboriginal.

During World War II, Mataranka was a military camp, ammunition dump, and a base workshop for all kinds of repairs.

Slab foundation remnants of the Sergeants' Mess, built in 1942, and other relics in the bush are wartime reminders. The first race meeting was run in 1943, and judging by the pedigrees of the horses supplied by local stations, the event was less than serious: 'Parched Throat' by 'Canteen' out of 'Grog'; 'Home Leave' by 'Hard to Get' out of 'Seldom Seen'; and 'Hitler' by 'Doubtful' out of 'Dam Unknown' were some.

ATTRACTIONS

Mataranka Homestead and Mataranka Thermal Springs Pool (Elsey National Park) . See under *Mataranka Homestead* listing.

Bitter Springs. A recently opened up section of Elsey National Park features a thermal pool (Bitter Springs) and day use area of tropical rainforest tracts along the course of the Middle Roper River. Activities include bush walking, picnicking and swimming. An adjacent commercial establishment, Mataranka Cabins, offers secluded farm-stay type cabin accommodation on a 70 acre (28ha) property ($60 double). Its located 2km from the Stuart Highway along Martin Road, just to the north of the township, credit cards accepted, pets allowed, ph. (08) 8975 4838.

Elsey Cemetery. The graves of the Elsey Station pioneers and *We of the Never Never* fame, including Aeneas Gunn, Muluka who was head of the property, and Henry Peckham ('Fizzer') the mailman, lie in the cemetery. Located 8km (4 miles) east of the Stuart Highway, from the turn-off 13km (8 miles) south of the township. A further 500m from the cemetery is the original homestead site, marked by a cairn. Because of frequent water shortages at this site, the homestead was relocated at McMinns Bar on the Roper River, in 1906.

Elsey National Park. Situated to the east of the Mataranka township, the 13,840 hectare (34,185 ac) park incorporates the well-known Mataranka thermal pool and protects large natural areas of the Roper and Waterhouse River catchments. During the

Dry Season, the rivers flow gently through large waterholes, tumbling over rocks and tuffa dams which divide the Roper into sections of waterways and braided channels. The Wet Season herald often raging torrents which swell the channels. Since the thermal pool lies adjacent to the Mataranka Homestead, a description is included under the homestead listing. Activities include camping, boating, canoeing, fishing, wildlife spotting, walking and picnicking in idyllic, lush tropical landscapes.

Facilities within the park include a campground at 12 Mile Yards managed by **Clearwater Canoe Camp**. It has grassed, shaded tent and caravan sites (adults $5, children $2), no powered sites, generators not allowed, hot showers, toilets, BBQs and a kiosk. No pets allowed, for details telephone (08) 8975 4789. Canoes are available for hire.

Walking tracks, ranger guided walks and day use areas with picnic, wood BBQ and toilet facilities are located at Bitter Springs, 12 Mile Yards and Mulurark. A boat ramp and canoe launching area is located at 12 Mile Yards and Mataranka Homestead. Locations of other features of the park are illustrated on the map, *Elsey National Park*. The **Ranger Station**, located just south of Mataranka on the Stuart Highway, has displays and is a useful introduction to the park, ph. (08) 8975 4560.

The Stockyard Gallery. The gallery also functions as a visitor centre for the Mataranka Region and offers a range of useful information. It features a good collection of Aboriginal artifacts, leather sculptures, buffalo horns and outback bronzes as well as a range of souvenirs and a shady tea garden. It's open daily, located in the town centre, ph (08) 8975 4430.

Other attractions include Barramundi feeding at **Territory Manor**, the **Museum of the Never Never** with outdoor displays and photographic gallery and the **Termite Mound** in the centre of town.

TOURS

Brolga Tours conduct a 4 hour *Roper River Adventure Cruise* through the historic Elsey Station to Red Lily Lagoon and branches of the Roper River. Freshwater crocodiles, prolific birdlife and flora of the Never Never lands are sightseeing highlights. It costs $55 p.p., bookings at the *Stockyard Gallery*, ph (08) 8975 4530.

EVENTS

In keeping with its colourful cattletown image, Mataranka hosts *Back to the Never Never Festival* (May), which showcases the best the region offers from bush tales and rodeo to sports and husband calling competition. The *Mataranka Bushmans Carnival* (August) is another notable event.

ACCOMMODATION

Mataranka Cabins (see under *Attractions, Bitter Springs*).
Mataranka Homestead Tourist Park (see separate listing).
Territory Manor (ph 08 8975 4516) offers more upmarket style with a relaxed retreat atmosphere and swimming pool. Motel - $65 single, $77 double; caravan section $18 powered site for two persons.
The Old Elsey Roadside Inn (ph 08 8975 4512) has motel units $60 double, $50 single, backpackers $11 p.p.
Mataranka Roadside Shell (ph. 08 8975 4571) has motel units from $53 single, $63 double and cabins $63; caravan sites $5 p.p. with $4 extra for power. Pets welcome.
The Mobil Service Station (ph 08 8975 4761) has powered caravan sites $10, unpowered sites $2 p.p.
Clearwater Canoe Camp (see under *Elsey National Park*).

EATING OUT

Territory Manor features open-air/indoor dining, and meals (barramundi, buffalo, beef) from around $20 at their licensed restaurant.
Old Elsey Inn: the colourful old pub serves good value counter meals (seafood, roasts, steaks - $8-$12). A truckies breakfast is also of unbelievable generosity ($8).

Kellys home-made pies are legendary for their superb quality.
Mataranka Homestead (see separate listing).

SERVICES AND FACILITIES

Hotel, restaurant, take-away food, supermarket (open 7 days),
store, 3 fuel outlets (all fuels including autogas), camping gas, oil,
vehicle repairs and towing (Willy's Auto, ph 08 8975 4583), health
centre, police station, post office and airstrip. Credit cards widely
accepted and EFTPOS facilities available at most establishments.

MATARANKA HOMESTEAD TOURIST RESORT

LOCATION

On the Waterhouse River, abutting Elsey National Park, 9km (5
miles) east of Mataranka Township.

CHARACTERISTICS

Set amidst tropical woodlands and bounded by the rainforest lined
Waterhouse River, this delightfully treed and grassed resort is an
ideal spot to relax and 'take the waters' of the thermal pool. Also,
it's a good base from which to explore some magnificent Roper
River scenery, or try some barra fishing.

Excellent campsites, an open tropical bar and restaurant, casual
family oriented atmosphere, a sense of history, wildlife, including
freshwater crocodiles, and plenty of activities, are the major features
offered. The homestead was purchased and established as a resort
after World War II by ex-serviceman H.V. Smith, who, during his
wartime service, had recognised its enormous tourist potential.

ATTRACTIONS

Mataranka Thermal Springs (Elsey National Park). Located next
to the homestead, the natural thermal spring and pool is
surrounded by a shady tract of tropical rainforest. It's a beautiful
place for a relaxing swim and, while the therapeutic powers of the

waters are debatable, it's still an invigorating experience. The waters rise crystal clear from the deep Rainbow Spring at a rate of 16,495 litres per minute, or 23,753,945 litres (5 million gallons) a day, and maintain a constant temperature of 34C (93F). In the pool, you may see any one of four species of tortoise (Elseya spp. and Chelodina spp), as well as a variety of small fish.

Fringing the pool are the pandanus (Pandanus aquaticus and P. spiralis), cabbage tree palms (Livistona sp. and near relatives of the ancient palms in the Red Centre's Finke Gorge), paper-barks (Melaleuca spp) and yellow passionfruit (Passiflora foetida).

Birdlife is plentiful, including the colourful and noisy red-tailed black cockatoo (Calyptorhynchus magnificus), sulphur-crested cockatoo (Cacatua galerita), rainbow lorikeet (Trichoglossus haematodus), azure kingfisher (Alcyone azurea) and blue-winged kookaburra (Dacelo leachii). Thousands of black fruit bats, or flying foxes, hang from the palms and use their wings as a fan to keep cool. They darken the sky in the evening as they swarm off to feed.

The weir was constructed during World War II to provide recreational facilities for soldiers stationed in the area, and its original 'R and R' function is little changed today, as visitors use the homestead and pool as a few days' resting place before resuming their journey up or down 'The Track'.

Elsey Homestead Replica. Located at the entrance to the resort, the replica houses a fascinating pictorial, photographic and written display that provides an insight into early droving days and cattle station life at The Elsey. Open all day. Nearby are Aboriginal Gunyas, built with the advice of the elders from the local Yangman/Mangari Clan. Free, historic homestead walking tours operate daily from May to September. During the tourist season, theres some live country and western music every night.

ACTIVITIES

Bush walks, swimming (thermal pool and Stevies hole), fishing (barramundi, bream, catfish, sleepy cod, freshwater crayfish on the Roper and Little Roper Rivers), canoeing (hire from *Waterhouse River Jetty*), bird watching, croc spotting, tours, horse riding, helicopter and scenic flights.

ACCOMMODATION

Motel - $65 single, $77 double. Family rooms and cabins from $82; budget $60 twin share. Backpacker $16 per person; $30 double.
Caravan Park - powered sites $18 x 2, unpowered sites $14 x 2. Sites shaded, grassed; some secluded waterfront sites. Pets are not allowed.

SERVICES AND FACILITIES

Bar, restaurant (steaks, buffalo, barramundi - main course around $17), take-away food, ice, general store, souvenirs, hire canoes, fuel (LP), oil, camping gas, picnic/shaded/BBQ areas (gas operated), wood BBQs (BYO wood), and airstrip (1000m, south-west approach). *Open 6am-midnight*, daily, credit cards accepted, EFTPOS facility, ph (08) 8975 4544.

PINE CREEK

Population 560

LOCATION

On the Stuart Highway, 226km (140 miles) south of Darwin, and 113km (70 miles) north of Katherine.

CHARACTERISTICS

Pine Creek is a relatively unspoilt small town in an undulating landscape setting and retains strong reminders of its frantic gold rush origins. Relics of old mine workings, and a number of original buildings, make Pine Creek a significant architectural and historic site that is well worth visiting. Gold mining by large companies, tourism, pastoral and horticultural activities, sustain a thriving community today.

HISTORY

Overland Telegraph Line builders first unearthed gold here in 1870 when digging holes for the line's construction. It triggered a gold rush. A telegraph office was opened in 1874, and in the same year, Europeans decided to import Chinese coolies to do the tough, physical work under the oppressive climatic conditions. Alluvial gold discoveries in 1877 resulted in a great influx of Chinese, so that by the 1880s, Pine Creek resembled more of a Chinatown than a European settlement. At this time, the Chinese population was about 1500, while Europeans numbered 100. Ping Que was the most astute. He not only held many mining leases, he also owned many stores and butcher's shops. European fear of Chinese dominance led to laws being passed in 1888, forbidding entry of Chinese into the Northern Territory (laws later rescinded).

In 1888, the township was officially named Playford; its present name is derived from the stands of pines that used to grow along the creek. The railway linking the town to Palmerston (Darwin) was completed in 1889. By 1905, the town consisted of a collection of galvanised iron buildings; railway station which incorporated the post office and telegraph station; police station; hotel; houses; and business premises, as well as tin shanties and Aboriginal bark humpies.

A period of stagnation occurred between the two world wars, and revitalisation came in the 1960s and 1970s with the development of short-lived uranium and iron ore mining ventures. Renewed interest in gold mining, and the advent of tourism provide a sound economic base for the town today.

ATTRACTIONS

The Repeater Station. Constructed at Burrundie in 1888, this iron building was dismantled and re-erected here in 1913. It is the oldest surviving pre-fabricated structure in the Territory, and is now owned by the National Trust. *The Pine Creek Museum* is housed here. It's located on Railway Terrace.

Playford Club Hotel. Opened in 1889, it is the earliest example of a Territory galvanised iron pub still surviving. Reference is made to it in Mrs Aeneas Gunn's book *We of the Never Never* - on their way to Elsey Station in 1902, the Gunns stayed here. It is now a private residence, located on Main Terrace.

Railway Precinct. Built in 1888-89, it is of historic and architectural interest, and includes the station, goods shed, employees' residences, weighbridge, crane, and water tank. The railway closed in 1976. Adjacent is a Miners Park with an interesting array of relic mining equipment. Its location is on Main Terrace.

Historic Sites. A number of sites of historic significance have been identified in the area by the National Trust as well as a few other heritage buildings including the old bakery. Sites include old Chinese workings and mine shafts. The National Trust has devised a Heritage Trail for visitors - guides are available from the Museum.

Mary River. Pine Creek is also the southern gateway to Kakadu National Park, via the Kakadu Highway. Locals go to the picturesque Mary River where fishing is one of the main activities (barramundi, black bream, catfish).

Other features of interest include the Copperfield Recreation Reserve, Mine Lookout, Miners Park, Water Gardens and Gun Alley Gold Mine where you can pan for gold, ph (08) 8976 1221.

EVENTS
The Pine Creek Races are held in late May. *The Pine Creek Goldrush Festival* celebrates the pioneering heritage of the town in a number of colourful events held in early May. *The Rodeo* is an action-packed event and includes country music, stalls and foods. It's held in June.

ACCOMMODATION
All establishments accept credit cards and most have EFTPOS.
Boonrook Lodge offers air-conditioned hotel rooms from $68 - $162 in a rural setting 7kms south of the town on the Stuart Highway. Facilities include an a la carte restaurant and lounge bar,

2 swimming pools and spa and horse-riding is available including overnight camps. For further details, ph (08) 8976 1232.

Diggers Rest Motel, has self-contained, air-conditioned cabins, $60 single, $70 for two persons and $75 for 3-5 persons, ph (08) 8976 1442.

Pine Creek Hotel/Motel has rooms from $69 single, $79 double, twin $84, triple $89. The hotel has a dining room with steak and seafood emphasis in its good value menu offering. There are also two rooms for disabled guests and the bar has pokies, ph (08) 8976 1288.

BP Service Station offers single rooms $36, double $48. Camping; powered sites $18x2, unpowered $12x2. Sites are grassed, pets allowed, dogs leashed. The service station also sells takeaway food. Ph (08) 8976 1217.

Lazy Lizard Tourist Park features a roadhouse, tavern, restaurant and has camping facilities - powered sites $17x2, unpowered $13x2. Facilities include swimming pool and BBQ area. Pets allowed, dogs leashed, ph (08) 8976 1244.

SERVICES AND FACILITIES

Police station, medical centre, post office, hotel, church (used by all denominations), supermarket and general store, bank agency (Commonwealth at Post Office), all fuels, repairs and spares, towing service and a good selection of eating out places (hotel and accommodation places). Credit cards are widely accepted and most establishments have EFTPOS.

ROPER BAR

Population 11

LOCATION

On the Roper Highway, 185km (115 miles) east of the Stuart Highway, from the turn-off just south of Mataranka.

CHARACTERISTICS

Glyn and Veronica run the store/motel at this attractive tropical outpost on the Roper River, called simply "The Roper" by the locals (station people). The area is rich in exploration and pastoral history, and it is a popular boating and fishing spot for the prized barramundi. But, be careful as both salt-water and freshwater crocodiles inhabit the waters. The store is also the last fuel stop for those heading down to Borroloola. It should be noted that the store is not a pub and does not sell any alcoholic beverages. If you travel this way, best advice is to bring your own.

HISTORY

Its European discoverer was Leichhardt and his party in 1845, and the river and bar were named after one of the expedition members, John Roper. Described as *"a tall, vague, hungry-looking man"*, Friedrich Wilhelm Ludwig Leichhardt arrived in Australia in 1841 and succeeded in the greatest overland expedition in the country's history - an epic 5000km (3100 miles) trek from near Brisbane to Port Essington via the Gulf of Carpentaria and Arnhem Land. The party discovered and crossed the Roper on October 19, 1845. In an area where fruit bats were abundant and easily caught, Leichhardt tossed some into the stew-pot and, after eating them, commented, *"... a little strong"*! While he did not have a university degree, Leichhardt was an expert naturalist, and his botanical skills enabled the party to 'graze' well on the hazardous trip. It could even be said that he was Australia's original European 'bush tucker man'! Leichhardt disappeared in an expedition in 1848 - it is thought he perished in the Simpson Desert fringes. His favourable pastoral-potential reports led to the establishment of large cattle runs in the Roper region in later years.

The Roper River was part of the main supply route for the construction of northern sections of the Overland Telegraph Line; the Bar marks the navigable point of the river, originally known as Leichhardt's Crossing, and the rock bar was constructed in the early 1900s.

ATTRACTIONS

Barramundi fishing. Best times are just after the Wet (April, May), and when they are 'running', the causeway is a popular spot. Other attractions are its remoteness, crocodiles, flora and fauna.

Glyn and Veronica offer individualised tours, and they can tell you much more about the area's history and landscape.

HOW TO GET THERE

By road, it is sealed for 140km (87 miles); the last 45km (28 miles) is a formed gravel surface suitable for conventional vehicles. From Roper Bar to Borroloola local advice is 4WD for the often rough road.

ACCOMMODATION

Motel - $35 single, $45 double.

A **camping/caravan park** with unpowered sites, $5.00 per person. Shaded, grassed sites, pets allowed, dogs leashed.

SERVICES AND FACILITIES

The general store is well provisioned, take-away food, ice, Commonwealth Bank agency, information, boat ramp, airstrip, fuel (LP, ULP, diesel), camping gas. Credit cards accepted, EFTPOS facility, *open daily 9am-7pm*, ph (08) 8975 4636.

TIMBER CREEK

Population 100

LOCATION

On the Victoria Highway, 285km (176 miles) south-west of Katherine, and 227km (141 miles) east of Kununurra.

CHARACTERISTICS

An historic settlement, consisting of two road houses, caravan park, old police station/museum, police station, and youth hostel, nestles quietly near the Victoria River in an open woodland setting at the base of the Newcastle Range foothills. The Ngaringman people live nearby in four camps. Bougainvillea adds a splash of colour to the dry township, and there are some idyllic tropical tracts along the river for fishing, but watch out for crocodiles. Timber Creek is in the heart of legendary cattle country, while to the south is the broad expanse of Gregory National Park.

HISTORY

The HMS *Beagle* sailed some 200km (124 miles) up the river, reaching a point on November 3, 1839 that was to become the Victoria River Depot. The river was named in honour of Queen Victoria, and explorer Augustus Gregory is credited with naming the township. In 1855, the expedition's ship, the *Tom Tough* was severely damaged when grounded on one of the river's many shoals, and timber found locally to repair the damage prompted the name Timber Creek. Gregory later went on to explore much of the Victoria River region, and his favourable reports led to the establishment of great pastoral holdings and European settlement.

The vast 41,155 sq km (15,638 sq miles) Victoria River Downs Cattle Station was the largest of the first leases granted in the early 1880s (see under *Victoria River Downs* in Barkly Region). Nat 'Bluey' Buchanan overlanded the first cattle for the station from Queensland, in an epic drove lasting many months (see *Newcastle Waters* listing, Barkly Region for an outline on drovers).

A police station was established in 1898 at Timber Creek in response to hostile Aborigines, and a general feeling of mistrust existed between the races. M.C. O'Keefe, along with Aboriginal trackers, were the first police here. Today, two police officers serve an area about the size of Tasmania! Horses were the only transport, and these were busy times for officers in dealing with murders, cattle killing and racial conflicts. The original 'bough hut' station was replaced in 1908 with a more solid structure that today houses the museum.

The Victoria River Depot was established in 1891 at the furthest navigable spot along the river, where it functioned as a port for cattle station supplies. A store also made it a focal point for trade and social activity, and the Depot served the region until 1940. The first roadhouses were established at Timber Creek in the 1950s.

ATTRACTIONS

Police Station Museum. Houses reminders of the police remount station days, and staff give informal accounts of events.

Victoria River Depot. The old port that is also an Historical Reserve. About 8km (4 miles) from the town.

Gregory's Tree Historical Reserve. The explorer's initials are carved on a boab tree near the site where their ship was damaged. It's located west of the town.

Gregory National Park. The park is situated in a transition zone between tropical and semi-arid environments. It protects a wide range of flora and fauna including rare species of plants and animals, and birdlife that is prolific. The park covers an area of approximately 12,800 sq km (8000 sq miles), encompassing the rugged Victoria River district terrain. The main part of the park is accessible from Timber Creek. The eastern portion surrounds the Victoria River Crossing settlement, and features the river and gorge which cut through some spectacular sandstone formations. The sheer gorge walls glow vividly at the rise and set of sun.

Throughout the area are the traces of Aboriginal culture, European exploration and pastoral settlement.

A number of 4WD tracks have been established within the Park, but other roads are accessible by conventional vehicles. Towing trailers or caravans is not recommended. All roads, including the Victoria Highway may be impassable during the Wet Season. Road conditions can be obtained from the Timber Creek Ranger Station on (08) 8975 0888.

Permits are required if you are intending to go on an extended bushwalk within the Park. Check with the Ranger Station.

Camping areas have been established throughout the Park, with facilities that include BBQ, picnic tables and pit toilets. A nominal camping fee applies.

Activities include boating, canoeing, fishing (barramundi) and walking. Facilities are marked on the map, and boat owners

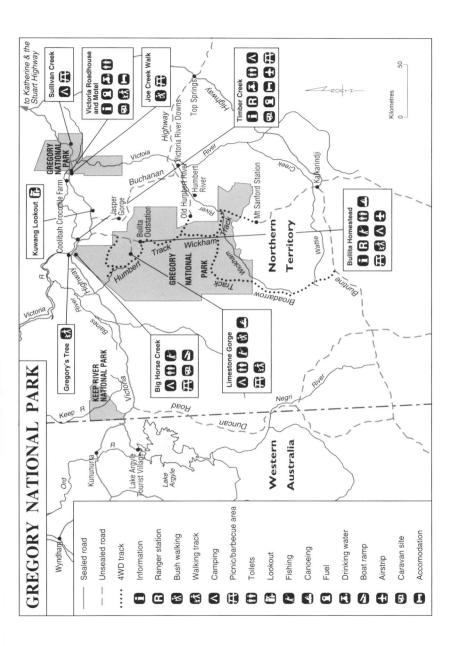

GREGORY NATIONAL PARK

Map legend:

- Sealed road
- Unsealed road
- 4WD track
- Information
- Ranger station
- Bush walking
- Walking track
- Camping
- Picnic/barbecue area
- Toilets
- Lookout
- Fishing
- Canoeing
- Fuel
- Drinking water
- Boat ramp
- Airstrip
- Caravan site
- Accomodation

Locations:

Sullivan Creek

Victoria Roadhouse and Motel

Joe Creek Walk

Timber Creek

Kuwang Lookout

Bullita Homestead

Gregory's Tree

Big Horse Creek

Limestone Gorge

GREGORY NATIONAL PARK

KEEP RIVER NATIONAL PARK

Northern Territory

Western Australia

Kilometres 0 — 50

to Katherine & the Stuart Highway

should note that the sluggish waters of the Dry season become raging torrents during the Wet.

Do not swim in any natural waterways as the Victoria River and its tributaries are the home of the salt-water and freshwater crocodiles.

EVENTS

Timber Creek Races and Campdraft. The colourful event is held in early September. *The KGFC Big Horse Creek Barra Classic* is a family fishing competition with prizes for biggest barramundi. It's held in early May.

TOURS

The **Gregory Explorer and Max's Victoria River Boat Tours** run cruises on the Victoria River and explore wildlife, history and geography in the course of these adventure trips. Ph (08) 8975 0850 for details.

ACCOMMODATION

The Timber Creek Hotel offers a range of room types - motel $70, basic rooms $30, self contained cabins $65, dormitory style sleeping 3-8 persons from $50.

The hotels **Circle F Caravan Park** has powered sites $16x2; unpowered $7.50. The hotel/caravan park complex has a swimming pool, shaded sites, pets allowed, dogs leashed. It's open daily, ph (08) 8975 0722.

The Wayside Inn has motel rooms from $79; budget rooms $55 x3 and $48x2. Powered camp sites $12, unpowered $4 p.p. The complex has a swimming pool, shaded sites, pets allowed, dogs leashed. It's open daily, ph (08) 8975 0732.

SERVICES AND FACILITIES

Timber Creek has a Police station, post office, medical clinic, restaurants (hotels), two supermarkets, two service stations (all fuels, 24 hours, mechanical repairs), takeaway food, ice, souvenirs, artifacts and hire boats. There's an airfield (scenic flights), tours, poker machines (Wayside Inn), boat ramp, marine and fishing services. Credit cards widely accepted, EFTPOS at both accommodation establishments.

UMBRAWARRA GORGE NATURE PARK

972ha (2400 acres)

LOCATION
25km (15 miles) south-west of Pine Creek.

CHARACTERISTICS
Rugged gorge scenery and a series of pools make Umbrawarra an idyllic location for bush camping. Aboriginal art sites add to the character of the Gorge area, where bush walking, swimming and photography are the main activities. A narrow walking track winds through the steep-sided gorge for about a kilometre after which the rest of the gorge can only be reached by wading, swimming and rock hopping. Along the way Aboriginal art can be seen on the rock walls and wildlife includes the short-eared Rock Wallaby, butterflies, native fish and plenty of birds. A climb up the cliffs is rewarding for magnificent views over this isolated nature park. The car park located near the park entrance was the site of a tin mine in the early 1900s.

HOW TO GET THERE
About 3km south of Pine Creek, an unsealed road turns south-west off the Stuart Highway. The 22km of road can become dusty and corrugated and it has steep dips and dry creek crossings. The park can be reached by all vehicles in the dry season (May-September), but in the Wet (October-April), after rain, the road is often closed. It is not recommended that caravans be brought into the park.

FACILITIES
Camping is allowed. Facilities include picnic, wood barbecues and toilet. No animals are allowed. A camping fee of $1 p.p. ($3 family) should be deposited into the honesty box. No water is provided at the Park.

VICTORIA RIVER CROSSING

Population 5

LOCATION

On the Victoria Highway, 196km (121 miles) west of Katherine.

CHARACTERISTICS

The settlement consists of the Victoria River Roadhouse which is attractively sited by the crossing and gorge tract of the Victoria River. Rugged sandstone cliff faces and flat-topped ranges provide an impressive backdrop to what has been described as the 'flashiest pub in the scrub'. It's a delightful camping spot, frequented sometimes by wild brolgas. Attractions include the *Gregory National Park*, the eastern segment of which surrounds the roadhouse, and features the scenic Victoria River Gorge and sandstone ranges. It's thought that their unusual shapes have been the result of massive erosion of an uplifted, ancient marine bed. The gorge scenery is best seen by boat. (Refer to *Timber Creek* listing for outline of Gregory National Park.) Salt-water and freshwater crocodiles inhabit waters of the Victoria river, so swimming is not advisable. Barramundi and bream fishing are popular river pursuits. The roadhouse also runs gorge cruises.

ACCOMMODATION

The **roadhouse** offers budget rooms $25 single; motel rooms $40 single, $60 double.

Campsites - powered $15x2, unpowered $3 p.p Sites are grassed and shaded, pets allowed, dogs leashed.

SERVICES AND FACILITIES

General store, dining room (mixed grills $14), bar, take-away food, ice, artifacts, souvenirs, showers for travellers ($2), picnic/BBQ area, tourist information, airstrip, all fuels. Credit cards accepted, EFTPOS facility, *open daily 7am-11pm*, ph (08) 8975 0744.

The Kimberley Region, Western Australia

See map inside back cover.

CHARACTERISTICS

The least unexploited frontier of Australian wilderness occupies the ancient lands behind the great swirl of the north-west coast of the continent. It covers 421,450 sq km (162,680 sq miles), or one sixth of Western Australia's total area - a size which is twice that of Great Britain. Named because of its similarity to its counterpart in South Africa, the images evoked do not disappoint; nor do the grand-sounding names of the inlets and bays, ranges and gorges.

A remote region that is little known in the broader Australian sense, the Kimberley is a land of spectacular contrasts. The coast is deeply indented with numerous gulfs, in which the tides have a variation of up to 10 metres. Knots of rugged ranges, deep gorges, plateau country, sandstone massifs, and some rich red plains, give the landscape a unique, savage beauty. The savannah-like open woodland and tall grasslands present some real safari country.

The Kimberley is mainly a cattle domain, with nearly a hundred leases occupying over half its area. The people who work the huge one-million-acre-plus runs are renowned for their indomitable spirit and adventurous lifestyle. While a sparsely populated area, the region has a vibrant economy based on the pastoral, agricultural, mining and tourist industries. Towns with colourful pasts provide interesting discoveries for the adventurous and curious.

The Kimberley has infinite variety, plenty of characters, and above all, the stunning Purnululu landforms (Bungle Bungle) and the memorable fiery-red of the Cockburn Range ramparts at sunset.

CLIMATE

The Kimberley experiences two seasons - the Wet and the Dry - but there are some differences when compared to the Top End region of the Northern Territory. Here the Wet comes a bit later, and rainfall is not so high, although temperatures can be searing. Geographical differences are noticeable, too. The northern towns generally have higher maximum temperatures, and humidity is high throughout the summer period, when the monsoons arrive. The exception is Broome, where the climate is tempered and best described as balmy. Occasional tropical cyclones form off the north-west coast during this time.

The winter brings long, dry, rainless days and loads of sunshine. For most, this is the ideal time to visit, but the Wet or green season brings a lushness to the landscape that is also worth seeing. Rivers rise and recede quickly and are not the hazards they were when roads were tracks. The climate table for Broome indicates patterns.

FLORA AND FAUNA

A broad range of tropical vegetation is in evidence, and specialist flora is found in the mangrove belt along the sheltered coastline, amongst the sandstone gorges of the King Leopolds, and in the vine thickets of the Mitchell Plateau. A notable difference from other areas of the Outback is the Pindan, a complex flora association of acacias, eucalypts and the boab tree. The baobab (shortened to boab) in Australia is peculiar to the Kimberley and Ord-Victoria regions (a few grow elsewhere in the Northern Territory), has an immense bottle-shaped trunk, and reaches a height of 25m (82 ft). It should not be confused with the

Queensland bottle tree. It also grows in South Africa, and it is thought seeds may have washed up thousands of years ago to produce the species here.

Details of the prolific and colourful birdlife, and other wildlife, are included in the listings for various places.

HAZARDS

Salt-water crocodiles inhabit coastal and inland waterways, and the only safe coastal swimming is around Broome (refer to *Top End Region Introduction* for information on crocodiles). The lethal fish-eating cone shell is another hazard (see *Broome* listing for details). Tides are enormous - up to 10m (over 30 ft) - and the navigation of northern inlets is definitely dicey. Check tide charts and seek advice if sailing these waters, or fishing along the coast. Fire in the sweeping savannah landscapes can cause enormous damage. Be aware of the danger, highlighted dramatically when 4 million hectares (9,880,000 acres) of the Mitchell Plateau was razed by a 5-month-long fire in 1988.

High temperatures, often searing in places, require sensible precautions and plenty of compensatory fluid intake, particularly on walks in areas like the Purnululu National Park (Bungle Bungle).

TOURING SUGGESTIONS

Kununurra is a good base for East Kimberley exploration, and allows a taste of the Gibb River Road attractions at Jacks Waterhole, Home Valley and El Questro Stations.

For the adventurous and self-sufficient, the Kimberley offers much from the Purnululu (Bungle Bungle) to the Mitchell Plateau country. This is 4WD experience at its best. Highly recommended too is a flight over Purnululu, which offers not only rare views of the range, but also the raw beauty of the Kimberley landscape. The gorges of the Western Kimberley are a must, and Broome and Derby should not be missed. Whichever way you come, both the East and West Kimberley have much to offer.

PLACES AND ATTRACTIONS

BROOME

Population 10,500

LOCATION

On the north-west coast, on Roebuck Bay, 220km (136 miles) south-west of Derby, and 610km (379 miles) north-east of Port Hedland.

CHARACTERISTICS

This delightful, tropical Nor'West town sits astride a peninsula and is bounded by the turquoise, mangrove-fringed coast of Roebuck Bay on one side, while the sweep of Cable Beach and the Indian Ocean bound the other. It has had a colourful past as the former pearling capital of the world, has been bombed by the Japanese, and blasted by several cyclones. Broad-leafed tropical vegetation, the fragrance of frangipani, tropical architecture, the old corrugated iron and timber Chinatown, the jetty area, and the beautiful white sands of Cable Beach, are characteristics of this easy-going town.

Once a wild boom town, Broome has a lively economy today, based on tourism, pearling, meat processing, fishing, agriculture and pastoral activities, and mining exploration.

The rapidly growing centre is a tourist mecca in the winter season, partly because it has the only safe swimming beach in the Kimberley, and also for its romantic atmosphere and balmy climate.

HISTORY

The first authenticated European visit was by William Dampier in 1699, and he named the bay after his ship, the HMS *Roebuck*. There is some evidence that the Portuguese may have visited Napier Bay in the 1500s, and likely early visitors were Malays and other Asians on turtle, dugong and oyster shell collecting voyages.

The settlement was named after Sir Frederick Napier Broome, the then Governor of Western Australia, in 1883. Pearling was the catalyst for the boom in the early 1900s, when Broome became the undisputed pearling capital of the world, with a fleet of nearly 400

BROOME

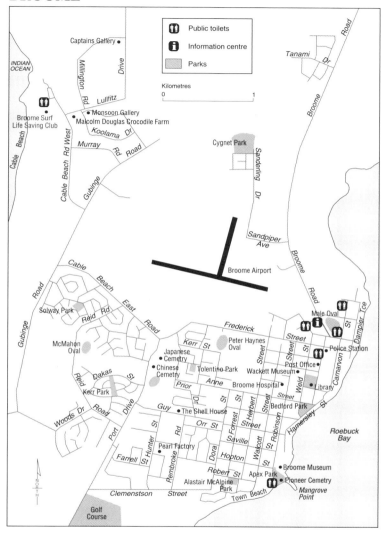

luggers. While natural pearls were prized, the real profit was in collecting pearl shells for 'mother of pearl'. Broome became the world's leading supplier of the shell. World markets collapsed in 1914, particularly when the first synthetic buttons appeared on the market. Despite this, the demand for cultured pearls sustained a much smaller but viable industry. In 1956, a pearl farm was established at Kuri Bay, further north, and luggers supplied live shells for 'seeding'.

Broome has seen its fair share of natural disasters: cyclones of 1893, 1908 and 1910 resulted in the loss of many lives, and the sinking of a number of luggers. Seventy people were killed by Japanese bombing raids in 1942. There are many reminders of its colourful past, all of which contribute to the unique character of this isolated Kimberley town.

INFORMATION

There is a very active **Broome Tourist Bureau**, located on the corner of Bagot Road and Great Northern Highway. Open daily, Christmas and Good Friday excepted. Hours - April to October, Mon-Fri 8.00am to 5.00pm, Sat and Sun 9.00am - 4.00pm; November to March, same hours Mon-Fri, Sat 9.00am - 1.00pm and Sun 9.00am - 12.00pm; ph (08) 9192 2222.

The **Shire of Broome** produces an excellent Community Information booklet, while the **Tourist Bureau** has a wealth of local literature.

ATTRACTIONS

Chinatown. Originally a mixture of pearling sheds, Japanese boarding houses, Chinese eating houses, billiard saloons and the Pearlers' Rest Hotel, formed the town's commercial centre. Pearling houses still operate, with many sheds converted into retail pearl and shell centres. It is a colourful area of town, with interesting shops, and lots to see, including the world's oldest operating open-air theatre, Sun Pictures, ph (08) 9192 1677, where current movies are shown seven nights a week, and kiosk facilities are available.

Historical Museum. Located in Saville Street, it houses a display of pearling history and relics, including diving gear. Admission is $2 adults, 50c children.

Pearl Shell and Pearls. Shell displays, pearls and curios can be seen at the *Historical Museum*; *Shell House*, in Guy Street; *Paspaley Pearling Co* in Short Street; *Broome Pearls*, and *Linneys Pearls* in Dampier Terrace; and *Anastasia's Pearl Gallery* in Carnarvon Street. Pearls and the like may be purchased from some of these places.

Captain Gregory's House. Captain Gregory built the largest and most profitable pearling enterprise in the town. The house, now in Carnarvon Street, has been restored, and is part of *Matso's Gallery and Cafe*.

Anglican Church. Known as the *Little White Church*, and built in 1903, it features a mother of pearl decorated chancel, dedicated to divers who lost their lives in the 1908 cyclone.

Streeters Jetty. Built in 1879, when 400 pearl luggers served the pearling industry. Today there are only three or four.

Court House. On the corner of Hamersley and Frederick Streets, and featuring an unusual architectural design. It was the Broome telegraph station for the telegraph cable from Banjuwangi in the Dutch East Indies to Perth in 1889.

Library. In the *Shire Gardens* on Hamersley Street, it is housed in a building that reflects the charm of early Broome architecture.

Matso's Store and Broome Brewery. The old *Union Bank* building, now located on the corner of Hamersley and Anne Streets, has been moved twice in its history; first by Sam Male and then again in 1986 when it was relocated and renovated. It now houses *Matso's Art Gallery*, and the only boutique brewery in the Kimberley.

Flying Boats. At Roebuck Bay at extremely low tides, several wrecks of Allied (Dutch Dornier) flying boats lie half-submerged - the result of a Japanese air raid in 1942. Care should be taken and protective footwear worn.

Japanese Cemetery. Located in Port Drive are the graves of Japanese pearlers, the earliest of which date from the 1890s.

Pioneer Cemetery. Near the old jetty is the resting place of early pioneers.

Broome Heritage Trail. For finer details of this 2km town walk which features buildings and sites of historic interest, check with the Tourist Bureau.

Raou Broome Bird Observatory. Established in 1988 for research and recreational purposes, it features 247 different species of birds, and thousands of waders can be seen between October and April. The Observatory has no caged birds. Located in Crab Creek Road, off Great Northern Highway, 18km south-east of Broome.

Malcolm Douglas Broome Crocodile Park, Cable Beach Road, ph (08) 9192 1489. It is one of the few crocodile parks in WA, with over 500 reptiles (freshwater, salt-water and the exotic alligator). Open daily April-Oct 10am-5pm, with feeding tours at 3pm. Check with the Tourist Bureau for opening times Nov-April. *Admission is $10 adults, $5 children, $25 family, and $8 seniors.*

Cable Beach. A 22km (14 miles) white beach with beautiful waters, where you can swim safely and see magnificent sunsets.

Staircase to the Moon. This romantic phenomenon can be viewed from between the *Mangrove Hotel* and *Seaview Shopping Centre*, as the moon rises after dark. This coincides with the low-water spring tide, and is the result of moonlight reflected from the ocean bed. Check with the Tourist Bureau.

Staircase Markets. Evening markets are held at *Town Beach* on the nights when the full moon and very low tides create the optical illusion of a staircase reaching to the moon. It features local fare, crafts and talented local entertainers. Dates are available at the Tourist Bureau.

Dinosaur Tracks. Beautifully coloured and sculptured sandstone cliffs surround the area where footprints of a dinosaur, made 130 million years ago, are revealed at extremely low tides at *Gantheaume Point*. Cement casts of it are displayed near the beacon on the cliff.

Anastasia's Pool. A small man-made rock pool fills at high tide, and is believed to have been gouged out by a former lighthouse occupant for his crippled wife named Anastasia. Located at Gantheaume Point.

Deepwater Port. At Entrance Point, deepwater anchorage for overseas ships features a 800m long jetty. There is a beach where you can swim and picnic.

Buccaneer Rock. In Roebuck Bay, at the entrance to Dampier Creek, is a beacon and memorial to William Dampier - a colourful navigator.

Willie Creek Pearl Farm, Willie Creek, about 35km (22 miles) north of Broome. The farm produces south sea cultured pearls from the silver-lipped oyster Pinotada Maxima. Tours are offered which include the history of the pearling industry, a demonstration of seeding live half pearl shell, and a video of divers collecting shells. Coach tours cost $39, or self-drive $17.50 p.p. Check with the Tourist Bureau for tour times.

Swimming. *Cable Beach* for surfing; *Riddell Beach*; *Town Beach*; and *Gantheaume Point*.

Wildlife. The coastal location is habitat to a number of water birds, including great knots, tattlers, large sand plovers, Mongolian plovers, terek sandpipers, red knots, ruddy turnstones, curlew sandpipers, and red-necked stints, as well as migratory birds from Siberia, Malaysia, Indonesia and south of Australia. Land-based wildlife includes euros, wallabies, goannas and snakes. There is a great variety of birds - bustard or Australian turkey, brolgas, parrots, finches, eagles, falcons and kites can be seen.

Riddell Beach. Fortress-shaped rocks, coral reef and rock pools.

Fishing. Recreation fishing requires a licence. Check with the Fisheries Department in Broome. Fishing is good all year. Species include - threadfin salmon, trevally, queenfish, skipjack, catfish, mulloway, barracuda or Spanish mackerel, whiting, flathead, barramundi and mud crabs. The jetty is a popular spot, and most waters are good places. Check with locals or the Fisheries Department.

TOURS

A wide range of tours of varying duration are available. These include Bush Walks and Natural History Tours, Astronomy, Wildlife, Camel treks, Aboriginal Art and Culture, Scenic Air Tours, Day Adventure Tours, Fishing and Pearl Farm Tours, extended boat and yacht cruises and 4WD safaris.

Check with the Tourist Bureau for details of these excellent offerings which allow unique opportunities to explore magnificent wilderness coast and inland areas.

EVENTS

Shinju Matsuri (Festival of The Pearl): an annual event held August/September, the traditional time of various Asian celebrations. It features 10 days of parades, performing arts, fairs and exhibitions.

Mango Festival: celebrates the ripening of the mango fruit, and is held in November-December. Events include Mardi Gras, mango tasting and the "Great Chefs at Broome Mango Cook-off".

Other events include a colourful *Race Round*, culminating in the Broome Cup in July; Fishing Tournaments (*Sailfish Fly Rod Challenge* in July and *Broome Game Fishing Tournament* in August/September); the *Fringe Arts Festival* in June and the *Rotary Dragon Boat Classic* in April.

HAZARDS

Tides. Tidal range is extreme. Boaties and other fishermen, in particular, should have tide charts. Equinox or King Tides occur twice per year (March-April, September-October) with variations of 9m (30ft) or more, on a 12.5 hour cycle. Contact the Tourist Bureau for information.

Cone Shells. These occur on local beaches, and must not be touched. Stings from these are traumatic, and can be lethal. Venom attacks the nervous system and causes pain and dizziness, and death can result from respiratory failure. Apply expired-air resuscitation, and seek urgent medical help. Wear protective footwear on rocky and mud flat beaches.

Coastwatch and sea safety planes patrol the coast daily.

To avoid the discomfort of ***mosquito bites*** (October-March), apply insect repellent. Campers are advised to use mosquito candles or coils. Best advice is to cover exposed skin at dawn and dusk for protection. *Sandflies* can be annoying too, on high tides, and the same prevention methods are applicable.

HOW TO GET THERE

By Air: daily flights (Ansett and Airlink) from Perth and Darwin, and other states.

By Coach: Greyhound-Pioneer operates regular express services from Darwin and Perth.

By Road: Broome is easily accessed by sealed road, 30km (19 miles) to the west of Highway 1.

ACCOMMODATION

The telephone area code is (08)

Hotels, Motels and Resorts.

Seasonal rates apply and all offer restaurants, bars and swimming pools.

Cable Beach International Resort. Cable Beach Road, ph 9192 0400 - offers luxury accommodation and a range of tariffs and packages from $225 at its beach front location.

Mangrove Hotel. Carnarvon Street, ph. 9192 1303 - has great Roebuck Bay views, with a number of room options from $120 for doubles.

Mercure Inn-Continental. Weld Street, ph 9192 1002 - a modern establishment with rates from $105 for doubles.

Palms Resort. Hopton Street, ph 9192 1898 - is set in 6 acres of tropical gardens and offers studios to apartments from $106-$224.

Roebuck Bay Hotel Motel. Carnarvon Street, ph 9192 1221 - offers good, honest accommodation from $60 for doubles.

Budget/B&B
A number of options are available.

Broometime Lodge, Forrest Street, ph. 9193 5067 - from $40.

Broome's Last Resort, Bagot Street, ph 9193 5000 - bunkhouse from $13 p.p. Cable Beach Backpackers, Napier Terrace, ph 9193 5511, dormitory type from $15 p.p.

Roebuck Bay Back-Packers, Napier Terrace, ph 9192 1183 - dormitory type from $12 p.p., rooms from $40.

Kimberley Club, Frederick Street, ph 9192 3233 - dormitory from $14 p.p., rooms from $40.

Manse B&B, Anne Street, ph 9192 1162 - from $40 per night.

Nature/Wilderness Experience
Broome Bird Observatory, 25 kms from Broome, ph 9193 5600 - has rates from $22 and range accommodation style and campsites from $12.

Eco Beach, Cape Villaret (130 km from Broome), ph 9192 4844 - has single cabins, $100 p.p., and twin share $50 p.p.

Kooljaman, Cape Leveque (220 km from Broome, 4WD access only) ph 9192 4970 - has cabins from $70 for 2 people, family units from $60, beach shelters from $20 for 2 people and camping from $8 p.p.

Self-contained

There's a good selection available. Some examples are:

Broome Beach Resort, ph 9158 3300 - has one bedroom apartments from $90.

Palm Grove, Cable Beach, ph 9192 3336 - has two bedroom cabins from $85.

Tabbita Court, ph 9193 6026 - with apartments from $75.

Camping

Broome Caravan Park, Broome Road, ph 9192 1776 - has powered site, x 2 from $14, on-site vans from $35, and camping x 2 from $10.

Cable Beach Caravan Park, ph 9192 2066 - caravan sites from $18 x 2, camping from $15 x 2.

Roebuck Bay Caravan Park, ph 9192 1366 - van sites from $18 x 2, tent sites from $7 p.p., on-site vans from $40.

Tarangau Art Village Caravan Park, Cable Beach, ph 9193 5084 - van sites from $18 x 2, camping from $12 x 2, on-site vans from $29 x 2.

EATING OUT

The balmy climate and open-air eating go together well, and there is plenty of interesting food fare. There is a choice of take-away, and the ubiquitous fish and chips. Many restaurants have a seafood emphasis (not surprising), and pubs offer excellent, affordable meals. A wide variety of licensed and BYO restaurants provides plenty of reasonably-priced choices, particularly in the number of Asian establishments.

NIGHT LIFE

Centres mainly around the hotels and nightclubs. The Aboriginal community has the *Mamabulanjin*, where dances and social evenings are held. The *Sun Pictures Open Air Cinema* is also popular.

SERVICES AND FACILITIES

A full range of services and facilities are available. All shopping centres have supermarkets and many specialty shops. Credit cards are widely accepted.

A hospital and full medical services; full vehicle services including all fuel (super, ULP, diesel, autogas); banks (Challenge, Commonwealth and ANZ all with auto tellers); post office; police; churches (Anglican, Uniting, Catholic, Shiloh Pentecostal Church, Assembly of God); hire vehicles; bicycle hire from Chinatown Bike Hire; boat ramps; golf course; tennis; diving; and races, are some of the facilities.

Radio stations: ABC 6BE 675; 102.9 FM; Tourist Radio 88AM.

DERBY

Population 5000

LOCATION

On King Sound, 220km (136 miles) north-east of Broome.

CHARACTERISTICS

A pleasant sprawling town on a coast of mainly extensive mirage-producing mud flats, backed by a zone of open woodland and savannah vegetation. A wide main street, boabs, an interesting port area where there is an average annual tidal variation between 10m and 6m, and a friendly, comfortable town atmosphere, greet the visitor. It functions as an administrative centre, as well as serving a rich pastoral, agricultural and mining hinterland. It also services local Aboriginal communities, and a healthy tourist industry. While 42km (26 miles) north from the highway, a turn-off is well worth while for another dimension of the Kimberley and The Gateway to The Gorges.

HISTORY

Although William Dampier visited Cygnet Bay in 1688, it wasn't until after 1879 that the area was settled by Europeans. Explorer

Alexander Forrest led an overland expedition through the area in 1879, and filed favourable pastoral assessments. Before the Europeans came, these were the traditional lands of the Warwa people and, as in many other Outback places, initial contact between the two races resulted in conflict. Derby was no exception. During the 1880s, hostilities were experienced, and the story of the activities of the outlaw 'Pigeon' are well told in a Heritage Trail that starts in the town. This well-presented trail gives interesting historic insights into earlier, tougher Kimberley days. In 1942, an air raid by Japanese bombers gave the town a brief experience of war.

INFORMATION

Derby Tourist Bureau is located in Clarendon Street, ph (08) 9191 1426, open Mon-Fri 8.30am - 4.30pm, Weekends 9am - 1pm (Easter to September). Check here for tours and good tourist literature.

ATTRACTIONS

Pigeon Heritage Trail. Starts in the town and outlines the legendary events of the time.

Boab Prison Tree. With a girth of 14m (46 ft), this hollow boab was used as an overnight 'lockup'. It is a popular photography spot, located 7km south of the town.

Myall's Bore. Located near the Prison Tree, this lengthy cattle water-trough is said to be the longest in the world at 120m (394 ft). It was used to water stock in the days of the cattle droves and drovers.

Cultural Centre. This magnificent state library and art gallery is well worth visiting. Located in Clarendon Street. Alongside is a botanic garden.

The Old Port and Jetty. A long wooden jetty, wharf building, relic machinery, and old cattle races are evidence of much busier live cattle export days, when men had to sometimes round up strays in the mud at low tide.

Fishing. The old jetty is a popular spot. Salmon start to run in May, skipjack in June. Others include groper, barramundi (Nov-Jan), snapper, bream and catfish. Check with the local tourist centre, and beware of hazards - big tides and salt-water crocodiles. The Fitzroy River is good for barra.

Wildlife. An interesting variety includes kangaroo, wallaby, echidna (spiny anteater), dingo and flying fox. Reptiles include 5 species of python (including the tree snake), brown snake and death adder, gecko, skink, goanna, frill-necked lizard, and bungarra. Birdlife includes magpies, larks, honeyeaters, budgerigars, parrots, lorikeets, galahs, finches and wood swallowes. Kites, falcons, eagles and kestrels are the main birds of prey. They live generally in the Pindan - a complex vegetation association of acacias, eucalypts and the extraordinary boab tree.

Wharfinger's House. An historic house in Lock Street is now a museum and art gallery. Check at the tourist bureau.

Swimming. The public pool is the only safe place to swim in town. Estuarine crocodiles inhabit coastal areas and inland waters.

Outlying Attractions include *Windjana Gorge* and *Tunnel Creek National Parks* - these are listed separately.

TOURS
West Kimberley Tours, ph (08) 9193 1442, and *Bush Track Safaris*, ph (08) 9191 4644, are the local ground tour operators.
Boat tours are provided by *Buccaneer Sea Safaris*, ph (08) 9191 1991, and *Kimberley Thousand Island Charters*, ph (08) 9191 1851.
For scenic flights contact *Aerial Enterprises*, ph (08) 9191 1132, or *Derby Air Service*, ph (08) 9193 1375.
  Contact the Tourist Bureau for details of all tours.

EVENTS

The *Boab Festival* runs for two weeks in mid-July, with such activities as mud football, races, rodeo, mardi gras, country music, and arts and crafts. The *Country Music Festival* is also held in July. *Boxing Day Sports* feature cockroach and frog 'derbies'.

HOW TO GET THERE

By Air: Derby Airport has daily flights by **Skywest** to Broome, to connect with Ansett and Qantas.
By Coach: Daily services by Greyhound-Pioneer.
By Road: a sealed road from the main highway leads to the town.

ACCOMMODATION

The telephone area code is (08).
King Sound Resort Hotel, ph 9193 1044 - single $90, double $100, family $150; pool.
Boab Inn, ph 9191 1044 - budget from $50, double from $90; pool.
West Kimberley Lodge, ph 9191 1031 - rooms from $40, communal kitchen, pool.
Spinifex Hotel, ph 9191 1233 - rooms from $40, units $65 double.
Backpackers Aboriginal Hostel, ph 9191 1867 - from $12 p.p.,
Kimberley Entrance Caravan Park, ph 9193 1055 - powered sites from $16 for 2, unpowered sites from $13 for 2. Shaded, grassy sites. Pets allowed, dogs leashed.

EATING OUT

There is a good choice - **The Boab Inn**, **Derby Sportmen's Club**, A Chinese restaurant, **The King Sound Resort Hotel** (mains from $10), **Spinifex** and **Wharfs Restaurant**.

SERVICES AND FACILITIES

Most tourist needs are well catered for with EFTPOS facilities, and credit cards are widely accepted. It has a hospital, doctor, dentist, chemist, banks (ANZ, Bankwest, Commonwealth agency), police station, post office, supermarket, take-away food, ice, boat ramp, all vehicle services (fuel - LP, ULP, diesel, LPG for cars, camping gas, aviation gas) and repairs, churches (Anglican, Catholic, Uniting, Derby Community Church, Assemblies of God, Baptist Fellowship).

Hire vehicles - Avis, ph 9191 1357, and Budget, ph 9191 2044.

Recreational facilities include swimming pool, golf course, squash, tennis and bowls.

Radio stations: ABC 6DB 873; 107.5 FM.

DEVONIAN REEF NATIONAL PARKS

LOCATION

Near Fitzroy Crossing (Geike Gorge), extending in a north-westerly direction to near the Gibb River Road. Geike is 18km (11 miles) north-east of Fitzroy Crossing; Windjana Gorge is 145km (90 miles) north-west of Fitzroy Crossing and the same distance east of Derby; Tunnel Creek is 110km (68 miles) from Fitzroy Crossing and 180km (112 miles) from Derby. Check road conditions, as the unsealed surfaces can become corrugated.

THE PARKS

Geike Gorge (3135ha-7746 acres), *Windjana Gorge* (2134ha-5271 acres) and *Tunnel Creek* (91ha-225 acres) National Parks protect the fascinating, exposed faces of a giant 350 million-year-old horseshoe-shaped 'great barrier reef'. This reef once extended for over 1000km (620 miles) beyond the current coastline, to join similar formations at Kununurra. Parts of it are now exposed in a series of limestone ranges, stretching for some 300km (186 miles) along the margins of the Canning Basin, south-east of Derby, once part of a shallow tropical sea. Weathering and erosive action of water have created some stunning features that are well worth seeing. The three parks are Dry season only - April to October.

GEOLOGY

In this vast warm sea, a barrier reef belt grew, built by various lime-secreting organisms that had the ability to erect wave

DEVONIAN REEFS NATIONAL PARKS

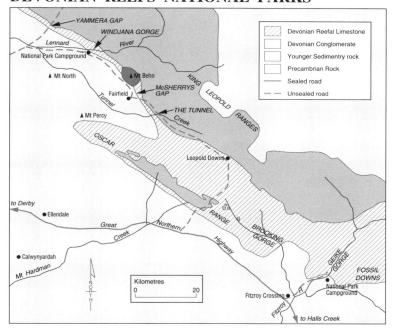

resistant structures close to sea level. These organisms included calcareous algae, stromatoporoids and corals. Stromatoporoids, now extinct, resembled modern corals, except for their internal structure. Other contributors, now seen as fossils, are sponges, bivalve, brachiopod, gastropod, coral (Argutastrea), horn coral, and algal stromatolites, to name some. Limestone deposits, up to 2000m (6562 ft) thick and 20km (12 miles) wide, were built up by these organisms.

The limestone reefs and their associated deposits wind across the landscape, reaching some 50-100m above the adjoining plains, in much the same way that they stood above the ancient sea floor. From the air, the reef is clearly delineated, aided by a complex series of geological occurrences since the seas withdrew: sedimentation, uplift and erosion over millions of years. The clear topographic landform results from shales and soft sediments bedded on the ocean floor in front of the reefs, having eroded to form valleys and leaving the resistant limestone reefs exposed as ranges. Except for an extensive outcrop in the Oscar Range, the reefs are backed by the ancient pre-Cambrian rock structures (see map). Many reefs grew nearly vertically, but some grew outwards, advancing over their own marginal slope deposits. Reef scarps were the result of slow subsidence; a black-reef limestone platform is the structure exposed and shaped by erosion and river action.

FLORA AND FAUNA

Trees in the gorges are mainly cadjeputs (tropical paperbarks), river red gums, native fig, and freshwater mangrove (distinctive for its sprays of red flowers). Surrounding vegetation is typical of the Kimberley, but with dense fringes of riverine forest near the permanent waters.

Aquatic fauna includes freshwater crocodiles in Geike and Windjana Gorges (give them plenty of space); sawfish and stingrays, whose marine ancestors, trapped by the receding seas, journeyed up the Fitzroy and adapted to a freshwater habitat; and archer fish, which shoot down insects from foliage with a jet of water. While most indigenous mammals are small, nocturnal and shy, you may see the agile wallaby, euro and rock wallaby. There is a variety of birdlife, from parrots to water birds. In fact rangers have a checklist of over 100 species at Geike Gorge alone.

CONSERVATION

Please be aware of the sensitivity and uniqueness of these parks. Pets and firearms are not permitted. All litter must be properly disposed of. Gas BBQs are available. Rangers on site are only too pleased to answer any questions you may have.

GEIKE GORGE

CHARACTERISTICS

The gorge was named after British geologist, Sir Archibald Geike in 1883. It features part of the Fitzroy River slashing through the

Geike Range, exposing a fine section of the Devonian Reef. The gorge is 14km (9 miles) long, divided into two sections of approximately equal length, with several atoll-type reefs in the Copley Valley area. The 30m high walls are bleached white by sun and water to a height of about 10-12m above normal river level, and fossils embedded in the limestone may be seen. Most of the gorge in its southern part is cut through back-reef limestone, while to the north, the river slices through marginal slope deposits which contain some conspicuous bivalve shells. The contact between steeply inclined margin-slope deposits and horizontally bedded reef and back-reef deposits, is well illustrated 2km south of Sheep Camp Yard.

OTHER FEATURES

The colours, reflections, freshwater crocodiles, fish, and freshwater stingrays, add to the park's fascinating landforms. Many people swim off the sandbank, but care is needed. There are also walking tracks.

The Sanctuary. Because of their significance, both banks of the river have been declared a sanctuary - no-one is allowed within 200m of either bank, and the only permitted area runs along the west bank, from the southern boundary of the park to the beginning of the west wall of the gorge.

HOW TO GET THERE

The road is sealed for the 18km (11 miles) from Fitzroy Crossing. It is suitable for conventional vehicles, trailers and caravans.

SERVICES AND FACILITIES

Ranger station, permanently manned; the rangers run boat tours 8am, 11am, 3pm ($18 adults, $2 children); park interpretative centre.

Facilities include boat ramp, information, BBQs, picnic areas, drinking water, and toilets (including those for the disabled). Day-use park only, no pets. Open Dry season only. Ph (08) 9191 5121.

TUNNEL CREEK

CHARACTERISTICS

Tunnel Creek flows through the Napier Range in an amazing tunnel cave about 750m (2460 ft) long. The creek, once on the surface, created an underground 'channel', by solution enlargement along joints in the marginal-slope limestone, to form this rather remarkable geological feature. A bench in the tunnel, 8m above the present floor, marks an older underground creek level.

  You can walk through the 3m to 12m high tunnel: it is about waist-deep at the beginning, then about 0.6m-1m in the various pools along its length. It is also dark, so a torch is advised, and after about 300m, a roof collapse allows in light and fresh air. Bats frequent the tunnel, and cave paintings can be seen at the northern entrance.

HOW TO GET THERE

The formed, gravel road is suitable for conventional vehicles during the Dry Season, but caution is advised.

FACILITIES

It is a day-use, Dry season only park, open 6am-6pm. No camping is allowed, and pets are prohibited. The water is cold. Display panels, and toilet are the only facilities provided.

WINDJANA GORGE

CHARACTERISTICS

An attractive, narrow canyon carved by the Lennard River through the Napier Range. It is about 3.5km (2 miles) long, and up to 100m deep, with near vertical walls for most of its length. Isolated pools have fish and freshwater crocodiles, and vegetation mutes the sharp geological formations. It is of great scientific interest due to the range of complex reef structures exposed. The fossil remains of huge extinct crocodiles and turtles were found in a small cave in the gorge wall, and remains of the giant marsupial Diprotodon (resembling a giant wombat) have been recovered from the river gravels.

With its sheer walls and calm pools, it is an ideal wilderness spot for the family, encouraging an appreciation for the remarkable geology of this ancient landform area. Swimming is dubious because of the water quality and restricted space for crocs. Dry season only (April to October).

HOW TO GET THERE

With care, the road is suitable for conventional vehicles during the Dry Season.

FACILITIES

Walking tracks, water (be careful, it is from the river), camping allowed ($7 per adult, $1 child), generator areas (restricted times), toilets, showers (cold), picnic, display panels, gas BBQs (fires being discouraged). No pets allowed. One ranger is in residence during Dry Season only.

EIGHTY MILE BEACH

Population 7

LOCATION

10km (6 miles) west of the Great Northern Highway, from the turn-off 45km (28 miles) south of Sandfire.

CHARACTERISTICS

A 10km (6 miles) dirt track leads through huge sand ridges to provide access to this isolated caravan park and store, established in 1986 by Sandfire Roadhouse. Set behind a primary dune, the camping area is a great base for exploring and enjoying an incredible stretch of wide, white sands, and the sweep of the Indian Ocean. The beach, particularly after storms and infrequent cyclones, becomes a beachcomber's paradise, with its colourful washed-up shells.

Fishing is excellent for the threadfin salmon, but you have to be a smart angler - sharks like them too, when conveniently caught on the line! Talk with park managers about the fishing. Even though the water looks great, it is full of sharks and sea-snakes, so swimming should be avoided. The beach is a delight for walkers who enjoy solitude and glorious sunsets. The huge 202,429ha (500,000 acres) Wallal Station surrounds the park.

HOW TO GET THERE
The turn-off is well sign-posted, 45km (28 miles) south of Sandfire Flat, and the gravel surface road is suitable for conventional vehicles, trailers and caravans.

ACCOMMODATION
Camping - powered sites $16 x 2 persons, unpowered sites $12 x 2 persons, cabins from $55.
   There is shade, BBQs and grass. Pets allowed, dogs leashed.

SERVICES AND FACILITIES
The park has a shop selling basic provisions, ice, bait, fishing tackle and souvenirs. There is 24-hour power, and well-appointed toilet and shower facilities. It is *open all year 7am-7pm*, and credit cards are accepted, ph (08) 9176 5941.

FITZROY CROSSING

Population 1230

LOCATION
On the Great Northern Highway alongside the Fitzroy River, 260km (161 miles) east of Derby, and 288km (179 miles) west of Halls Creek.

CHARACTERISTICS
An old town with a tough reputation, situated on the shady banks of a river of the same name. It has had a vibrant history, and today, is a service town for local Aboriginal communities, stations, and the more recent Western Metals mining development at Cadjebut

and other sites. The nearby Geike Gorge National Park has added an important tourist function.

HISTORY

The settlement was established in the 1890s, when Joseph Blythe built one of the first structures: a shanty inn and store to serve the prospectors, bullock teamsters, drovers and the stations. It was a harsh life too, with fires, floods and droughts to contend with, as well as the hardships associated with isolation and distance.

Explorer Alexander Forrest's expedition in 1879 provided stimulus for further exploration and settlement. His favourable pastoral reports attracted pioneers from the west, and the first sheep runs at Meda River and Yeeda were stocked by overlanding livestock from Beagle Bay. By 1882, there were six stations operating in the Fitzroy area. Easterners became interested too. An exploratory trip led to the epic droves of the Duracks (Queensland), Emanuels, MacDonalds and McKenzies (all from NSW) to stock their new holdings. While they were assembling herds for the 5600km (3500 miles) trek, in 1883, Nat Buchanan, the Gordons and Paddy Cahill were already on the 'Gulf Route', basically Leichhardt's exploration route to Port Essington. It was a trek of incredible hardship and losses, but the Duracks arrived at Argyle in September 1885, while the MacDonalds struck the junction of the Fitzroy and Margaret Rivers with only 300 cattle and few horses left. The latter ended the longest and hardest cattle drove of all time at the property they called Fossil Downs.

The Fitzroy River was discovered in 1837 by George Grey in the *HMS Beagle*, and he named it after a former commander of the ship, Captain Robert Fitzroy, RN. The river flows through rugged hills and plains for 750km (465 miles), draining an area of 90,000 sq km (54,750 sq miles), before discharging into King Sound, south of Derby. While docile for most of the year, it erupts into a raging torrent up to 15km (9 miles) wide, when the rains come. It has one of the highest discharge rates of any river in Australia, with estimated flood flow rates of 30,000 cubic metres per second.

The deeply gouged channel and torn up trees seen in the Dry, are reminders of its awesome power, and the pub profited considerably in the early days, when floods stranded travellers.

INFORMATION
The Area Code is (08).
The **Fitzroy Crossing Tourist Bureau** features an art gallery, books, tours and offers a good range of local information. It's *open weekdays 9am-4.30pm, Sat 9am-12noon* (daily during season) ph 9191 5355.

ATTRACTIONS
In the town. The old *Crossing Inn*, the old single-roomed tin police station, the old low level river crossing, the pioneer cemetery and post office (now Backpackers), are the main features.

Outlying. *Geike Gorge* is a major attraction (see separate listing). The river is a good spot for some barramundi fishing. On the natural scene, large river red gums and paperbarks line the river, and wildlife includes freshwater crocodiles, varied birdlife (heron, ibis, cormorants, kites, brolgas) and flying foxes, wallabies and dingoes.

TOURS
Geike Air Charter, ph 9191 5068.
Fitzroy Crossing Charter Tours, ph 9191 5355.
Geikie Gorge Boat Tours and *Bungoolee Tours* 9191 5353 are C.A.L.M. and Danggu heritage cruises.

EVENTS
Two *Rodeos* (July and October) are lively affairs and draw truckloads of people from the outlying cattle stations.

HOW TO GET THERE
By Air: Ord Air Charter operates a local feeder service into the town from Derby, Halls Creek and Kununurra.
By Road: Greyhound-Pioneer provides a daily service.

ACCOMMODATION

The Area Code is (08)

Crossing Motor Inn, ph 9191 5080 - motel single around $60, double $85; camping - powered sites from $13.

Fitzroy River Lodge and Caravan Park, ph 9191 5141 - motel single from $100, double $135; safari - tented accommodation single from $85, double $100; caravan park - powered sites $18 for two, campsite $8 per adult.

Tarunda Caravan Park, Forrest Street, ph 9191 5044 - powered/unpowered sites from $10.

Darlngunaya Backpackers, Old Townsite (former Post Office), ph 9191 5140 - beds from $12 per person. Camping $6 p.p.

SERVICES AND FACILITIES

Tourist Bureau, Hotel, Restaurant (pub - good value meals at Fitzroy Lodge with mains from $14), take-away food, supermarket, post office, police, medical (hospital), ANZ and Commonwealth bank agencies, all fuels at *Shell Roadhouse* and *BP Ngiyali Roadhouse*, repairs, spares, tyres and tubes, camping gas, and airfield. Credit cards generally accepted; EFTPOS facilities.

GIBB RIVER AND KALUMBURU ROADS REGION

CHARACTERISTICS

The road crosses one of the most exciting wilderness areas in Australia, and offers the adventurous a rare view of one of the world's last remaining frontiers. The Gibb River Road, completed as a beef road for the large road trains connecting the remote Kimberley stations to the ports of Derby and Wyndham, spans 667km (414 miles) through the heart of the Kimberley. From Derby in the west, it traverses the rugged escarpments of the

Napier and King Leopold Ranges, and crosses creeks and broad valleys through some magnificent gorge, ridge and sweeping savannah landscapes. "Bold and beautiful," "raw and rugged," sum up this great track.

The Kalumburu Road strikes north, 419km (260 miles) from Derby, or 250km (155 miles) from the Great Northern Highway between Wyndham and Kununurra. This natural earth road ends at Kalumburu Mission nearly on the coast, 271km (168 miles) from the Gibb River Road turn-off. It traverses beautiful terrain of the Mitchell Plateau, and offers some of the most isolated features in the Kimberley. There are many attractions along the way to discover, and many fine camping spots, too.

ROAD CONDITIONS

The first 60km (37 miles) from Derby are sealed. The surface then changes to gravel, then natural earth, due to the rocky nature of the land. It is essentially 4WD, although some people risk conventional vehicles (high clearance essential). It is particularly severe on tyres, and 2 spares should be carried. While there are basic services at points along the way (have cash too, as EFTPOS and credit card facilities are limited), extra fuel, food and water is strongly advised, and the best time to travel is between May and November. Contact authorities in Derby or Kununurra for up-to-date road reports and advice, or phone 1800 013 314 (Main Roads Dept). Self-sufficiency, a well-equipped, mechanically sound vehicle, and a sense of adventure, are essentials for this part of the world. Towing caravans or trailers is not advised. Access is not recommended during Wet or Green Season (Dec-April) due to flooding. Check availability of services prior to leaving.

HAZARDS

Be on the lookout for road trains and straying stock, and take extreme care with fire. And beware of saltwater crocodiles in waterways.

CAMPING

Be exceptionally careful with fire. Please be courteous and environmentally-respectful in this wilderness region. Camp in designated areas only.

TOURS

Some coach companies operate tours through this region from Australian capital cities. Local tour operators are in evidence, too: Check with the Tourist Bureau in Derby and Kununurra. All travellers to this region are strongly advised to get a copy of the Derby Tourist Bureau's 8 page guide to the Gibb River and Kalumburu Road, including Mitchell Plateau for the most up-to-date information. Write to PO Box 48, Derby 6728 or ph (08) 9191 1426.

ALONG THE GIBB RIVER ROAD

Places offering accommodation and services are detailed following this outline.

From Derby

km (miles)	Features
0	Junction Derby Highway and Gibb River Road. Information Bay.
35(21)	Meda Station turn-off. May River. Fishing, picnic, camping, watch out for salt-water crocodiles.
64(39)	End of bitumen.
73.4(45)	Kimberley Downs Station turn-off (4km). No access.
123.2(76)	Turn right to Fairfield, Leopold Downs Windjana Gorge National Park (21km), Tunnel Creek National Park (51km) and Great Northern Highway.
124(77)	Lennard River Bridge.
133(82)	'Queen Victoria's Head' on left of pass through Napier Range.

134(83)	Napier Downs Homestead (no access).
189(117)	Inglis Gap.
190(117)	Mt Hart Homestead (50km rough road). Accommodation (no camping)
197 (122)	Lennard River Gorge turn-off (4WD only-8km rough road). A 5km gorge, waterfall and pool. A delightful spot.
227(138)	Bell Gorge turn-off at Silent Grove Station (4WD 29km rough road) - 4WD, camping, Resident Ranger, camp fee. This area designated to become part of the 770,000 ha King Leopold Range National Park.
229(141)	Imintji Store and Community - good range of foodstuffs.
255(158)	Mt House Homestead (store, food available). Accommodation.
255(158)	Old Mornington Stockcamp turnoff (100km), Sir John Gorge, Dimond Gorge, 40 kms, Fitzroy River frontage. Offers a range of services.
259(160)	Beverley Springs Homestead. Accommodation.
275(176)	Adcock Gorge (5km). The 3 walls exceed 30m. Waterfall tumbles down stepped rock face into a small pool beside.
293(181)	Galvans Gorge turn-off (700m).
301(187)	Manning Gorge and Mt Barnett Roadhouse - range of services.
328(204)	Barnett River Gorge turn-off (3km).
338(209)	Mt Elizabeth Homestead turn-off (30km). Accommodation
406(252)	Junction with Gibb River-Kalumburu Road (see listing after *Gibb River*).
451(279)	Campbell Creek. No camping.
476(295)	Ellenbrae Station (6km). Accommodation, services.
496(307)	Durack River, no camping.

513(318)	Rollies' Jump Up - steep descent.
524(326)	Jack's Waterhole. Large permanent waterhole; camping, swimming, services.
525(326)	Gregory's Jump Up - steep descent.
562(349)	Bluey O'Malley's Crossing, Bindoola Creek. No camping.
580(360)	Lookout, Cockburn Range, Gulf and twin rivers, Pentecost and Durack.
581(360)	Home Valley Station turn-off (1km); camping, homestead accommodation, services
590(366)	Pentecost River, water upstream of crossing, good fishing downstream in tidal section. Salt-water crocodiles. No camping.
614(381)	El Questro Station (16km); accommodation, services Chamberlain Gorge.
623(388)	Emma Gorge, accommodation, services.
630(391)	King River, no camping
645.9(400)	Great Northern Highway. 48km (30 miles) to Wyndham; 52km (32 miles) to Kununurra.

SERVICES, FACILITIES AND FEATURES - GIBB RIVER ROAD

These are arranged in order from Derby. All stations have an airstrip.

Mount Hart Homestead, ph (08) 9191 4645 - Homestead accommodation, dinner Bed and Breakfast package from $98 pp. ($50 child). Swimming (waterhole), BBQ, bushwalks are features of the homestead located in the Leopold Ranges. Bookings are essential.

Bell Gorge, (Silent Grove Station) - Conservation and Land Management Dept. Administered area. Camping along Bell Creek or Silent Grove. ($6 per adult, $1 child). Resident Ranger - Dry Season.

Imintji Store and Community, ph (08) 9191 9474 - the general store has a good range of foodstuffs, cold drinks, ice and diesel fuel only. EFTPOS facility.

Mount House Station, ph (08) 9191 4649 - located on the banks of the Adock River at the base of a curious tabletop mountain, the working cattle station offers dinner/bed/breakfast packages from $77 p.p., and camping ($15 per vehicle). It has a store (good range of foodstuffs), fuel (diesel and ULP) and a mechanical and tyre repair service.

Old Mornington Stock Camp, ph (08) 9191 7035 - the camp has 40 kms of Fitzroy River frontage and has local tours (Sir John and Dimond Gorges), including scenic air flights. Comfortable tent accommodation (from $85 pp. including meals), camping from $8 p.p., bush kitchen, fishing, swimming, canoe hire, meals, licensed bar and good toilet facilities are available. Prior bookings advised.

Beverley Springs Homestead, ph (08) 9191 4646 - the working station has a number of accommodation options - camping ($8), chalets and homestay (from $80 all inclusive), self contained homes ($85 per house for 4 people), and facilities for groups. There are a number of scenic attractions.

Mount Barnett Roadhouse, ph (08) 9191 7007 - is the gateway to the Manning Gorge and Falls, and a number of natural pools. The station is owned and run by the Kupingarri Aboriginal Community and features a well-stocked store, takeaway food, ice, artifacts, disabled facilities (toilet, shower), vehicle services (repairs, tyres and tubes), fuel (LP, ULP, Diesel). Camping in gorge area $5 pp., family $10.

Mt Elizabeth Station, ph (08) 9191 4644 - offers dinner/bed/breakfast packages ($90 adult, $45 child), camping (adult $7, child $1). Access to some remote country and coastline is possible through their tour offerings - safari style and scenic air flights. The station has a store and picnic/BBQ facilities. Bookings are essential for homestead accommodation.

Ellenbrae Station, ph (08) 9161 4325 - located between two tree fringed billabongs, the homestead has a restful setting and offers homestay packages D/B/B from $80 and camping (adult $7, child $1). Local crafts are available for purchase. Bookings essential for homestay.

Jacks Waterhole, ph (08) 9161 4324 - an excellent stop for a swim in a huge natural pool by the Durack River or as a base for Kimberley exploration. It offers D/B/B from $75 pp., camping from $6 pp., and tours - the Oomaloo Falls Safari, or fishing safaris are popular. It has good facilities including a store.

Home Valley Homestead, ph (08) 9161 4322 - the large working cattle station has a beautiful setting on the tree-lined Pentecost River, with a backdrop of the startling Cockburn Range. The homestead exudes plenty of Kimberley character and offers D/B/B packages around $80 pp., camping (adult $6, child $1). It has a shop and runs a number of tours. Homestead bookings advised.

El Questro Station and Wilderness Park, ph (08) 9169 1777 - on this working 1 million acre cattle property, you can join in on various aspects of station life. Activities include horse-riding, scenic helicopter flights, fishing (barramundi) or relaxing in some beautiful natural thermal pools. This Tourism Award winning property caters for all budgets and offers wonderful heritage and natural insights into the Kimberley.

Chamberlain Gorge features some Wandjina Paintings (some Bradshaw figures - see under Drysdale River National Park). Accommodation includes camping $10 per adult (children free), bungalow (single $105, double $140), homestead (minimum two nights) all inclusive $640 pp. twin share per day.

The *Brumby Base* is a rustic "outstation" from which there is access to rock art, thermal pools, waterfalls and boating - costs $20 per adult (min, 2 nights). The station has a store, steakhouse (open for meals - mains from $17)) and fuel (ULP, Diesel, Avgas). Credit cards accepted, EFTPOS facility.

Emma Gorge Resort, ph (08) 9169 1777 - the Gorge area (part of El Questro Station) has facilities which include a fully licensed bar and restaurant, luxury tented cabins (single from $70, double $105, family $155). It is a short walk to the stunning Emma Gorge. Bookings essential.

ALONG THE KALUMBURU ROAD

Places offering services are listed following this outline.

From Gibb River Road

km(miles)	Features
0	Junction Gibb River Road and Kalumburu Road
3(2)	Gibb River Crossing, picnic and camping.
16(10)	Plain Creek, picnic and camping.
59(36)	Drysdale River Homestead left 1km, accommodation and services.
	Drysdale River Homestead is the last service point and information stop before the turn-off to the Mitchell Plateau. Trailers and caravans can be left at the homestead; the road past this point is unsuitable for most caravans.
62(38)	Miners Pool, turn right 3.5km; picnic and camping ($3 adult, $1 child).
63(38)	Drysdale River Crossing; picnic, no camping.
96(60)	Doongan Station - no access.
135(84)	Old Mitchell River Station Road - no access.
162(101)	Mitchell Plateau turn-off left 70km. The Mitchell Plateau area is one of extreme importance from a biological viewpoint, This is an isolated area; you must be totally self-sufficient before entering.
198(124)	Theda Homestead - no access.

247(153)   Carson River Crossing.
250(155)   Carson River Homestead turn-off. Drysdale
                National Park - 4WD road access, permit required.
267(165)   Kalumburu Aboriginal Community; range
                of services

SERVICES, FACILITIES AND FEATURES - KALUMBURU ROAD

Drysdale River Homestead, (08) 9161 4326 - the working cattle station has a general store, fuel (ULP, LP, Diesel), emergency mechanical repairs and EFTPOS facility. It offers daily scenic flights (Dry Season) and for those visiting the Mitchell Plateau, trailers/caravans can be left here for $2 per day. Accommodation includes units (shared facilities), adult $30, child $20; Homestead Guest House, dinner/bed/breakfast adult $80, child $50; riverside camping, adult $3, child $1.

Mitchell Plateau. The plateau is of high cultural (Aboriginal heritage) and environmental significance. The palm, Livistonia eastoni, is the most striking vegetation feature on the plateau where it thrives amongst an open eucalypt association of woolleybutt, stringybark and bloodwoods. Features include The Mitchell Falls These are a spectacular feature located 3km from nearest vehicle parking area. The walking track into the falls takes 4-6 hours return and is not well marked over its rough course. Exercise caution and keep a close watch on children near cliffs. Take plenty of water and equip yourself sensibly. The first falls encountered are Mertons Falls. The Mitchell Falls drop over five levels and you need to cross the river and walk along the gorge to see the extent of the falls. Saltwater crocodiles frequent the pools below the falls, so don't swim here! Heliwork (ph. 08 9168 1811) operates scenic flights from the car park (prices from $50). Near the delightful King Edward River, Kimberley Horse Experience offers guided wilderness rides. Contact local tourist Bureau for details.

Camping. Campsites are limited. Aboriginal people (the traditional owners often camp on the plateau, so please respect them). You can camp at King Edward River and as firewood is scarce, gas is preferred. Camping is allowed at the Mitchell Falls Car Park. Kimberley Coastal Camp (7km by boat from Walsh Point, Port Warrender, Mitchell River, or by helicopter or float plane), offers a luxurious way of appreciating the wonders of the plateau and coast. All- inclusive accommodation cost $250 per day. It includes guided fishing and sightseeing. Telephone 015 778 840.

 Access Road. Remember the Mitchell Plateau is an isolated area. You must be totally self-sufficient before entering. The road is narrow, very rough, with steep inclines. A 4WD is essential. A major hazard is other vehicles travelling too fast and speeds of 20kph are advised for safety. Allow plenty of time - 3 days is a minimum.

Drysdale River National Park. One of the most remote parks in Australia, protecting a pristine wilderness. River, escarpment and gorge landscapes, along with waterfalls and variety of vegetation and wildlife, give it a unique appeal. It covers 448,264 ha and is one of the locations of some extraordinary Aboriginal Rock Art Galleries - the ancient Bradshaw art figures and the more recently discovered mysterious Wandjina art figures. The Bradshaw figures are named after the first European who discovered them in the 1890s - Joseph Bradshaw. He described them in this way: "the bodies and limbs were attenuated and represented as having numerous tassel-shaped adornments appended to the hair, neck, waist, arms and legs, but the most remarkable fact in connection with these drawings is that wherever a profile face is shown, the features are of a most pronounced aquiline type, quite different from those of any native we encountered." These mysterious paintings are further evidence of the richness of Aboriginal artistic expression, making the Kimberley one of the greatest ancient rock art galleries in the world. Visits to the sites are not possible.

 Access requires prior permission to cross the Aboriginal owned Carson River Station - one week's notice is required from

Kalumburu Aboriginal Community. The road is rough, 4WD only, and for details of campsites and fees, contact the CALM office at Kununurra (08) 9168 0200, or Tourist Bureau.

Kalumburu Aboriginal Community. The settlement is located close to the coast and has a picturesque setting with giant mango trees and coconut palms surrounding the historic, former Catholic Mission buildings.

It is recommended that an *Entry Permit* be obtained prior to arrival at Kalumburu.

The settlement has a well stocked store, Aboriginal artworks and fuel. Check opening times for the store. Campsites are available and there is an entry fee of $25 per vehicle. Provided plenty of notice is given, a variety of activities (fishing, trekking and scenic flights) can be arranged. You must report to the office on arrival. For further details, phone (08) 9161 4300 during office hours - 7am-12noon weekdays.

HALL'S CREEK

Population 1350

LOCATION
On the Great Northern Highway, 544km (338 miles) east of Derby, and 359km (223 miles) south of Kununurra.

CHARACTERISTICS
The old town, 14km (9 miles) away, was the site of Western Australia's first gold rush. Since those wild days, the new town has become the centre of a vast beef industry, and is the gateway to a number of tourist attractions. Services to mineral exploration companies, Aboriginal communities, and more recently, tourists, are its prominent functions.

HISTORY

A second Forrest expedition to the Kimberley in 1883, reported favourable pastoral lands, and the suggestion that gold might be found in the rocks. Charlie Hall rode across from Roebourne and discovered the magical ore in 1855, on the creek that now bears his name. He returned to the coast two months later with his mate, Jack Slattery, and 200 fine ounces of gold. Another prospector found a 22oz nugget, and the rush was on. Between 1885 and 1887, about 10,000 men came to the Kimberley from all over Australia and overseas. Sailing vessels, luggers and schooners tied up at the fledgling ports of Derby and Wyndham, while the overlanders arrived by horse, wagon, camel, or on foot. Fierce heat, waterless landscapes, resentful Aborigines, fever, thirst, starvation and loneliness, were experienced by those desperadoes as they trekked across the hundreds of kilometres of unknown terrain. Hall's Creek became a tough town consisting of wood, stone, canvas, tin, bark and spinifex structures, including a couple of pubs, among this ramshackle collection of buildings. In 1955, the town was relocated to less rugged land, so that expansion could take place - a far cry from the former shanty town of old Hall's Creek.

INFORMATION

Hall's Creek Tourist Information Centre, Main Street (opposite Shell Roadhouse), ph (08) 9168 6262.

ATTRACTIONS

Aboriginal Art. The Halls Creek Art Centre display works from local Aboriginal communities.

Old Hall's Creek. The remnants of the original gold town can be seen, and include the old post office, and ruins of many other buildings.

China Wall. A near vertical quartz vein projects above the surrounding rocks to form a startling white stone wall. Along with its block-like structure, it appears like a miniature Great Wall of China - hence the name. Located off Duncan Road.

Old Mines. Mt Bradley (off Duncan Road) is one of the original gold mine shafts, where care is needed as the shafts are deep. Ruby Queen Mine is a later one, (access by 4WD only).

Palm Springs. A natural spring used once as a local water supply. An ideal picnic and swimming spot is where the Black Elvire River crosses the Duncan Highway.

Russian Jack Memorial. Commemorates the heroic gold rush character who, for over 300km, carried a sick friend in a bush wheelbarrow to find medical help. Located at Shire Offices on Thomas Street.

Caroline Pool. A natural waterhole near Old Hall's Creek.

Sawpit or Saw Tooth Gorge. A popular fishing and swimming spot is located off Duncan Road, where the Black Elvire River has cut through a ridge. A shaded tree-flanked pool has a sandy beach and inviting waters.

Outlying Attractions include *Purnulu National Park* (Bungle Bungle Range) and *Wolfe Creek Crater Reserve* (see separate listings for both).

Fossicking. Check with the Mines Department for areas.

TOURS
Safaris to Purnulu National Park, Geike and Windjana Gorges; and scenic flights are available. Tour operators are: *Hall's Creek Bungle Bungle Tours*, ph (08) 9168 6217; *Kingfisher Aviation*, ph (08) 9168 6162; *Ord Air Charter*, ph (08) 9161 1335; and *Oasis Air*, ph (08) 9168 6462.

EVENTS

Agricultural Show is held in July, and the *Rodeo* is held in August.

HOW TO GET THERE

By air: Ord Air Charter connects to main airports at Derby and Kununurra.

By coach: Greyhound-Pioneer.

By road: sealed surfaces connect all main centres in the Kimberley.

ACCOMMODATION

Area code is (08)

Kimberley Hotel/Motel, Roberta Avenue, ph 9168 6101 - motel units singles from $80, double from $95; dormitory (share facilities) from $15 per person per night.

Hall's Creek Hotel, Great Northern Highway, ph 9168 6001 - single from $65, double $80.

Shell Roadhouse, McDonald Street, ph 9168 6060 - cabins from $50, backpacker $15.

Hall's Creek Caravan Park, Roberta Avenue, ph 9168 6169 - powered sites from $14, unpowered $6, on-site vans $38; cabins from $48. Shaded, grassed sites.

At Old Halls Creek (16km from Halls Creek) is Halls Creek Lodge which offers powered van sites $12; tent sites $7; and rooms from $38. Facilities include restaurant and kiosk. Telephone 9168 8999.

SERVICES AND FACILITIES

Most basic services are available, including: hospital, police, post office, bank agency, supermarket, taxi, all vehicle needs and fuel, camping gas, ice, restaurant (Shell Roadhouse), take- away food and airfield. Credit cards widely accepted, EFTPOS facility. Radio Stations: ABC 106.1 and 107.7 FM.

KUNUNURRA

Population 6000

LOCATION

Near the Northern Territory border in the north-east of the Kimberley region, 480km (298 miles) west of Katherine, and 1057km (655 miles) east of Broome.

CHARACTERISTICS

Although it is a relatively new town, Kununurra, meaning 'big waters', presents a few delightful surprises from its lakeside setting, where it blends comfortably into lush tropical bushland overlooked by the rocky outcrop of Kelly's Knob. The compact town centre is dotted with palms, and provides all the necessary facilities and services for comfortable living and travelling in the tropics. Climate, as with most towns in the classic Wet/Dry climate regions of the tropical north, brings magnificent contrasts to Kununurra and its surrounding landscape. The luxuriant greenery of the Wet changes as the relentless sun of the Dry Season browns and dusts. Whitened grasses sharpen landscape tones and emphasise the raw beauty. During this time, the startling green of the town centre's well-watered lawns give it an oasis quality.

There is much to see and do. The Lake offers excellent fishing and a range of water based activities. If you can't make it to the Purnululu National Park (Bungle Bungle), then visit the Mirima National Park (Hidden Valley) miniature. The Ord scheme, the dam of Lake Argyle, the Gibb River Road, and various wildlife, are a few of its attributes.

Kununurra functions as a service centre for government administration of agricultural, (including research based on the Ord Irrigation Scheme), pastoral, mining and tourism industries. This might well be enough for most small, tropical towns, but

Kununurra has another jewel; it is Australia's diamond centre, based on the huge Argyle mine, 200km (124 miles) to the south.

Above all, Kununurra is an ideal, friendly base from which to explore a range of near and outlying attractions of the vast East Kimberley region.

HISTORY

Western Australian sheepmen and Queensland cattlemen were attracted to the region by explorer Alexander Forrest's promising description, in 1879, of the pastoral potential of the Ord and Fitzroy river valleys. Long before Forrest's expedition, Miriwun and Katjerong Aboriginal people from the broader based Dj'eragum Language Group ('Tribal' groupings and distribution are based on language more than any other characteristic), occupied these lands. Their cultural richness can be seen in art sites around Kununurra.

Alexander Forrest failed to find the Ord River outlet, and was forced to strike east for the Overland Telegraph Line in the Northern Territory (see *Daly Waters,* Barkly Region). Pastoralists established stations in the region in the 1880s. Among the pioneers were the Duracks who established Lissadell, Argyle, Rosewood and Ivanhoe Stations. The latter homestead was destroyed by fire and rebuilt at Ivanhoe Crossing, while a replica of the Argyle Homestead, (the original was located in the area flooded by the Ord Scheme), was built on a higher site. The Duracks and the Kimberley are synonymous, and Mary Durack's book *Kings in Grass Castles* gives a vivid account of the early pastoral days (refer also to *Fitzroy Crossing* and *Lake Argyle* for further history).

Apart from similarities in geology, space and climate to the Northern Territory, the trails of the early explorers, pastoralists and drovers, and the outlooks spawned, also strengthen the unity between these two great Outback regions.

After tropical agricultural research, the Western Australian Government began the Ord Irrigation Scheme. In 1963, the town was established to service the irrigation area, where over 12,000ha (29,640 acres) of rich, black alluvial soil supports peanuts, sorghum, fodder crops, sunflower and high protein beans, while fruit and vegetables include bananas, mangoes, paw paw, melon, cucumbers and beans. In recent times, sugar cane has become the dominant crop. The diversity of crops is the major reason why authorities are so strict, and ban fruits, etc, at the border in order to keep out pests and diseases. Other agricultural ventures include feedlots where cattle are fattened before being exported live from Wyndham.

INFORMATION

A very active *Tourist Bureau* is open daily, and located in the town centre at 75 Coolibah Drive. It has an excellent range of tourist literature, ph (08) 9168 1177.

The *Department of Conservation and Land Management* has offices in Konkerberry Drive, with good park information, maps and literature. Telephone (08) 9168 0200.

ATTRACTIONS

Kelly's Knob. The lookout is ideal for orientation and some fine views of the town and Ord Valley. Located 2.4km (1.5 miles) from town on Speargrass Road.

Mirima (Hidden Valley) National Park. Known as the 'Mini Bungle Bungle', the park protects a valley of rugged cliffs that suffuse with colour and landform features that include amphitheatres, gullies and ridges. Mirima is the Aboriginal name, and past usage by ancestors of the Miriwun can be seen in the fascinating depictions of figures, beings and animals in the rock paintings and engravings. These art sites are fully protected, and must not be interfered with in any way.

The spectacular landforms evolved during the Devonian Period (320 million years ago) from sands laid down under shallow seas, uplifted to great blocks and weathered to the shapes seen today.

The quartz sandstone shattered from the cliffs provides an ideal habitat for the agile and short-eared rock wallabies, while their droppings, containing boab seeds, explain how the small boabs that cling tenaciously high on the valley walls got there. There's a wealth of wildlife: frogs, tortoise, geckoes, goannas, snakes and other reptiles can be seen near Lily Creek; fruit bats, dingoes and echidna; while birdlife is colourful and prolific - brown quail, peaceful dove, white-quilled rock pigeon, red-collared lorikeet, little corella, red-backed kingfisher, blue-winged kookaburra, rainbow bee-eater, common koel, pheasant coucal, northern fantail, leaden flycatcher, black-faced cuckoo shrike, brown honeyeater, bowerbird and black kite are the main types. The Park features a number of walking tracks and has picnic facilities only.

Ivanhoe Crossing. A crossing at the Ord River near Ivanhoe Station Homestead forms a mini-waterfall, and was once part of the original road to Wyndham, before the advent of a new road across the Diversion Dam. The Ord, along with the Fitzroy and other rivers in the Kimberley, carries 86% of Western Australia's potential fresh water supply, and at a national level this comprises 16%. Before the new bridge was built, station people had to stock up prior to the Wet season, as later rains made roads and crossings impassable and gravel airfields were often unusable. Today, the crossing is closed to vehicular traffic, but remains a popular fishing spot. But be careful, it is very slippery.

Lake Kununurra. A man-made lake as a result of the Irrigation Scheme attracts an abundance of wildlife, including fish (black bream, catfish) and freshwater crocodiles and water birds. People swim here. Other activities are fishing, canoeing, windsurfing, sailing, boating, scuba diving, water skiing, and on the banks, picnicking.

Celebrity Tree Park. Located on the banks of the Lily Creek inlet of the Ord, the park contains trees planted by various celebrities visiting Kununurra. Plaques provide identification in this rather novel glade.

Black Rock Falls. A spectacular Wet season attraction where water thunders over a 30m semi-circular cliff into a pool below. Minerals in the water have stained the rockface black. Located just of Parry Creek Road, 4WD access only.

Middle Springs. A small Wet season pool and waterfall dominated by a large, slab-faced rock. Located off Parry Creek Road, 4WD access only.

Valentine's Pool. An interesting series of rock pools and sandy beaches, best seen during the Wet. A popular swimming spot.

Bandicoot Beach. A beach at Bandicoot Bar on the Ord River, just below the Diversion Dam wall. The grassy beach is a popular fishing spot. Swimming is not recommended below the dam wall as crocodiles are common.

Sleeping Buddha. A razorback ridge stands alongside the Ord River, and from a distance gives the appearance of a person lying down on his back. At the river end of the Sleeping Buddha, the rock resembles an elephant's head, complete with trunk. Best viewed on river cruises.

Waringarri Aboriginal Arts. Locally produced artifacts are on display and for sale. Located in Speargrass Road.

Pandanus Palm Wildlife Park and Zebra Rock Gallery. A range of birds, wallabies and other Australian wildlife adds interest to a drive through banana plantations of the irrigated agricultural zone, and the main feature, Zebra Rock. The only known deposits of this rock are found nearby in small reef outcrops of stratified claystone, with an estimated age of 600 million years. It is an attractive fine-grained siliceous argillite (indurated siltstone or claystone) with rhythmic patterns of red bands or spots on a white background. The workshop is interesting, and you can purchase the unique polished stone. A practical use can be seen at the hotel where the bar has a zebra rock base. Located off Packsaddle Road.

Arboretum. The Department of Conservation and Land Management has established a 50ha (124 acres) arboretum, with the first trees having been planted in 1980. It has both native and exotic species, and a self-guiding walk trail. Located between the irrigation channel and Ivanhoe Road, close to the town centre.

Fishing. Another great Kimberley place for the keen angler on inland or coastal waters. Types include barramundi, black bream, catfish, longtoms, mullet, tarpon, groper, threadfin salmon, archer fish and bony bream. Fishing sports are Bullocks Crossing (camping), access through Kimberley Research Station; Dunham River for barra - dam gates. Lake Kununurra and Ivanhoe Crossing are others. Check with locals for detailed advice, or the tackle shop in town. A licence is required for fishing.

Swimming. Apart from the places mentioned, the Kununurra Leisure Centre has an adventure pool, learners' pool and huge main pool and water slide. Located opposite the Tourist Bureau. Those using natural swimming places, beware of salt-water crocodiles below the Diversion Dam at Lake Kununurra

OUTLYING ATTRACTIONS

Argyle Diamond Mine. Located at the southern extremity of the Carr-Boyd Range, 200km (124 miles) south of Kununurra, is the huge open-cut mine, with its ultra-modern village close by. It is a formidable location for the operation, which was developed between 1983 and 1985 at a cost of $435 million, and produces about 17kg of diamonds a day (5 tonnes per annum). In terms of quantity, it is the largest in the world where 4 tonnes of rock are removed to produce one tonne of ore, and each tonne gives about 7 carats of diamonds; so 4 tonnes of rock produce 1gm of diamond. Only about 5% of the output is of gem quality, 45% near gem quality, while the balance finds an industrial use (for drills, saws, etc). The gem and near gem quality are finding an outlet in jewellery settings, as the world was made known of the fine 'cognac' or 'champagne' Argyle diamonds. The finest diamond found so far has been a rare 2.11 carat pink, valued at over $1 million.

The mine can now be visited through tour groups, and the magnificent gems can be seen and purchased at jewellery shops in town. Check with the Tourist Bureau for tour details. The mine can also be viewed on scenic flights from Kununurra to the Purnululu National Park.

Purnululu (Bungle Bungle) National Park. See separate listing, and under tours.

Gibb River Road. Highly recommended are El Questro Station (Chamberlain and Emma Gorges), and Mt Barnett (Manning Falls and Gorge). See separate listings.

TOURS

Short tours include Mirima National Park; Lake Argyle; Keep, Dunham and Ord Rivers; agricultural district; and town attractions.

Cruises are available on Lake Kununurra. Fishing safaris of 2-5 days on the Ord, or by floatplane or helicopter along the coast of the Timor Sea. Ground safaris vary from 2-8 days. Specialist tours (wildlife, fishing, bird watching). Tours to Gibb River Road and El Questro Stations are recommended.

Highly recommended is a 2 hour Purnululu flight. In what must be one of the best scenic flights in Australia, for variety and majestic landscapes, it covers the town, irrigation district, Ord Valley, Lake Argyle (including Dam and Durack Homestead), Argyle Diamond Mine and Purnululu.

A number of tour operators and tours stem from Kununurra. Check with the Tourist Bureau for details of air and other tours available.

EVENTS

Dam to Dam Regatta - April; *Kununurra Agricultural Show* - July; *Horse Racing* - August.

HOW TO GET THERE

By air: Ansett operates a daily jet service between Kununurra and Perth, Darwin and Alice Springs. The Darwin flight takes about 40 minutes. Ansett's 'milk-run' flight (early morning) into Kununurra and onto Darwin is a beauty - more like a scenic flight with the sun tinting the land in orange, pinks and reds. Ord Air Charter operates a regional feeder service to Hall's Creek, Fitzroy Crossing and Derby.

By coach: Greyhound-Pioneer services Kununurra daily.

By road: Kununurra is connected by an all-sealed road to other parts of Western Australia and the Northern Territory.

ACCOMMODATION

There is a good range, but Kununurra's increasing popularity as a tourist destination means it's advisable to book in advance. Area code is (08).

Kununurra Hotel, Messmate Way, ph 9168 1344 - single from $65-85, double $65-95; pool.

Mercure Inn-Kununurra, Duncan Highway, ph 9168 1455 - single/double from $98, family $110; pool.

Country Club Private Hotel, Coolibah Drive, ph 9168 1024 - from $130; pool.

Kununurra Backpackers, 111 Nutwood Crescent, ph 9168 1711 - $15 per person per night.

Kimberley Court, cnr River Fig Avenue and Erythrina Street, ph 9168 1411 - unit, B&B single from $74, double $84; full facilities for the disabled.

Lakeside Resort, ph 9169 1092, from $117.

Desert Inn, ph 9168 2702 - Backpackers from $14 single.

Camping

Town Caravan Park, Bloodwood Drive, ph 9168 1763 - Shire operated. No dogs, on-site vans from $50 x 2, powered sites from $11 x 2.

Kona Lakeside Park, Lake Kununurra setting, ph 9168 1031 - caravan sites $13 x 2, tent sites $10 x 2. No dogs.

Ivanhoe Village, ph 9169 1995, powered sites $10 x 2. Kimberleyland Holiday Park, Duncan Highway, ph 9168 1280 - dogs allowed, leashed; caravan sites $15 x 2, tent sites $12 x 2.

Hidden Valley Caravan Park, Weaber Plains Road, ph 9168 1790 - powered sites $14 x 2, unpowered sites $12 x 2.

EATING OUT

There is *Chicken Treat*, *Valentine's Pizza* and the fish and chips outlet in Konkerberry Street, in the convenience food line.

Hotel - counter meals in the **Green Room**. Bistro/smorgasbord in Dining Room (around $11).

The **George Room**, **Gulliver's Tavern**, **Cotton Tree Avenue**, ph 9168 1666 - a la carte in comparatively elegant Georgian atmosphere, with a Gulliver's Travels theme depicted in prints around the walls. Main course around $18. The Tavern has counter meals.

The Country Club in Coolibah Street, ph 9168 1024, has **Chop Sticks** - a Chinese restaurant in a delightful outdoor setting (around $16); and **Kelly's Bar and Grill** for steak and seafood.

Mercure Inn - a la carte. Good value with main course around $17.

SERVICES AND FACILITIES

Most services and facilities are offered, and credit cards are widely accepted. There is a hospital, full medical services, chemist, police, post office, supermarket, specialty shops, banks (National, Commonwealth, R&I), EFTPOS facilities, all vehicle fuels and services, camping gas, ice, airport, boat ramp, churches (Anglican, Catholic, Uniting, People's Church), rental vehicles; hire bicycles, fishing tackle.

Recreational facilities are provided by the *Leisure Centre*.

LAKE ARGYLE TOURIST VILLAGE

Population 20

LOCATION

70km (43 miles) south of Kununurra on Lake Argyle.

CHARACTERISTICS

Picturesquely sited on treed, grassed slopes near the lake, the Tourist Village, including an Inn, does not disappoint after a beautiful, mountainous and winding 37km (23 miles) drive from the Duncan Highway turn-off. Apart from the wonders of this huge man-made lake and associated water activities (fishing, water skiing, boating, canoeing), it is an ideal family place for relaxation that is particularly attractive during the Green Season.

Lake Argyle

The nearby dam was built as a vital part of the *Ord River Scheme*, designed to store the massive volumes of water in the Wet season so that up to 76,000ha (187,720 acres) of heavy soils could be irrigated for tropical agriculture. Despite initial setbacks and crop failures for unforeseen reasons (the scheme was branded in some quarters as a 'white elephant'), the development, apart from the agriculture it has fostered, has silenced the critics. A wide variety of crops are grown on small holdings around Kununurra, but its biggest success is in the opening up of the region for such activities as tourism, as well as encouraging prolific wildlife.

The dam creates a surface area of 740 sq km (286 sq miles) at storage level, rising to 2072 sq km (800 sq miles) during maximum floods. It is the largest lake of its type in Australia, with a volume of water nine times that of Sydney Harbour.

ATTRACTIONS

Magnificent Kimberley scenery, including drives to the dam and lookout, where in the evening there are plenty of rock wallabies.

Argyle Homestead Museum. This is the reconstructed homestead of the Durack Family, known as Argyle Downs Station. The homestead was in the area to be flooded when Lake Argyle was formed, but because of its historical significance, it now houses interesting pioneer days memorabilia, and implements from its higher ground location. A generalised history of the region is contained in the Kununurra listing.

Aquaculture Centre. It features a barramundi hatchery and displays of other native fish species in Lake Argyle. There is a $3 entry fee.

TOURS

Boat cruises are available. Contact *Lake Argyle Cruises* ph. (08) 9168 7361 for details. For other tours, including flights, see under *Kununurra*.

ACCOMMODATION

Motel - around $65 single/double.

Camping - sites $6 adult, $3 child; power - $3.50 per site. Shaded, grassed sites. Pets allowed, dogs leashed.

SERVICES AND FACILITIES

Hotel/motel, store (limited foodstuffs), restaurant (buffet style breakfast, counter meals, country style food), take-away food, ice, souvenirs, telephone, fuel (ULP, diesel), oil, camping gas, basic spares, picnic/bbq shaded area, tourist information, swimming pool, boat ramp, tennis court, mini golf course, pool table in bar, showers for travellers ($2). Open all year 7am-8.30pm. Credit cards accepted, ph (08) 9168 7360.

PURNULULU (BUNGLE BUNGLE) NATIONAL PARK

239,723ha (592,115 acres)

LOCATION
Approximately 180km (112 miles) by air south of Kununurra.

CHARACTERISTICS
Purnululu is a crowded maze of gigantic sandstone whorls that tower and taper to domes and spires over 300m above the surrounding savannah landscape. Startling orange and black bands etched into the stone highlight the curious domes. The scale of the abruptly rising 'beehives' is astounding, and matched only by the geological masterpiece of it all, Cathedral Gorge. Other deep chasms, pools and a variety of flora and fauna, add to what is undoubtedly one of Australia's most exciting landform features.

GEOLOGY
The range is a sandstone formation some 350 million-years-old, formed during the Devonian Period. A similar geological structure is found in the Mirima National Park, near Kununurra, but on a much smaller scale. The rounded beehive shapes resulted from weathering along the rectangular joints of the original block, where the corners eroded more easily from eons of torrential rain, wind and heat. It is possible from the air to see 'new Bungle Bungle' in the making, as the massif continues to erode. The weathering processes and the erosive power of water have formed deep gorges and steep-sided chasms.

The sandstone is quite fragile, despite its solid appearance, and will crumble easily under hand or foot. CALM does not permit climbing because of this and visitor safety. The orange and black striations that give the 'beehive' effect (best seen towards the south near Piccaninny Creek) consist of iron oxide (orange) and cyanobacteria (black). The latter is a primitive living organism,

PURNULULU NATIONAL PARK

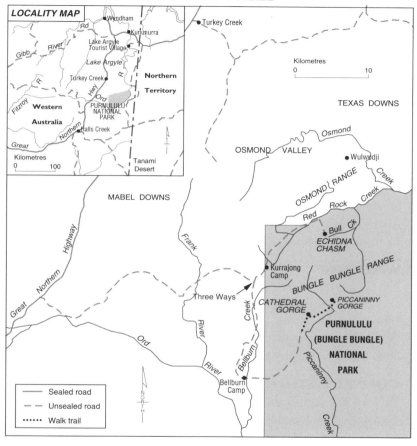

LOCALITY MAP

Wyndham
Rd
Kununurra
Lake Argyle
Tourist Village
Gibb
River
Lake Argyle
Turkey Creek
R
Ord
Hwy
Northern
Territory
Fitzroy
R
Western
PURNULULU
NATIONAL
PARK
Australia
Northern
Halls Creek
Great
Kilometres
0   100
Tanami
Desert

Turkey Creek

Kilometres
0   10

TEXAS DOWNS

Osmond
OSMOND   VALLEY
Wulwudji
Creek
OSMOND RANGE
MABEL DOWNS
Red   Rock   Creek
Bull Ck
ECHIDNA
CHASM
Highway
Frank
Kurrajong
Camp
BUNGLE BUNGLE RANGE
Three Ways
Creek
CATHEDRAL
GORGE
PICCANINNY
GORGE
Northern
River
Ord
River
Bellburn
PURNULULU
(BUNGLE BUNGLE)
NATIONAL
PARK
Piccaninny
Great
Bellburn
Camp
Creek

———— Sealed road
‑ ‑ ‑ ‑ Unsealed road
•••••• Walk trail

NORTH

formerly known as "blue-grey algae". Underneath, the sandstone is white to yellowish in colour.

HISTORY

To the Kija Aborigines, the area of the Bungle Bungle is known as Purnululu. The name Bungle Bungle is thought to have been coined as a corruption of either the Aboriginal name Purnululu or a common Kimberley grass found in the region, the bundle bundle grass. The area was opened up initially for cattle grazing around the turn of the century. In themselves, they were of little interest to the cattlemen, who probably had more to contend with in the harsh environment, than to explore the formidable range. While the actual area of the range is approximately 450 sq km, the large size of the park is designed to act as a buffer zone and conserve the landforms and habitats.

FEATURES

Individual features are *Echidna Chasm*, *Cathedral Gorge*, and for the energetic and adventurous, *Piccaninny Gorge*. Access is by walks of varying length and duration - one-way Cathedral Gorge is about 30 minutes, while Piccaninny is about 10 hours! Aboriginal art sites add much to the sense of timelessness evoked by these extraordinary landforms.

WALKING

A wide-brimmed hat, skin protection, comfortable footwear, and above all, drinking water, are requirements for all walks. Temperatures can be searing, partly due to the additional heat radiated from the surrounding rock. Advise the ranger of planned longer walks, and their advice should be taken.

CONSERVATION

This is a magnificent wilderness area, and to prevent fire devastation and ecological impact of wood collection, campfires are permitted only in fireplaces using only the wood supplied. It is preferable to use gas stoves for cooking. Please keep to designated tracks and parking areas, and do not interfere with any art sites. Firearms and pets are not allowed.

ENTRY AND FEES

An entry fee of *$8 per vehicle* is charged ($3 for motorcycles and holders of Seniors Cards). *Camping fees are $7 p.p. per night* ($1 for children under 16 years). The park is closed during the Wet season

(Jan 1 - Mar 31), partly due to the rains, but also because of the fierce heat (50C - 122F) and high humidity. Unseasonal rains at other times may temporarily close the park.

HOW TO GET THERE
By Road: it is 250km (155 miles) to the Purnululu turn-off from Kununurra, or 110km (68 miles) from Halls Creek.
By Air: scenic flights over the Purnululu from Kununurra (see Kununurra listing), Broome and Halls Creek, are available.
By Tour: tour operators from Kununurra, Halls Creek and other locations, offer ground tours. Check with local tourist centres.

ACCESS
4WD only due to rough road conditions. No caravans or trailers allowed, and a high clearance 4WD vehicle is needed. It is 55km (34 miles) to Threeways, and takes between 3-4 hours! Pick up information and maps from either Kununurra or Halls Creek for finer details.

FACILITIES
Two camping areas are *Kurrajong* (just north of Threeways), which has pit toilets, water and some shade, and *Walardi Camp*, with pit toilets and water. It is advisable to boil the water first before drinking. Helicopter flights are available. You need to be self-sufficient for a visit, in particular, carry extra fuel (much of the trip in is low ratio 1st and 2nd gear) and water. There is some shade, but you need to be early to get an ideal spot. There is no swimming area in the park.

ROEBUCK PLAINS

Population 6

LOCATION
On the Great Northern Highway, 35km (22 miles) east of Broome.

CHARACTERISTICS

A modernised Swagman Roadhouse serves both road users and the locals from nearby stations. It is a good meeting place for truckies, travellers and ringers, who add a touch of flavour to the bar. The large 303,643ha (750,000 acre) Roebuck Cattle Station, which is also a Brahman Stud, surrounds the roadhouse in an area characterised by both flat and undulating country, dotted with spinifex and eucalypts.

ACCOMMODATION

Basic units - $25 single, $40 double.
Camping - powered van sites $10, tent sites $6. Sites have some grass and shade. Pets allowed, dogs leashed.

SERVICES AND FACILITIES

It has a bar, restaurant (steak/grills from $15), take-away food, shop, ice, souvenirs, telephone, showers for travellers ($3), picnic/BBQ area, tourist information, fuel (super, ULP, diesel, autogas), oil, camping gas, tyres and tubes. Open all year, 24 hours. Credit cards are accepted, ph (08)9192 1880.

SANDFIRE

Population 13

LOCATION

On the Great Northern Highway, approximately 310km (192 miles) south of Broome, and 300km (186 miles) north of Port Hedland.

CHARACTERISTICS

One of the loneliest roadhouses in the north-west is located in the spinifex and acacia ridge country of the vast Great Sandy Desert. There is plenty of character here. The air-conditioned tavern has hundreds of shirt sleeves hanging from the ceiling, as a fund raising effort for the Royal Flying Doctor Service. You can join the club, too. Either donate about $10, or, for a $2 discount, rip off your sleeve and pin it up! The Norton family are the owners of this remarkable, remote roadhouse, and they have a store of tales about the area. Whether driving from south or north, Sandfire marks either the beginning of the Kimberley, or its memorable end.

HISTORY

The roadhouse was established in early 1970, when Ken Norton's father put the first bore down. Mr Norton Senior had read a diary of Ludwig Leichhardt (the explorer) and was struck by a reference to sand appearing to be on fire. Some years later, whilst broken down on the Great Northern Track, he saw what Leichhardt meant; the interplay of sun and desert fired the sands, hence the name. The original roadhouse was nothing more than a shed, but a very welcome stop for those heading north when the road was a treacherous track.

ATTRACTIONS

55km (34 miles) south is access to one of the longest, loneliest and most beautiful beachcombing sands in Australia, 80 Mile Beach (see separate listing).

HOW TO GET THERE

By road: it is a sealed all-weather road serviced by coach company, Greyhound- Pioneer.

ACCOMMODATION

Motel - double between $50 and $60.
Budget - single $20, double $30.
Camping - powered sites $12 x 2, unpowered $10 x 2. Grassed tent sites, limited shade. Pets allowed, dogs leashed.

SERVICES AND FACILITIES

The roadhouse has a tavern bar, restaurant (good Aussie meals, `steak & veg' $14, breakfast bacon and eggs $7.50), a shop selling basics, ice, take-away food, souvenirs, telephone, showers for travellers ($2), tourist information (80 Mile Beach), fuel (super, ULP, diesel), LPG for vehicles, oil, camping gas, emergency vehicle repairs, basic spares, and an airstrip. *Open all year 6am- midnight.* Credit cards are accepted, ph (08) 9176 5944.

TURKEY CREEK (WARMUN)

Population 550 (approximately)

LOCATION
On the Great Northern Highway, 196km (121 miles) south of Kununurra.

CHARACTERISTICS
A roadhouse (owned by the Warmun Community) that serves not only travellers and local stations, but also the nearby Warmun Aboriginal Community. It is a welcome stop after some magnificent Kimberley landscape, and also serves as the gateway to the Purnululu National Park.

ATTRACTIONS
The turnoff to Purnululu (Bungle Bungle) Range is 80km (50 miles) from here (see separate listing). Caravans and trailers can be left at the Roadhouse for those planning the 4WD-only journey into the Range. A modest fee is charged.

HOW TO GET THERE
By road: it is sealed, and serviced by Greyhound-Pioneer Coaches.

ACCOMMODATION
(Turkey Creek Roadhouse)
Motel style - single around $55, double around $65.
Single dongas (cabins) from $30; backpacker dormitory style from $17.50 per person.
Camping - powered sites around $20 x 2; camping $7.50 per person. Sites are grassed with limited shade. Pets, dogs leashed.

SERVICES AND FACILITIES

It has a general store/supermarket selling a surprisingly wide range, restaurant (a good meal at around $14), take-away food, ice, artifacts, souvenirs, tours, telephone, showers for travellers($2), picnic/BBQ area, swimming pool; tourist information, fuel (super, ULP, diesel, autogas), camping, oil, basic spares, and airfield. It is not licensed to sell alcohol. *Open all year, 6.30am - 8.00pm*. EFTPOS facility, credit cards accepted, ph (08) 9168 7882.

WILLARE BRIDGE

Population 7

LOCATION

On the Great Northern Highway, 56km (35 miles) south of Derby, and 155km (96 miles)of Broome.

CHARACTERISTICS

Only a good cast away from the barramundi in the Fitzroy River billabongs (actually 600m), the quaint squared roadhouse, set amidst shady trees and green lawns, is a pleasant overnight stopping or refuelling spot. There's good fishing and a bird-watching trail along the river banks. And the *Willare Cascade* is a fishing and boating competition held every year in May.

ACCOMMODATION

Old style Hotel rooms - Double $40, single $25.
Camping - powered sites $12 x 2, unpowered $8. Sites grassed, shaded. Pets allowed, dogs on leash.

SERVICES AND FACILITIES

The roadhouse has a licensed restaurant (home cooked meals), general store, ice, take-away food, telephone, picnic/BBQ shaded area, showers for travellers, fuel (super, ULP, diesel), camping gas, oil, basic spares, tyres and tubes, and fishing tackle. *Open daily all year, 6am-10pm*, allcards, ph (08) 9191 4775.

WOLFE CREEK METEORITE CRATER RESERVE

1460ha (2606 acres)

LOCATION

Approximately 130km (81 miles) south of Hall's Creek.

CHARACTERISTICS

The Reserve protects a huge crater, measuring about 850m in diameter and 50m deep, caused by the impact shock of a huge meteorite. To the Djaru people, who called the crater `Kandimalal', it is deeply symbolic. The winding paths of two rainbow serpents formed the nearby Sturt and Wolfe Creeks, and the crater is where one snake emerged from the desert sands. The first recorded European discovery was in 1947. It is the world's second largest meteorite crater. *The reserve is day-use only.*

ORIGIN

There is some doubt about how the crater was formed. Geologists are still pondering over the fascinating formation. One theory suggests that a meteor, weighing several thousand tonnes, and travelling at a speed of over 15km/sec, impacted at this location. Evidence of this includes the shape of the crater (despite its floor, which today lies 20m below the surrounding sandplain), meteorite fragments and iron oxide balls found scattered on its slopes. The explosion that caused the crater is thought to have occurred 300,000 years ago.

HOW TO GET THERE

With care, the formed gravel road is suitable for conventional vehicles during the Dry season (caravans not advised). Check at Hall's Creek for road conditions. The turn-off to the crater is 16km (10 miles) west of Hall's Creek from the Great Northern Highway. It's also the turn-off for the Canning Stock Route Track and the

Tanami Track to Alice Springs. The RAC Canning Stock Route Map is good for 4WD tracks and Wolfe Creek.

SERVICES AND FACILITIES

An information panel and basic picnic facilities are provided in this *day-use only* reserve. Please keep to the tracks. Camping and campfires are not permitted.

WYNDHAM

Population 1000

LOCATION

On the west arm of Cambridge Gulf, 101km (63 miles) north-west of Kununurra, at the end of the Great Northern Highway.

CHARACTERISTICS

An 18m (60 ft) long and 3m (10 ft) high "Big Croc" replica greets visitors at the entrance to Western Australia's most northerly town and port. It is a friendly town that has two sites; the original port site, and Wyndham East on the Great Northern Highway. The latter is the main shopping and residential area today. The older, frontier-town part has some of the original corrugated iron shops with hitching-rails outside, while benign boab trees dot the streetscape. The sense of history, and numerous things to see, make it worth visiting. The pub is a good place to meet the owners, and locals who will advise on fishing spots and other attractions.

HISTORY

Long before the Europeans came, the Djeidji, Dulngari and Aruagga people are thought to have been the traditional dwellers in the region. Lieutenant Phillip King sailed into the inlet he called Cambridge Gulf in 1819, while 1885 saw the arrival of the *Torinda Borstel* with a cargo for the Duracks.

The gold rush at Hall's Creek was the catalyst for settlement, and a rough and ready town was well-established by 1886, based on the port. The influx of miners prompted the rapid erection of six hotels, but when the gold fever died down, the slowness and remoteness of Wyndham returned. The town, named in honour of the son of Lady Broome, received new life in 1919, when the English land and livestock company, Vesteys, opened a meatworks. Chilled beef was exported, and Wyndham became the main port for the East Kimberley. The meatworks had a stop-go history, finally closing in 1987, and gutted by fire soon afterwards. A thriving port today is based on mineral, sugar and live cattle exports, while the town serves the pastoral, mining and tourism industries, as well as Aboriginal communities.

ATTRACTIONS

Five Rivers Lookout. A fine spot, at the peak of the Bastion Range, for Kimberley landscape appreciation and great orientation views of the town, port and, of course, the five rivers: King, Pentecost, Durack, Forrest and Ord. Best views are early morning, due to later haze.

Frontier-town Port site. Old buildings include the port post office and courthouse built in the early 1900s. The latter now appropriately houses the local historical society's museum. Near the wharf officesis a display of early trains which used to carry cargo to and from ships.

Gully and Bend Cemeteries. Headstones reveal much local history. Graves date back to the early 1880s.

Three Mile Valley. The valley has all the characteristics of the East Kimberley - red gorges, rock pools, rugged terrain, and open vegetation.

Boab Trees. An enormous boab tree is located in the Three Mile Caravan Park. A hollow one, situated on the King River Road, was used as a local 'lock-up' or prison.

The Grotto. This feature overlooks a clear pool, and has a certain mystique. A carved-stone staircase leads through the greenery fringing the rock-bound pool. It is a popular swimming spot.

King River Pools. Many fine pools offer barramundi fishing, particularly during the Wet, while along Parry's Creek Road, stone creek crossings give access to some good fishing holes, the most popular being Crocodile Hole.

Afghan Cemetery. Contains the graves of Afghan cameleers whose camel strings brought supplies to the region.

Aboriginal Paintings. Overhanging rock walls near the Moochalabra Dam have paintings in ochre of spriitual figures and animals. This is a protected site.

Parry's Lagoon Nature Reserve. This protects a series of lagoons 20km (12 miles) south of Wyndham. Like the wetlands of Kakadu, it hosts flocks of waterbirds, which come from as far afield as Siberia in Russia. It is an important breeding ground, too. Species include egrets, spoonbills, herons, ibis, magpie geese, raptors, pelicans, jabirus and brolgas, while aquatic life features both species of crocodiles and fish (barramundi, mullet, tarpon). Dawn and dusk are the best times to visit this sanctuary, when thousands of birds gather.

Crocodile Farm. Located on the old meatworks site, it offers visitors a close but safe view of these awesome reptiles. Check with the Information Centre (Mobil Service Station) for feeding times.

Fishing. Wyndham offers all-year fishing, both salt and freshwater. Barramundi, golden grunter, mangrove jack, threadfin salmon and huge groper, are the main types. The wharf is a popular spot, but check with the locals for others. Watch out for saltwater crocodiles.

Diggers Rest Station. An outlying attraction (approximately 30km south-west of Wyndham on King River Road), features an 8000 ha (20,000 ac) working cattle station where visitors are welcome to experience a muster, fish, bushwalk or just soak up some beautiful East Kimberley scenery. *Kimberley Pursuits* is the touring arm of the station, offering 2- to 11-day horse trek safaris. The station has bunkhouse accommodation from $12 pp; camping $5 pp and offers dinner and B & B packages. Access is via an unreliable gravel road. Care should be taken in conventional vehicles and no trailers attached. Telephone (08) 9161 1029.

TOURS
4WD safari style, fishing, scenic air flights and horse trek safaris (see *Diggers Rest* under Attractions) are among the local tour offerings. Check with the information centre at the Mobil Service Station (open daily) for details. Telephone (08) 9161 1281.

EVENTS
Parry's Creek Picnic - June long weekend; *Horse Racing* - August; *Billy- cart Derby* - mid-year.

HOW TO GET THERE
By air: services from Kununurra.
By road: Greyhound-Pioneer.

ACCOMMODATION
Wyndham Town Hotel, 19 O'Donnel Street, ph (08) 9161 1003 - self-contained rooms, single $40, double $80.

Wyndham Community Club, Great Northern Highway, ph (08) 9161 1130 - rooms single $50, double $60.

Three Mile Caravan Park, Baker Street, ph (08) 9161 1064 - powered sites from $15, unpowered from $6 pp. Pets must be supervised.

SERVICES AND FACILITIES

The town has a police station, post office, hospital, medical services (doctor, dentist),supermarkets, hotel, restaurant (hotel - counter meals, lunch and dinner from $8), take-away food, Commonwealth and Bankwest Banks, churches (Catholic, Uniting), ice, airfield, all vehicle services (fuel - super, ULP, diesel, autogas), camping gas. Recreational facilities include swimming pool, golf course and tennis courts. Everything is *open all year*, EFTPOS facility and credit cards are widely accepted.

INDEX

A tranquil waterhole fed by a thin waterfall in Kakadu National Park

The infamous saltwater crocodile; a prehistoric predator whose presence makes swimming in the Top End region hazardous

Maps

Some sandstone spires of the Bungle Bungles in Purnululu National Park rise more than 300m above the surrounding savannah landscape

THE KIMBERLEY

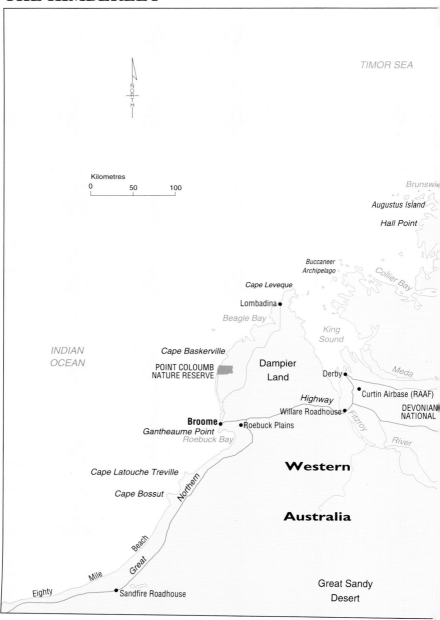

TIMOR SEA

Brunswi

Augustus Island

Hall Point

NORTH

Kilometres
0   50   100

Buccaneer
Archipelago

Collier Bay

Cape Leveque

Lombadina

Beagle Bay

King
Sound

INDIAN
OCEAN

Cape Baskerville

POINT COLOUMB
NATURE RESERVE

Dampier
Land

Derby

Meda

Curtin Airbase (RAAF)

Highway

DEVONIAN
NATIONAL

Willare Roadhouse

Fitzroy

Broome

Gantheaume Point

Roebuck Plains

River

Roebuck Bay

Western

Cape Latouche Treville

Northern

Australia

Cape Bossut

Beach

Great

Great Sandy
Desert

Mile

Eighty

Sandfire Roadhouse